Welcome to *NewWorld Online*.

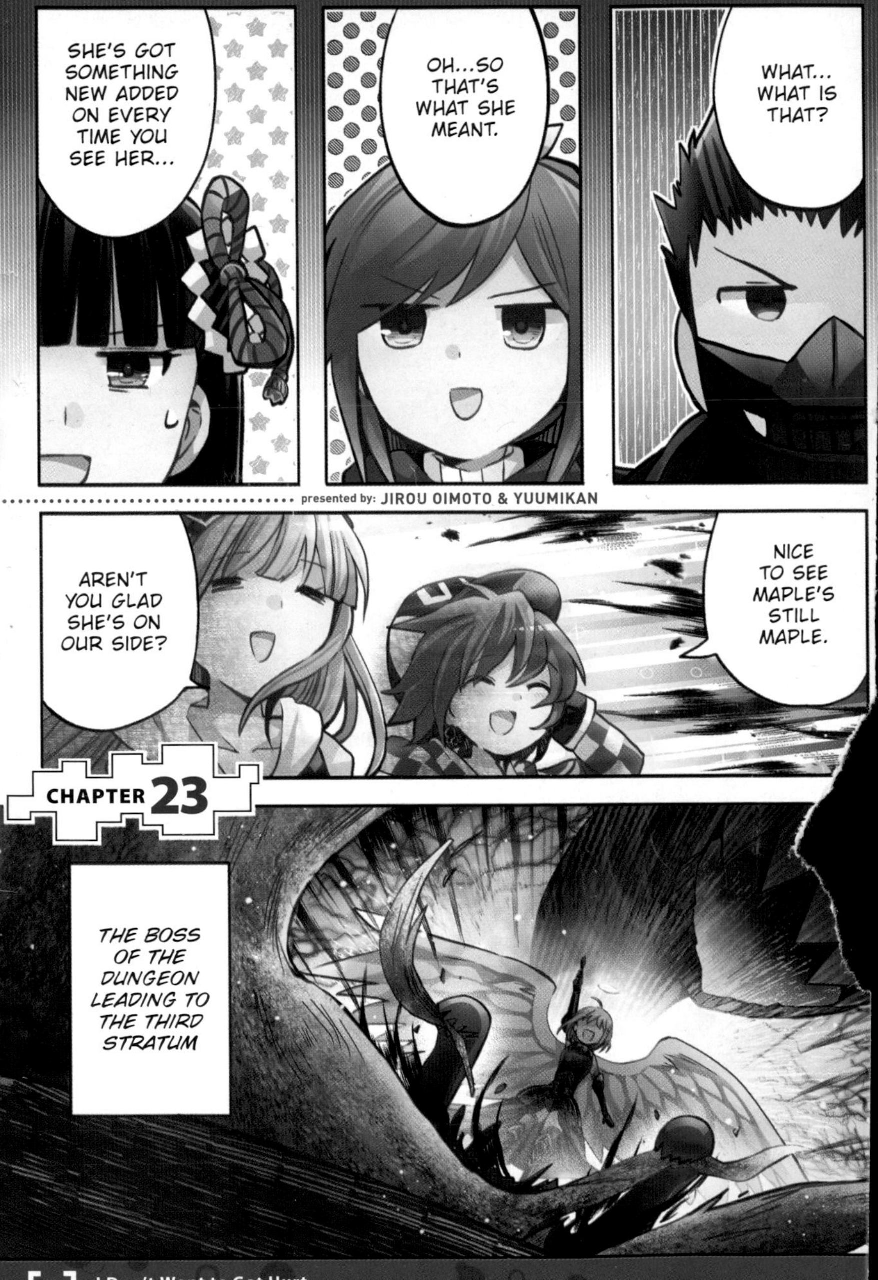
WHAT... WHAT IS THAT?
OH...SO THAT'S WHAT SHE MEANT.
SHE'S GOT SOMETHING NEW ADDED ON EVERY TIME YOU SEE HER...
presented by: JIROU OIMOTO & YUUMIKAN
NICE TO SEE MAPLE'S STILL MAPLE.
AREN'T YOU GLAD SHE'S ON OUR SIDE?
CHAPTER 23
THE BOSS OF THE DUNGEON LEADING TO THE THIRD STRATUM

[5] I Don't Want to Get Hurt, so I'll Max Out My Defense.

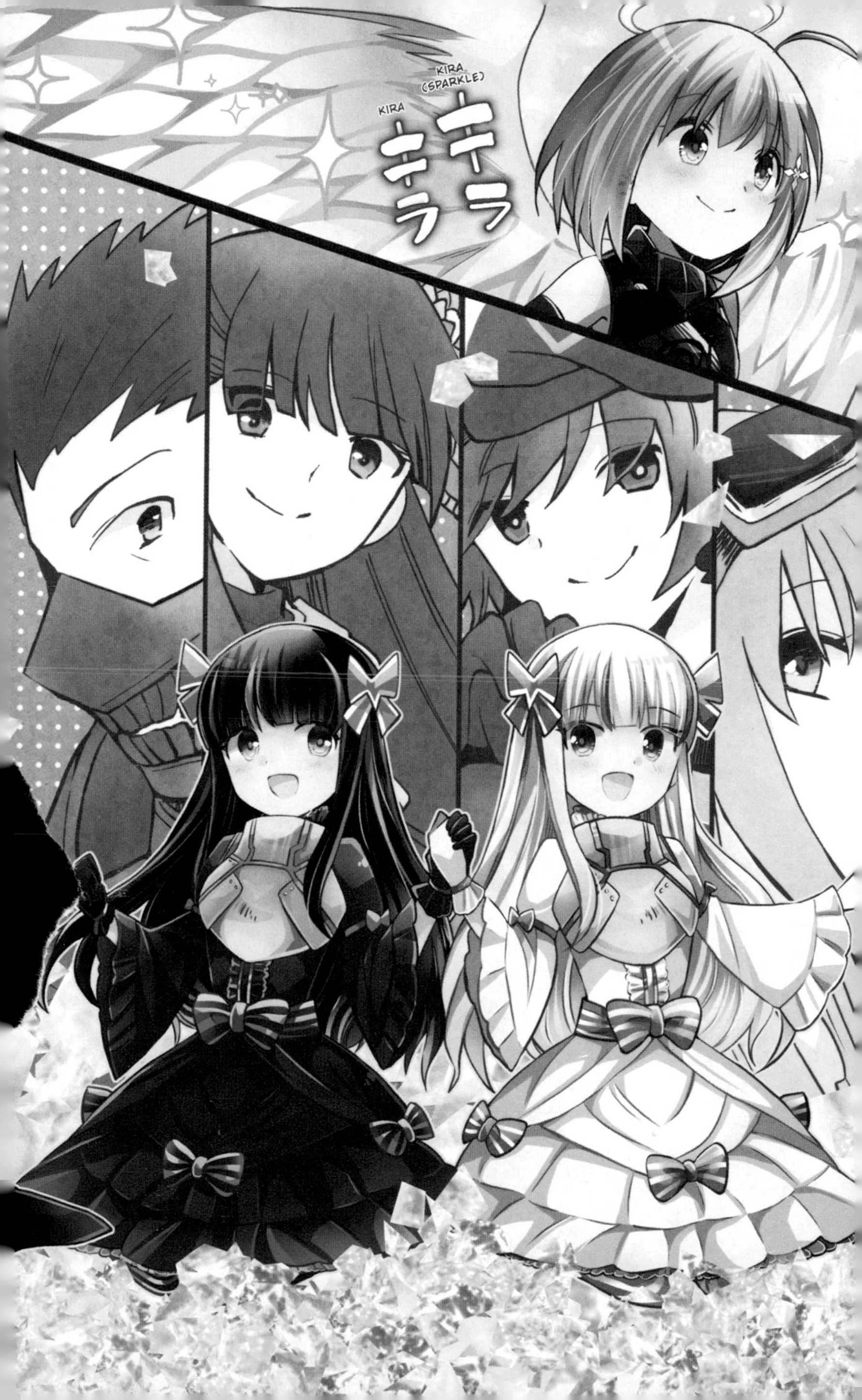
KIRA (SPARKLE)
キラ
KIRA
キラ

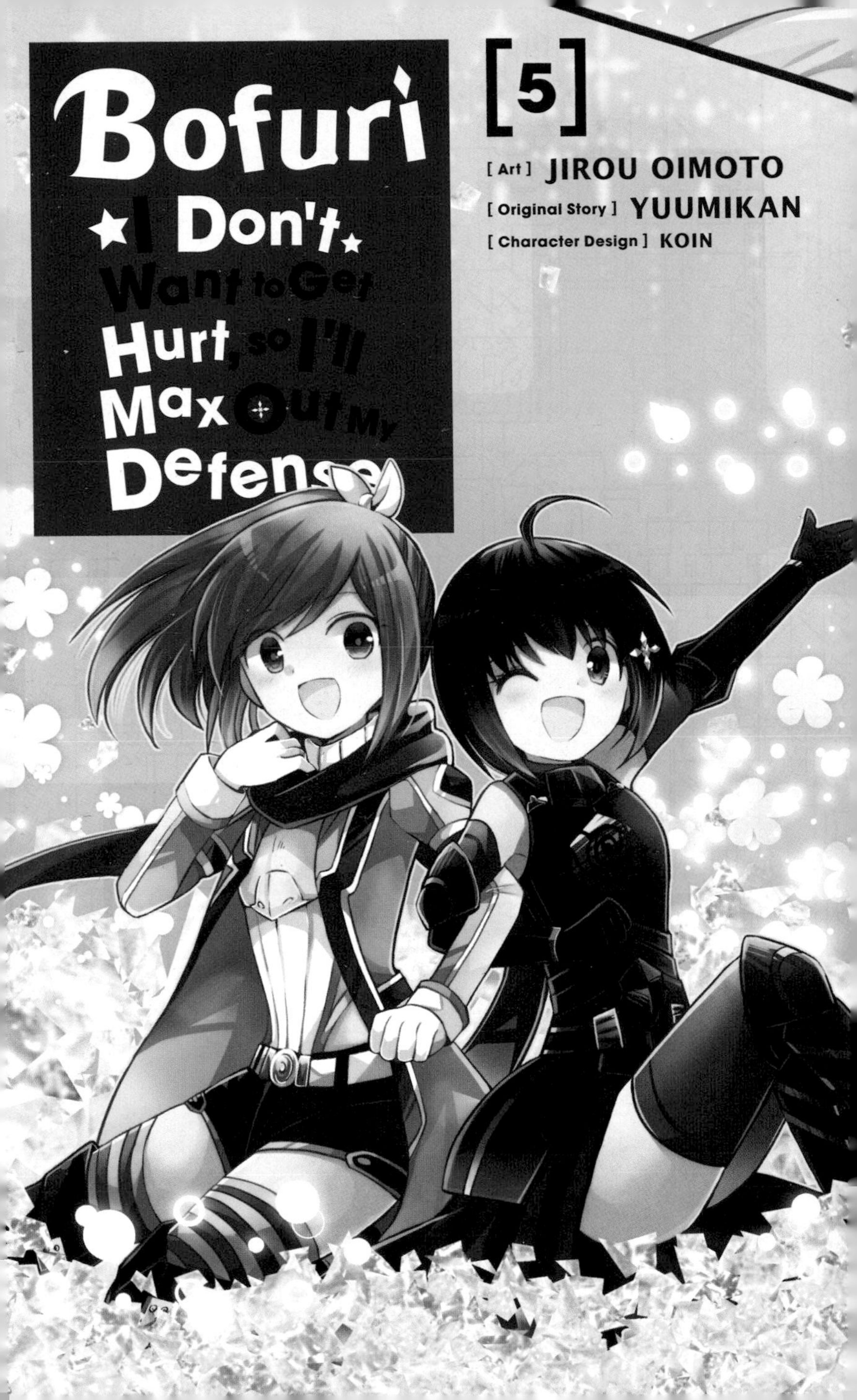
Bofuri
★I Don't★
Want to Get
Hurt, so I'll
Max Out My
Defense
[5]
[Art] JIROU OIMOTO
[Original Story] YUUMIKAN
[Character Design] KOIN

Welcome to
NewWorld Online.

CONTENTS

[5]

I Don't Want to Get Hurt,
so I'll Max Out My Defense.

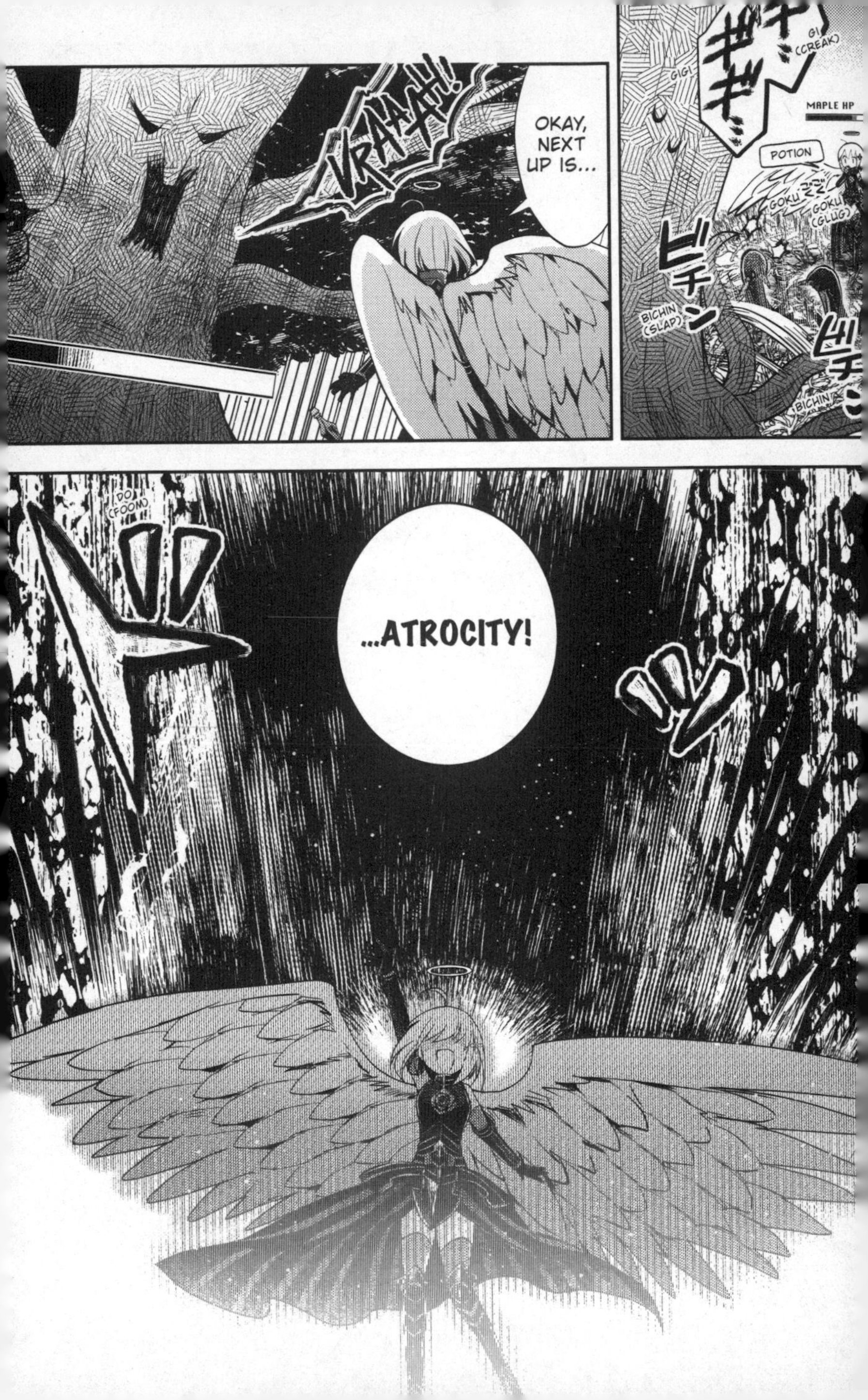

ギギ
GI (CREAK)
GIGI
MAPLE HP
POTION
GOKU
GOKU (GLUG)
ビチン
BICHIN (SLAP)
BICHIN
VRAAAH!
OKAY, NEXT UP IS...
DO (FOOM)
...ATROCITY!

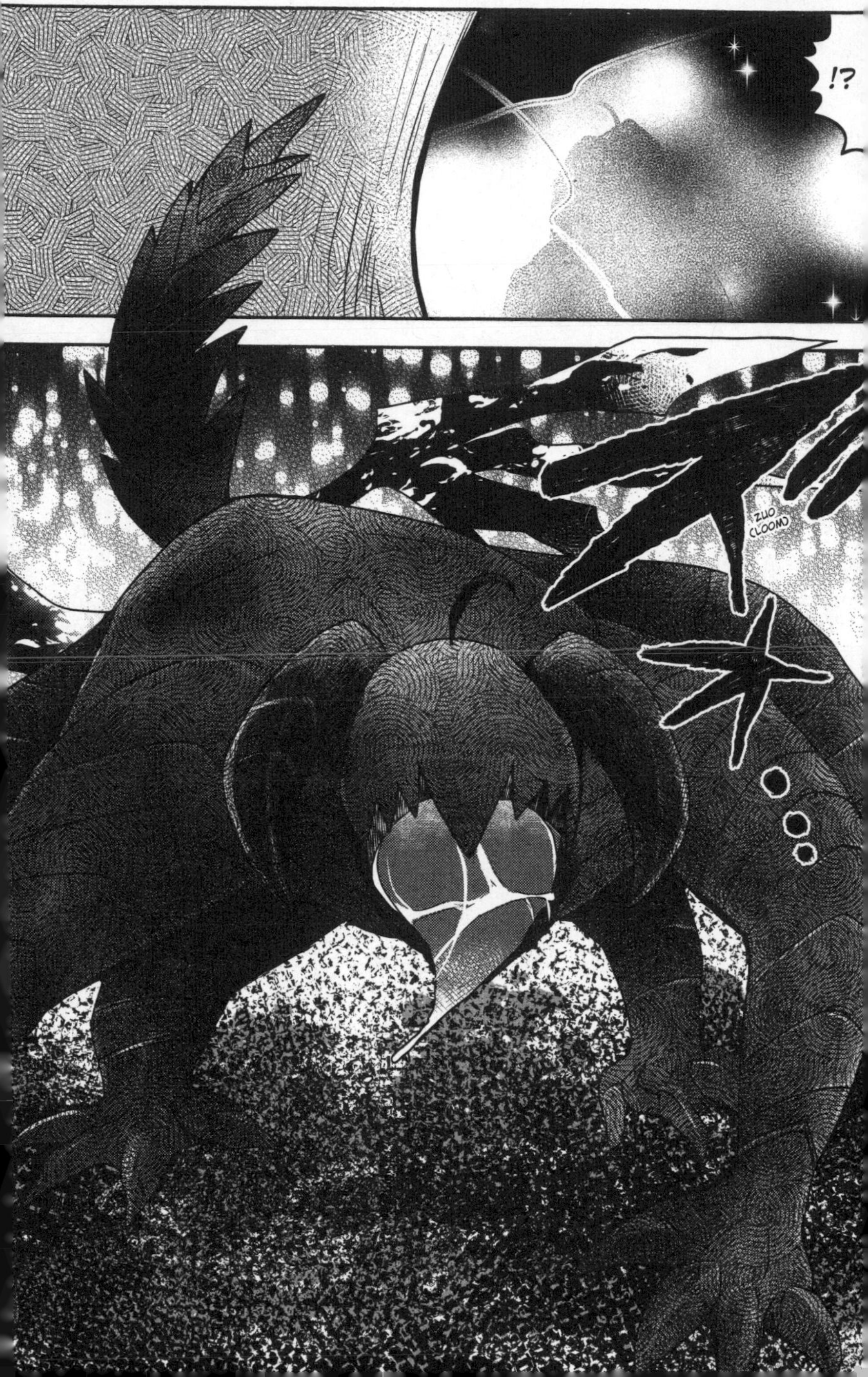
!?
ZUO (LOOM)

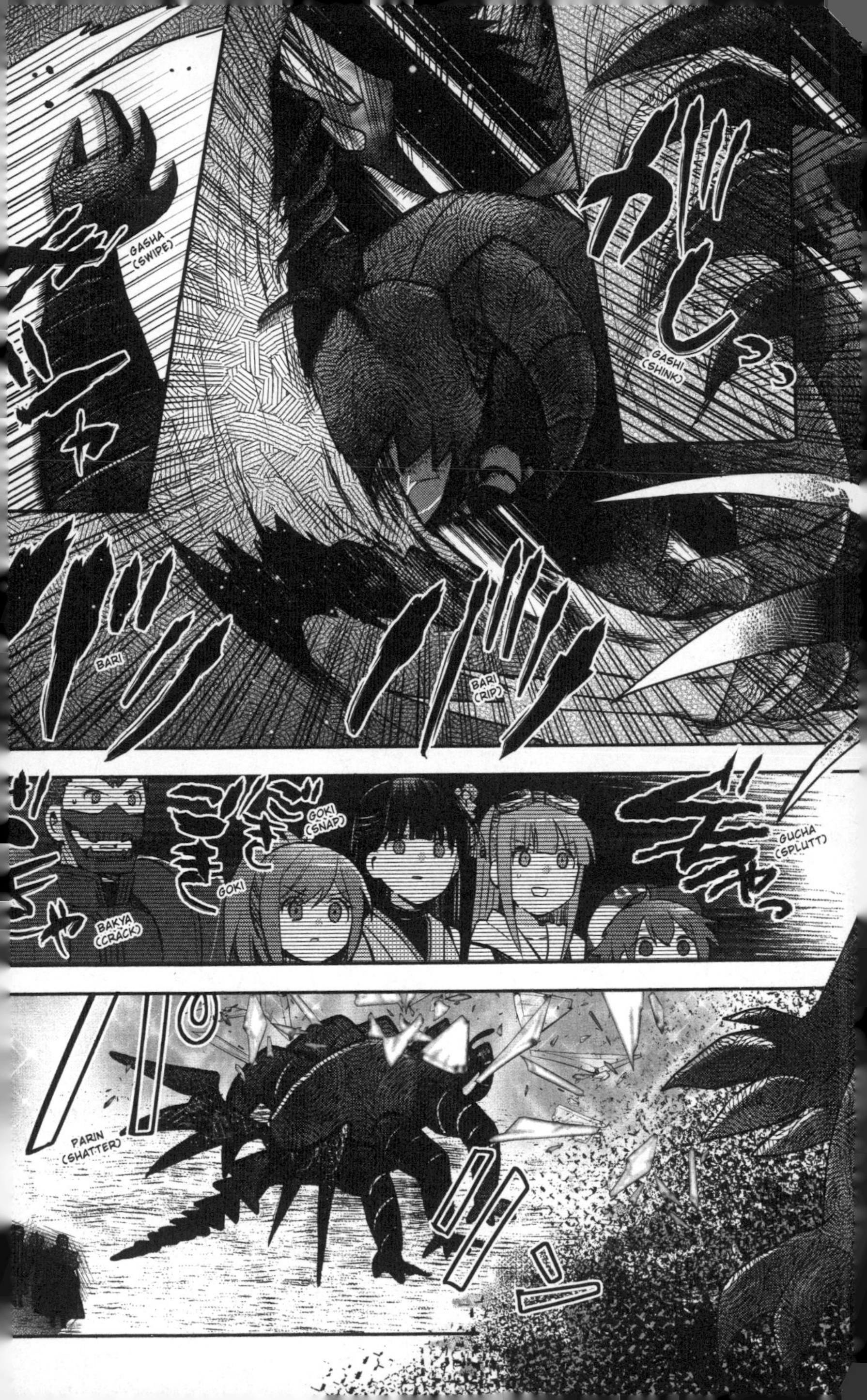
GASHI (SHINK)
GASHA (SWIPE)
BARI (RIP)
BARI
GUCHA (SPLUTT)
GOKI (SNAP)
GOKI
BAKYA (CRACK)
PARIN (SHATTER)

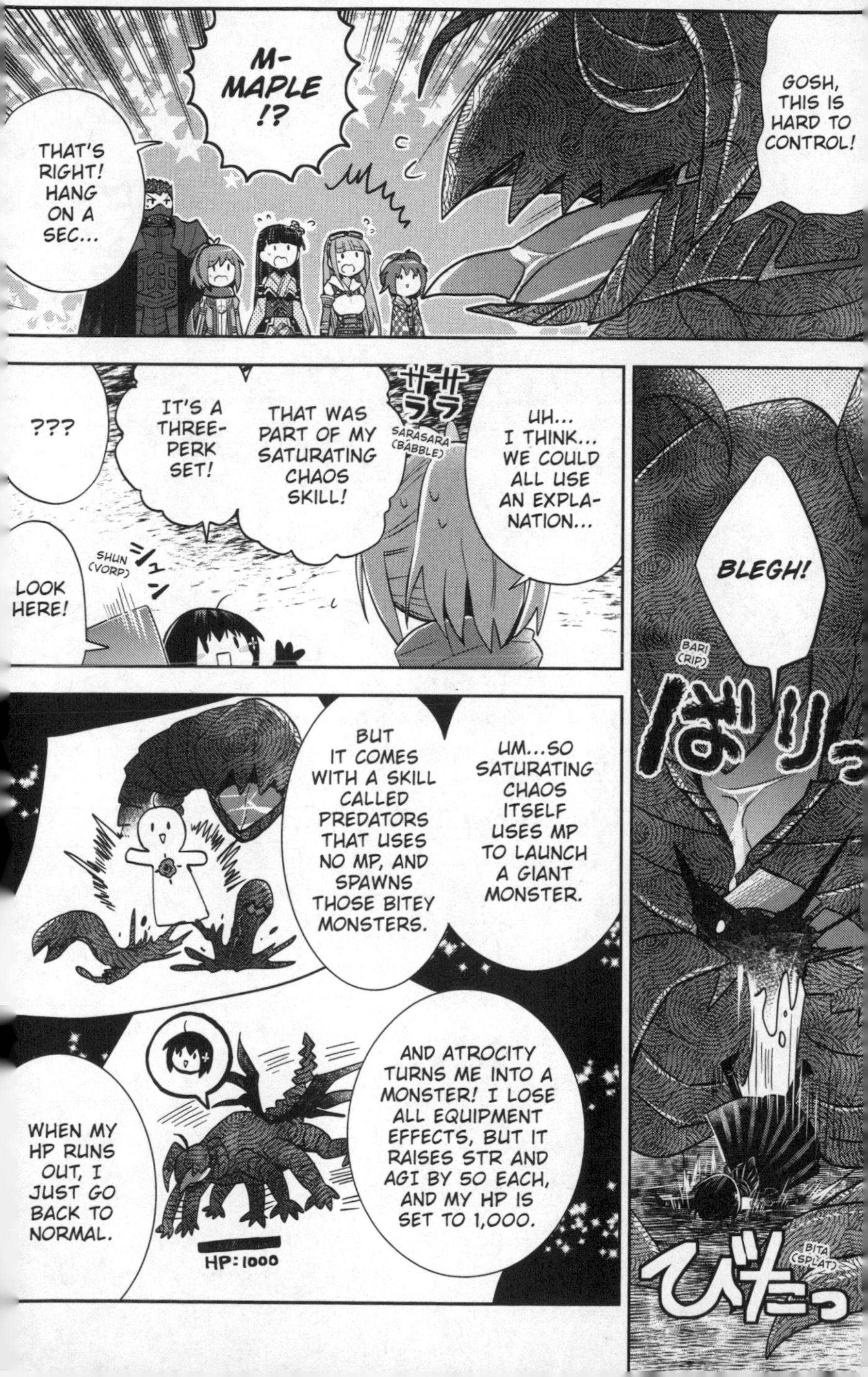
GOSH, THIS IS HARD TO CONTROL!
M-MAPLE!?
THAT'S RIGHT! HANG ON A SEC...
BLEGH!
BARI (RIP)
ぱりっ
BITA (SPLAT)
びたっ
UH... I THINK... WE COULD ALL USE AN EXPLANATION...
サラサラ
SARASARA (BABBLE)
THAT WAS PART OF MY SATURATING CHAOS SKILL!
IT'S A THREE-PERK SET!
???
SHUN (VORP)
シュン
LOOK HERE!
UM...SO SATURATING CHAOS ITSELF USES MP TO LAUNCH A GIANT MONSTER.
BUT IT COMES WITH A SKILL CALLED PREDATORS THAT USES NO MP, AND SPAWNS THOSE BITEY MONSTERS.
AND ATROCITY TURNS ME INTO A MONSTER! I LOSE ALL EQUIPMENT EFFECTS, BUT IT RAISES STR AND AGI BY 50 EACH, AND MY HP IS SET TO 1,000.
WHEN MY HP RUNS OUT, I JUST GO BACK TO NORMAL.
HP: 1000

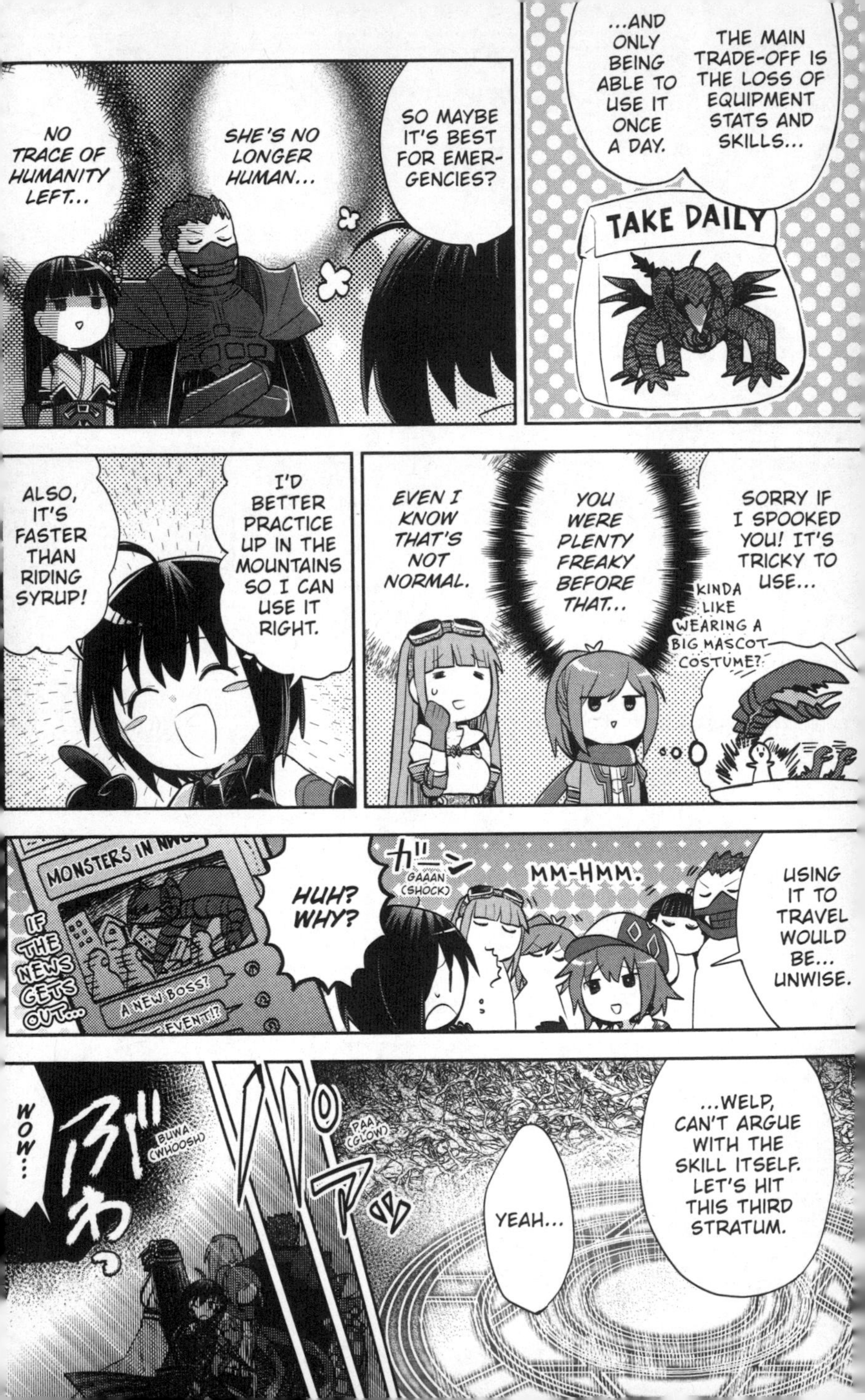
THE MAIN TRADE-OFF IS THE LOSS OF EQUIPMENT STATS AND SKILLS...
...AND ONLY BEING ABLE TO USE IT ONCE A DAY.
TAKE DAILY
SO MAYBE IT'S BEST FOR EMERGENCIES?
SHE'S NO LONGER HUMAN...
NO TRACE OF HUMANITY LEFT...
SORRY IF I SPOOKED YOU! IT'S TRICKY TO USE...
KINDA LIKE WEARING A BIG MASCOT COSTUME?
YOU WERE PLENTY FREAKY BEFORE THAT...
EVEN I KNOW THAT'S NOT NORMAL.
I'D BETTER PRACTICE UP IN THE MOUNTAINS SO I CAN USE IT RIGHT.
ALSO, IT'S FASTER THAN RIDING SYRUP!
USING IT TO TRAVEL WOULD BE... UNWISE.
MM-HMM.
ガーン
GAAAN (SHOCK)
HUH? WHY?
MONSTERS IN
A NEW BOSS?
EVENT!?
IF THE NEWS GETS OUT...
...WELP, CAN'T ARGUE WITH THE SKILL ITSELF. LET'S HIT THIS THIRD STRATUM.
YEAH...
パァ
PAA (GLOW)
ぶわっ
BUWA (WHOOSH)
WOW...

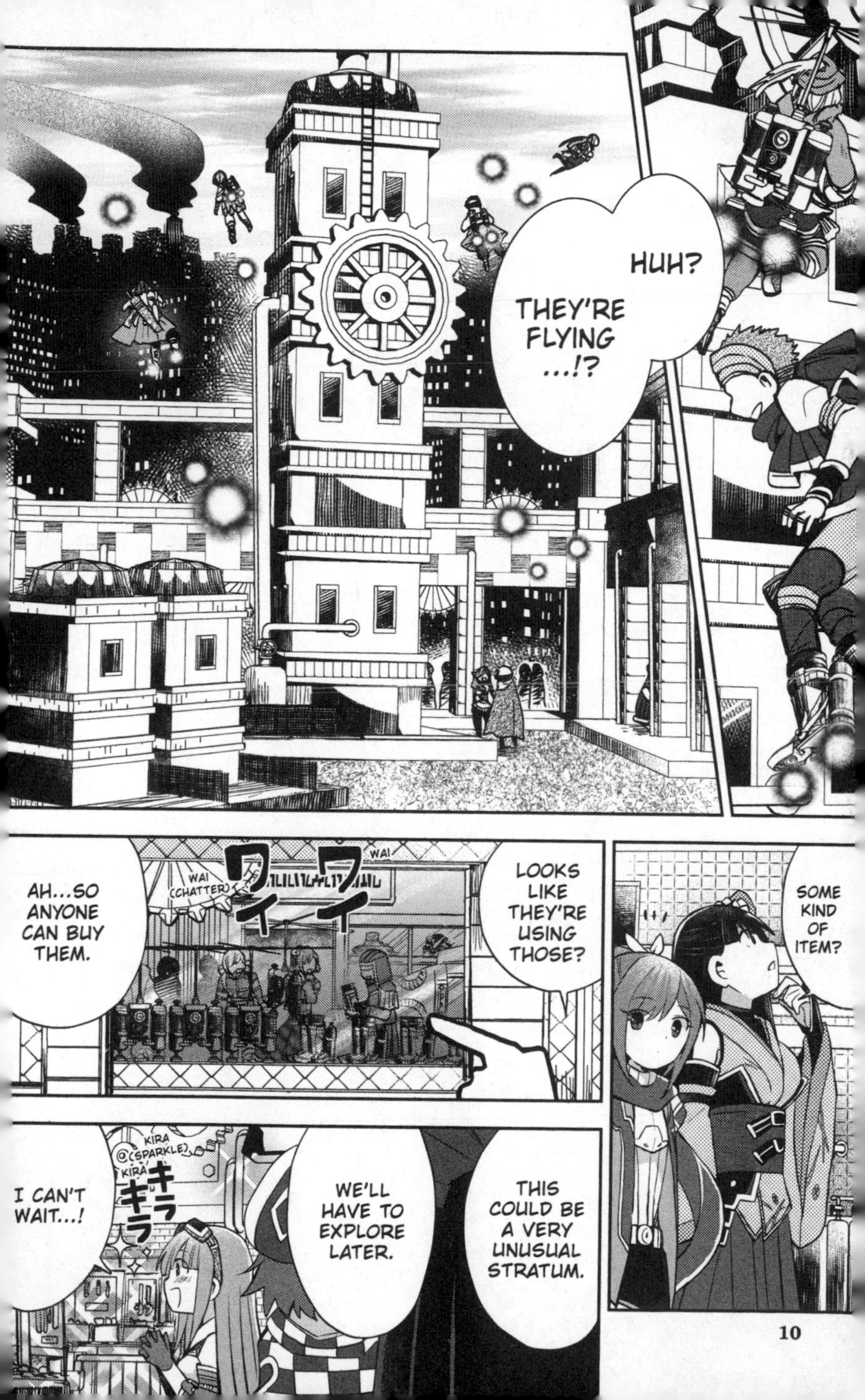
HUH?
THEY'RE FLYING...!?
SOME KIND OF ITEM?
LOOKS LIKE THEY'RE USING THOSE?
WAI WAI (CHATTER)
AH...SO ANYONE CAN BUY THEM.
THIS COULD BE A VERY UNUSUAL STRATUM.
WE'LL HAVE TO EXPLORE LATER.
KIRA KIRA (SPARKLE)
I CAN'T WAIT...!

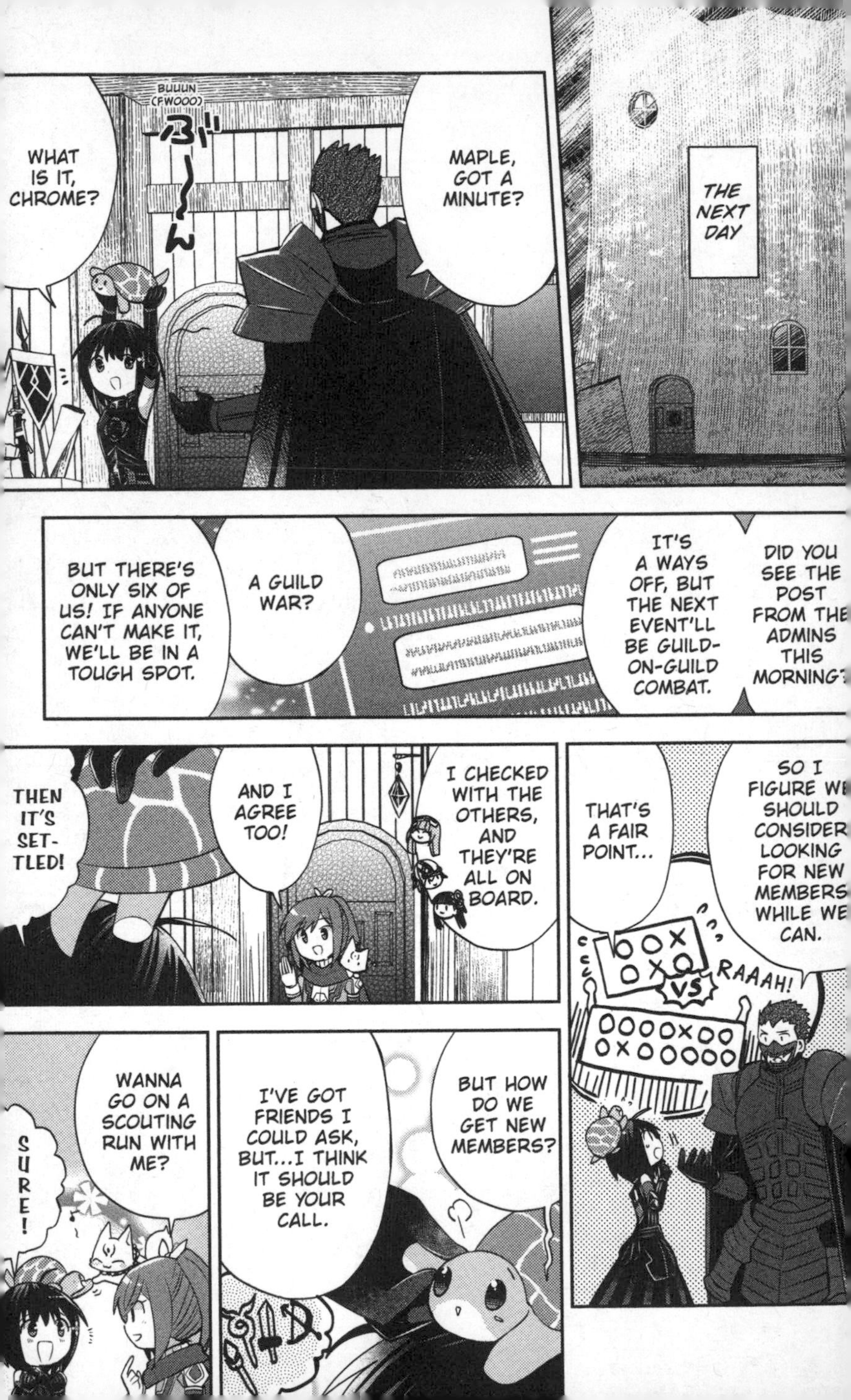
THE NEXT DAY
MAPLE, GOT A MINUTE?
BUUUN (FWOOO)
WHAT IS IT, CHROME?
DID YOU SEE THE POST FROM THE ADMINS THIS MORNING?
IT'S A WAYS OFF, BUT THE NEXT EVENT'LL BE GUILD-ON-GUILD COMBAT.
A GUILD WAR?
BUT THERE'S ONLY SIX OF US! IF ANYONE CAN'T MAKE IT, WE'LL BE IN A TOUGH SPOT.
SO I FIGURE WE SHOULD CONSIDER LOOKING FOR NEW MEMBERS WHILE WE CAN.
THAT'S A FAIR POINT...
VS
RAAAH!
I CHECKED WITH THE OTHERS, AND THEY'RE ALL ON BOARD.
AND I AGREE TOO!
THEN IT'S SET-TLED!
BUT HOW DO WE GET NEW MEMBERS?
I'VE GOT FRIENDS I COULD ASK, BUT...I THINK IT SHOULD BE YOUR CALL.
WANNA GO ON A SCOUTING RUN WITH ME?
SURE!

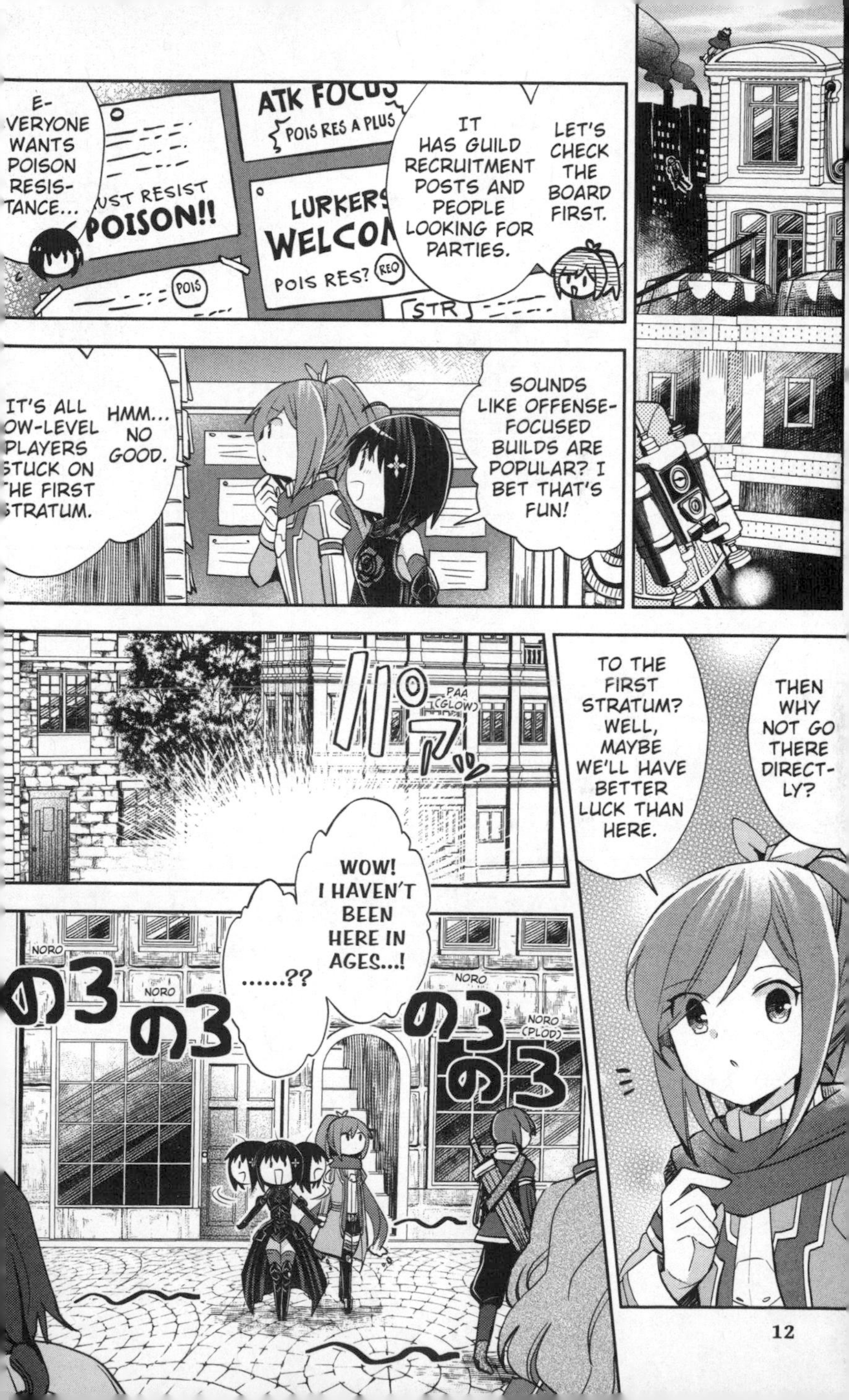
LET'S CHECK THE BOARD FIRST.
IT HAS GUILD RECRUITMENT POSTS AND PEOPLE LOOKING FOR PARTIES.
ATK FOCUS
POIS RES A PLUS
LURKERS WELCOM
POIS RES?
REQ
STR
UST RESIST POISON!!
POIS
E-VERYONE WANTS POISON RESIS-TANCE...
SOUNDS LIKE OFFENSE-FOCUSED BUILDS ARE POPULAR? I BET THAT'S FUN!
HMM... NO GOOD.
IT'S ALL OW-LEVEL PLAYERS TUCK ON HE FIRST TRATUM.
THEN WHY NOT GO THERE DIRECT-LY?
TO THE FIRST STRATUM? WELL, MAYBE WE'LL HAVE BETTER LUCK THAN HERE.
パァ
PAA (GLOW)
WOW! I HAVEN'T BEEN HERE IN AGES...!
......??
のろ
NORO
NORO
NORO
NORO (PLOD)

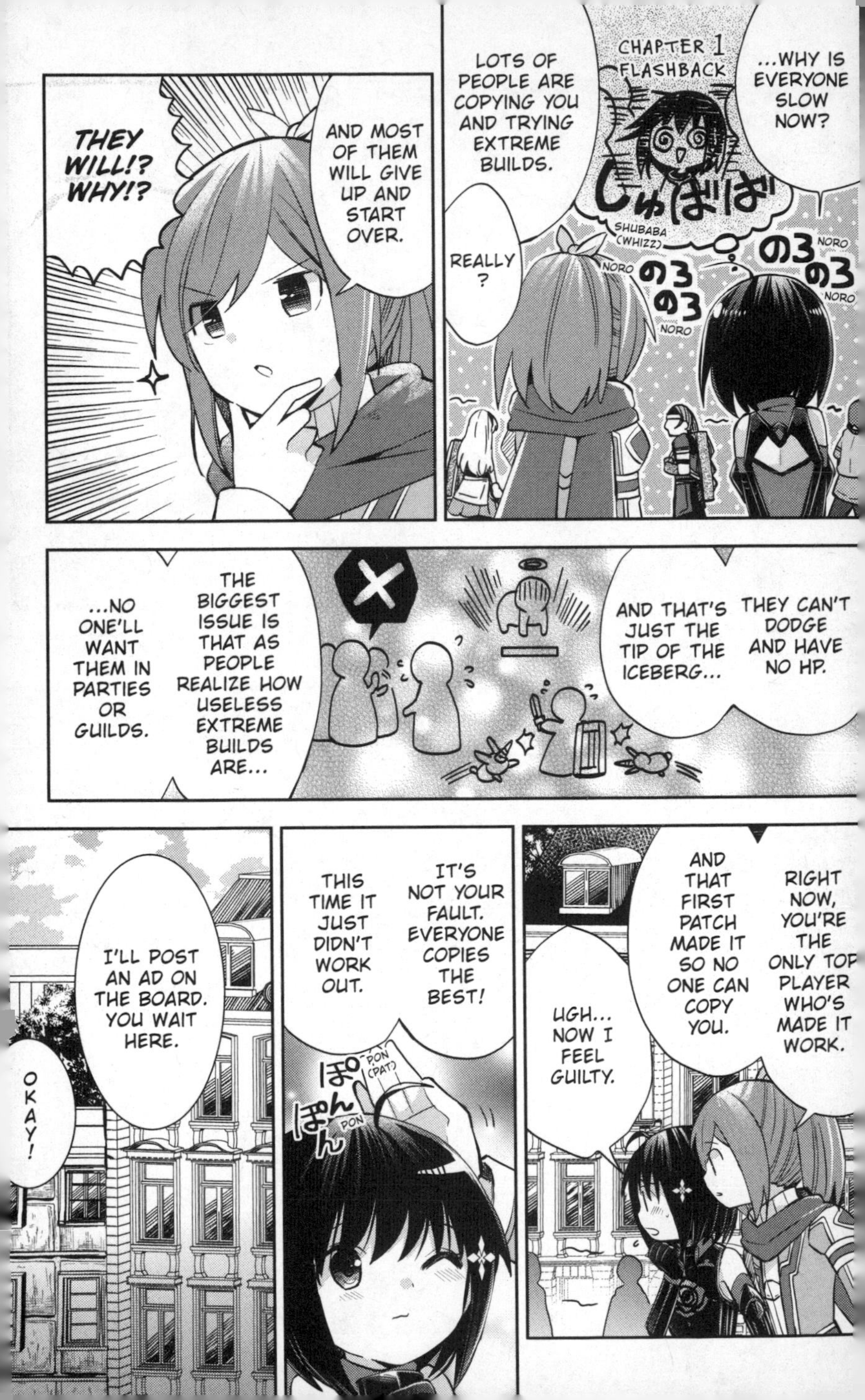
...WHY IS EVERYONE SLOW NOW?
CHAPTER 1 FLASHBACK
しゅばば
SHUBABA (WHIZZ)
LOTS OF PEOPLE ARE COPYING YOU AND TRYING EXTREME BUILDS.
REALLY?
のろのろ
NORO NORO
のろのろ
NORO NORO
AND MOST OF THEM WILL GIVE UP AND START OVER.
THEY WILL!? WHY!?
THEY CAN'T DODGE AND HAVE NO HP.
AND THAT'S JUST THE TIP OF THE ICEBERG...
THE BIGGEST ISSUE IS THAT AS PEOPLE REALIZE HOW USELESS EXTREME BUILDS ARE...
...NO ONE'LL WANT THEM IN PARTIES OR GUILDS.
RIGHT NOW, YOU'RE THE ONLY TOP PLAYER WHO'S MADE IT WORK.
AND THAT FIRST PATCH MADE IT SO NO ONE CAN COPY YOU.
UGH... NOW I FEEL GUILTY.
IT'S NOT YOUR FAULT. EVERYONE COPIES THE BEST!
THIS TIME IT JUST DIDN'T WORK OUT.
ぽん
PON (PAT)
ぽん
PON
I'LL POST AN AD ON THE BOARD. YOU WAIT HERE.
OKAY!

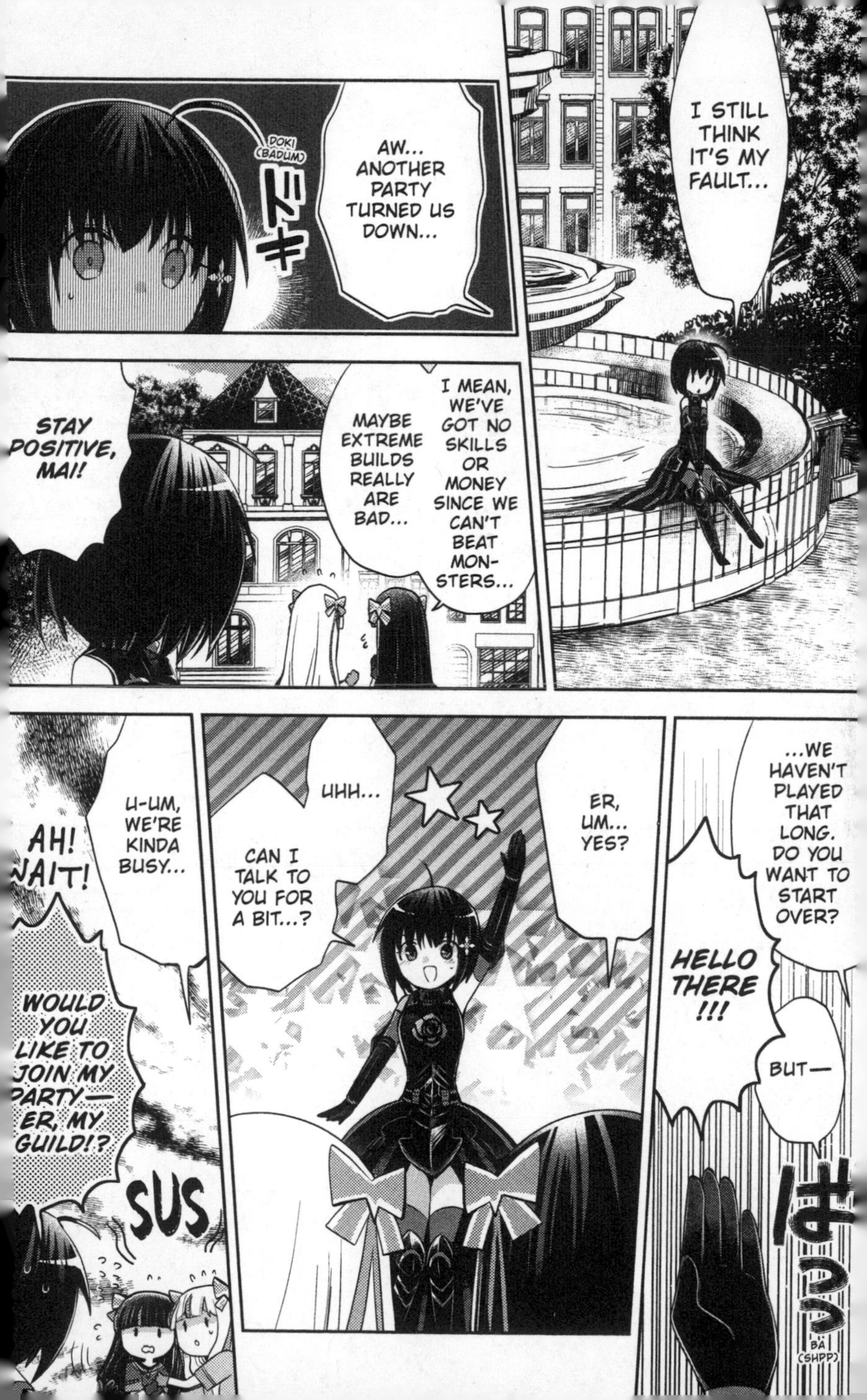
I STILL THINK IT'S MY FAULT...
DOKI (BADUM)
ドキ
AW... ANOTHER PARTY TURNED US DOWN...
I MEAN, WE'VE GOT NO SKILLS OR MONEY SINCE WE CAN'T BEAT MON-STERS...
MAYBE EXTREME BUILDS REALLY ARE BAD...
STAY POSITIVE, MAI!
...WE HAVEN'T PLAYED THAT LONG. DO YOU WANT TO START OVER?
BUT—
HELLO THERE!!!
はっ
BA (SHPP)
ER, UM... YES?
UHH...
CAN I TALK TO YOU FOR A BIT...?
U-UM, WE'RE KINDA BUSY...
AH! WAIT!
WOULD YOU LIKE TO JOIN MY PARTY—ER, MY GUILD!?
SUS

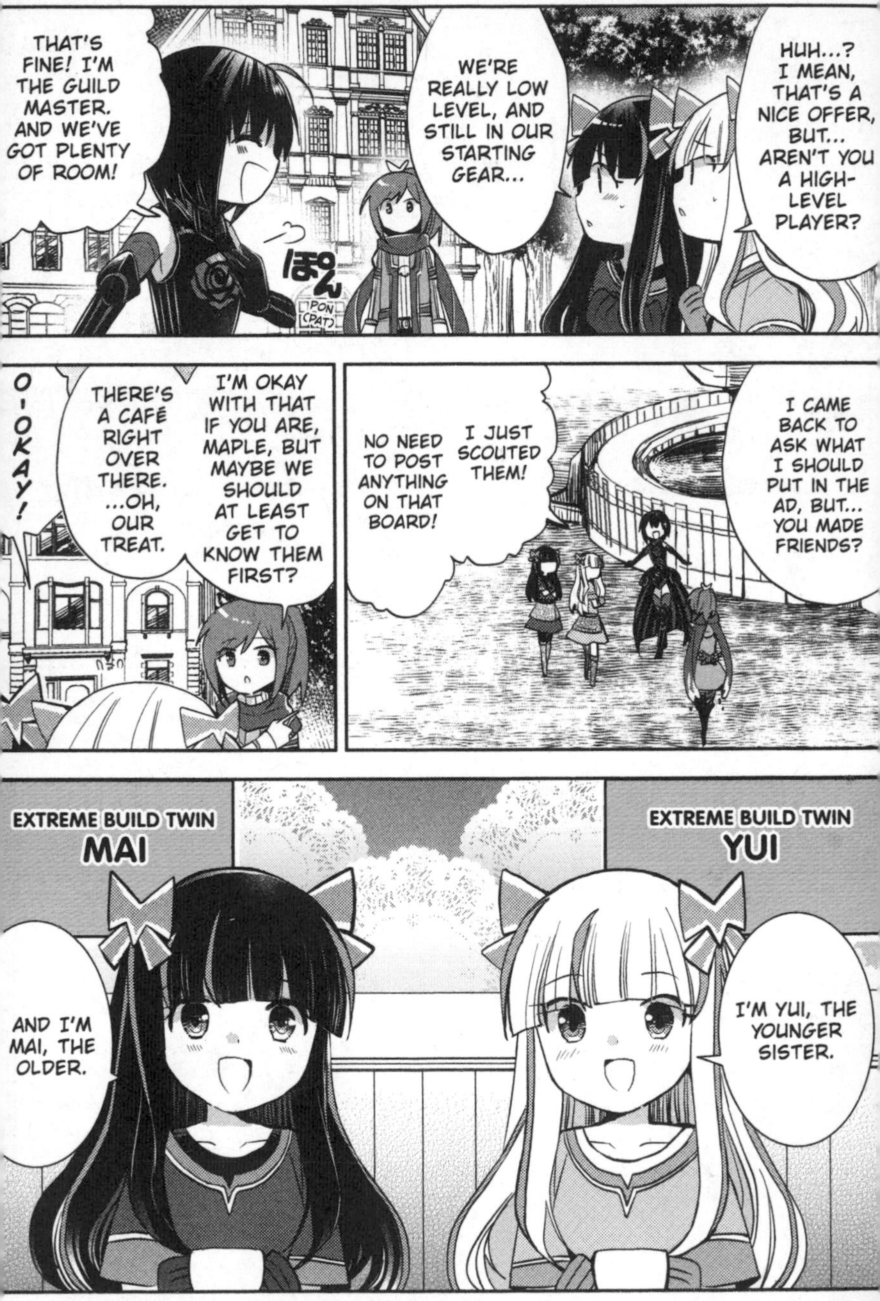
HUH...? I MEAN, THAT'S A NICE OFFER, BUT... AREN'T YOU A HIGH-LEVEL PLAYER?
WE'RE REALLY LOW LEVEL, AND STILL IN OUR STARTING GEAR...
THAT'S FINE! I'M THE GUILD MASTER. AND WE'VE GOT PLENTY OF ROOM!
ぽん
PON (PAT)
I CAME BACK TO ASK WHAT I SHOULD PUT IN THE AD, BUT... YOU MADE FRIENDS?
I JUST SCOUTED THEM!
NO NEED TO POST ANYTHING ON THAT BOARD!
I'M OKAY WITH THAT IF YOU ARE, MAPLE, BUT MAYBE WE SHOULD AT LEAST GET TO KNOW THEM FIRST?
THERE'S A CAFÉ RIGHT OVER THERE. ...OH, OUR TREAT.
O-OKAY!
EXTREME BUILD TWIN YUI
I'M YUI, THE YOUNGER SISTER.
EXTREME BUILD TWIN MAI
AND I'M MAI, THE OLDER.

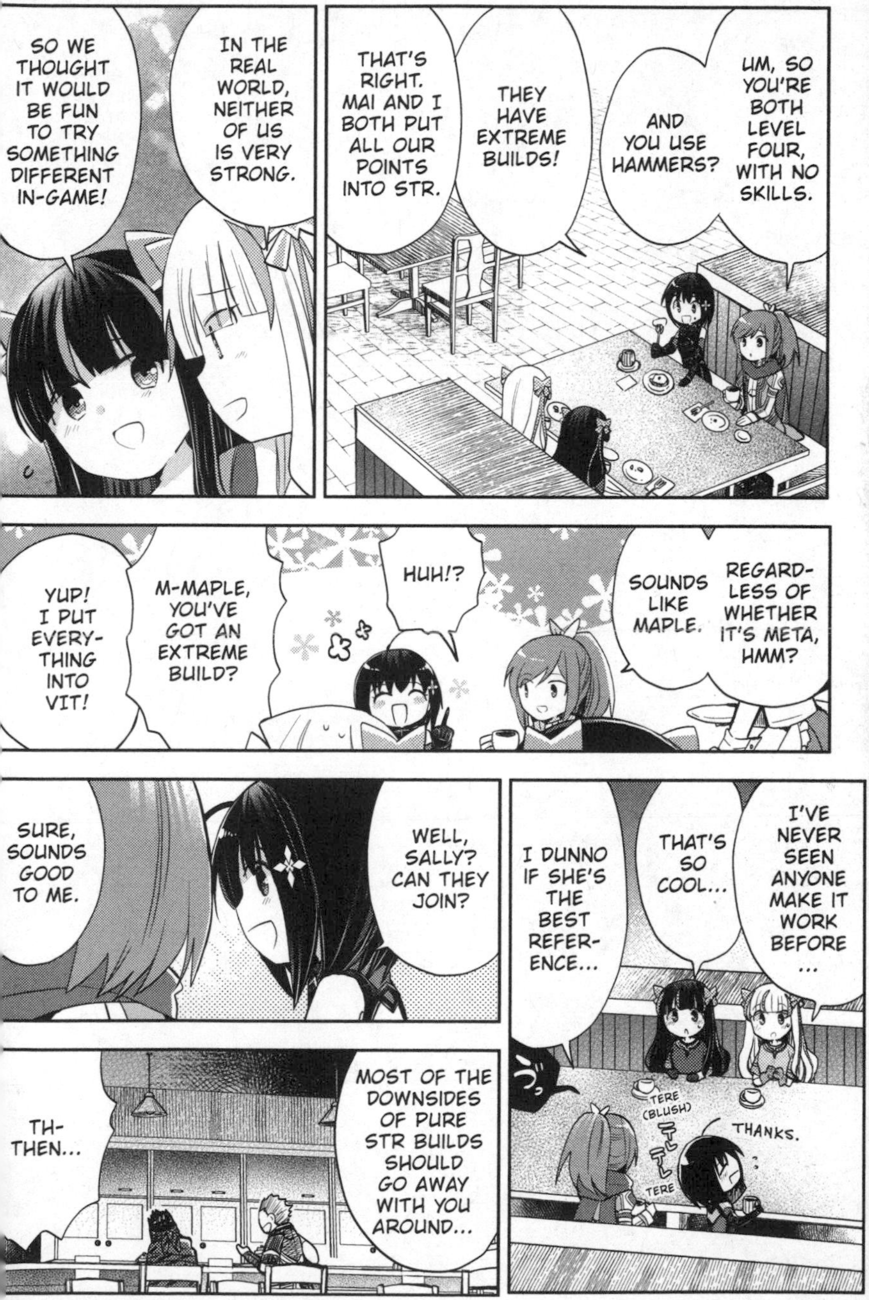
UM, SO YOU'RE BOTH LEVEL FOUR, WITH NO SKILLS.
AND YOU USE HAMMERS?
THEY HAVE EXTREME BUILDS!
THAT'S RIGHT. MAI AND I BOTH PUT ALL OUR POINTS INTO STR.
IN THE REAL WORLD, NEITHER OF US IS VERY STRONG.
SO WE THOUGHT IT WOULD BE FUN TO TRY SOMETHING DIFFERENT IN-GAME!
REGARDLESS OF WHETHER IT'S META, HMM?
SOUNDS LIKE MAPLE.
HUH!?
M-MAPLE, YOU'VE GOT AN EXTREME BUILD?
YUP! I PUT EVERYTHING INTO VIT!
I'VE NEVER SEEN ANYONE MAKE IT WORK BEFORE...
THAT'S SO COOL...
I DUNNO IF SHE'S THE BEST REFERENCE...
TERE (BLUSH)
TERE
THANKS.
WELL, SALLY? CAN THEY JOIN?
SURE, SOUNDS GOOD TO ME.
MOST OF THE DOWNSIDES OF PURE STR BUILDS SHOULD GO AWAY WITH YOU AROUND...
TH-THEN...

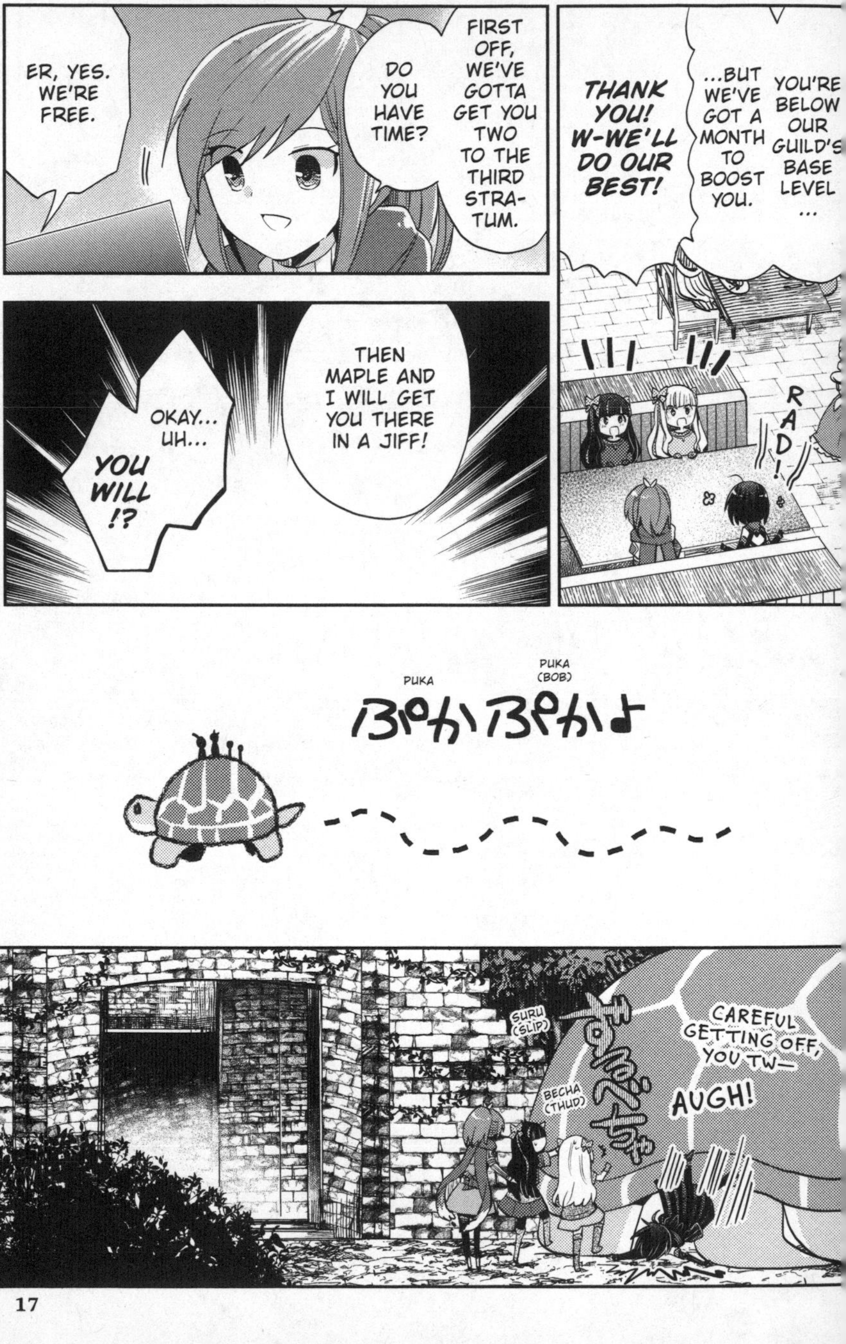
YOU'RE BELOW OUR GUILD'S BASE LEVEL...
...BUT WE'VE GOT A MONTH TO BOOST YOU.
THANK YOU! W-WE'LL DO OUR BEST!
RAD!
FIRST OFF, WE'VE GOTTA GET YOU TWO TO THE THIRD STRATUM.
DO YOU HAVE TIME?
ER, YES. WE'RE FREE.
THEN MAPLE AND I WILL GET YOU THERE IN A JIFF!
OKAY... UH...
YOU WILL!?
ぷかぷかよ
PUKA
PUKA (BOB)
CAREFUL GETTING OFF, YOU TW—
AUGH!
SURU (SLIP)
BECHA (THUD)

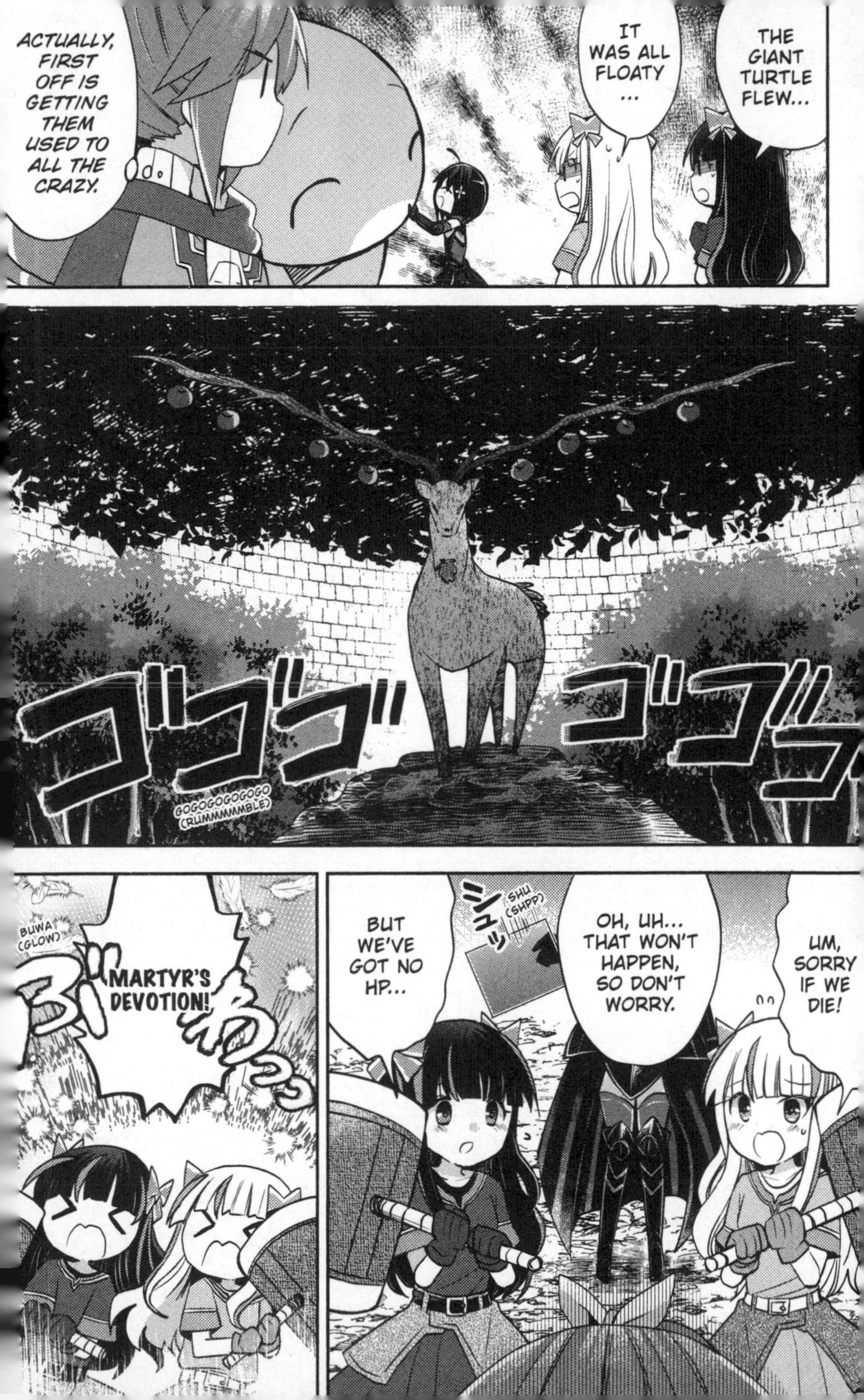
THE GIANT TURTLE FLEW...
IT WAS ALL FLOATY...
ACTUALLY, FIRST OFF IS GETTING THEM USED TO ALL THE CRAZY.
ゴゴゴ
ゴゴゴ
GOGOGOGOGOGO (RUMMMMMBLE)
UM, SORRY IF WE DIE!
OH, UH... THAT WON'T HAPPEN, SO DON'T WORRY.
シュッ
SHU (SHPP)
BUT WE'VE GOT NO HP...
ぶわっ
BUWA (GLOW)
MARTYR'S DEVOTION!

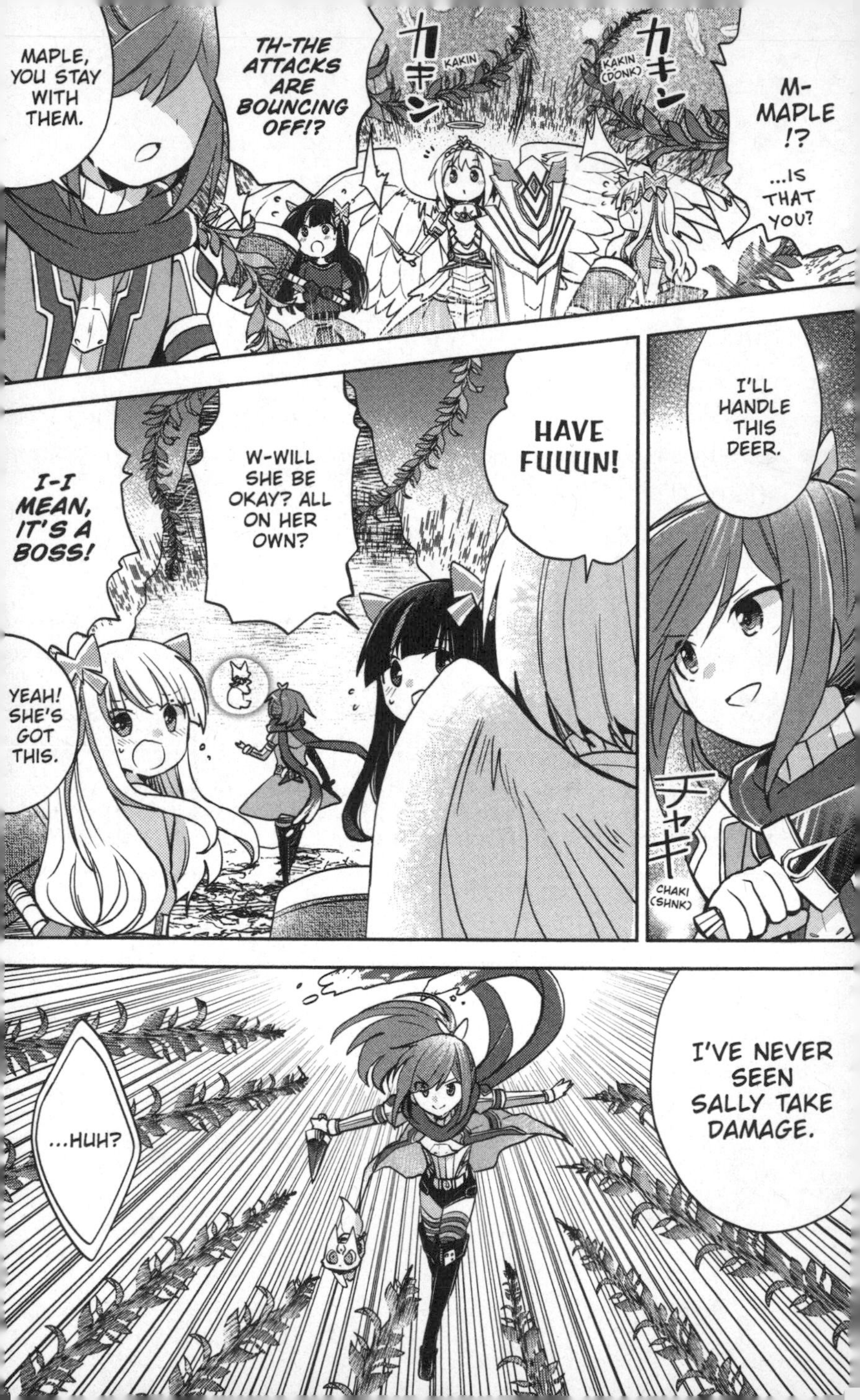
M-MAPLE!?
...IS THAT YOU?
カキン
KAKIN (DONK)
カキン
KAKIN
TH-THE ATTACKS ARE BOUNCING OFF!?
MAPLE, YOU STAY WITH THEM.
I'LL HANDLE THIS DEER.
チャキ
CHAKI (SHNK)
HAVE FUUUN!
W-WILL SHE BE OKAY? ALL ON HER OWN?
I-I MEAN, IT'S A BOSS!
YEAH! SHE'S GOT THIS.
I'VE NEVER SEEN SALLY TAKE DAMAGE.
...HUH?

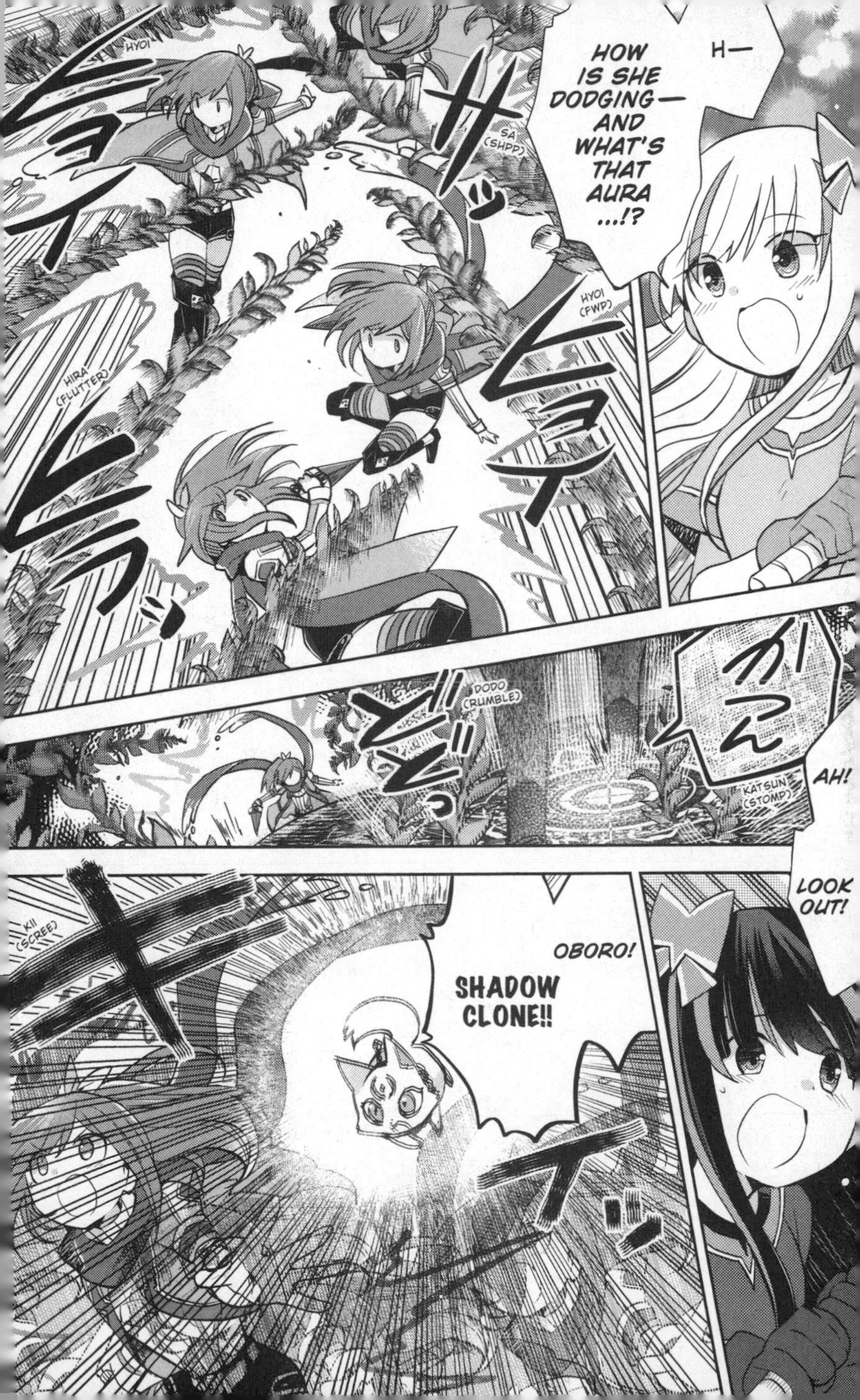
H—
HOW IS SHE DODGING—AND WHAT'S THAT AURA...!?
SA (SHPP)
HYOI
HYOI (FWP)
HIRA (FLUTTER)
KATSUN (STOMP)
AH!
DODO (RUMBLE)
LOOK OUT!
OBORO!
SHADOW CLONE!!
KII (SCREE)

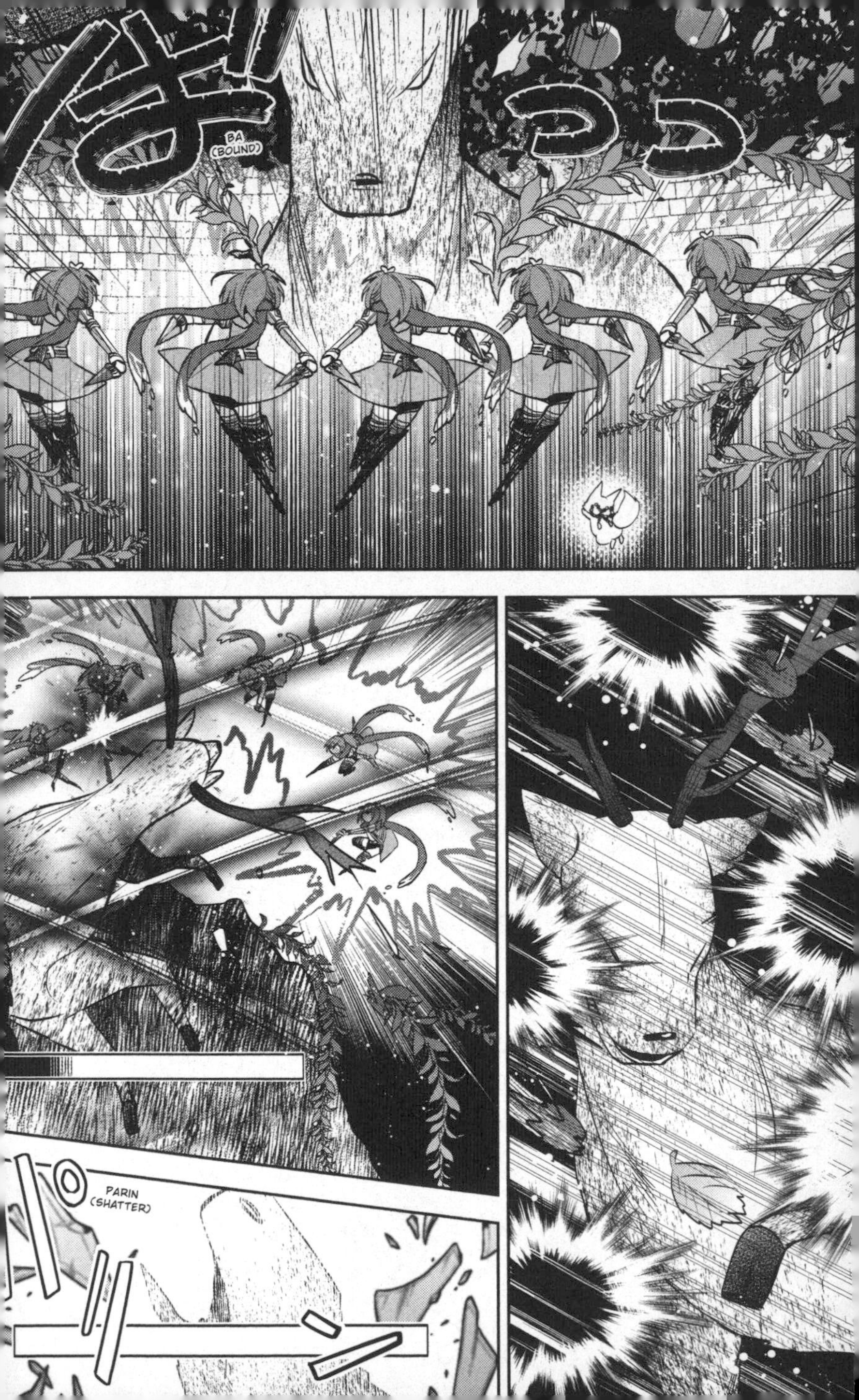
BA
(BOUND)
PARIN
(SHATTER)

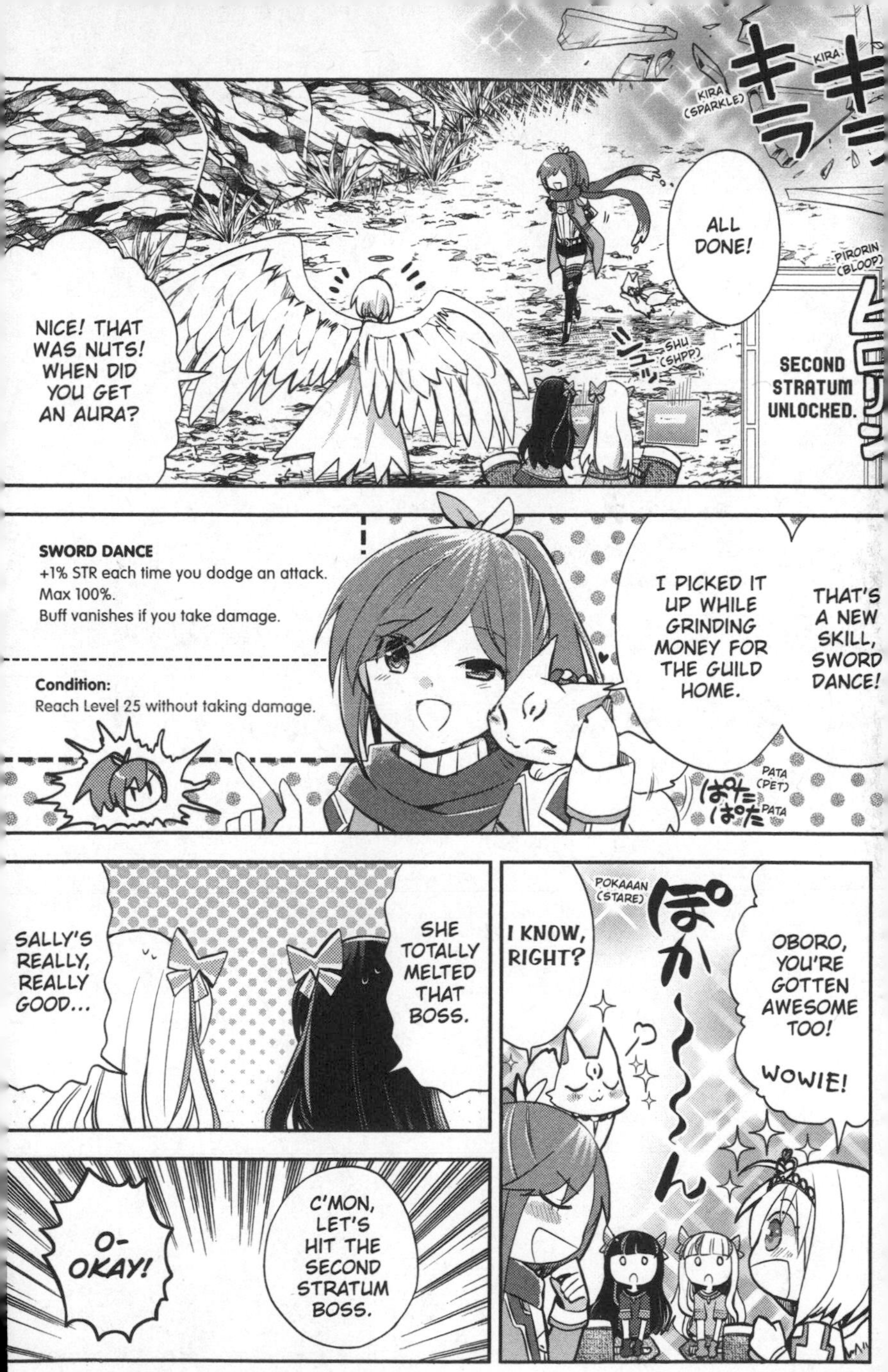
KIRA
KIRA (SPARKLE)
ALL DONE!
PIRORIN (BLOOP)
SECOND STRATUM UNLOCKED.
SHU (SHPP)
NICE! THAT WAS NUTS! WHEN DID YOU GET AN AURA?
THAT'S A NEW SKILL, SWORD DANCE!
I PICKED IT UP WHILE GRINDING MONEY FOR THE GUILD HOME.
SWORD DANCE
+1% STR each time you dodge an attack.
Max 100%.
Buff vanishes if you take damage.
Condition:
Reach Level 25 without taking damage.
PATA (PET) PATA
OBORO, YOU'RE GOTTEN AWESOME TOO!
WOWIE!
I KNOW, RIGHT?
POKAAAN (STARE)
SHE TOTALLY MELTED THAT BOSS.
SALLY'S REALLY, REALLY GOOD...
C'MON, LET'S HIT THE SECOND STRATUM BOSS.
O-OKAY!

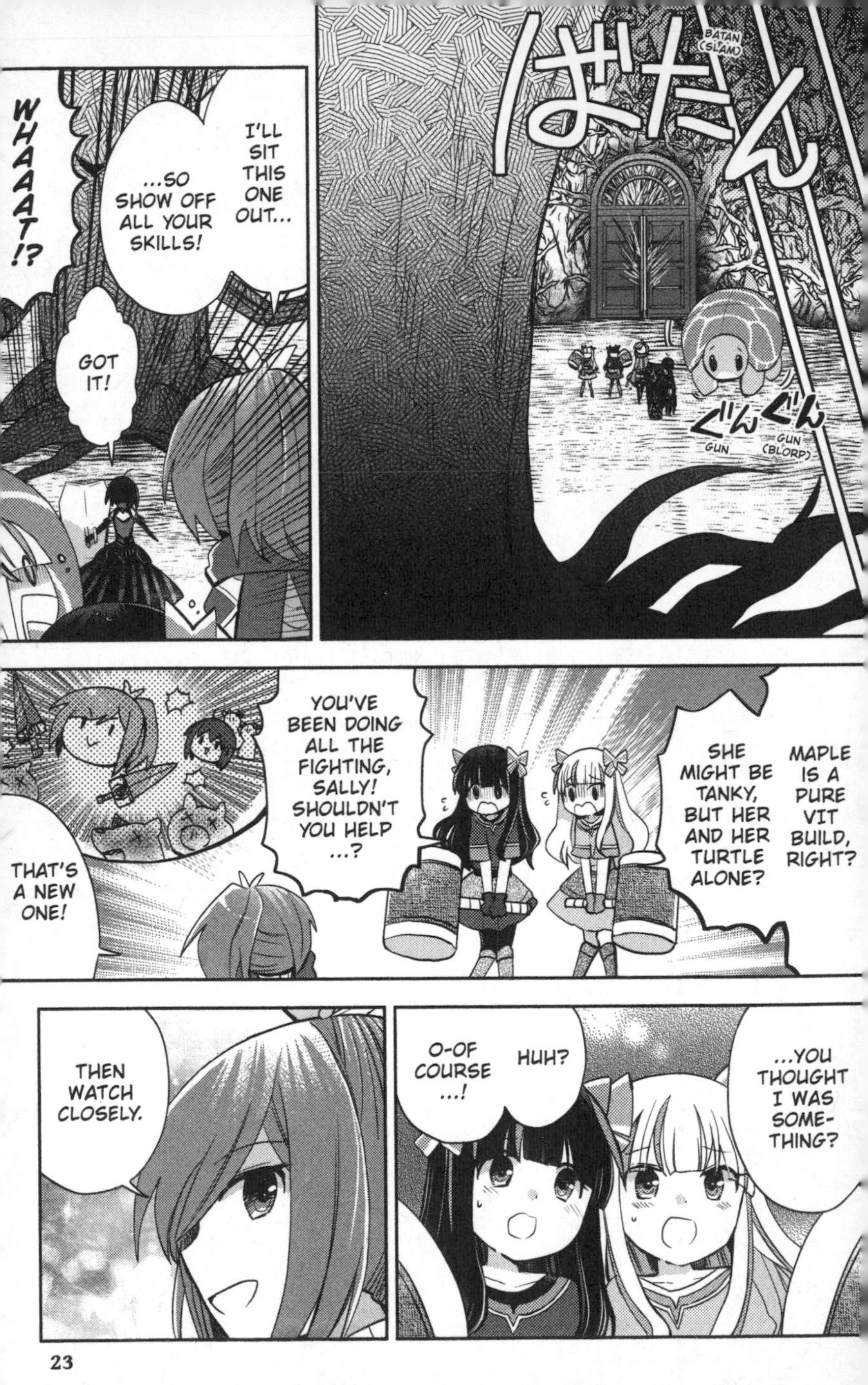
ばたん
BATAN (SLAM)
ぐんぐん
GUN (BLORP)
GUN
I'LL SIT THIS ONE OUT...
...SO SHOW OFF ALL YOUR SKILLS!
GOT IT!
WHAAAAT!?
MAPLE IS A PURE VIT BUILD, RIGHT?
SHE MIGHT BE TANKY, BUT HER AND HER TURTLE ALONE?
YOU'VE BEEN DOING ALL THE FIGHTING, SALLY! SHOULDN'T YOU HELP ...?
THAT'S A NEW ONE!
...YOU THOUGHT I WAS SOME-THING?
HUH?
O-OF COURSE ...!
THEN WATCH CLOSELY.

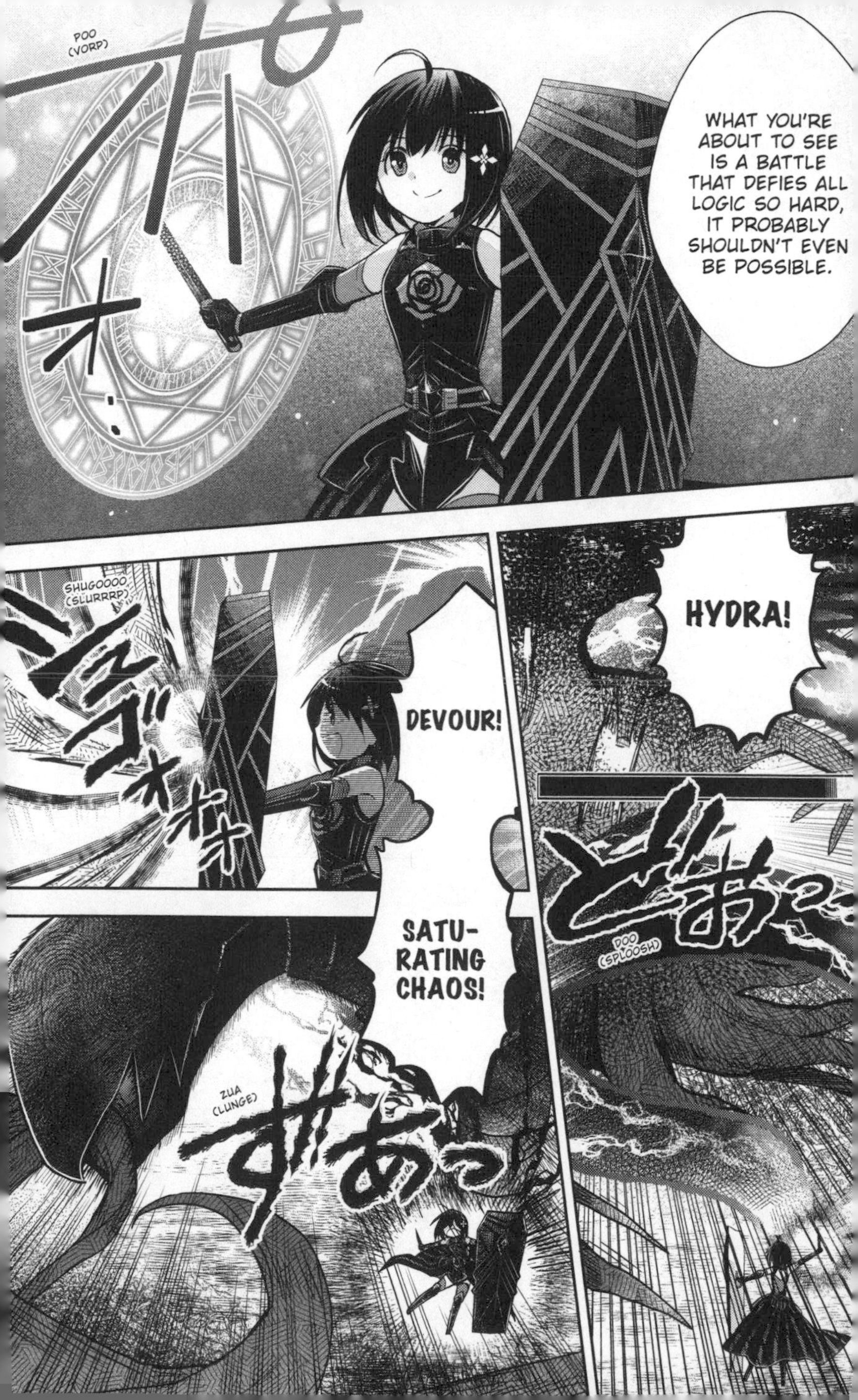
WHAT YOU'RE ABOUT TO SEE IS A BATTLE THAT DEFIES ALL LOGIC SO HARD, IT PROBABLY SHOULDN'T EVEN BE POSSIBLE.
POO (VORP)
HYDRA!
DOO (SPLOOSH)
SHUGOOOO (SLURRRP)
DEVOUR!
SATU-RATING CHAOS!
ZUA (LUNGE)

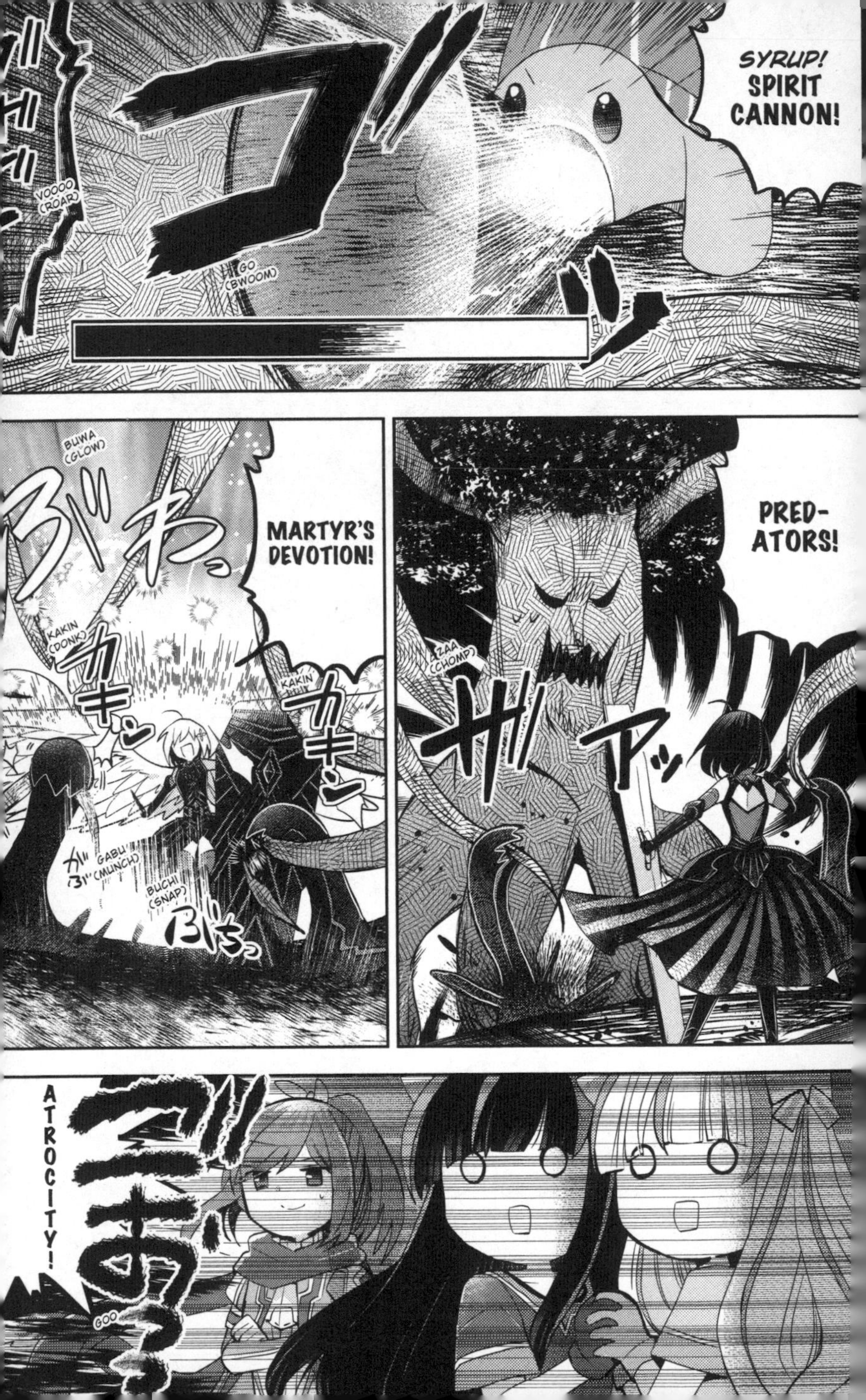
SYRUP! SPIRIT CANNON!
GO (BWOOM)
VOOOO (ROAR)
PRED-ATORS!
ZAA (CHOMP)
MARTYR'S DEVOTION!
BUWA (GLOW)
KAKIN
KAKIN (DONK)
GABU (MUNCH)
BUCHI (SNAP)
ATROCITY!
GOO

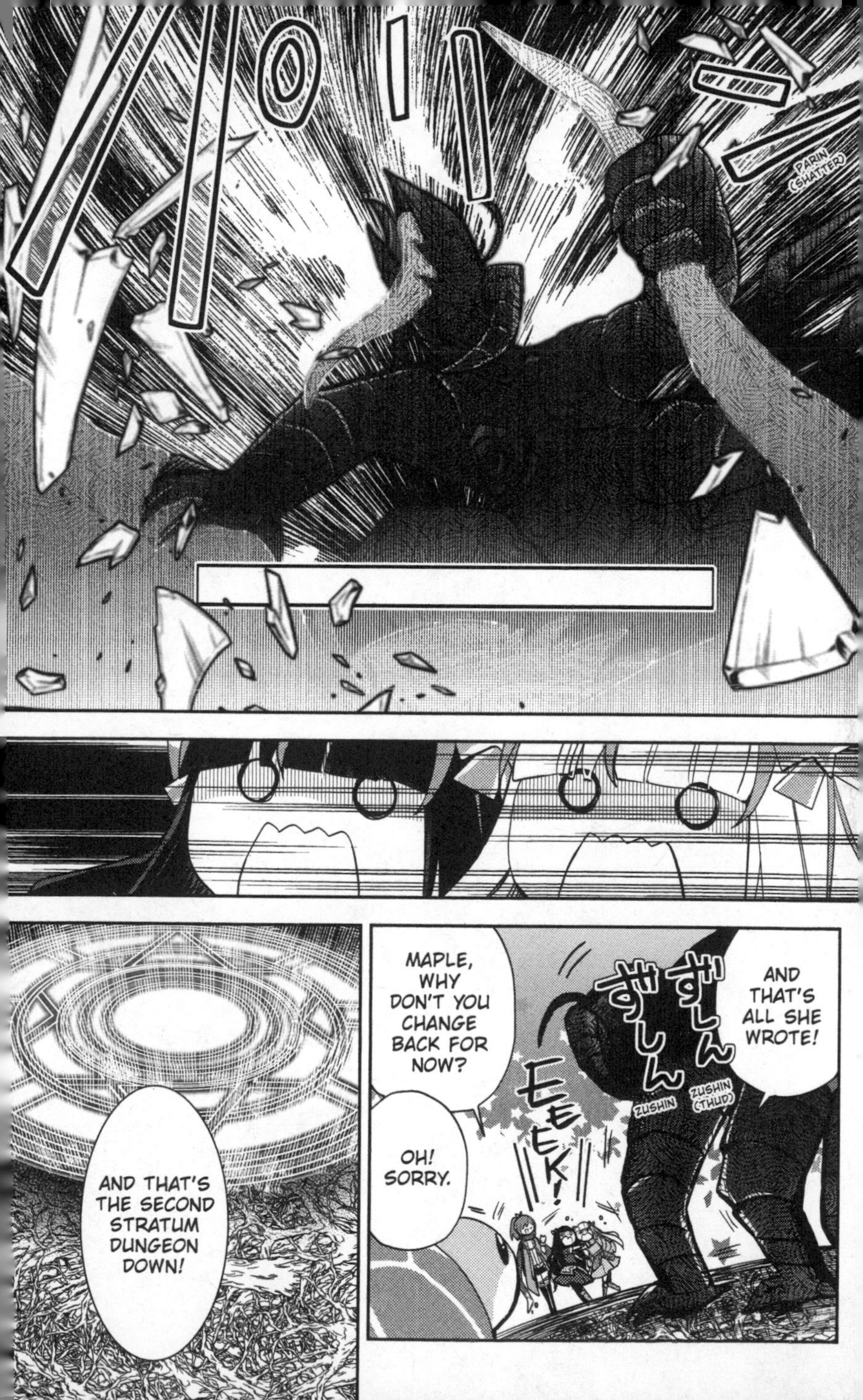
PARIN (SHATTER)
AND THAT'S ALL SHE WROTE!
ずしん
ZUSHIN (THUD)
ずしん
ZUSHIN
EEEK!
MAPLE, WHY DON'T YOU CHANGE BACK FOR NOW?
OH! SORRY.
AND THAT'S THE SECOND STRATUM DUNGEON DOWN!

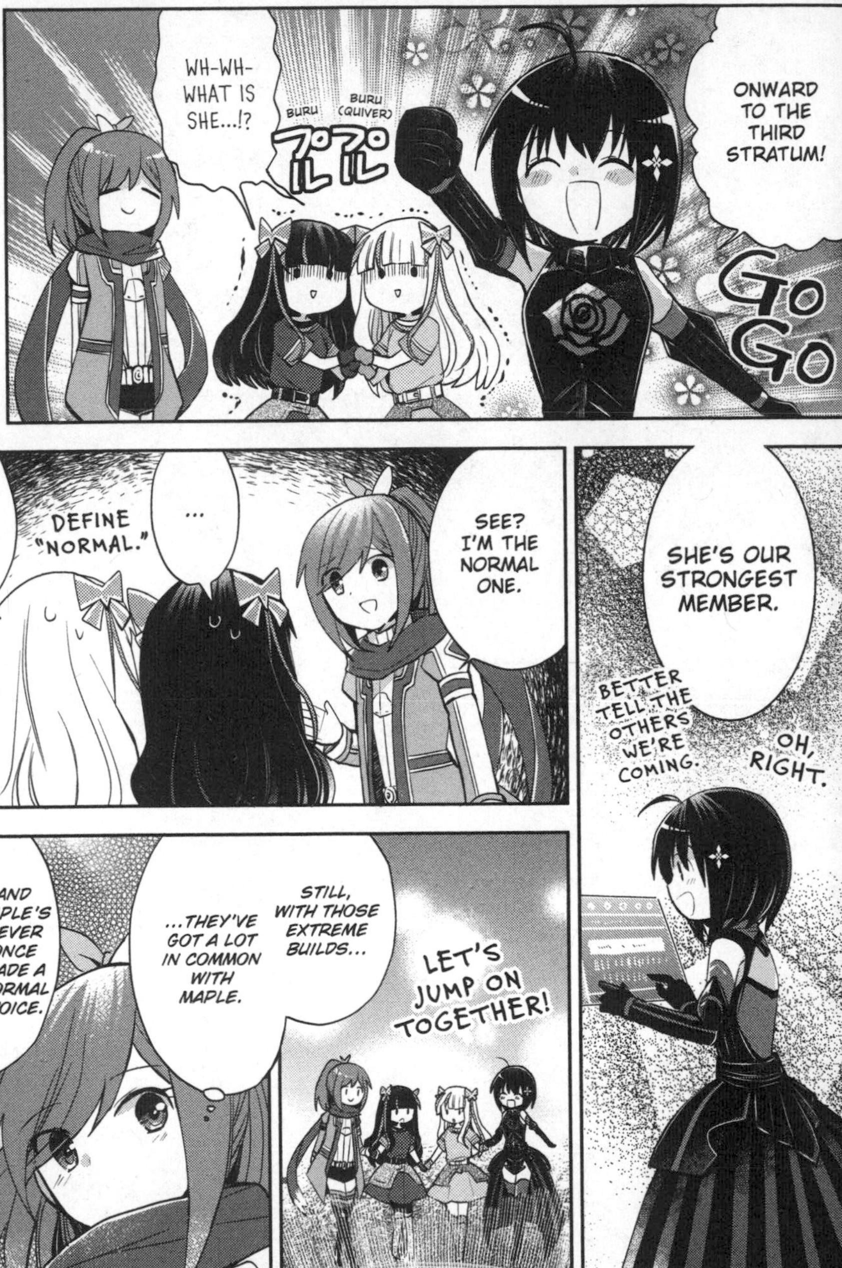
ONWARD TO THE THIRD STRATUM!
GO GO
WH-WH-WHAT IS SHE...!?
BURU BURU (QUIVER)
SHE'S OUR STRONGEST MEMBER.
OH, RIGHT.
BETTER TELL THE OTHERS WE'RE COMING.
SEE? I'M THE NORMAL ONE.
...
DEFINE "NORMAL."
...
LET'S JUMP ON TOGETHER!
STILL, WITH THOSE EXTREME BUILDS...
...THEY'VE GOT A LOT IN COMMON WITH MAPLE.
AND MAPLE'S NEVER ONCE MADE A NORMAL CHOICE.

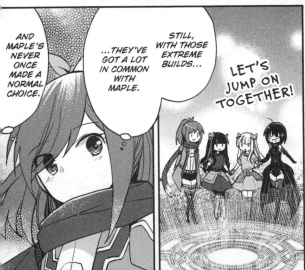

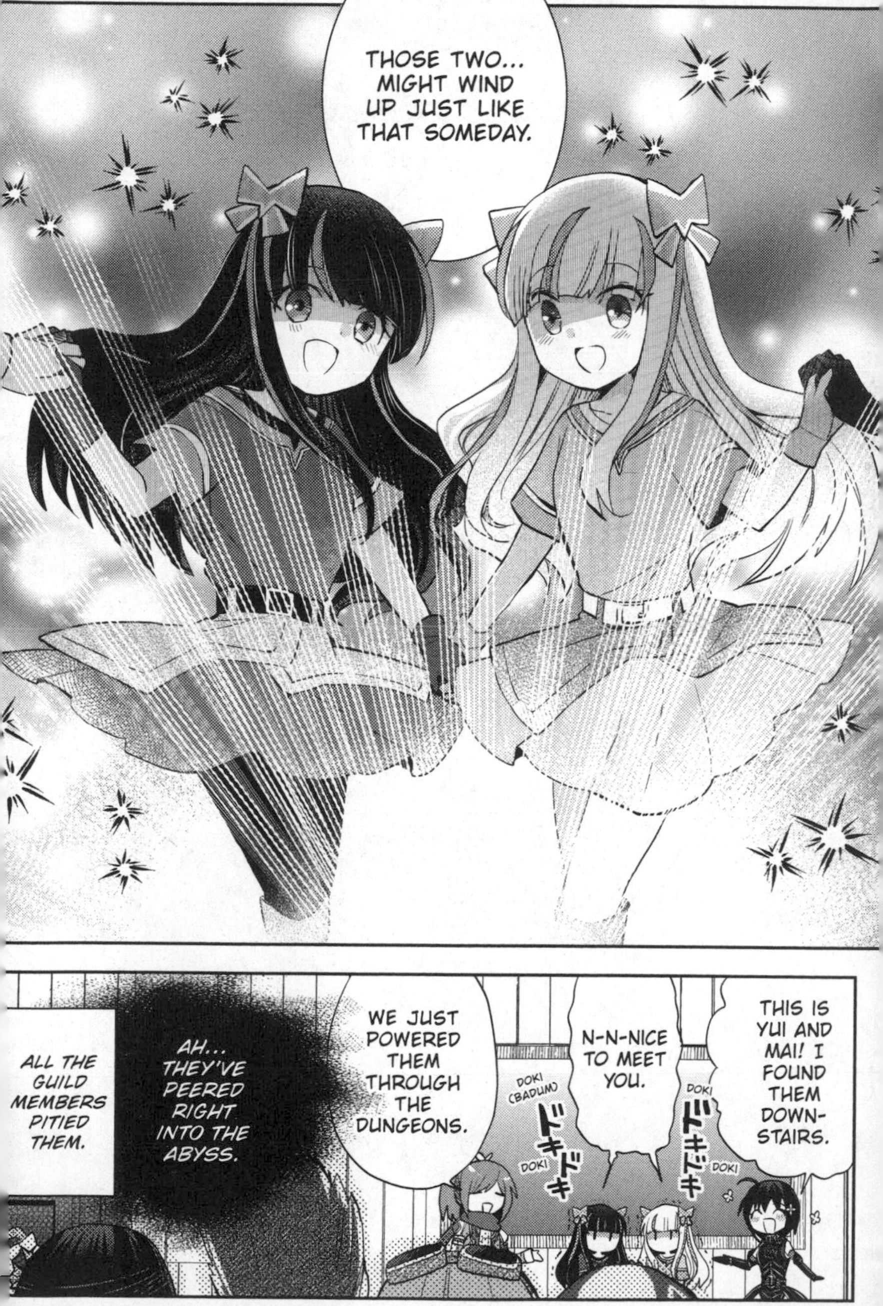
THOSE TWO... MIGHT WIND UP JUST LIKE THAT SOMEDAY.
THIS IS YUI AND MAI! I FOUND THEM DOWN-STAIRS.
DOKI
ドキドキ
DOKI
N-N-NICE TO MEET YOU.
DOKI (BADUM)
ドキドキ
DOKI
WE JUST POWERED THEM THROUGH THE DUNGEONS.
AH... THEY'VE PEERED RIGHT INTO THE ABYSS.
ALL THE GUILD MEMBERS PITIED THEM.

CHAPTER 24

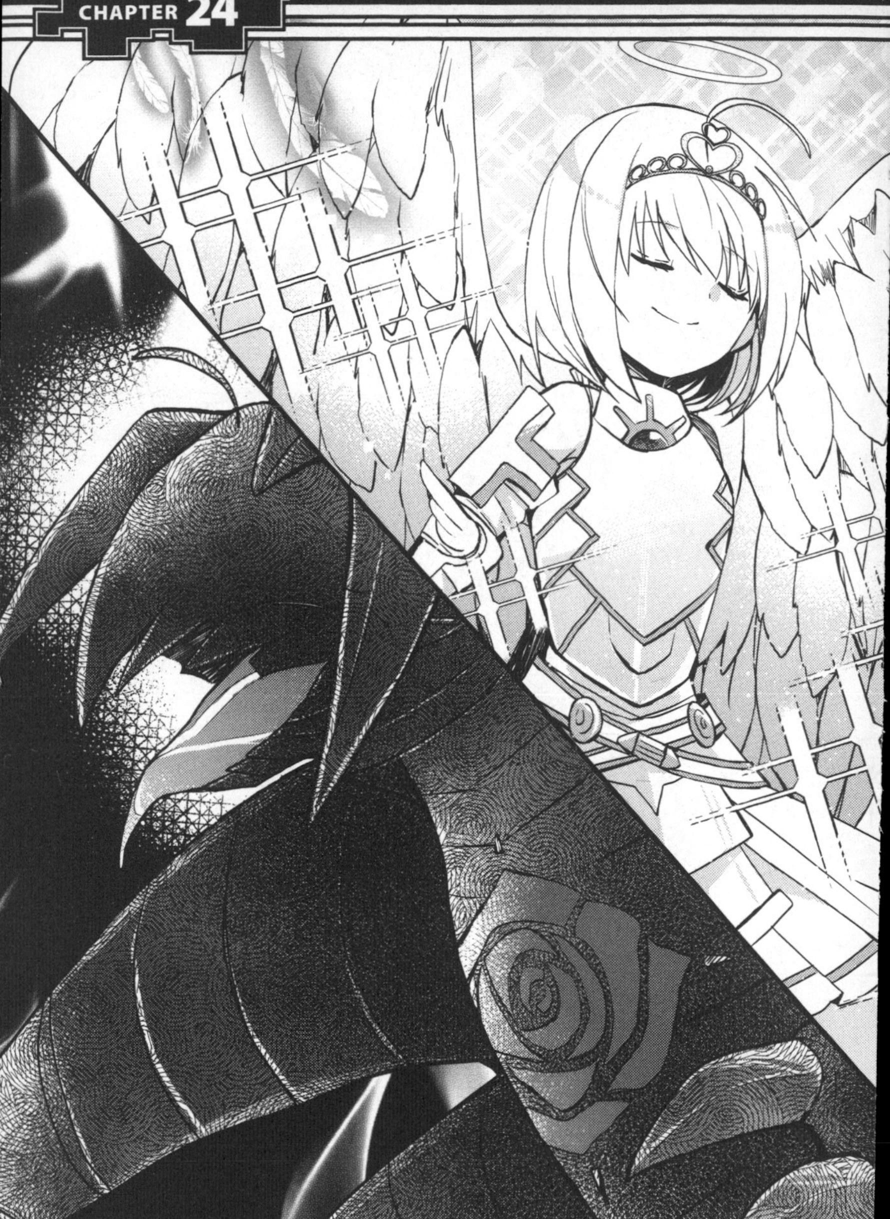

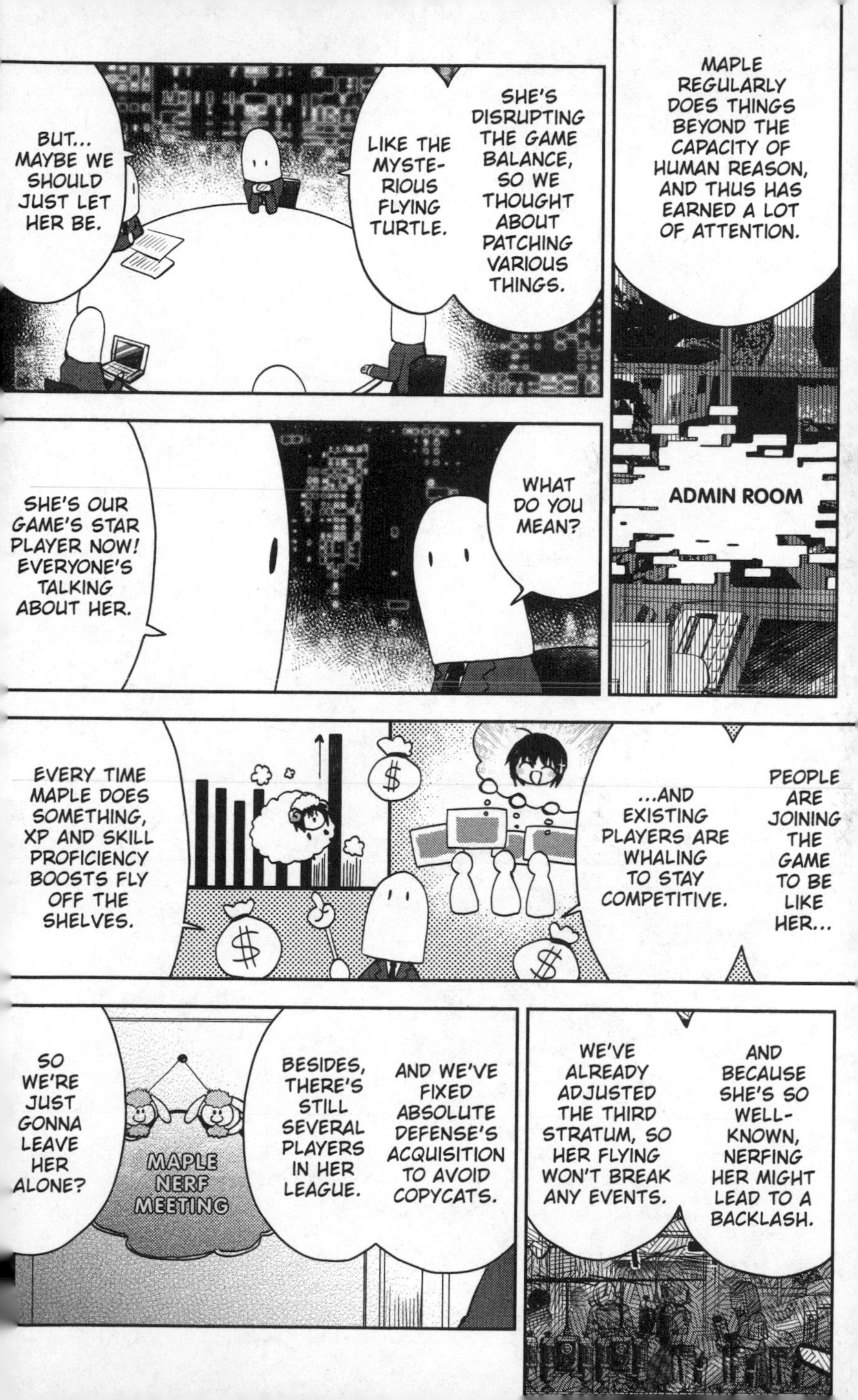
MAPLE REGULARLY DOES THINGS BEYOND THE CAPACITY OF HUMAN REASON, AND THUS HAS EARNED A LOT OF ATTENTION.
ADMIN ROOM
SHE'S DISRUPTING THE GAME BALANCE, SO WE THOUGHT ABOUT PATCHING VARIOUS THINGS.
LIKE THE MYSTE-RIOUS FLYING TURTLE.
BUT... MAYBE WE SHOULD JUST LET HER BE.
WHAT DO YOU MEAN?
SHE'S OUR GAME'S STAR PLAYER NOW! EVERYONE'S TALKING ABOUT HER.
PEOPLE ARE JOINING THE GAME TO BE LIKE HER...
...AND EXISTING PLAYERS ARE WHALING TO STAY COMPETITIVE.
EVERY TIME MAPLE DOES SOMETHING, XP AND SKILL PROFICIENCY BOOSTS FLY OFF THE SHELVES.
AND BECAUSE SHE'S SO WELL-KNOWN, NERFING HER MIGHT LEAD TO A BACKLASH.
WE'VE ALREADY ADJUSTED THE THIRD STRATUM, SO HER FLYING WON'T BREAK ANY EVENTS.
AND WE'VE FIXED ABSOLUTE DEFENSE'S ACQUISITION TO AVOID COPYCATS.
BESIDES, THERE'S STILL SEVERAL PLAYERS IN HER LEAGUE.
MAPLE NERF MEETING
SO WE'RE JUST GONNA LEAVE HER ALONE?

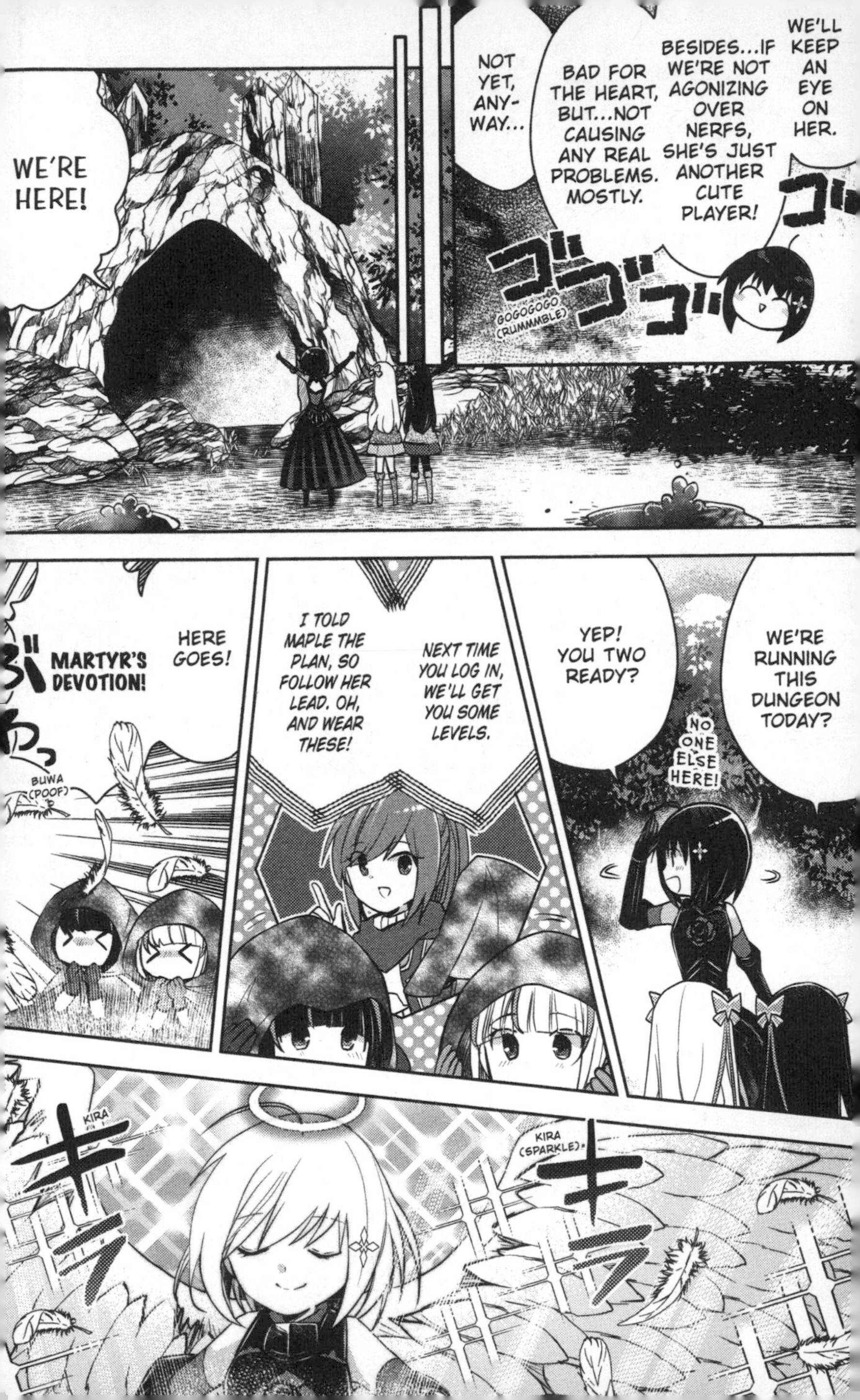
WE'LL KEEP AN EYE ON HER.
BESIDES...IF WE'RE NOT AGONIZING OVER NERFS, SHE'S JUST ANOTHER CUTE PLAYER!
BAD FOR THE HEART, BUT...NOT CAUSING ANY REAL PROBLEMS. MOSTLY.
NOT YET, ANY-WAY...
GOGOGOGO (RUMMMBLE)
WE'RE HERE!
WE'RE RUNNING THIS DUNGEON TODAY?
NO ONE ELSE HERE!
YEP! YOU TWO READY?
NEXT TIME YOU LOG IN, WE'LL GET YOU SOME LEVELS.
I TOLD MAPLE THE PLAN, SO FOLLOW HER LEAD. OH, AND WEAR THESE!
HERE GOES!
MARTYR'S DEVOTION!
BUWA (POOF)
KIRA (SPARKLE)
KIRA

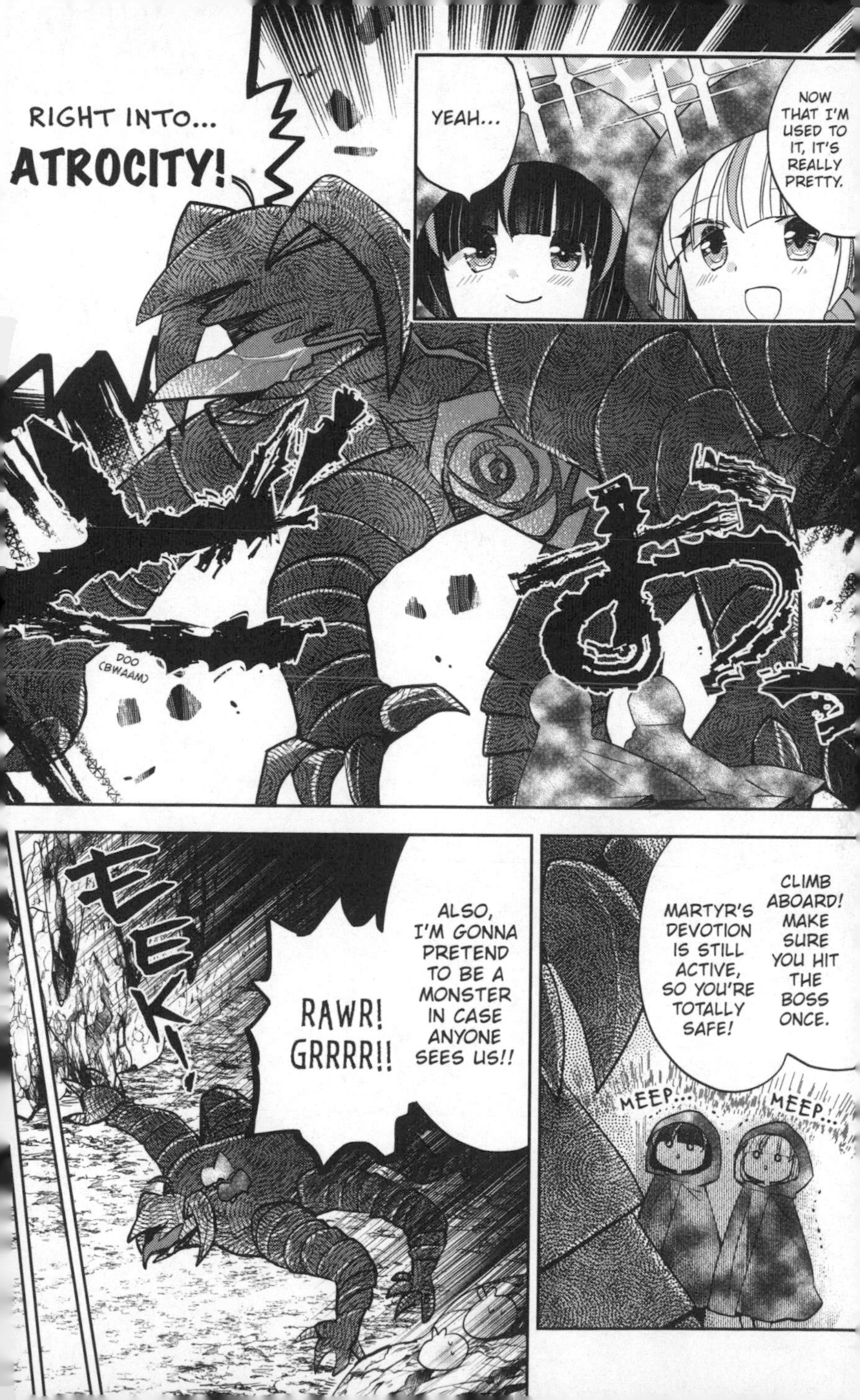
NOW THAT I'M USED TO IT, IT'S REALLY PRETTY.
YEAH...
RIGHT INTO... ATROCITY!
DOO (BWAAM)
CLIMB ABOARD! MAKE SURE YOU HIT THE BOSS ONCE.
MARTYR'S DEVOTION IS STILL ACTIVE, SO YOU'RE TOTALLY SAFE!
MEEP...
MEEP...
ALSO, I'M GONNA PRETEND TO BE A MONSTER IN CASE ANYONE SEES US!!
RAWR! GRRRR!!

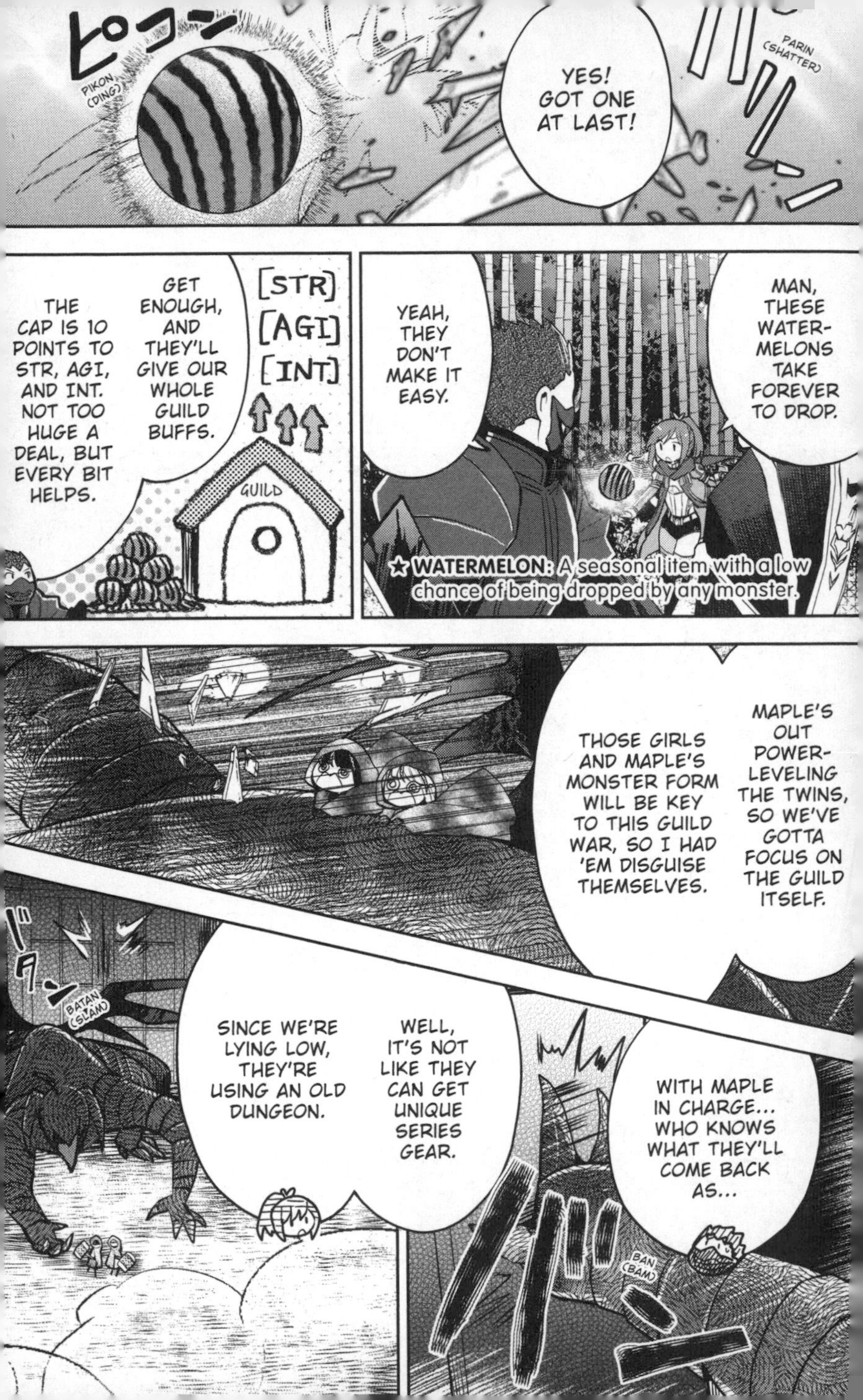
PARIN (SHATTER)
YES! GOT ONE AT LAST!
ピコーン
PIKON (DING)
MAN, THESE WATER-MELONS TAKE FOREVER TO DROP.
YEAH, THEY DON'T MAKE IT EASY.
★ WATERMELON: A seasonal item with a low chance of being dropped by any monster.
[STR]
[AGI]
[INT]
GET ENOUGH, AND THEY'LL GIVE OUR WHOLE GUILD BUFFS.
THE CAP IS 10 POINTS TO STR, AGI, AND INT. NOT TOO HUGE A DEAL, BUT EVERY BIT HELPS.
GUILD
MAPLE'S OUT POWER-LEVELING THE TWINS, SO WE'VE GOTTA FOCUS ON THE GUILD ITSELF.
THOSE GIRLS AND MAPLE'S MONSTER FORM WILL BE KEY TO THIS GUILD WAR, SO I HAD 'EM DISGUISE THEMSELVES.
WITH MAPLE IN CHARGE... WHO KNOWS WHAT THEY'LL COME BACK AS...
BAN (BAM)
WELL, IT'S NOT LIKE THEY CAN GET UNIQUE SERIES GEAR.
SINCE WE'RE LYING LOW, THEY'RE USING AN OLD DUNGEON.
BATAN (SLAM)

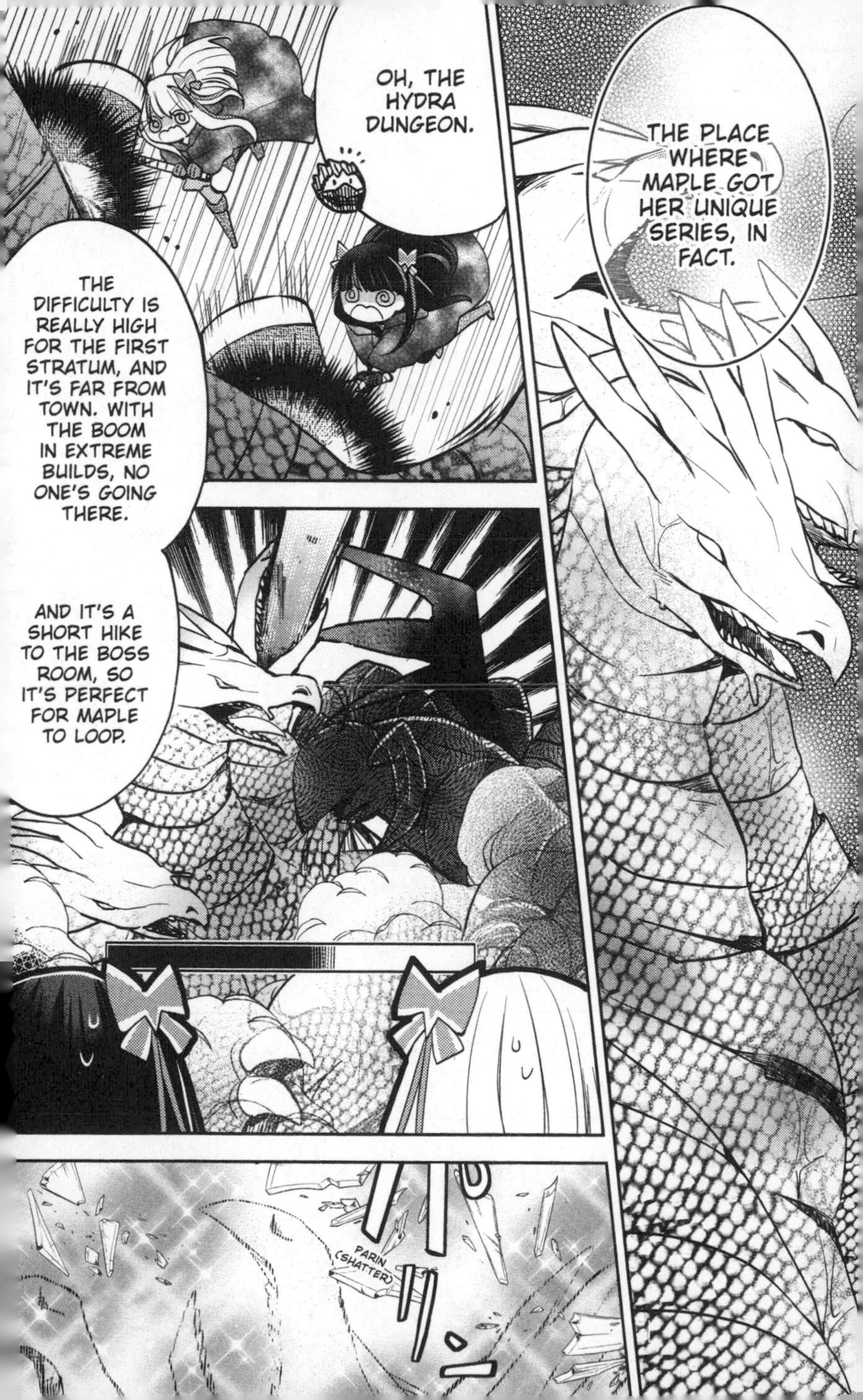
OH, THE HYDRA DUNGEON.
THE PLACE WHERE MAPLE GOT HER UNIQUE SERIES, IN FACT.
THE DIFFICULTY IS REALLY HIGH FOR THE FIRST STRATUM, AND IT'S FAR FROM TOWN. WITH THE BOOM IN EXTREME BUILDS, NO ONE'S GOING THERE.
AND IT'S A SHORT HIKE TO THE BOSS ROOM, SO IT'S PERFECT FOR MAPLE TO LOOP.
PARIN (SHATTER)

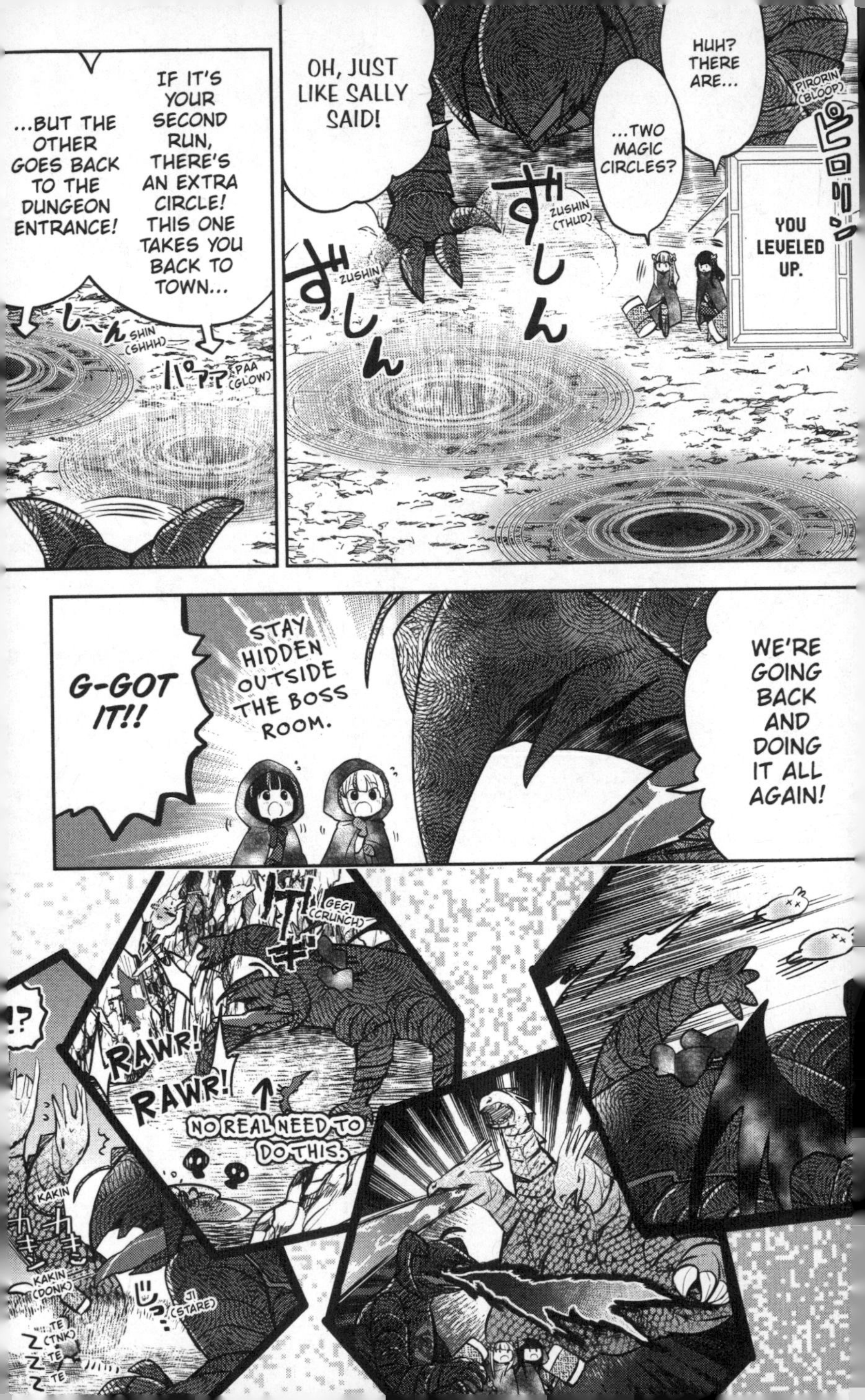
PIRORIN (BLOOP)
HUH? THERE ARE...
YOU LEVELED UP.
...TWO MAGIC CIRCLES?
ZUSHIN (THUD)
ZUSHIN
OH, JUST LIKE SALLY SAID!
IF IT'S YOUR SECOND RUN, THERE'S AN EXTRA CIRCLE! THIS ONE TAKES YOU BACK TO TOWN...
...BUT THE OTHER GOES BACK TO THE DUNGEON ENTRANCE!
SHIN (SHHH)
PAA (GLOW)
WE'RE GOING BACK AND DOING IT ALL AGAIN!
STAY HIDDEN OUTSIDE THE BOSS ROOM.
G-GOT IT!!
GEGI (CRUNCH)
RAWR!
RAWR!
NO REAL NEED TO DO THIS.
!?
KAKIN
KAKIN (DONK)
JI (STARE)
TE (TNK)
TE
TE

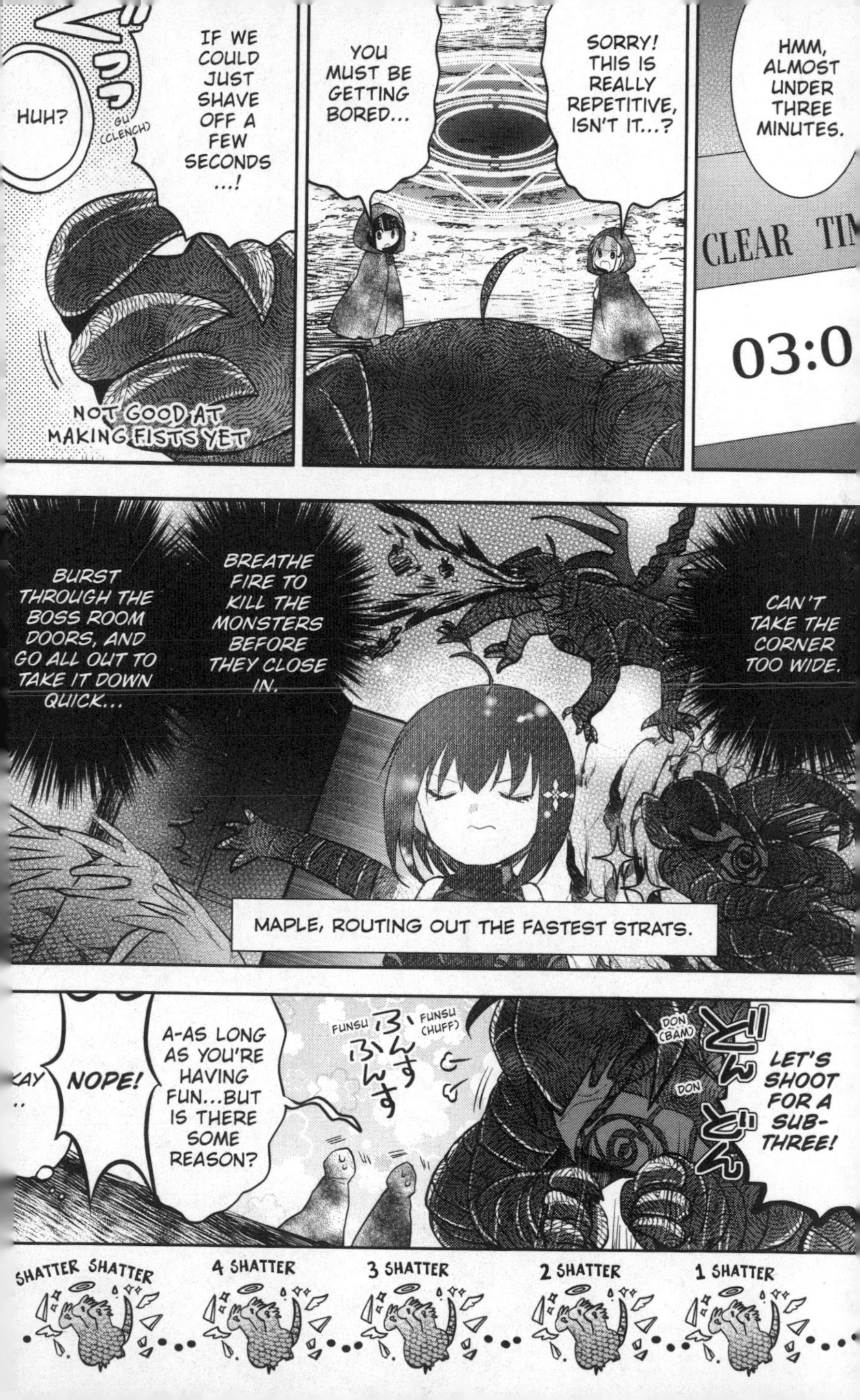
HMM, ALMOST UNDER THREE MINUTES.
CLEAR TIM
03:0
SORRY! THIS IS REALLY REPETITIVE, ISN'T IT...?
YOU MUST BE GETTING BORED...
IF WE COULD JUST SHAVE OFF A FEW SECONDS...!
GU (CLENCH)
HUH?
NOT GOOD AT MAKING FISTS YET
CAN'T TAKE THE CORNER TOO WIDE.
BREATHE FIRE TO KILL THE MONSTERS BEFORE THEY CLOSE IN.
BURST THROUGH THE BOSS ROOM DOORS, AND GO ALL OUT TO TAKE IT DOWN QUICK...
MAPLE, ROUTING OUT THE FASTEST STRATS.
LET'S SHOOT FOR A SUB-THREE!
どん どん
DON (BAM)
DON
ふんす ふんす
FUNSU (HUFF)
FUNSU
A-AS LONG AS YOU'RE HAVING FUN...BUT IS THERE SOME REASON?
NOPE!
1 SHATTER
2 SHATTER
3 SHATTER
4 SHATTER
SHATTER SHATTER

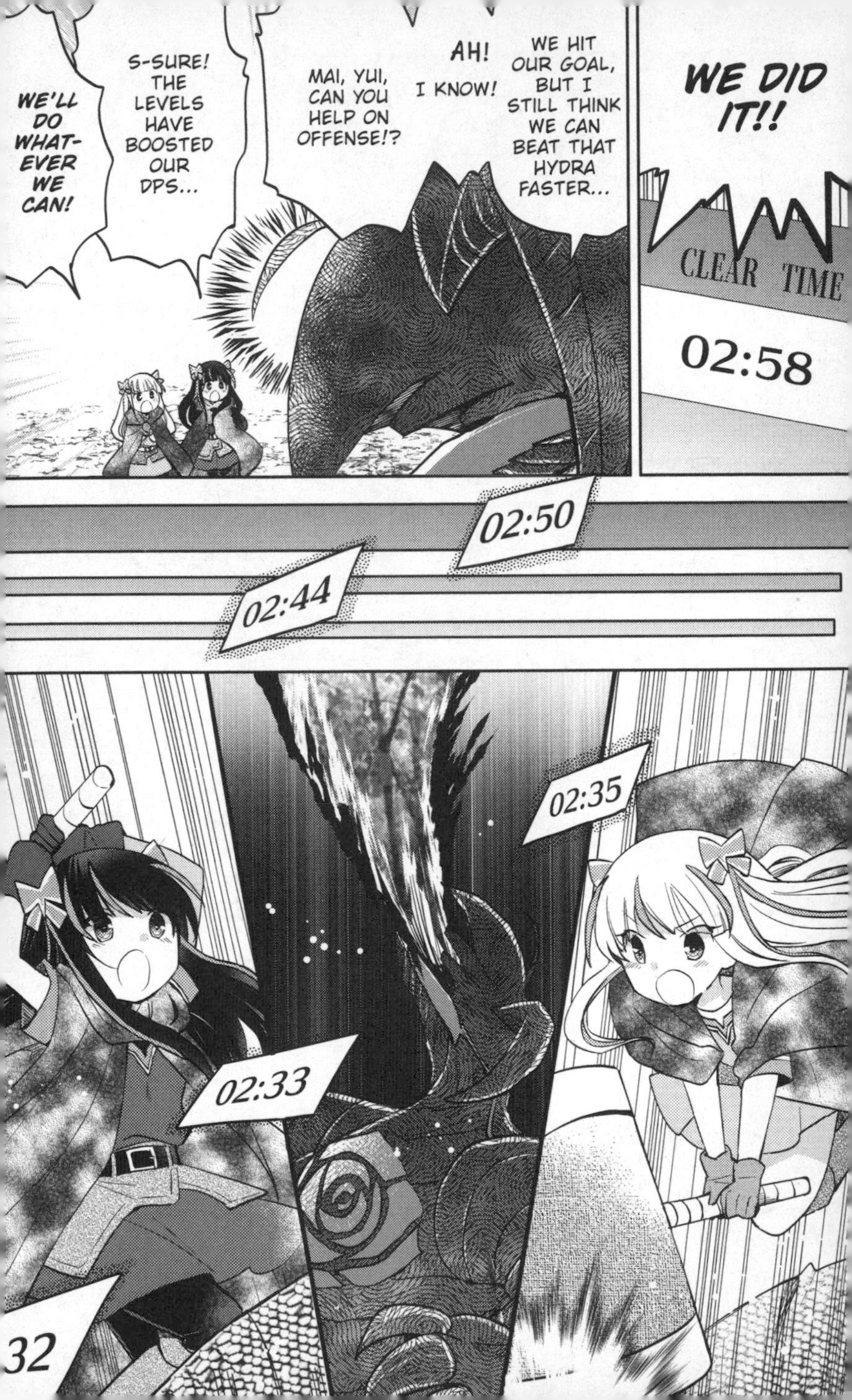
WE DID IT!!
CLEAR TIME
02:58
WE HIT OUR GOAL, BUT I STILL THINK WE CAN BEAT THAT HYDRA FASTER...
AH! I KNOW!
MAI, YUI, CAN YOU HELP ON OFFENSE!?
S-SURE! THE LEVELS HAVE BOOSTED OUR DPS...
WE'LL DO WHATEVER WE CAN!
02:50
02:44
02:35
02:33

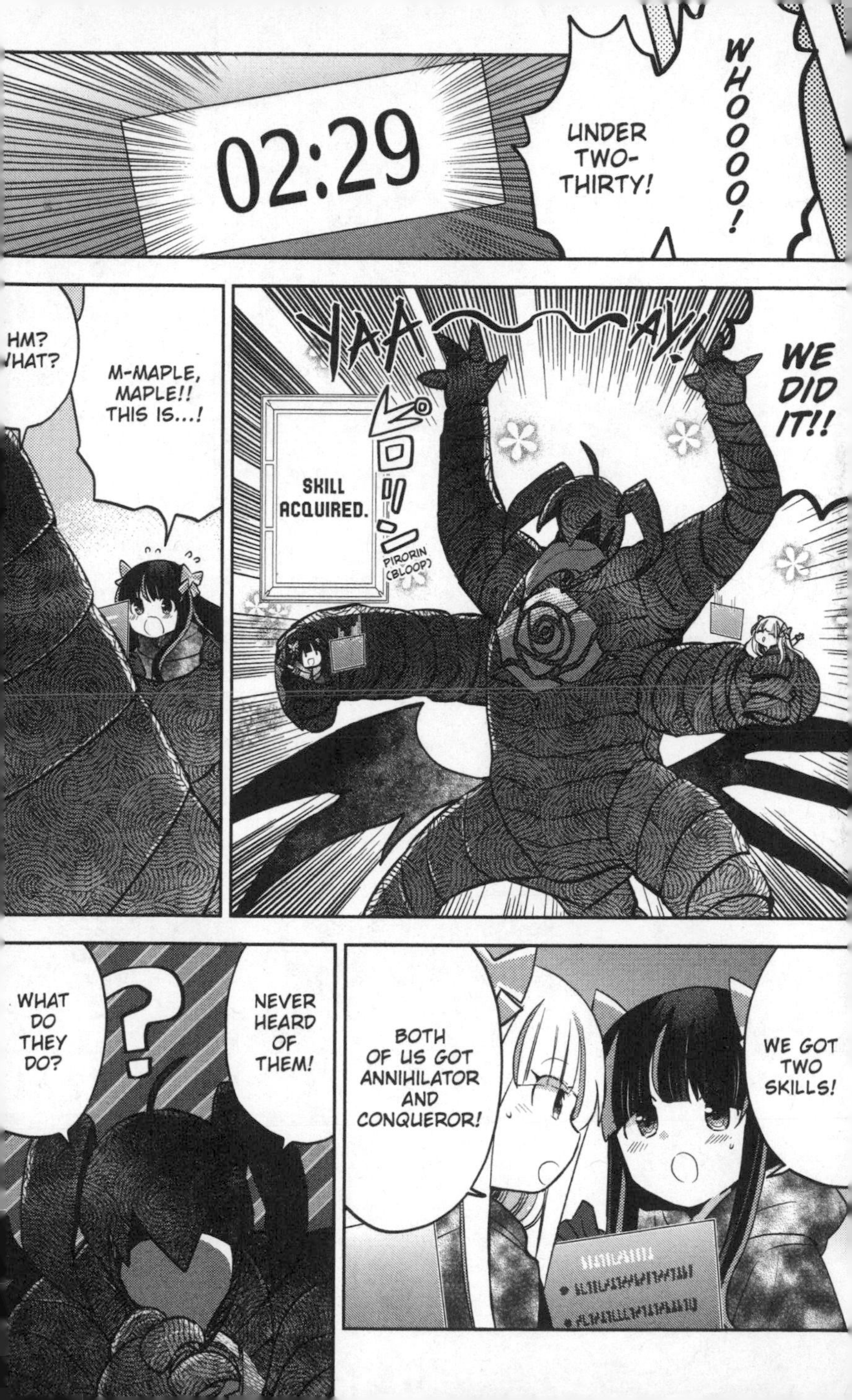
WHOOOOO!
UNDER TWO-THIRTY!
02:29
WE DID IT!!
YAA~~~AY!
SKILL ACQUIRED.
PIRORIN (BLOOP)
M-MAPLE, MAPLE!! THIS IS...!
HM?
WE GOT TWO SKILLS!
BOTH OF US GOT ANNIHILATOR AND CONQUEROR!
NEVER HEARD OF THEM!
WHAT DO THEY DO?

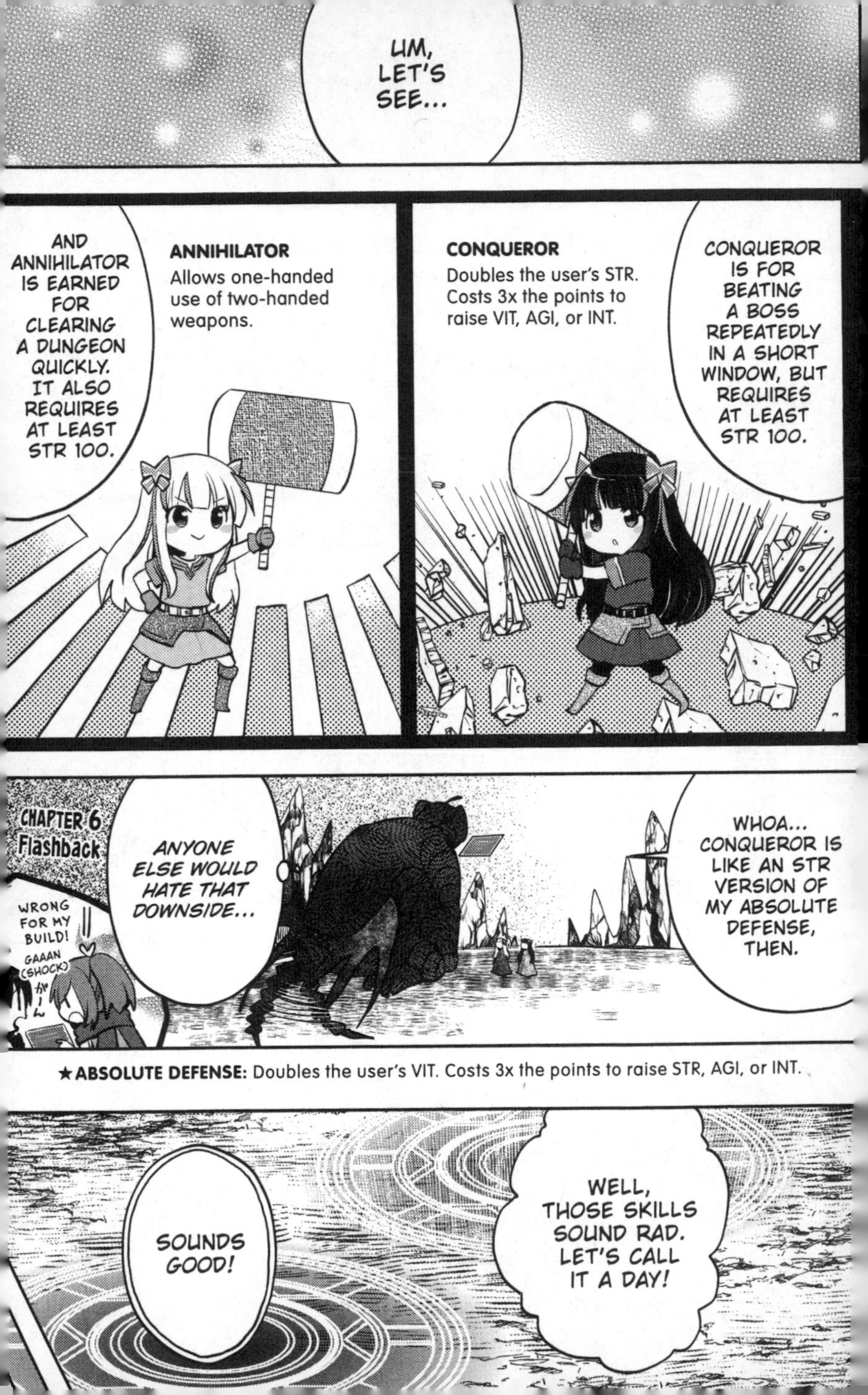
UM, LET'S SEE...
CONQUEROR IS FOR BEATING A BOSS REPEATEDLY IN A SHORT WINDOW, BUT REQUIRES AT LEAST STR 100.
CONQUEROR
Doubles the user's STR. Costs 3x the points to raise VIT, AGI, or INT.
ANNIHILATOR
Allows one-handed use of two-handed weapons.
AND ANNIHILATOR IS EARNED FOR CLEARING A DUNGEON QUICKLY. IT ALSO REQUIRES AT LEAST STR 100.
WHOA... CONQUEROR IS LIKE AN STR VERSION OF MY ABSOLUTE DEFENSE, THEN.
ANYONE ELSE WOULD HATE THAT DOWNSIDE...
CHAPTER 6 Flashback
WRONG FOR MY BUILD!
GAAAN (SHOCK)
★ABSOLUTE DEFENSE: Doubles the user's VIT. Costs 3x the points to raise STR, AGI, or INT.
WELL, THOSE SKILLS SOUND RAD. LET'S CALL IT A DAY!
SOUNDS GOOD!

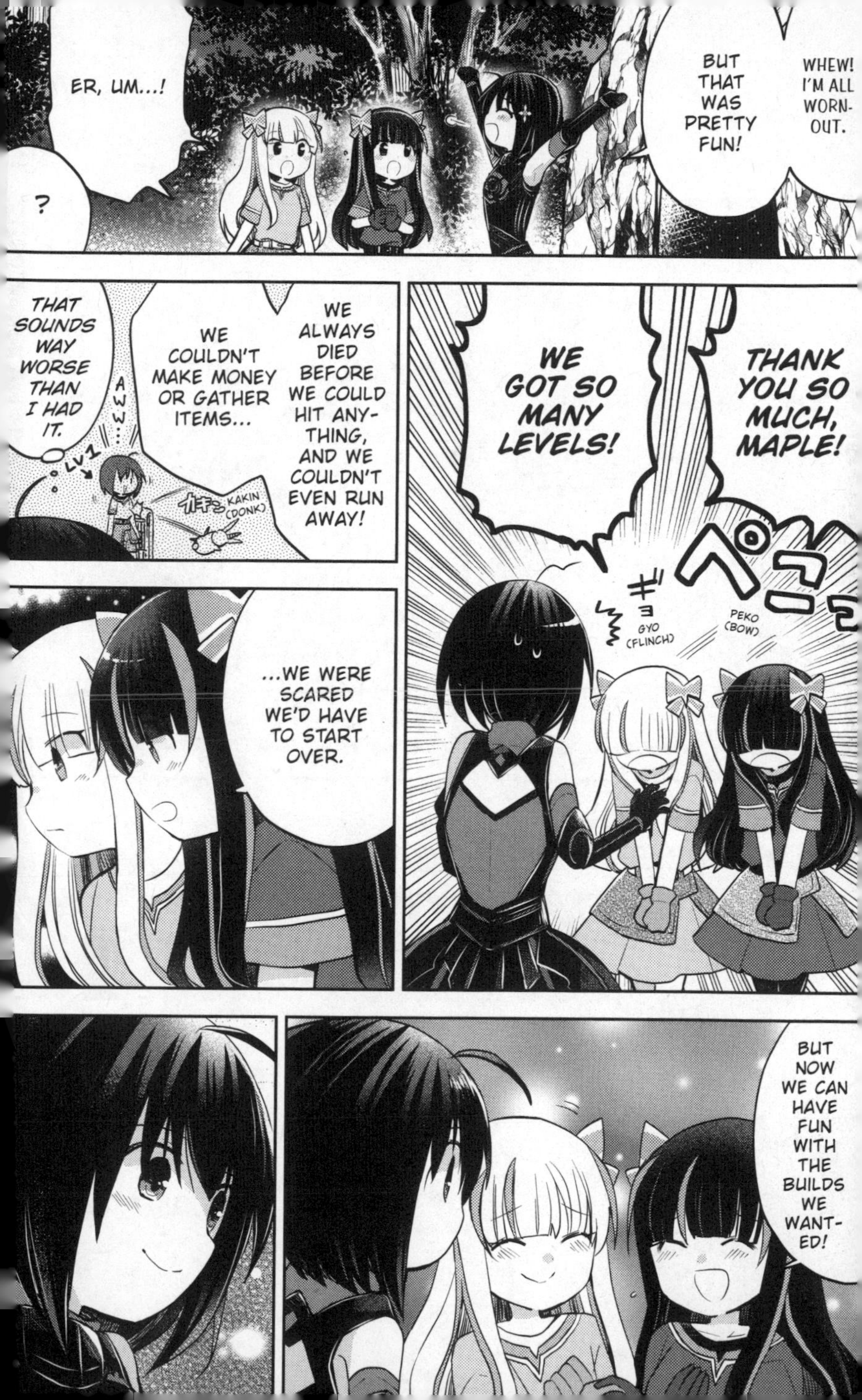
WHEW! I'M ALL WORN-OUT.
BUT THAT WAS PRETTY FUN!
ER, UM...!
?
THANK YOU SO MUCH, MAPLE!
WE GOT SO MANY LEVELS!
ペコー
PEKO (BOW)
ギョ
GYO (FLINCH)
WE ALWAYS DIED BEFORE WE COULD HIT ANY-THING, AND WE COULDN'T EVEN RUN AWAY!
WE COULDN'T MAKE MONEY OR GATHER ITEMS...
AWW...
THAT SOUNDS WAY WORSE THAN I HAD IT.
LV1
カキン
KAKIN (DONK)
...WE WERE SCARED WE'D HAVE TO START OVER.
BUT NOW WE CAN HAVE FUN WITH THE BUILDS WE WANT-ED!

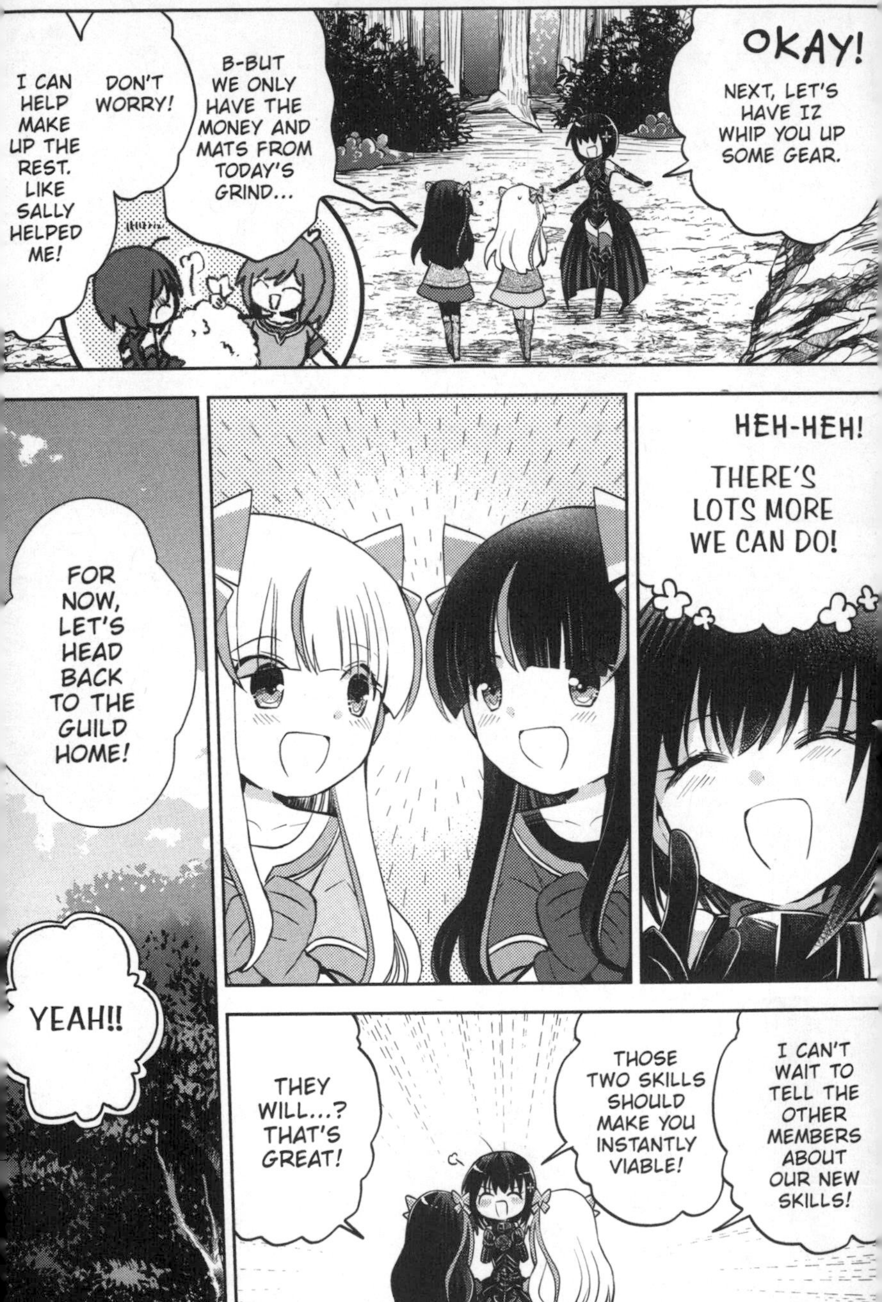
OKAY!
NEXT, LET'S HAVE IZ WHIP YOU UP SOME GEAR.
B-BUT WE ONLY HAVE THE MONEY AND MATS FROM TODAY'S GRIND...
DON'T WORRY!
I CAN HELP MAKE UP THE REST. LIKE SALLY HELPED ME!
HEH-HEH!
THERE'S LOTS MORE WE CAN DO!
I CAN'T WAIT TO TELL THE OTHER MEMBERS ABOUT OUR NEW SKILLS!
THOSE TWO SKILLS SHOULD MAKE YOU INSTANTLY VIABLE!
THEY WILL...? THAT'S GREAT!
FOR NOW, LET'S HEAD BACK TO THE GUILD HOME!
YEAH!!

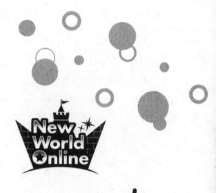

Welcome to *NewWorld Online*.

I Don't Want to Get Hurt,

so I'll Max Out My Defense.

presented by: **JIROU OIMOTO & YUUMIKAN**

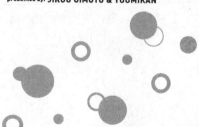

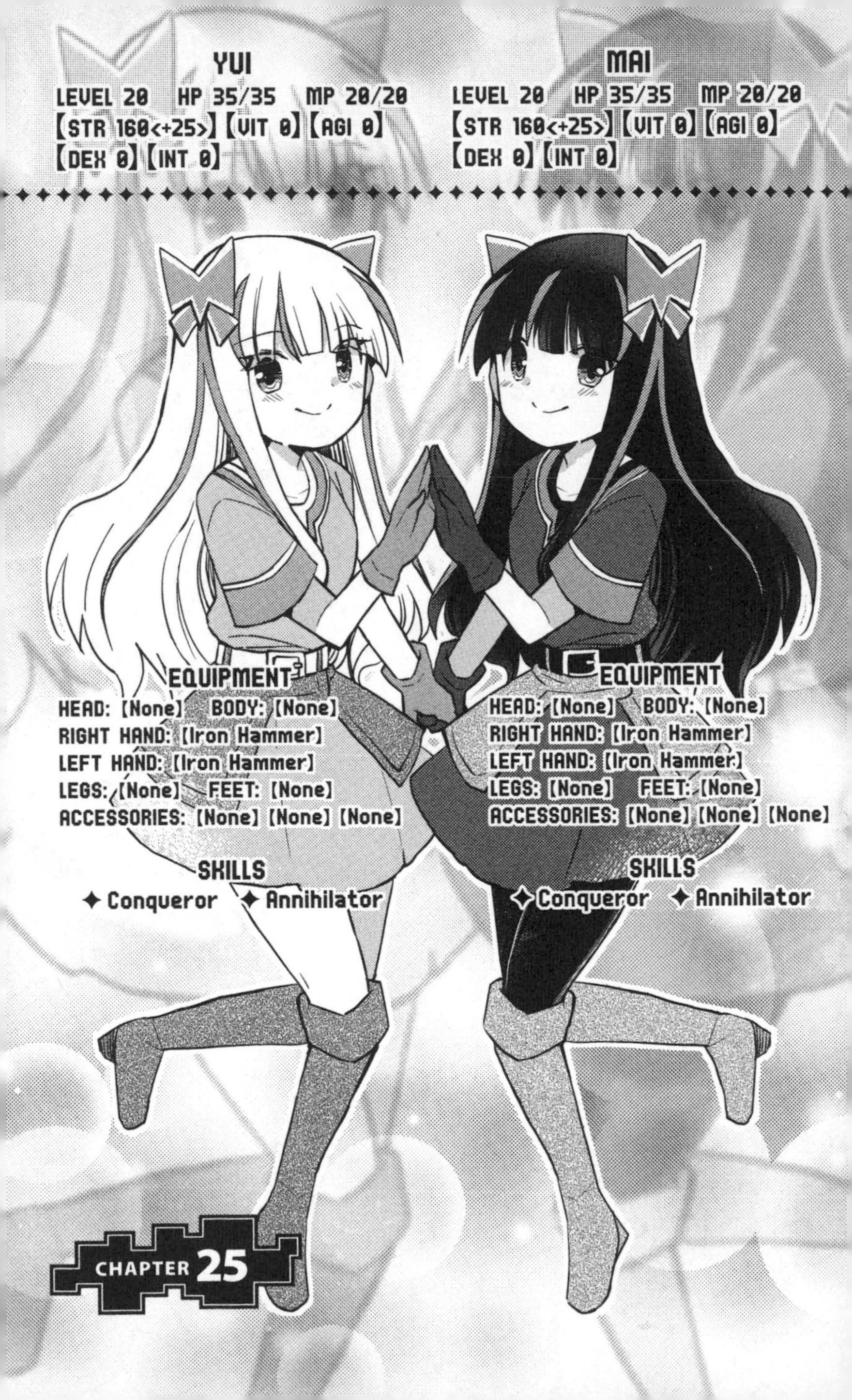
MAI
LEVEL 20 HP 35/35 MP 20/20
【STR 160<+25>】【VIT 0】【AGI 0】
【DEX 0】【INT 0】
EQUIPMENT
HEAD: 【None】 BODY: 【None】
RIGHT HAND: 【Iron Hammer】
LEFT HAND: 【Iron Hammer】
LEGS: 【None】 FEET: 【None】
ACCESSORIES: 【None】【None】【None】
SKILLS
✦Conqueror ✦Annihilator
YUI
LEVEL 20 HP 35/35 MP 20/20
【STR 160<+25>】【VIT 0】【AGI 0】
【DEX 0】【INT 0】
EQUIPMENT
HEAD: 【None】 BODY: 【None】
RIGHT HAND: 【Iron Hammer】
LEFT HAND: 【Iron Hammer】
LEGS: 【None】 FEET: 【None】
ACCESSORIES: 【None】【None】【None】
SKILLS
✦Conqueror ✦Annihilator
CHAPTER 25

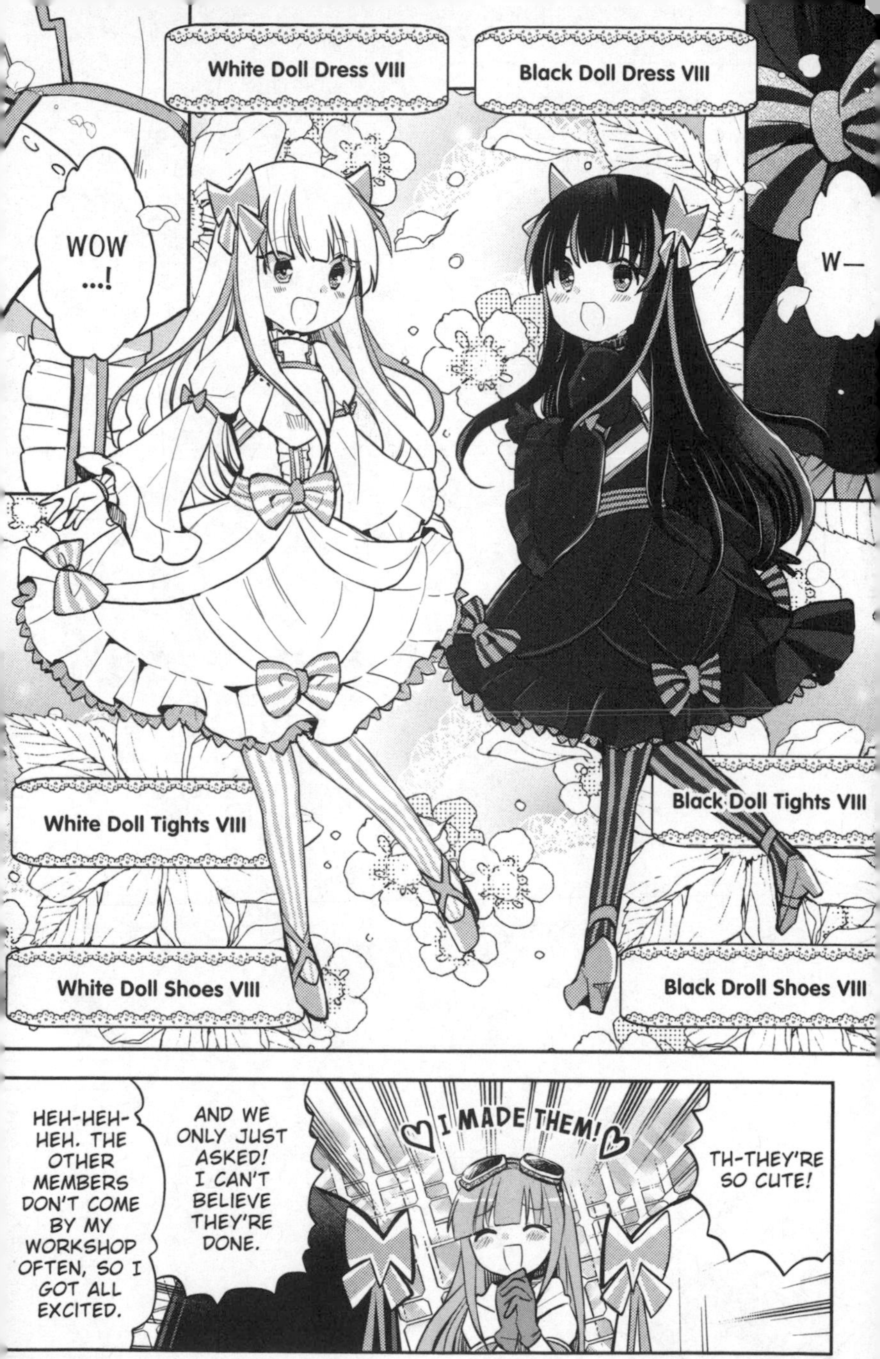
W—
Black Doll Dress VIII
White Doll Dress VIII
WOW ...!
Black Doll Tights VIII
White Doll Tights VIII
Black Droll Shoes VIII
White Doll Shoes VIII
TH-THEY'RE SO CUTE!
I MADE THEM!
AND WE ONLY JUST ASKED! I CAN'T BELIEVE THEY'RE DONE.
HEH-HEH-HEH. THE OTHER MEMBERS DON'T COME BY MY WORKSHOP OFTEN, SO I GOT ALL EXCITED.

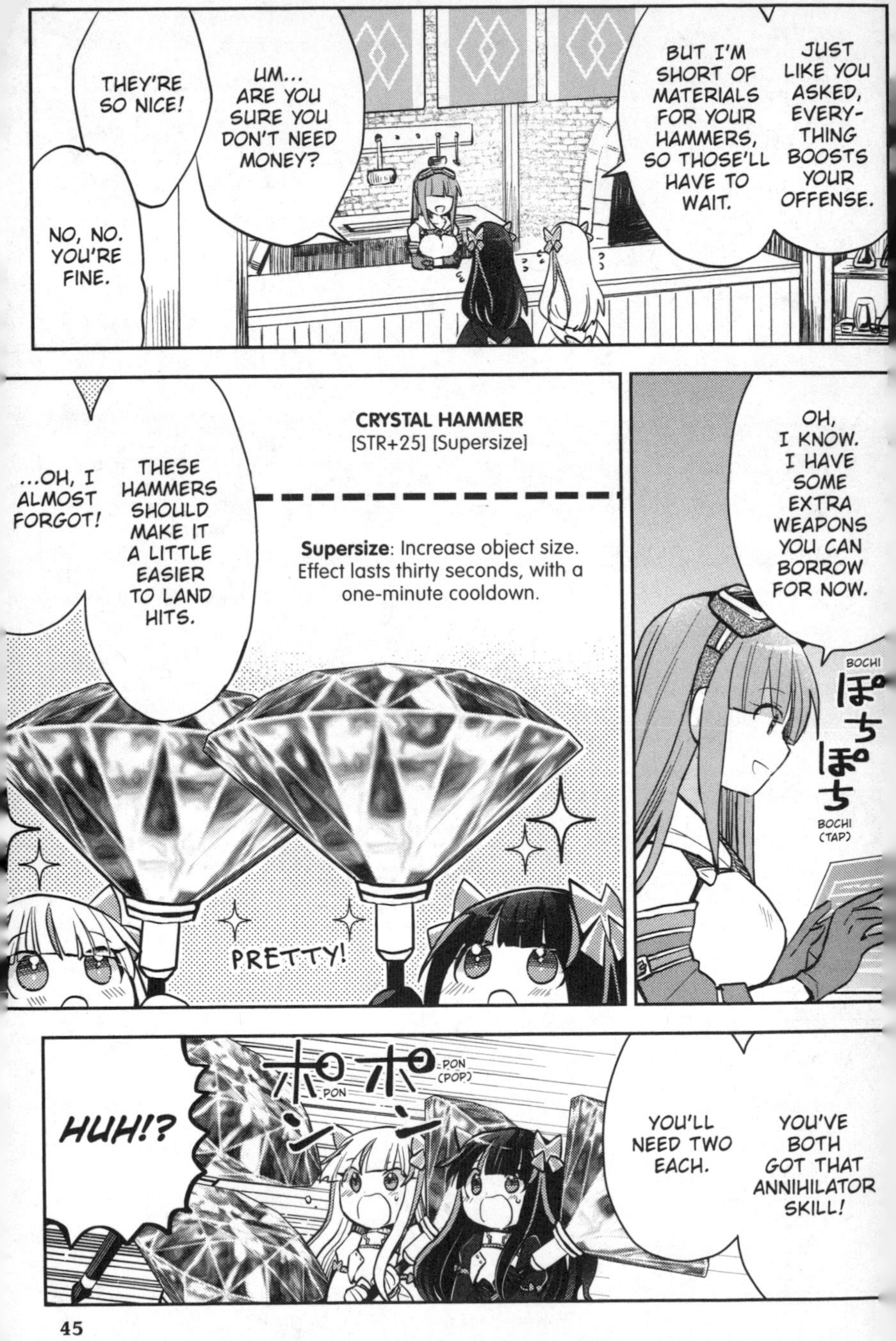
JUST LIKE YOU ASKED, EVERYTHING BOOSTS YOUR OFFENSE.
BUT I'M SHORT OF MATERIALS FOR YOUR HAMMERS, SO THOSE'LL HAVE TO WAIT.
UM... ARE YOU SURE YOU DON'T NEED MONEY?
THEY'RE SO NICE!
NO, NO. YOU'RE FINE.
OH, I KNOW. I HAVE SOME EXTRA WEAPONS YOU CAN BORROW FOR NOW.
BOCHI
ぽちぽち
BOCHI (TAP)
CRYSTAL HAMMER
[STR+25] [Supersize]
Supersize: Increase object size. Effect lasts thirty seconds, with a one-minute cooldown.
THESE HAMMERS SHOULD MAKE IT A LITTLE EASIER TO LAND HITS.
...OH, I ALMOST FORGOT!
PRETTY!
YOU'VE BOTH GOT THAT ANNIHILATOR SKILL!
YOU'LL NEED TWO EACH.
ポンポン
PON PON (POP)
HUH!?

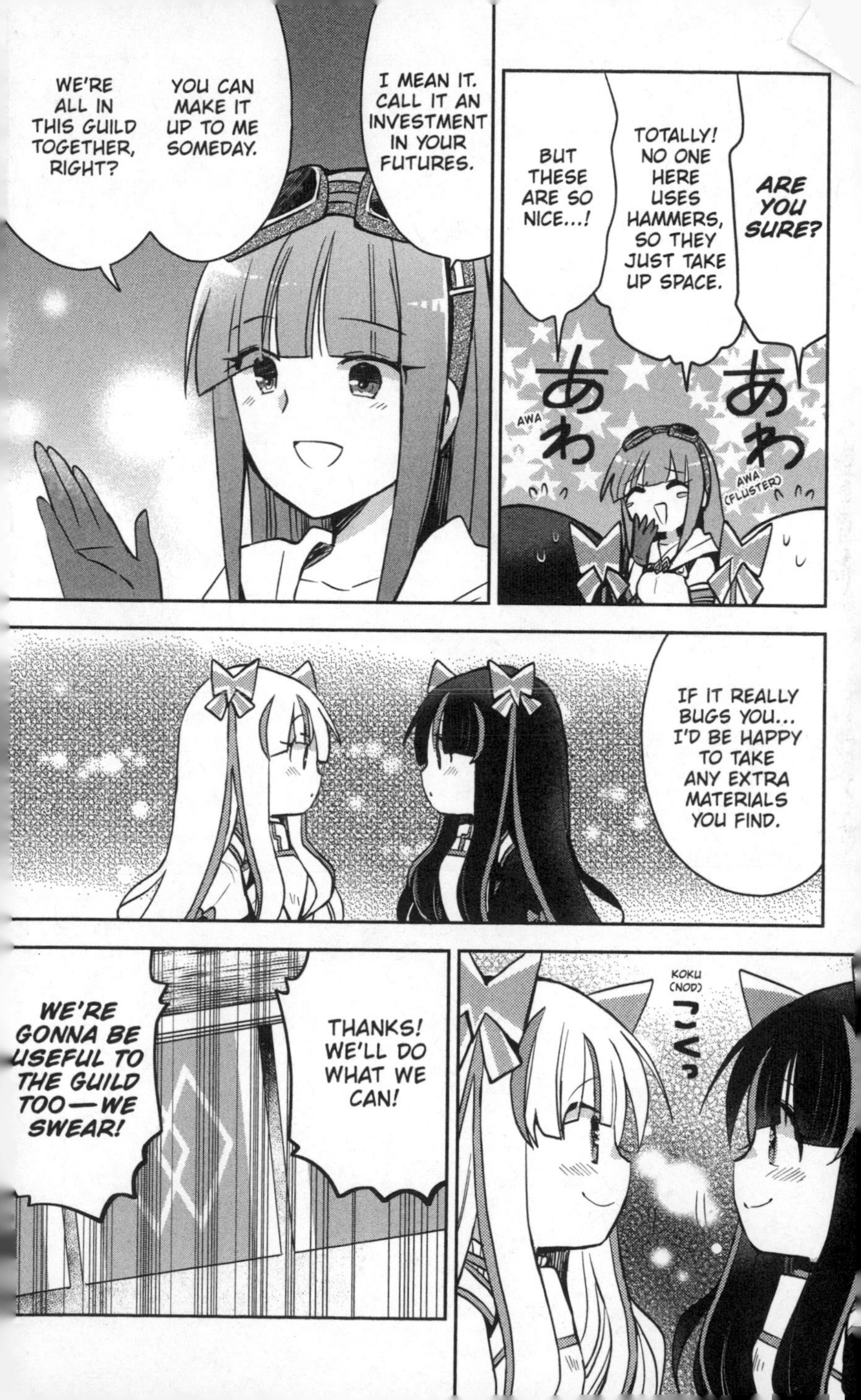
ARE YOU SURE?
TOTALLY! NO ONE HERE USES HAMMERS, SO THEY JUST TAKE UP SPACE.
BUT THESE ARE SO NICE...!
あわ
AWA (FLUSTER)
あわ
AWA
I MEAN IT. CALL IT AN INVESTMENT IN YOUR FUTURES.
YOU CAN MAKE IT UP TO ME SOMEDAY.
WE'RE ALL IN THIS GUILD TOGETHER, RIGHT?
IF IT REALLY BUGS YOU... I'D BE HAPPY TO TAKE ANY EXTRA MATERIALS YOU FIND.
KOKU (NOD)
こく
THANKS! WE'LL DO WHAT WE CAN!
WE'RE GONNA BE USEFUL TO THE GUILD TOO—WE SWEAR!

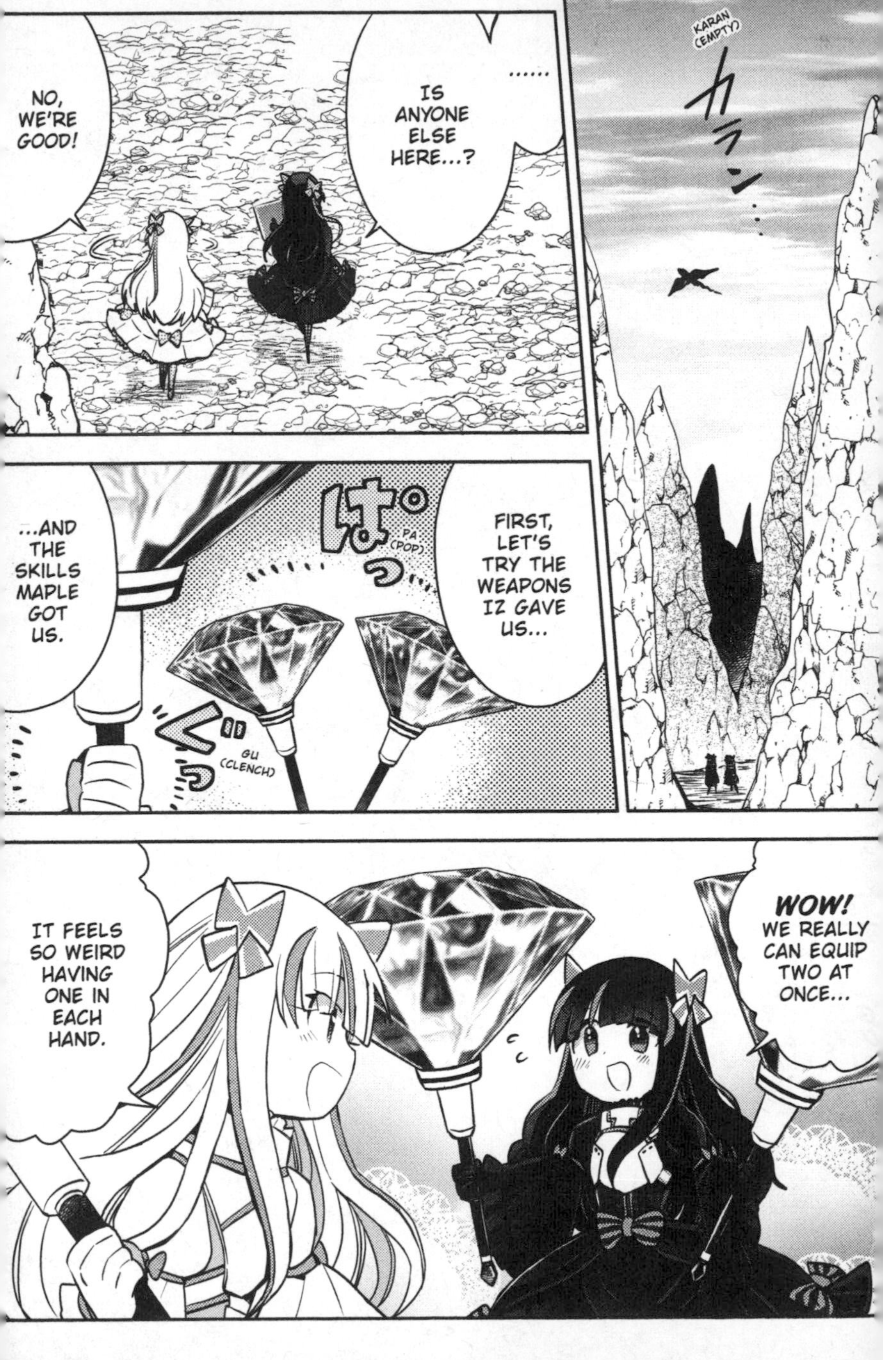
KARAN (EMPTY)
カラン
......
IS ANYONE ELSE HERE...?
NO, WE'RE GOOD!
はっ
PA (POP)
FIRST, LET'S TRY THE WEAPONS IZ GAVE US...
...AND THE SKILLS MAPLE GOT US.
ぐっ
GU (CLENCH)
WOW! WE REALLY CAN EQUIP TWO AT ONCE...
IT FEELS SO WEIRD HAVING ONE IN EACH HAND.

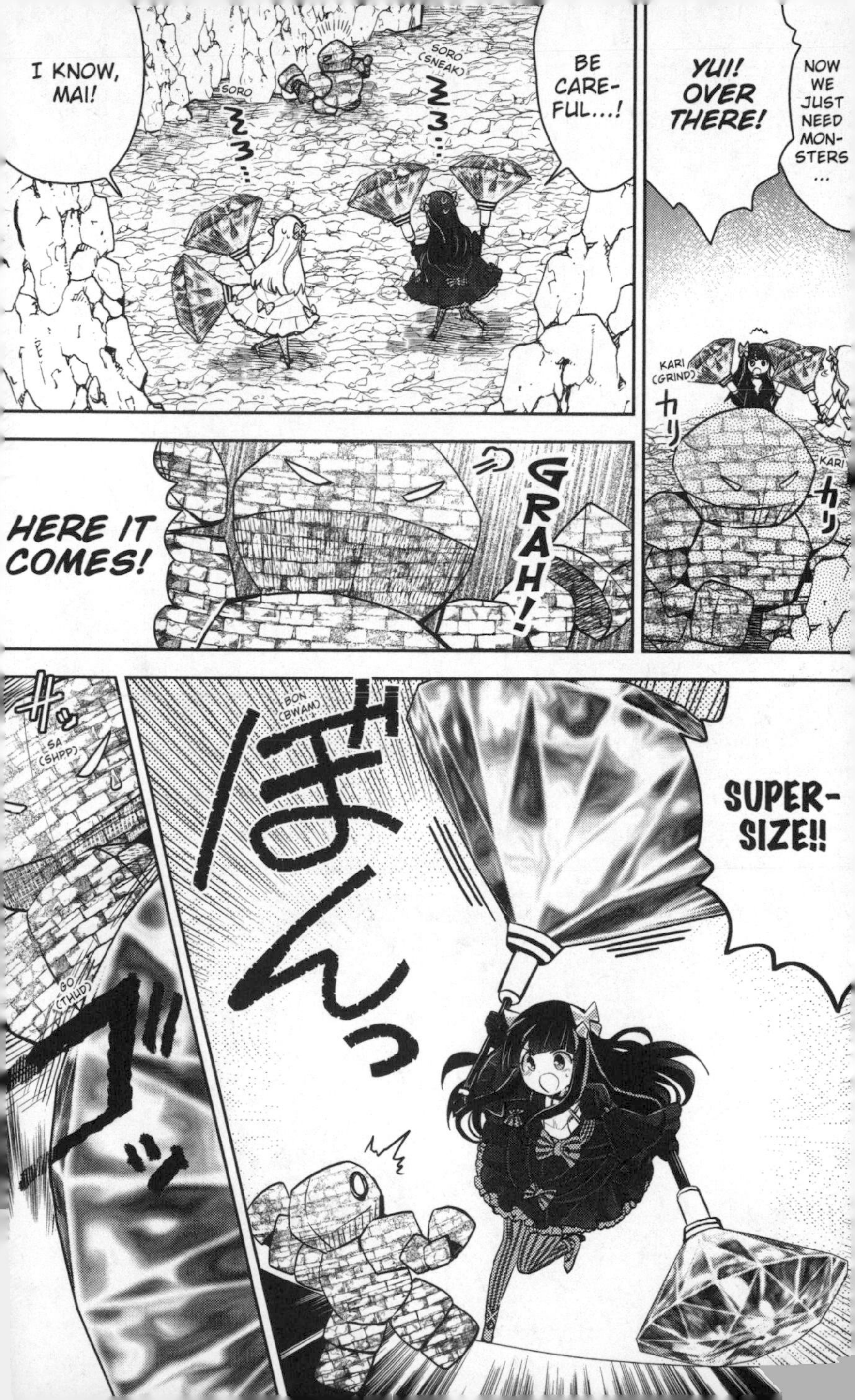
NOW WE JUST NEED MONSTERS...
YUI! OVER THERE!
KARI (GRIND)
KARI
BE CAREFUL...!
SORO (SNEAK)
SORO
I KNOW, MAI!
GRAH!
HERE IT COMES!
SUPER-SIZE!!
BON (BWAM)
SA (SHPP)
GO (THUD)

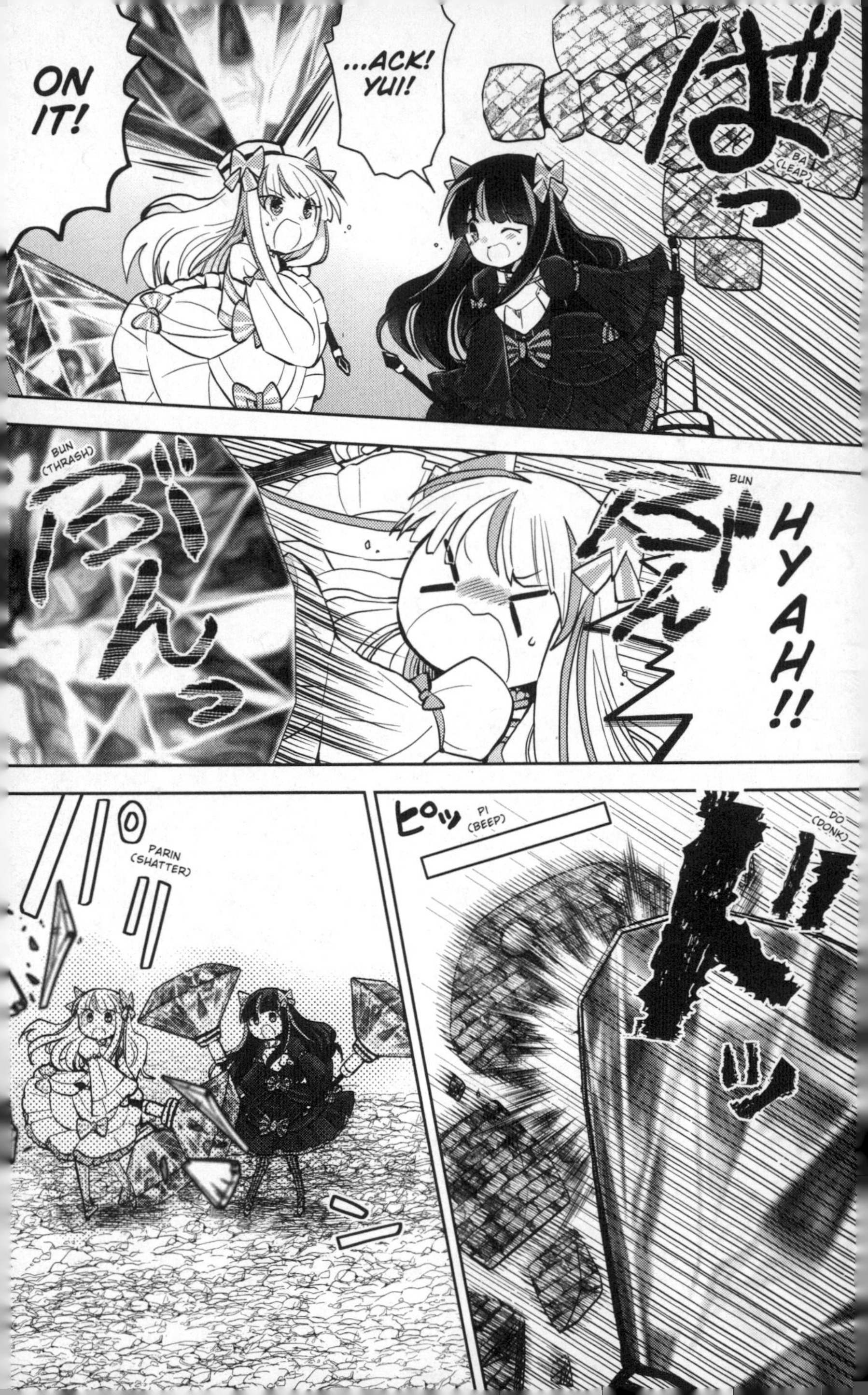

ばっ
BA (LEAP)
...ACK! YUI!
ON IT!
HYAH!!
ぶん
BUN
ぶんっ
BUN (THRASH)
ドッ
DO (DONK)
ピッ
PI (BEEP)
PARIN (SHATTER)

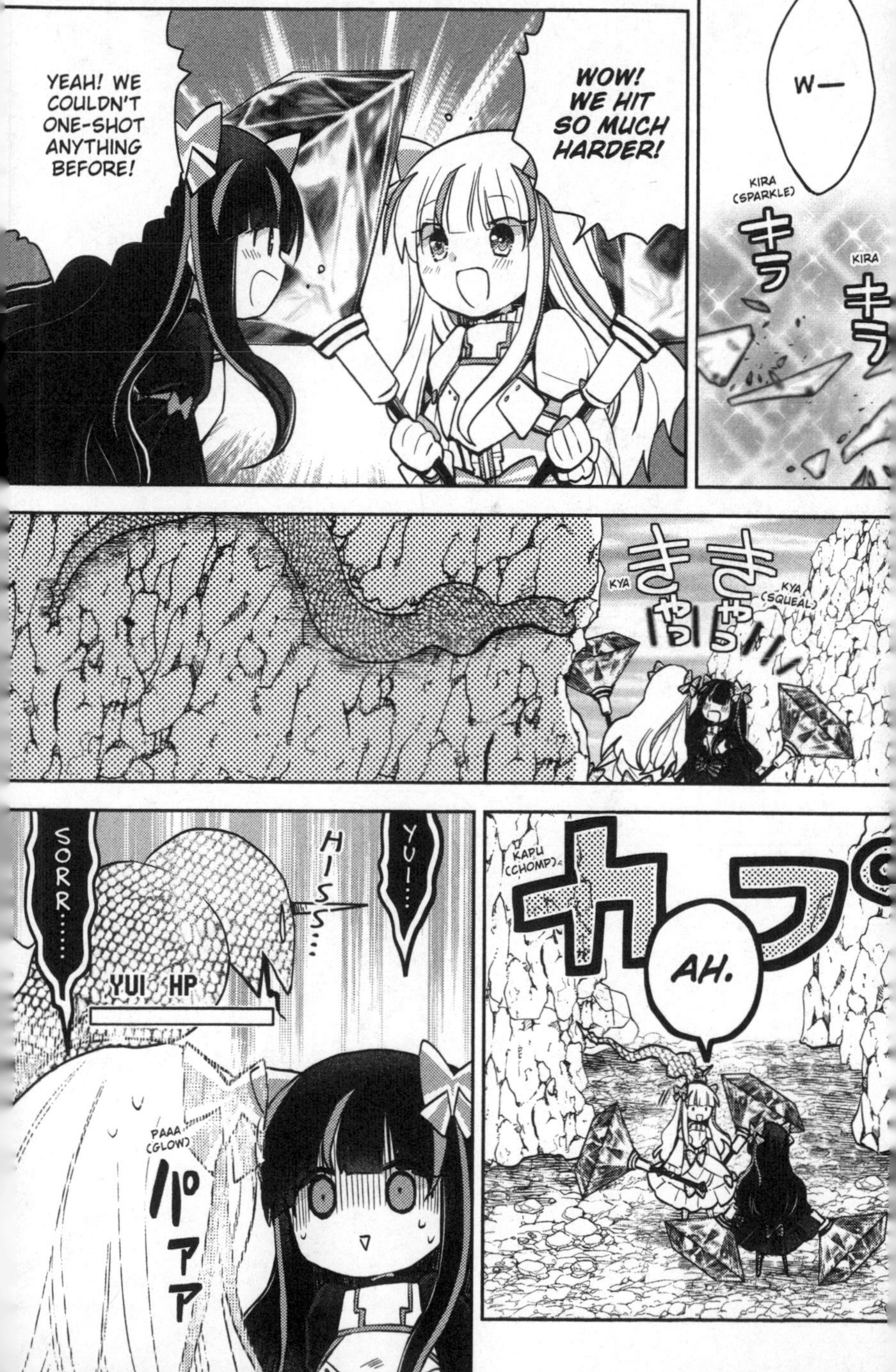
W—
KIRA (SPARKLE)
キラ
KIRA
キラ
WOW! WE HIT SO MUCH HARDER!
YEAH! WE COULDN'T ONE-SHOT ANYTHING BEFORE!
KYA (SQUEAL)
きゃっ
KYA
きゃっ
KAPU (CHOMP)
カプ
AH.
YUI......
HISS...
SORR......
YUI HP
PAAA (GLOW)
パァア

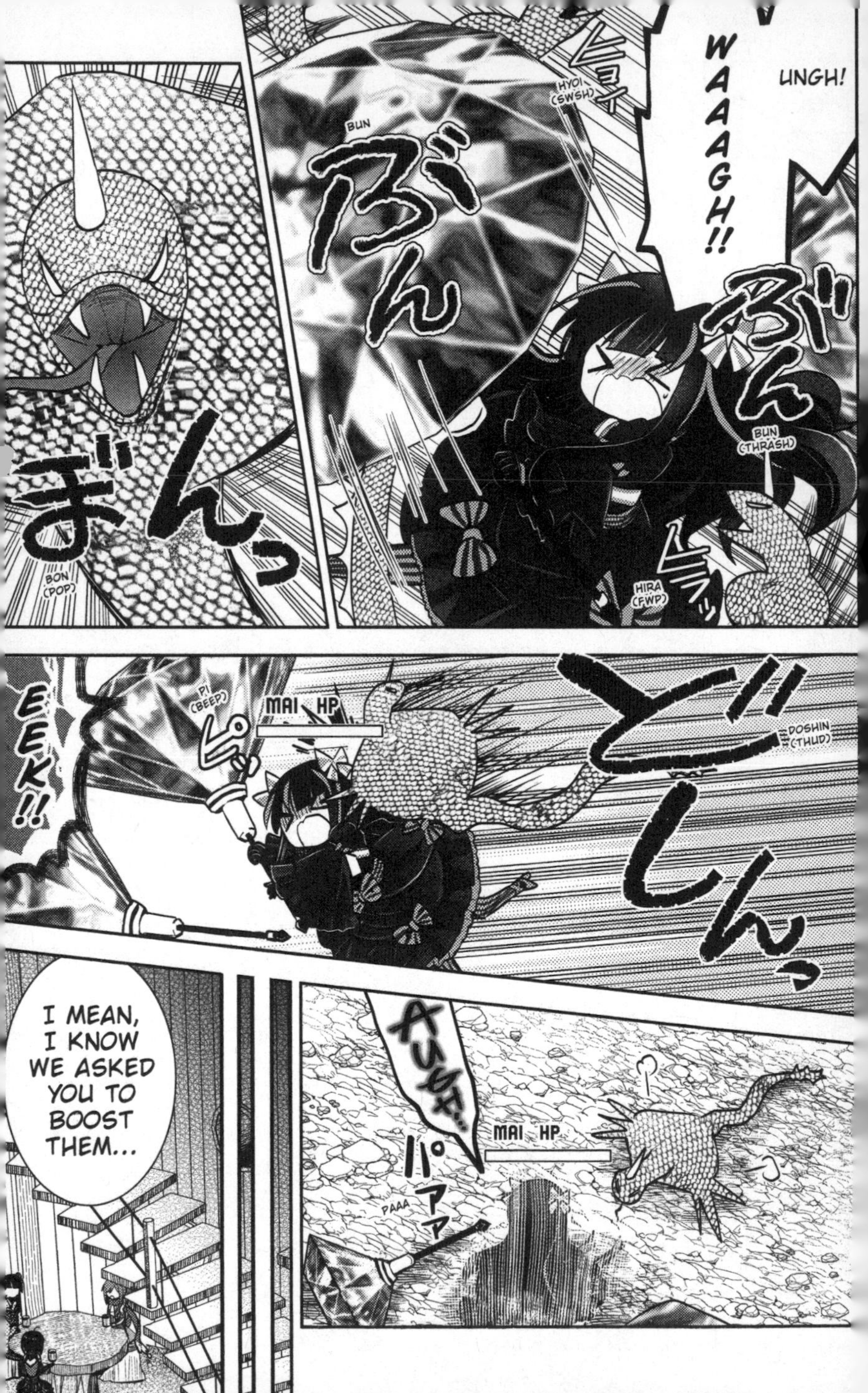
UNGH!
WAAAAGH!!
ヒョイ
HYOI (SWSH)
ぶん
BUN
ぶん
BUN (THRASH)
ヒラ
HIRA (FWP)
ぼんっ
BON (POP)
どしんっ
DOSHIN (THUD)
EEK!!
MAI HP
ピ
PI (BEEP)
AUGH...
MAI HP
パァア
PAAA
I MEAN, I KNOW WE ASKED YOU TO BOOST THEM...

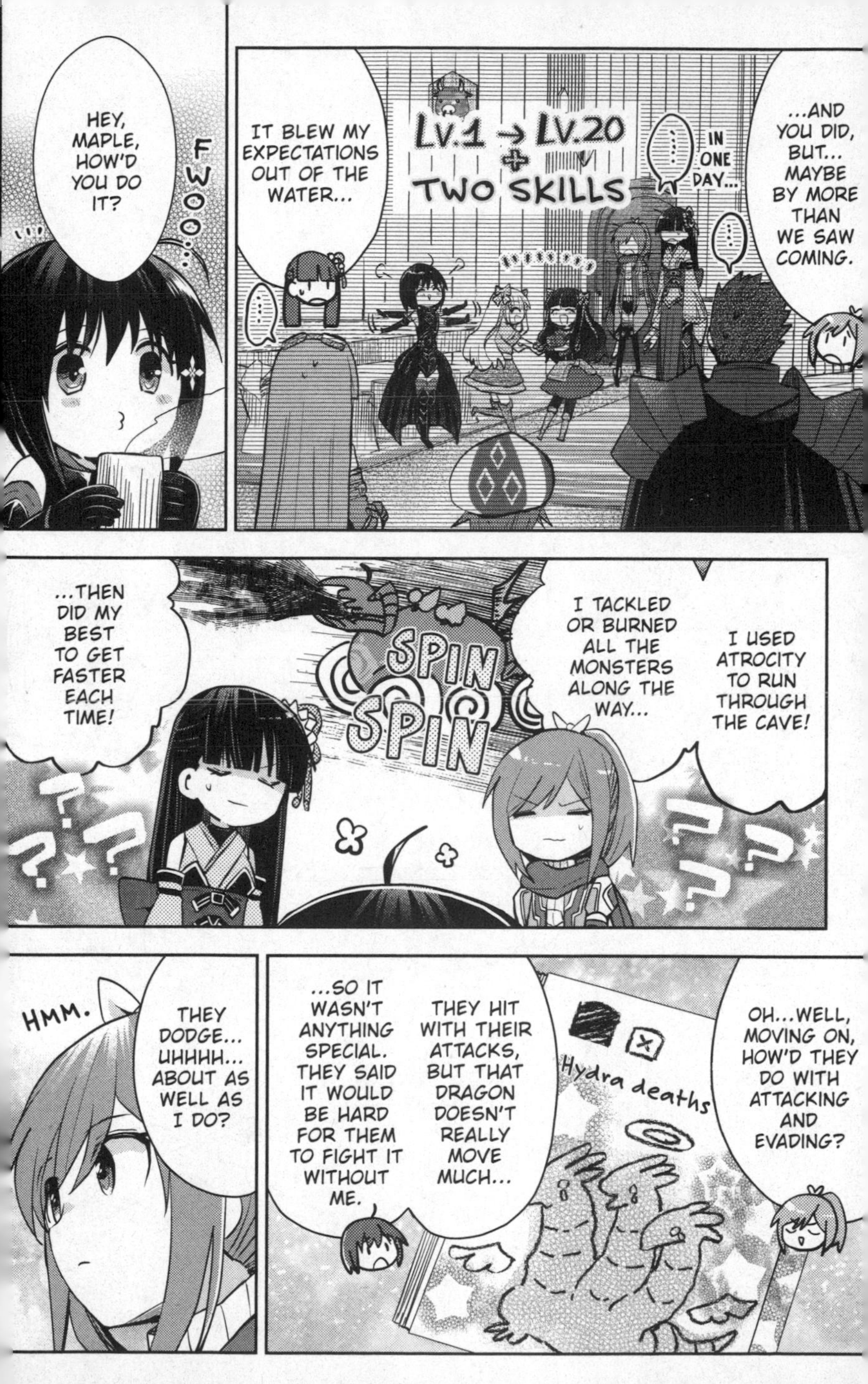
...AND YOU DID, BUT... MAYBE BY MORE THAN WE SAW COMING.
IN ONE DAY...
Lv.1 → Lv.20 + TWO SKILLS
IT BLEW MY EXPECTATIONS OUT OF THE WATER...
FWOOO...
HEY, MAPLE, HOW'D YOU DO IT?
I USED ATROCITY TO RUN THROUGH THE CAVE!
I TACKLED OR BURNED ALL THE MONSTERS ALONG THE WAY...
SPIN SPIN
...THEN DID MY BEST TO GET FASTER EACH TIME!
OH...WELL, MOVING ON, HOW'D THEY DO WITH ATTACKING AND EVADING?
Hydra deaths
THEY HIT WITH THEIR ATTACKS, BUT THAT DRAGON DOESN'T REALLY MOVE MUCH...
...SO IT WASN'T ANYTHING SPECIAL. THEY SAID IT WOULD BE HARD FOR THEM TO FIGHT IT WITHOUT ME.
THEY DODGE... UHHHH... ABOUT AS WELL AS I DO?
HMM.

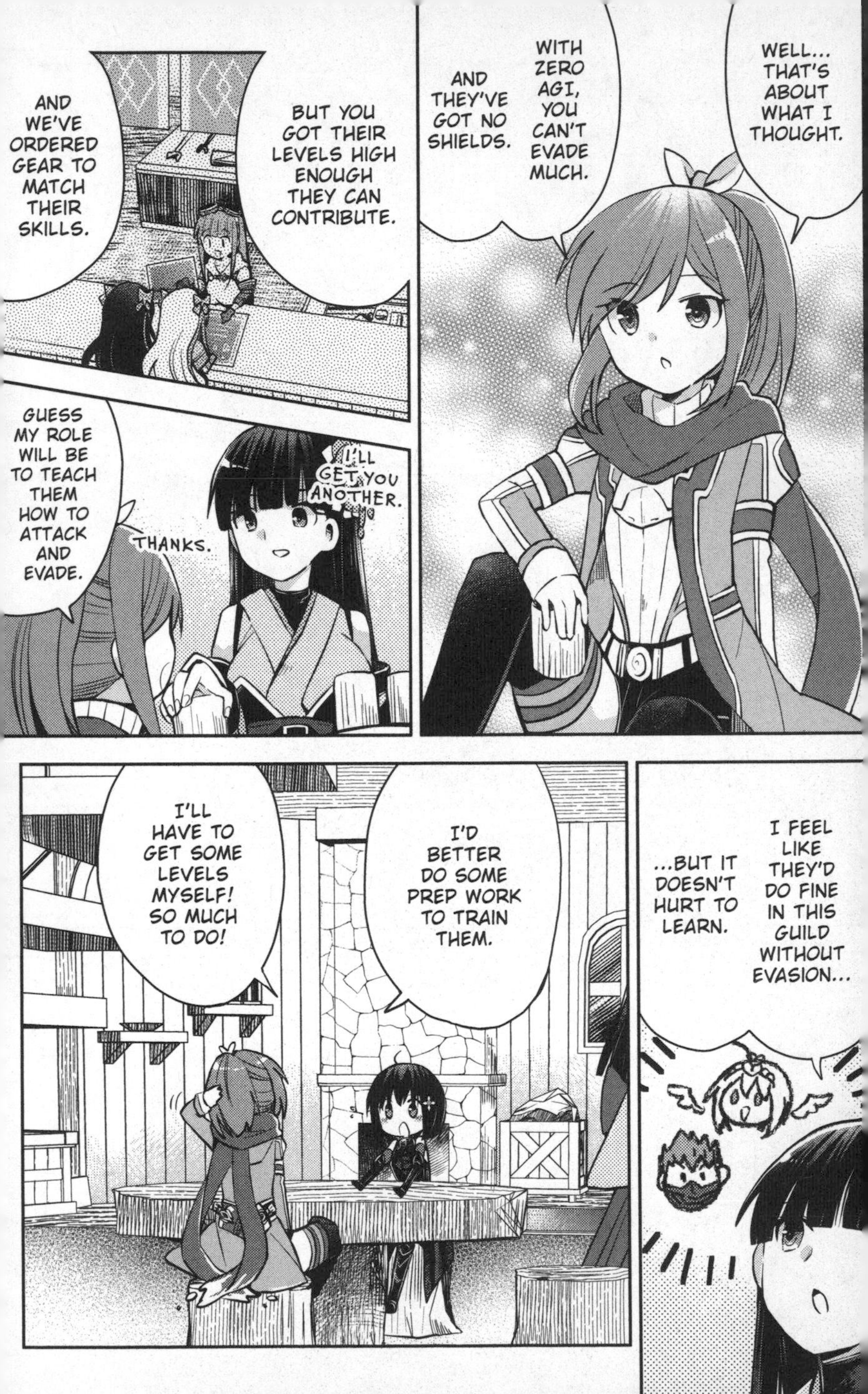
WELL... THAT'S ABOUT WHAT I THOUGHT.
WITH ZERO AGI, YOU CAN'T EVADE MUCH.
AND THEY'VE GOT NO SHIELDS.
BUT YOU GOT THEIR LEVELS HIGH ENOUGH THEY CAN CONTRIBUTE.
AND WE'VE ORDERED GEAR TO MATCH THEIR SKILLS.
I'LL GET YOU ANOTHER.
THANKS.
GUESS MY ROLE WILL BE TO TEACH THEM HOW TO ATTACK AND EVADE.
I FEEL LIKE THEY'D DO FINE IN THIS GUILD WITHOUT EVASION...
...BUT IT DOESN'T HURT TO LEARN.
I'D BETTER DO SOME PREP WORK TO TRAIN THEM.
I'LL HAVE TO GET SOME LEVELS MYSELF! SO MUCH TO DO!

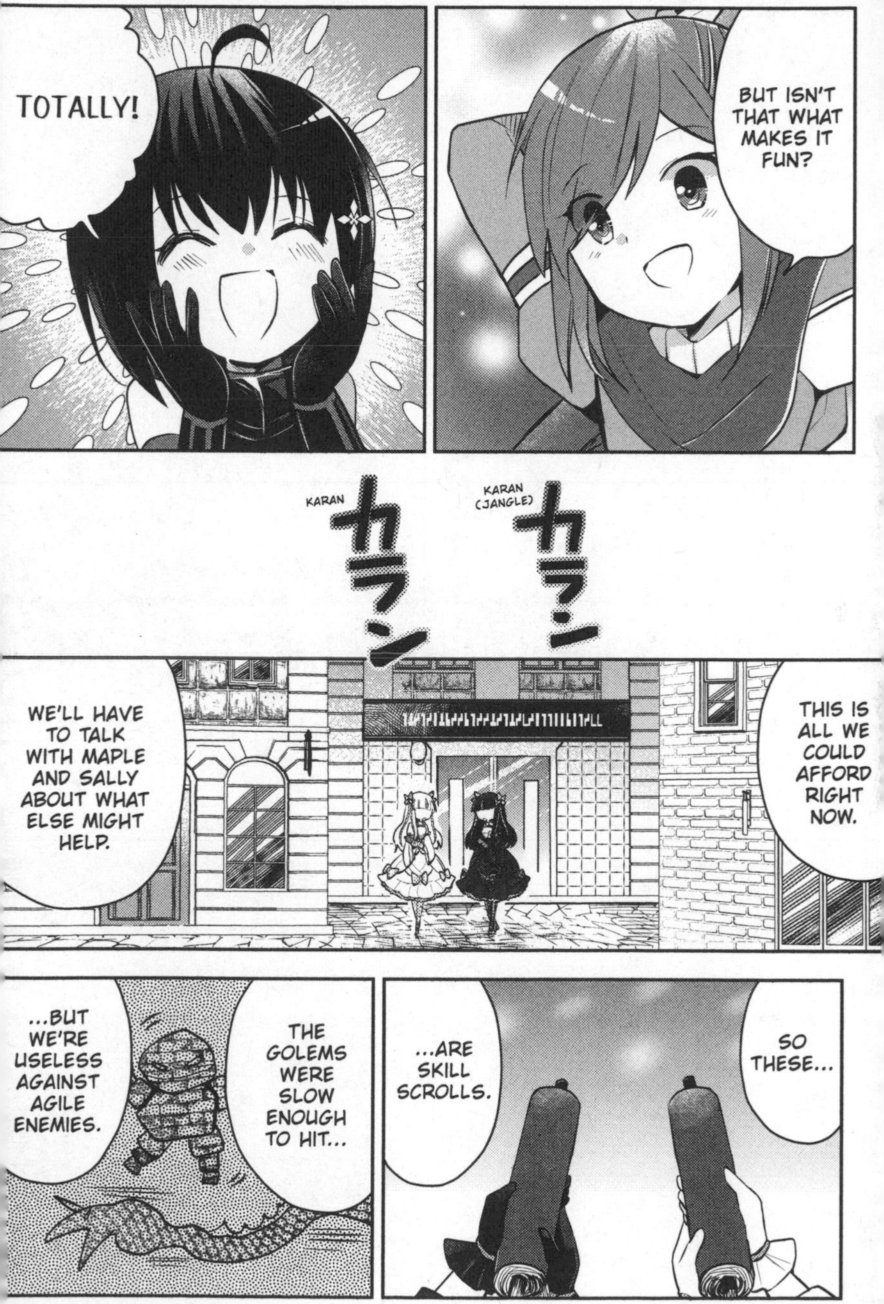
BUT ISN'T THAT WHAT MAKES IT FUN?
TOTALLY!
カラン
KARAN (JANGLE)
カラン
KARAN
THIS IS ALL WE COULD AFFORD RIGHT NOW.
WE'LL HAVE TO TALK WITH MAPLE AND SALLY ABOUT WHAT ELSE MIGHT HELP.
SO THESE...
...ARE SKILL SCROLLS.
THE GOLEMS WERE SLOW ENOUGH TO HIT...
...BUT WE'RE USELESS AGAINST AGILE ENEMIES.

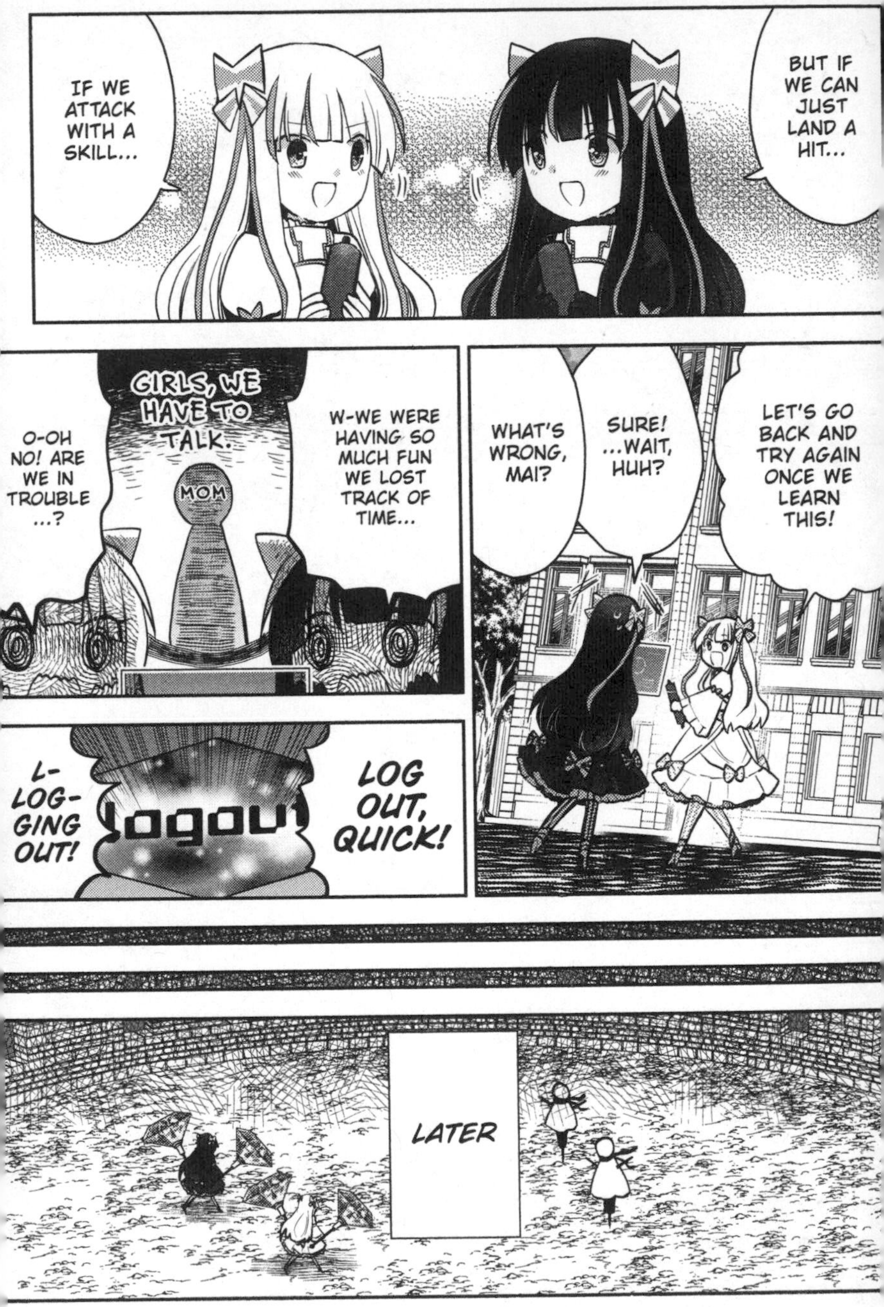
BUT IF WE CAN JUST LAND A HIT...
IF WE ATTACK WITH A SKILL...
LET'S GO BACK AND TRY AGAIN ONCE WE LEARN THIS!
SURE! ...WAIT, HUH?
WHAT'S WRONG, MAI?
W-WE WERE HAVING SO MUCH FUN WE LOST TRACK OF TIME...
GIRLS, WE HAVE TO TALK.
MOM
O-OH NO! ARE WE IN TROUBLE ...?
LOG OUT, QUICK!
logout
L-LOGGING OUT!
LATER

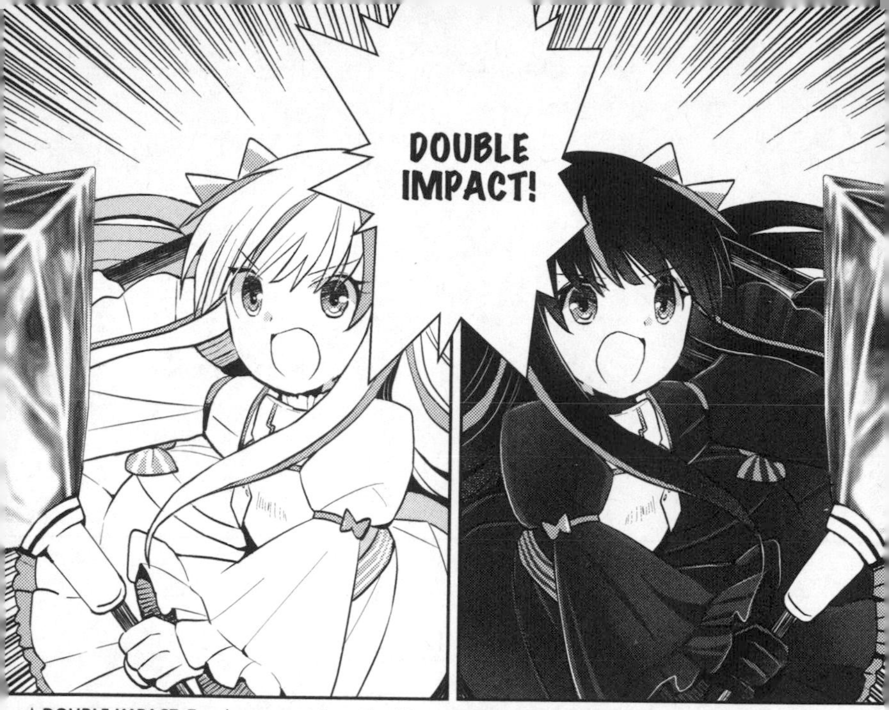
DOUBLE IMPACT!

★ **DOUBLE IMPACT:** Two hammer strikes. The blows create small shock waves, dealing extra damage.

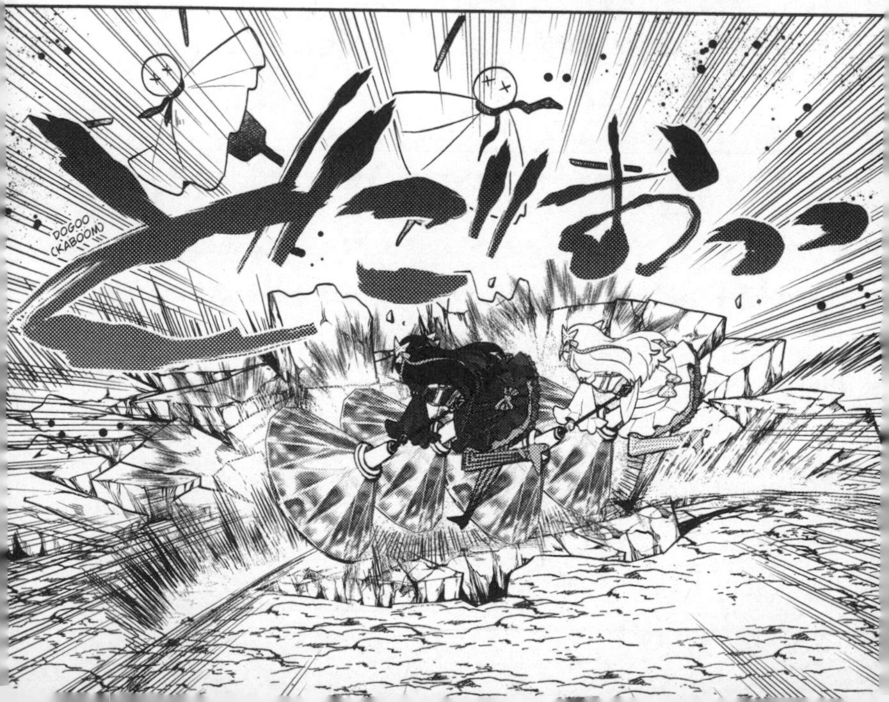
DOGOO (KABOOM)

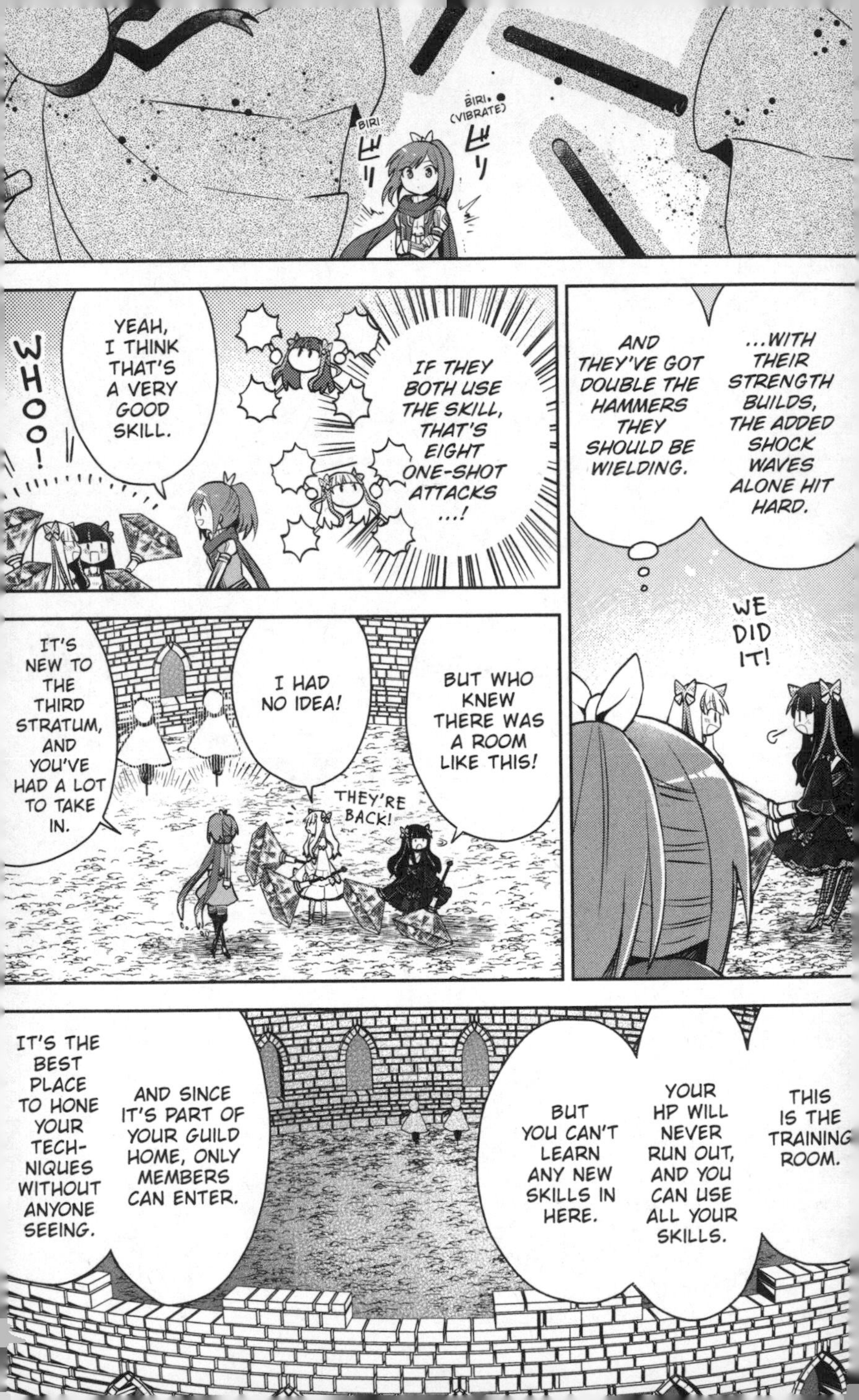
BIRI (VIBRATE)
BIRI
ビリ
ビリ
...WITH THEIR STRENGTH BUILDS, THE ADDED SHOCK WAVES ALONE HIT HARD.
AND THEY'VE GOT DOUBLE THE HAMMERS THEY SHOULD BE WIELDING.
WE DID IT!
IF THEY BOTH USE THE SKILL, THAT'S EIGHT ONE-SHOT ATTACKS ...!
YEAH, I THINK THAT'S A VERY GOOD SKILL.
WHOO!
BUT WHO KNEW THERE WAS A ROOM LIKE THIS!
THEY'RE BACK!
I HAD NO IDEA!
IT'S NEW TO THE THIRD STRATUM, AND YOU'VE HAD A LOT TO TAKE IN.
THIS IS THE TRAINING ROOM.
YOUR HP WILL NEVER RUN OUT, AND YOU CAN USE ALL YOUR SKILLS.
BUT YOU CAN'T LEARN ANY NEW SKILLS IN HERE.
AND SINCE IT'S PART OF YOUR GUILD HOME, ONLY MEMBERS CAN ENTER.
IT'S THE BEST PLACE TO HONE YOUR TECH-NIQUES WITHOUT ANYONE SEEING.

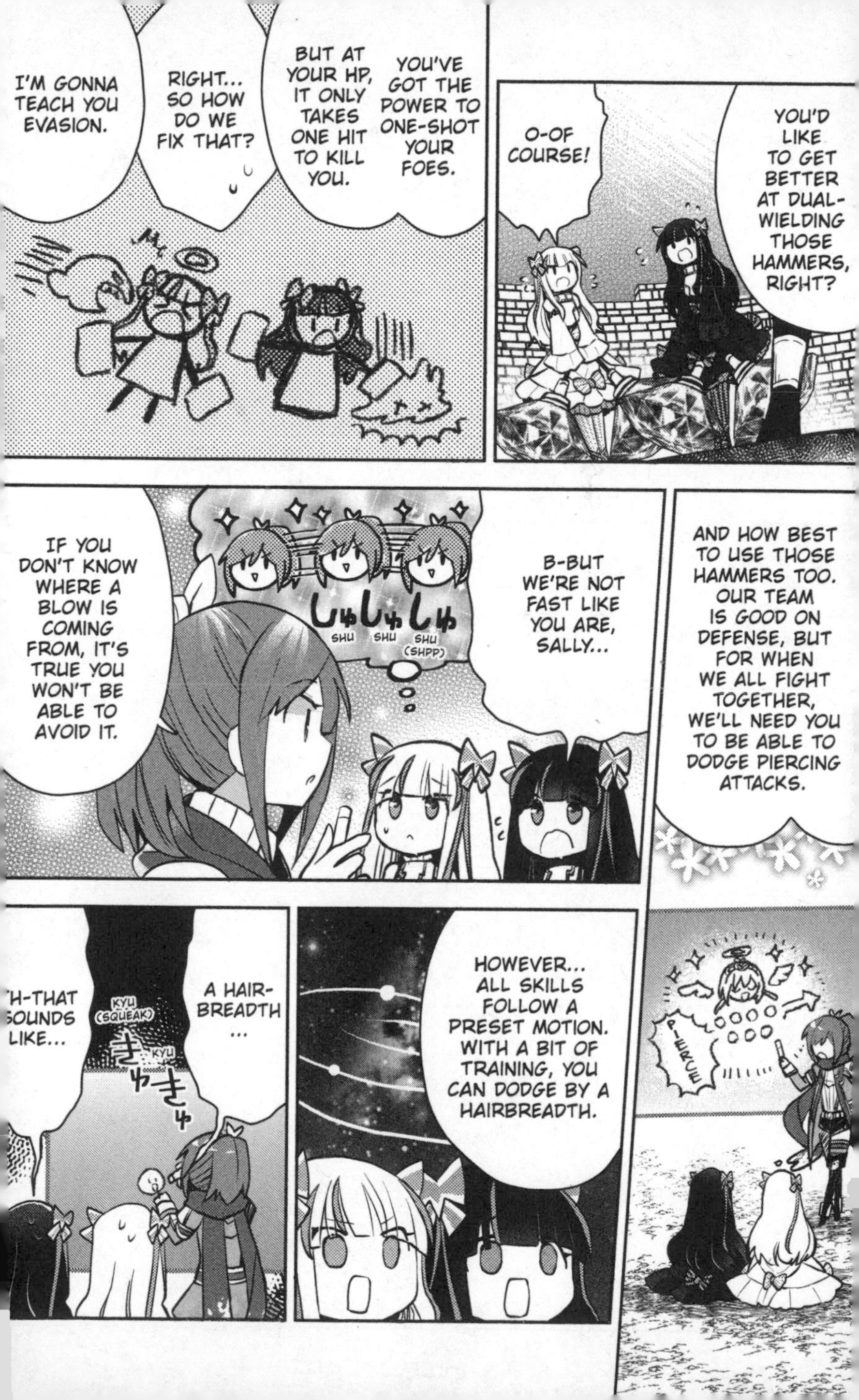

YOU'D LIKE TO GET BETTER AT DUAL-WIELDING THOSE HAMMERS, RIGHT?
O-OF COURSE!
YOU'VE GOT THE POWER TO ONE-SHOT YOUR FOES.
BUT AT YOUR HP, IT ONLY TAKES ONE HIT TO KILL YOU.
RIGHT... SO HOW DO WE FIX THAT?
I'M GONNA TEACH YOU EVASION.
AND HOW BEST TO USE THOSE HAMMERS TOO. OUR TEAM IS GOOD ON DEFENSE, BUT FOR WHEN WE ALL FIGHT TOGETHER, WE'LL NEED YOU TO BE ABLE TO DODGE PIERCING ATTACKS.
PIERCE
B-BUT WE'RE NOT FAST LIKE YOU ARE, SALLY...
しゅしゅしゅ
SHU SHU SHU (SHPP)
IF YOU DON'T KNOW WHERE A BLOW IS COMING FROM, IT'S TRUE YOU WON'T BE ABLE TO AVOID IT.
HOWEVER... ALL SKILLS FOLLOW A PRESET MOTION. WITH A BIT OF TRAINING, YOU CAN DODGE BY A HAIRBREADTH.
A HAIR-BREADTH...
きゅきゅ
KYU (SQUEAK) KYU
TH-THAT SOUNDS LIKE...

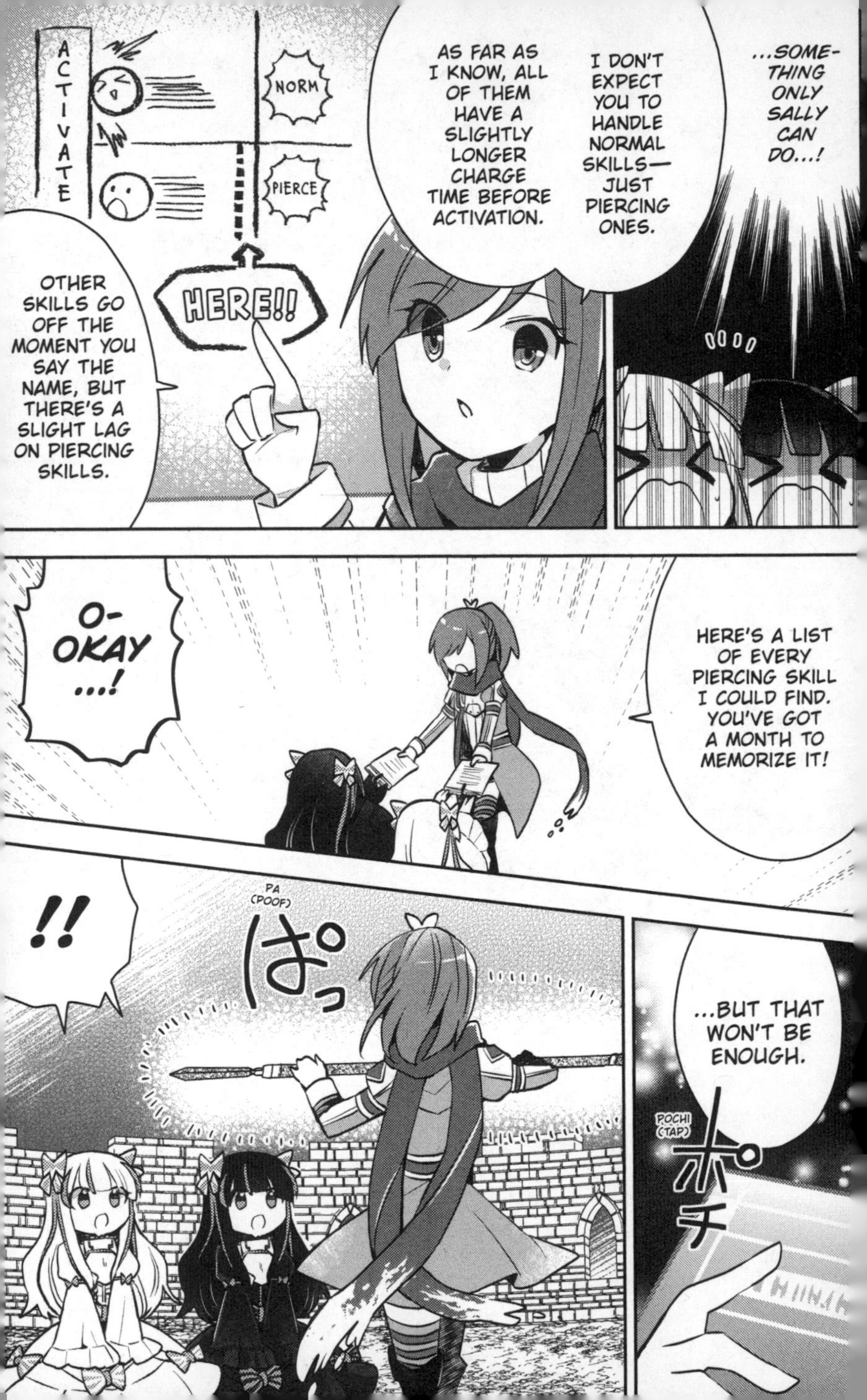

...SOME-THING ONLY SALLY CAN DO...!
I DON'T EXPECT YOU TO HANDLE NORMAL SKILLS—JUST PIERCING ONES.
AS FAR AS I KNOW, ALL OF THEM HAVE A SLIGHTLY LONGER CHARGE TIME BEFORE ACTIVATION.
NORM
PIERCE
ACTIVATE
HERE!!
OTHER SKILLS GO OFF THE MOMENT YOU SAY THE NAME, BUT THERE'S A SLIGHT LAG ON PIERCING SKILLS.
HERE'S A LIST OF EVERY PIERCING SKILL I COULD FIND. YOU'VE GOT A MONTH TO MEMORIZE IT!
O-OKAY...!
...BUT THAT WON'T BE ENOUGH.
ポチ
POCHI (TAP)
ぱっ
PA (POOF)
!!

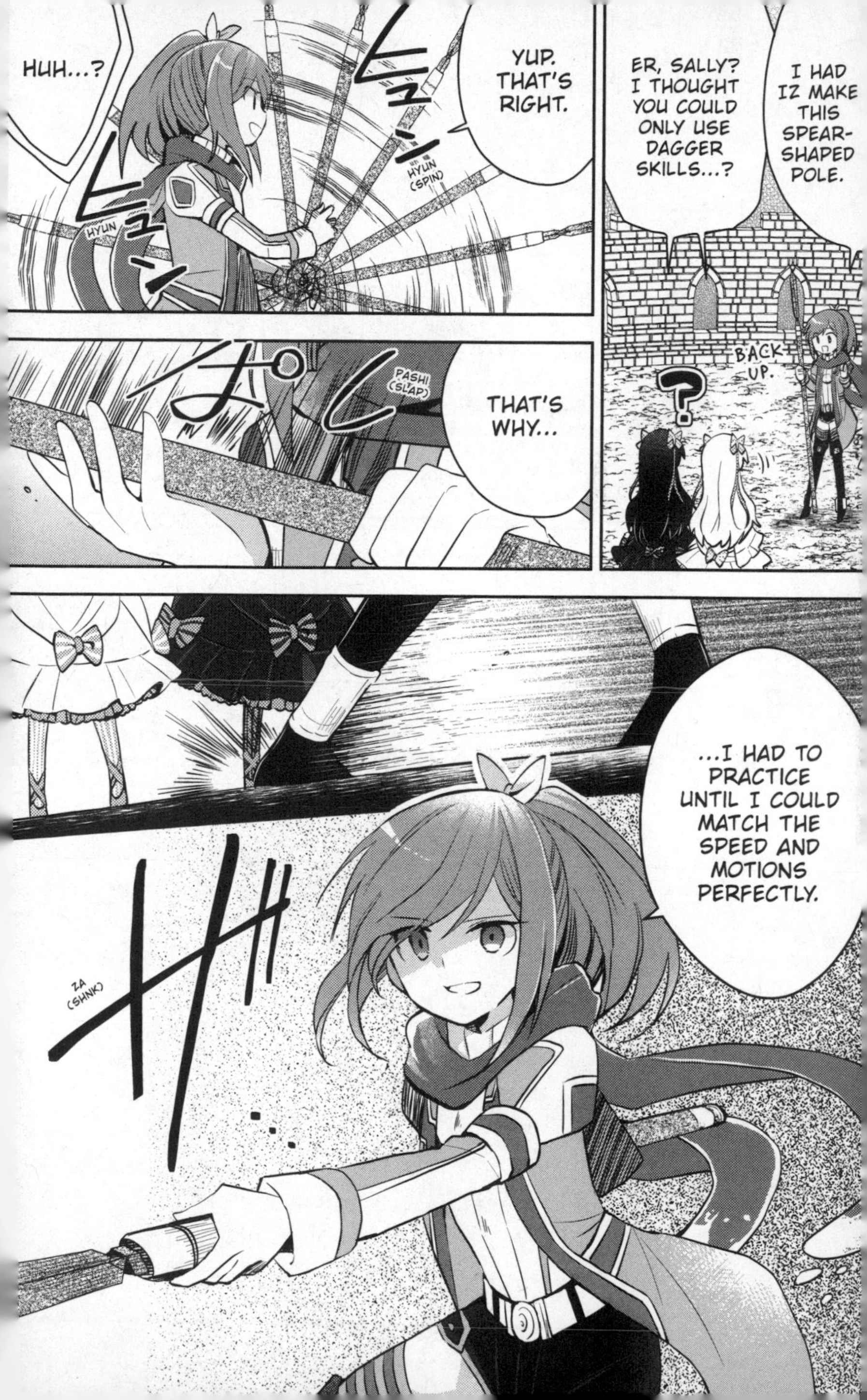
I HAD IZ MAKE THIS SPEAR-SHAPED POLE.
ER, SALLY? I THOUGHT YOU COULD ONLY USE DAGGER SKILLS...?
BACK UP.
?
YUP. THAT'S RIGHT.
HYUN (SPIN)
HYUN
HUH...?
PASHI (SLAP)
THAT'S WHY...
...I HAD TO PRACTICE UNTIL I COULD MATCH THE SPEED AND MOTIONS PERFECTLY.
ZA (SHNK)
...

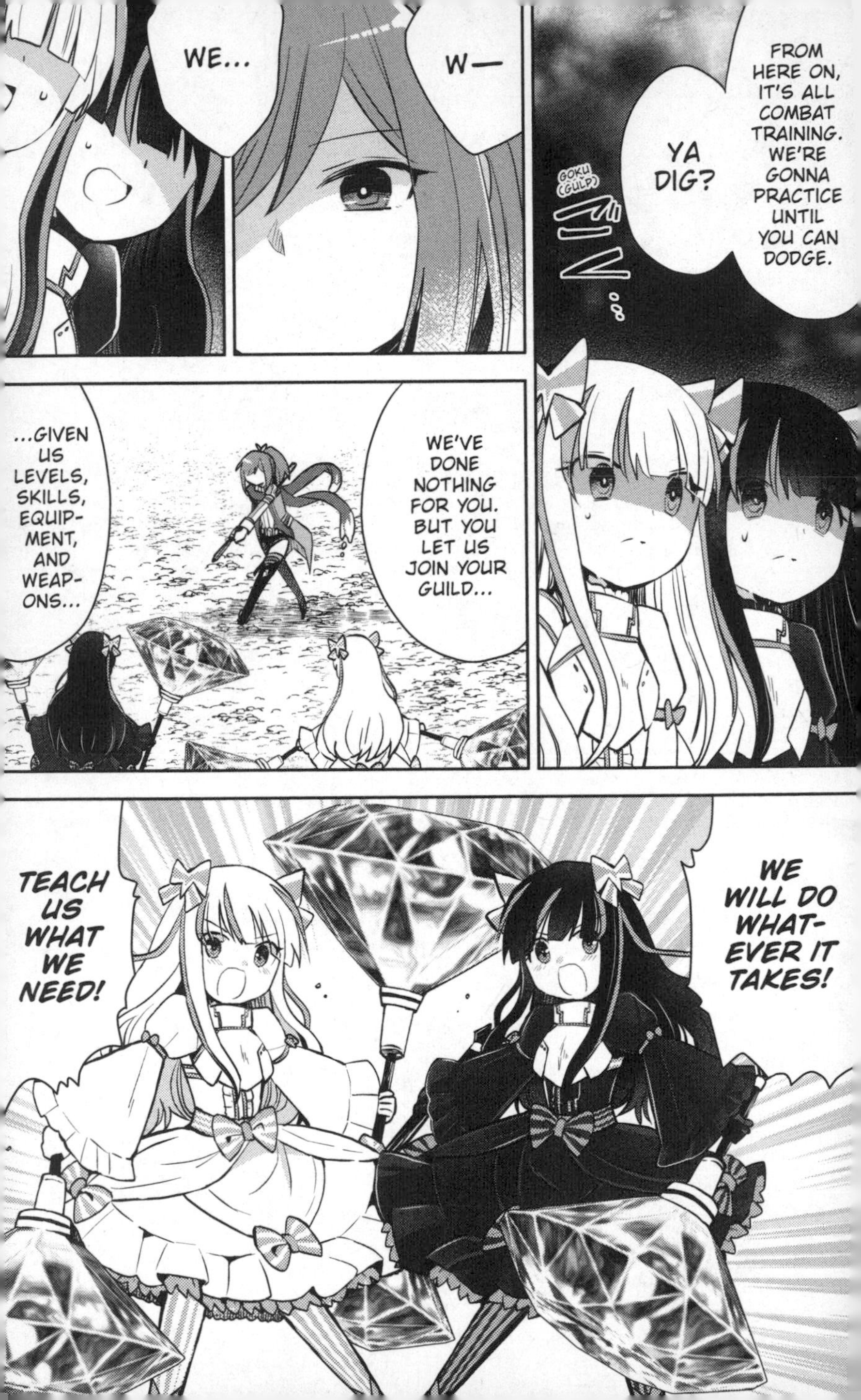
FROM HERE ON, IT'S ALL COMBAT TRAINING. WE'RE GONNA PRACTICE UNTIL YOU CAN DODGE.
YA DIG?
GOKU (GULP)
W—
WE...
WE'VE DONE NOTHING FOR YOU. BUT YOU LET US JOIN YOUR GUILD...
...GIVEN US LEVELS, SKILLS, EQUIPMENT, AND WEAPONS...
WE WILL DO WHATEVER IT TAKES!
TEACH US WHAT WE NEED!

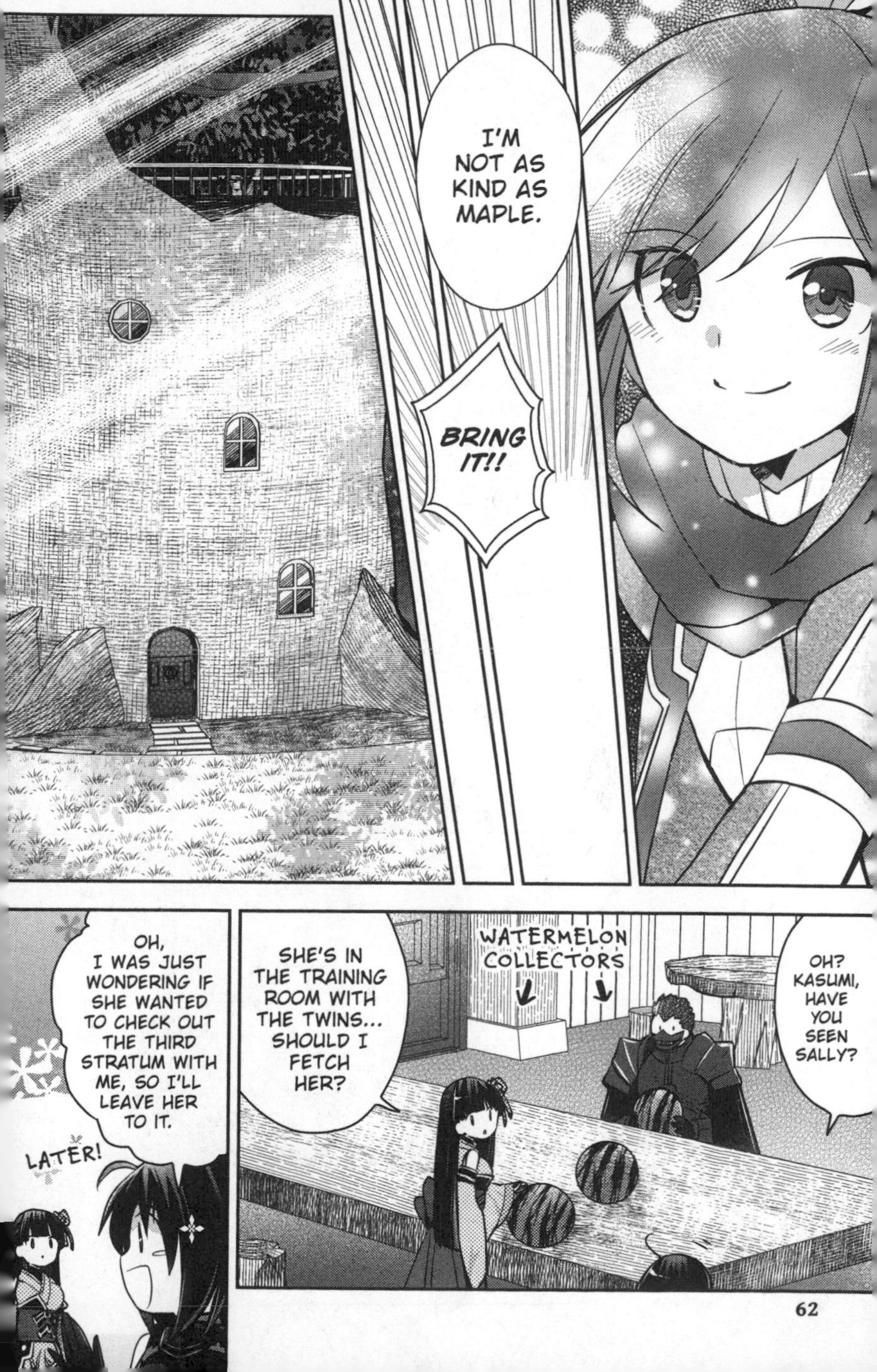
I'M NOT AS KIND AS MAPLE.
BRING IT!!
OH? KASUMI, HAVE YOU SEEN SALLY?
SHE'S IN THE TRAINING ROOM WITH THE TWINS... SHOULD I FETCH HER?
WATERMELON COLLECTORS
OH, I WAS JUST WONDERING IF SHE WANTED TO CHECK OUT THE THIRD STRATUM WITH ME, SO I'LL LEAVE HER TO IT.
LATER!

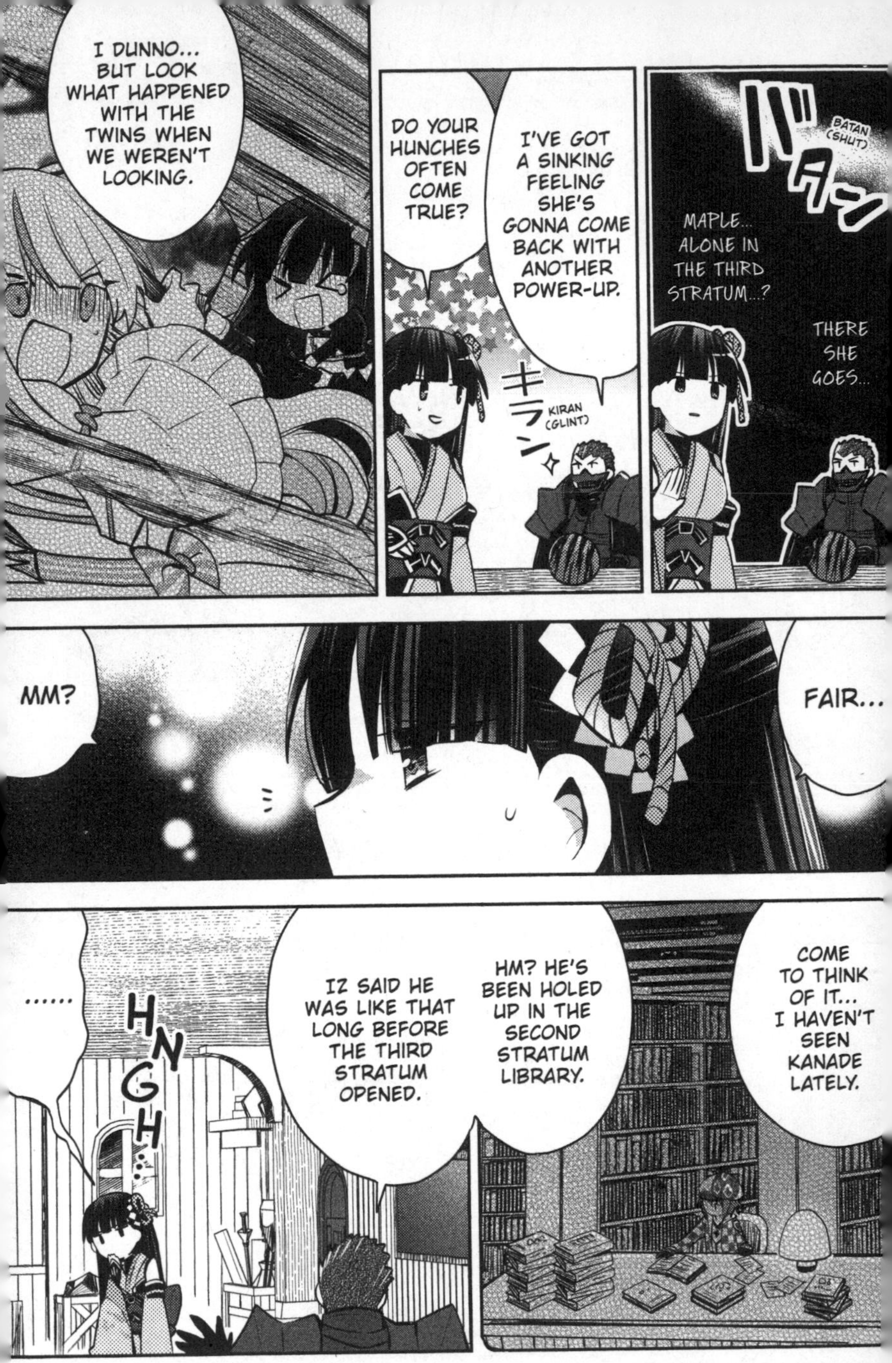

バタン
BATAN (SHUT)
MAPLE... ALONE IN THE THIRD STRATUM...?
THERE SHE GOES...
I'VE GOT A SINKING FEELING SHE'S GONNA COME BACK WITH ANOTHER POWER-UP.
キラン
KIRAN (GLINT)
DO YOUR HUNCHES OFTEN COME TRUE?
I DUNNO... BUT LOOK WHAT HAPPENED WITH THE TWINS WHEN WE WEREN'T LOOKING.
FAIR...
MM?
COME TO THINK OF IT... I HAVEN'T SEEN KANADE LATELY.
HM? HE'S BEEN HOLED UP IN THE SECOND STRATUM LIBRARY.
IZ SAID HE WAS LIKE THAT LONG BEFORE THE THIRD STRATUM OPENED.
......
HNGH...

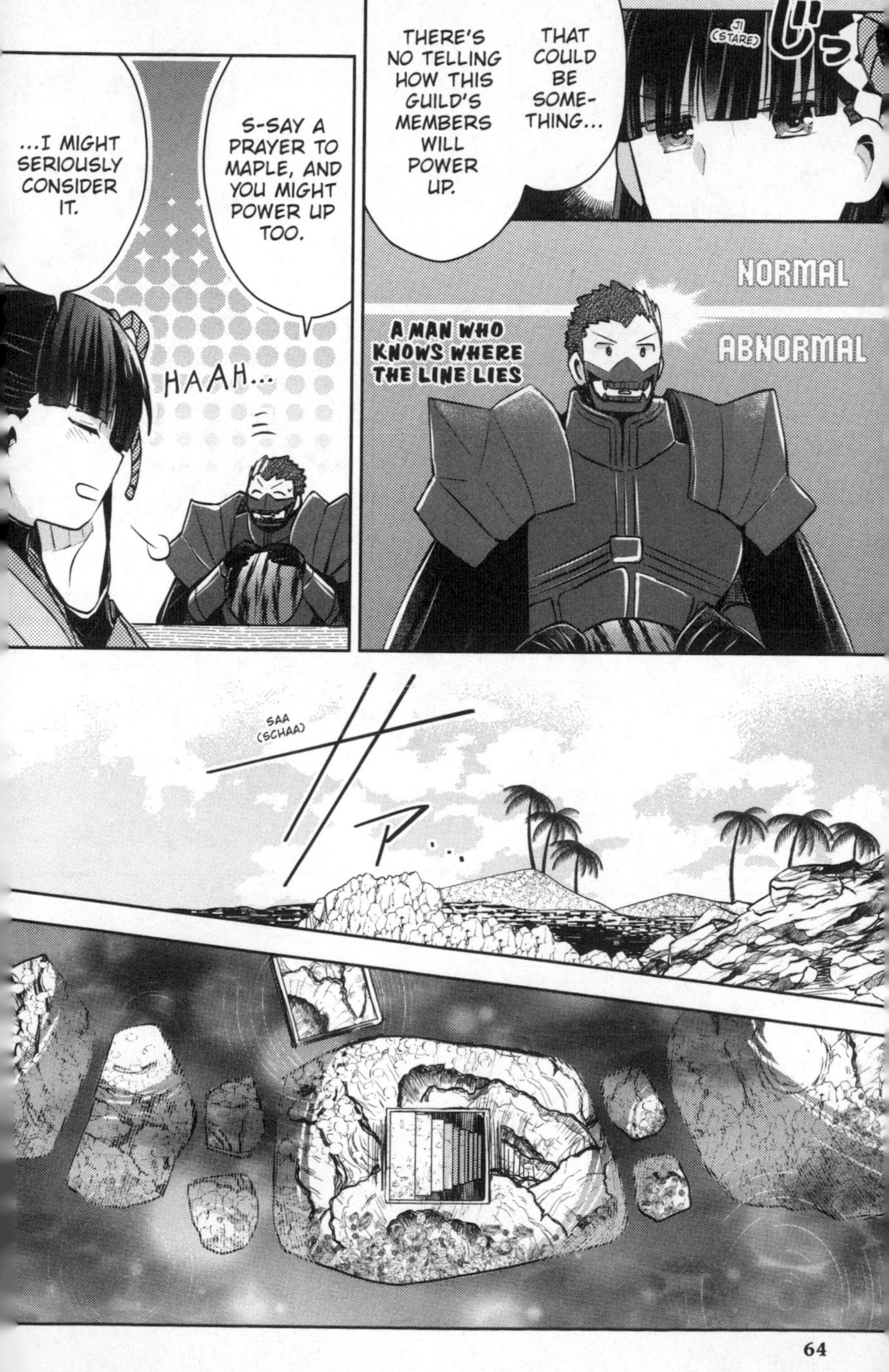
JI (STARE)
THAT COULD BE SOME-THING...
THERE'S NO TELLING HOW THIS GUILD'S MEMBERS WILL POWER UP.
NORMAL
ABNORMAL
A MAN WHO KNOWS WHERE THE LINE LIES
S-SAY A PRAYER TO MAPLE, AND YOU MIGHT POWER UP TOO.
...I MIGHT SERIOUSLY CONSIDER IT.
HAAH...
SAA (SCHAA)

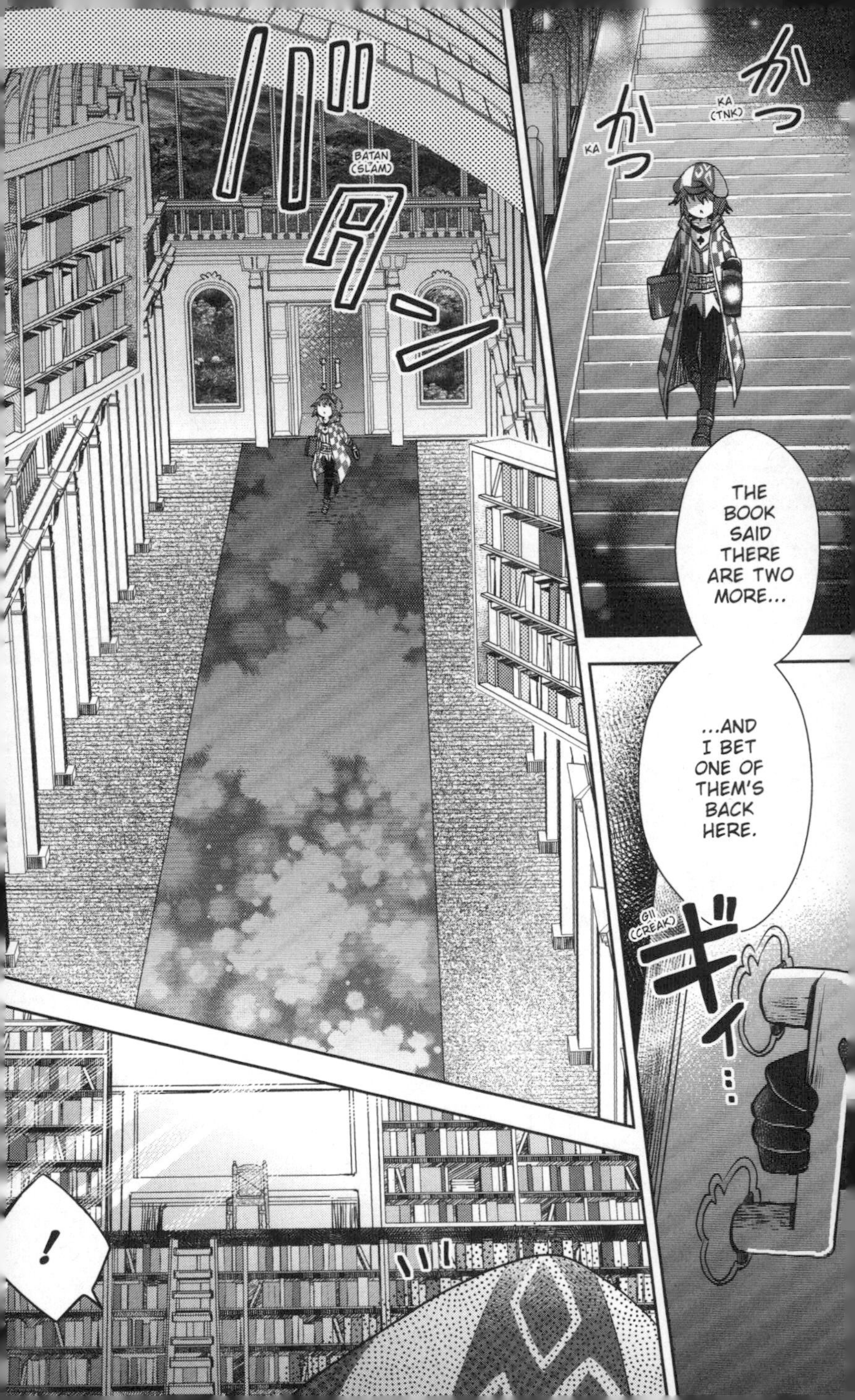
かっ
KA (TNK)
かっ
KA
THE BOOK SAID THERE ARE TWO MORE...
...AND I BET ONE OF THEM'S BACK HERE.
ギィ…
GII (CREAK)
バターン
BATAN (SLAM)
!

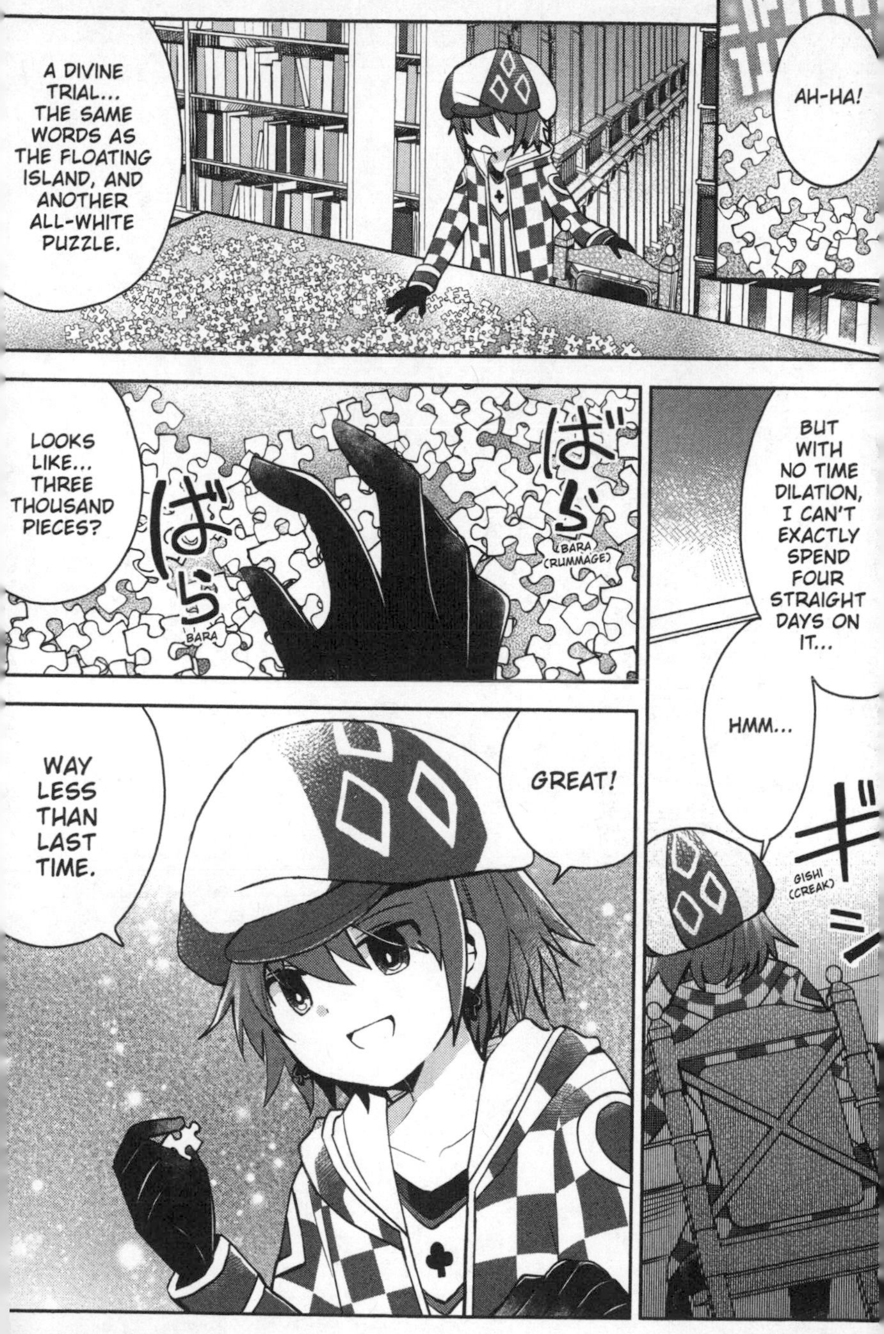

AH-HA!
A DIVINE TRIAL... THE SAME WORDS AS THE FLOATING ISLAND, AND ANOTHER ALL-WHITE PUZZLE.
BUT WITH NO TIME DILATION, I CAN'T EXACTLY SPEND FOUR STRAIGHT DAYS ON IT...
HMM...
ギシ
GISHI (CREAK)
LOOKS LIKE... THREE THOUSAND PIECES?
ばら
BARA (RUMMAGE)
ばら
BARA
GREAT!
WAY LESS THAN LAST TIME.

CHAPTER 26

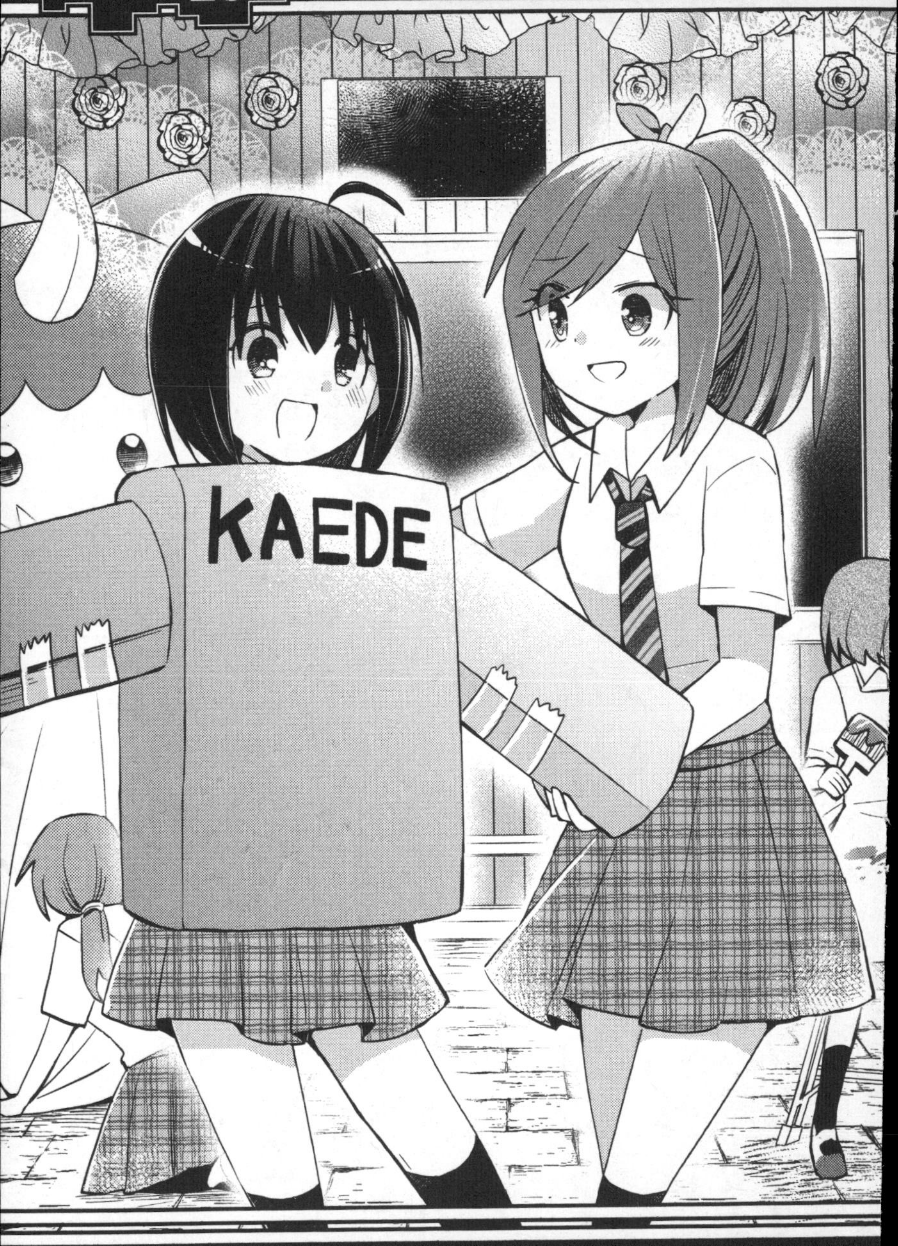

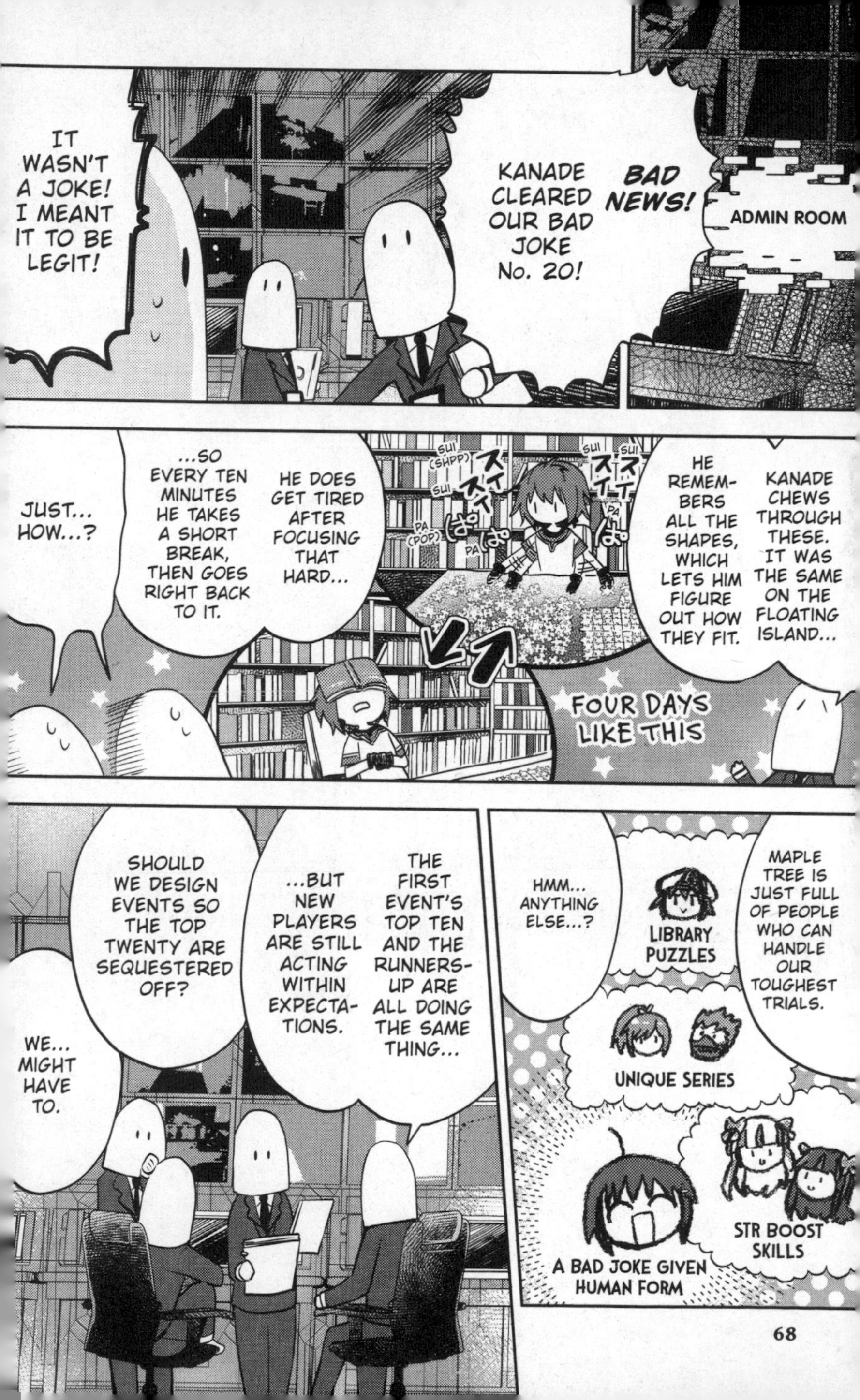
ADMIN ROOM
BAD NEWS!
KANADE CLEARED OUR BAD JOKE No. 20!
IT WASN'T A JOKE! I MEANT IT TO BE LEGIT!
KANADE CHEWS THROUGH THESE. IT WAS THE SAME ON THE FLOATING ISLAND...
HE REMEMBERS ALL THE SHAPES, WHICH LETS HIM FIGURE OUT HOW THEY FIT.
SUI スイ SUI スイ
PA ぱ
SUI (SHPP) スイ SUI スイ
PA (POP) ぱ PA ぱ
HE DOES GET TIRED AFTER FOCUSING THAT HARD...
...SO EVERY TEN MINUTES HE TAKES A SHORT BREAK, THEN GOES RIGHT BACK TO IT.
JUST... HOW...?
FOUR DAYS LIKE THIS
MAPLE TREE IS JUST FULL OF PEOPLE WHO CAN HANDLE OUR TOUGHEST TRIALS.
HMM... ANYTHING ELSE...?
LIBRARY PUZZLES
UNIQUE SERIES
STR BOOST SKILLS
A BAD JOKE GIVEN HUMAN FORM
THE FIRST EVENT'S TOP TEN AND THE RUNNERS-UP ARE ALL DOING THE SAME THING...
...BUT NEW PLAYERS ARE STILL ACTING WITHIN EXPECTATIONS.
SHOULD WE DESIGN EVENTS SO THE TOP TWENTY ARE SEQUESTERED OFF?
WE... MIGHT HAVE TO.

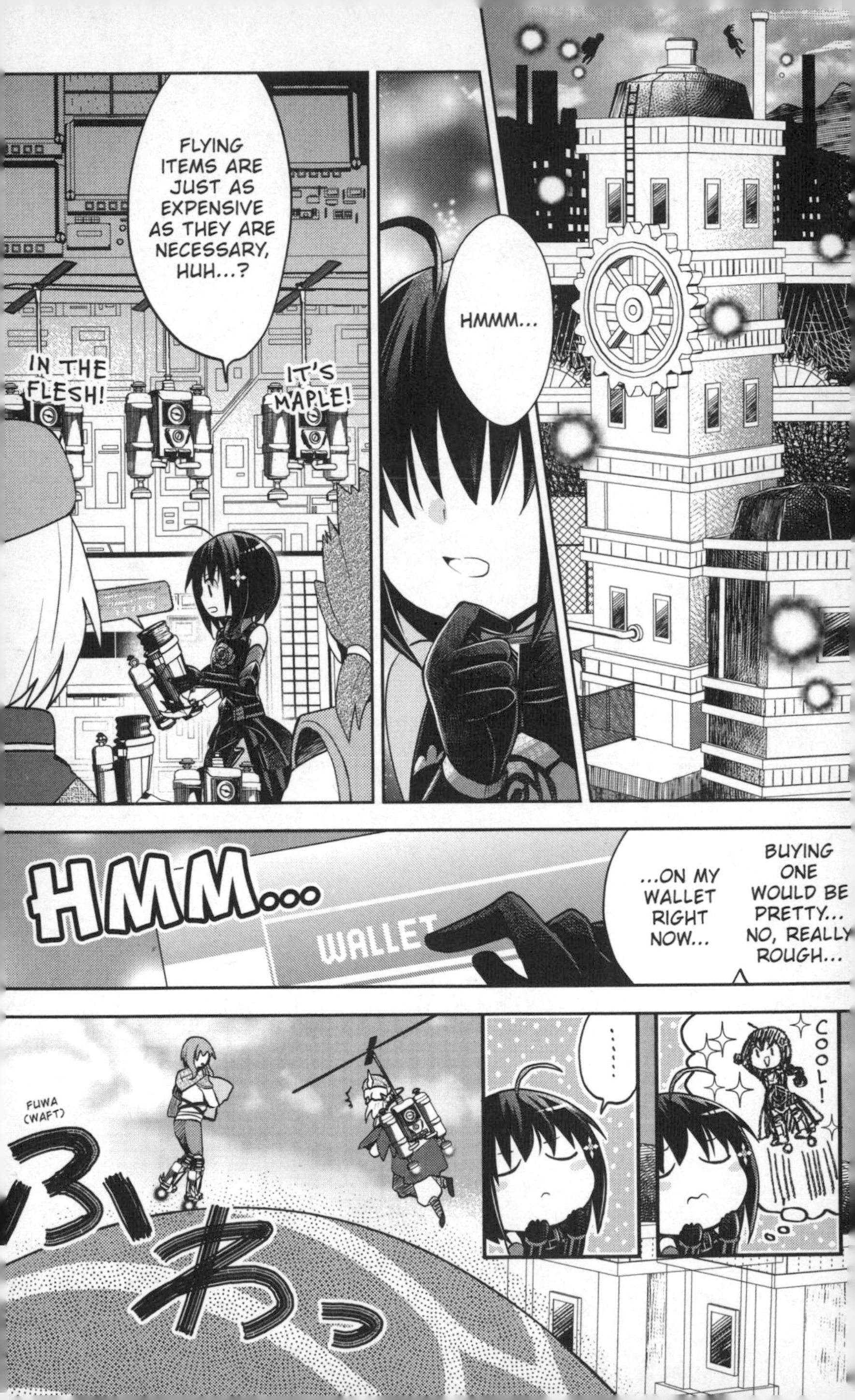
HMMM...
FLYING ITEMS ARE JUST AS EXPENSIVE AS THEY ARE NECESSARY, HUH...?
IT'S MAPLE!
IN THE FLESH!
BUYING ONE WOULD BE PRETTY... NO, REALLY ROUGH...
...ON MY WALLET RIGHT NOW...
WALLET
HMM...
COOL!
......
FUWA (WAFT)
ふわっ

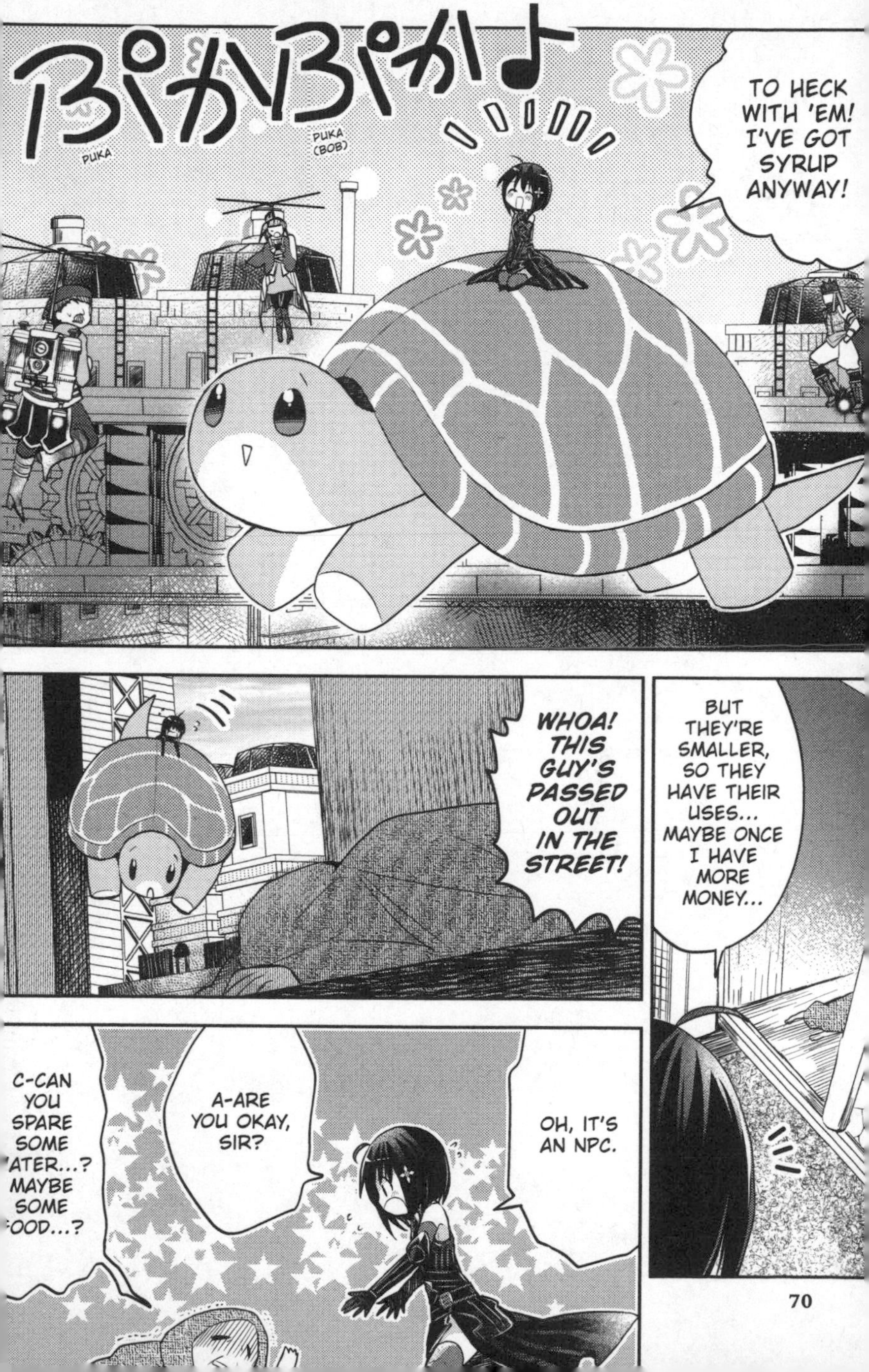
TO HECK WITH 'EM! I'VE GOT SYRUP ANYWAY!
ぷかぷか♪
PUKA (BOB)
PUKA
BUT THEY'RE SMALLER, SO THEY HAVE THEIR USES... MAYBE ONCE I HAVE MORE MONEY...
WHOA! THIS GUY'S PASSED OUT IN THE STREET!
OH, IT'S AN NPC.
A-ARE YOU OKAY, SIR?
C-CAN YOU SPARE SOME ATER...? MAYBE SOME OOD...?

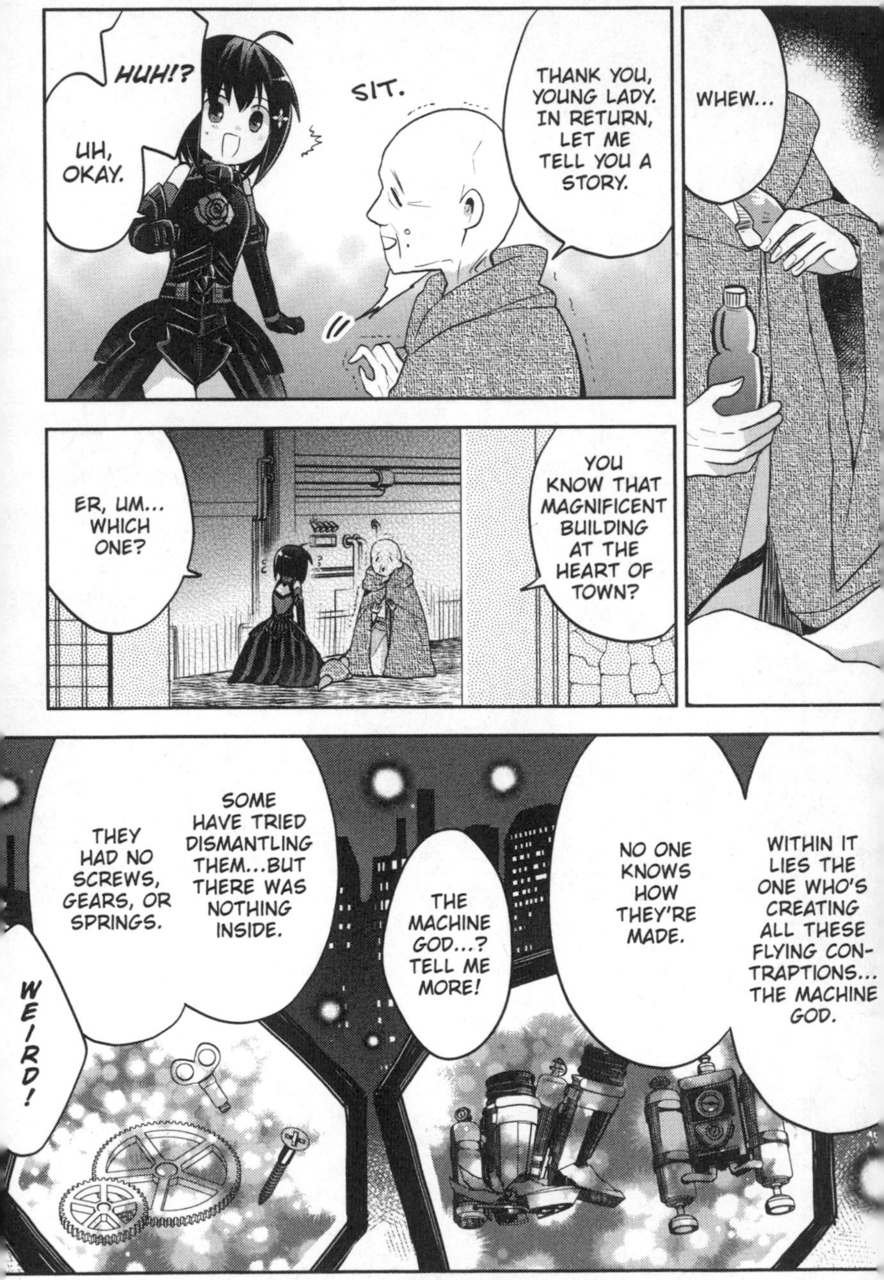
WHEW...
THANK YOU, YOUNG LADY. IN RETURN, LET ME TELL YOU A STORY.
SIT.
HUH!?
UH, OKAY.
YOU KNOW THAT MAGNIFICENT BUILDING AT THE HEART OF TOWN?
ER, UM... WHICH ONE?
WITHIN IT LIES THE ONE WHO'S CREATING ALL THESE FLYING CONTRAPTIONS... THE MACHINE GOD.
NO ONE KNOWS HOW THEY'RE MADE.
THE MACHINE GOD...? TELL ME MORE!
SOME HAVE TRIED DISMANTLING THEM...BUT THERE WAS NOTHING INSIDE.
THEY HAD NO SCREWS, GEARS, OR SPRINGS.
WEIRD!

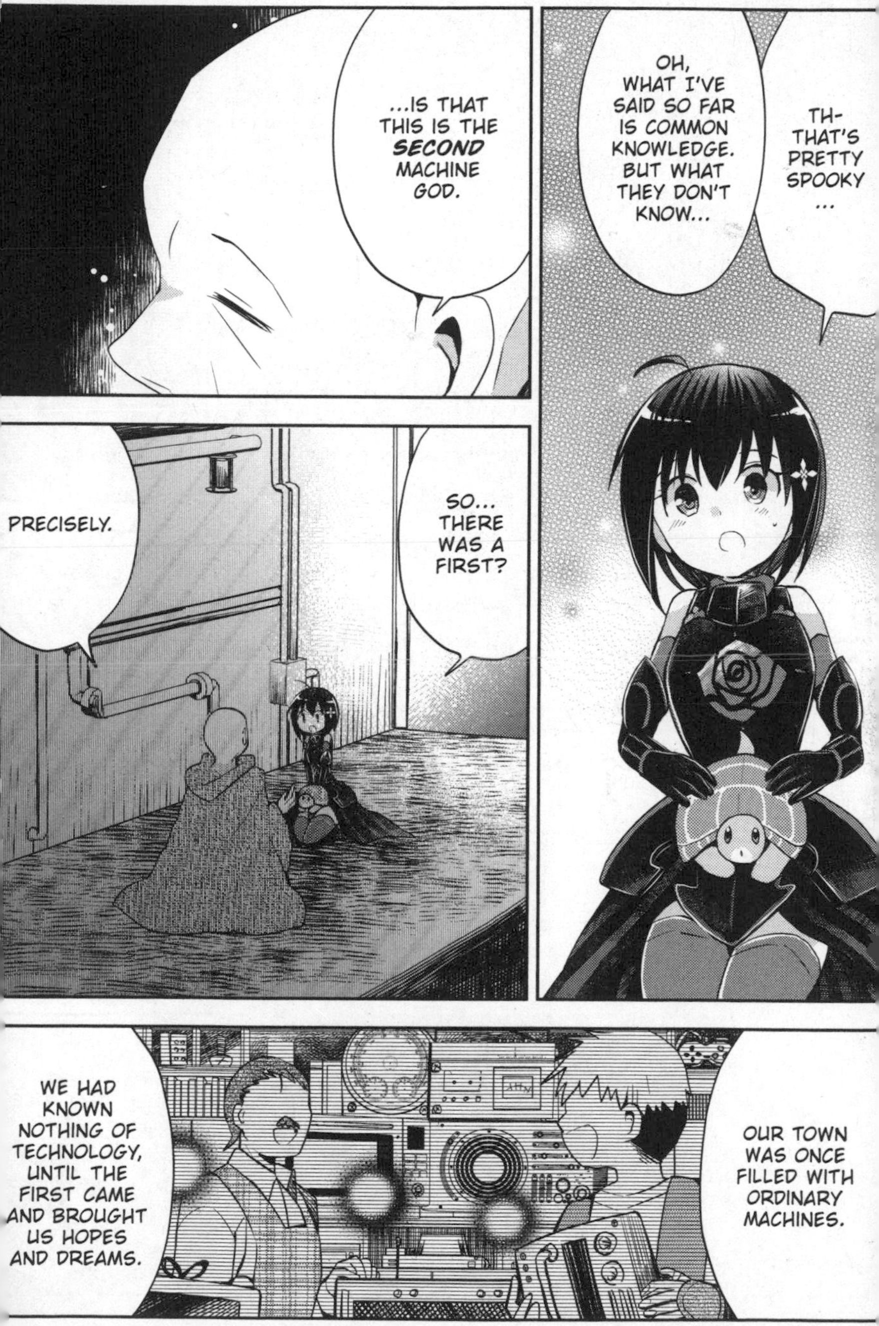
TH-THAT'S PRETTY SPOOKY...
OH, WHAT I'VE SAID SO FAR IS COMMON KNOWLEDGE. BUT WHAT THEY DON'T KNOW...
...IS THAT THIS IS THE SECOND MACHINE GOD.
SO... THERE WAS A FIRST?
PRECISELY.
OUR TOWN WAS ONCE FILLED WITH ORDINARY MACHINES.
WE HAD KNOWN NOTHING OF TECHNOLOGY, UNTIL THE FIRST CAME AND BROUGHT US HOPES AND DREAMS.

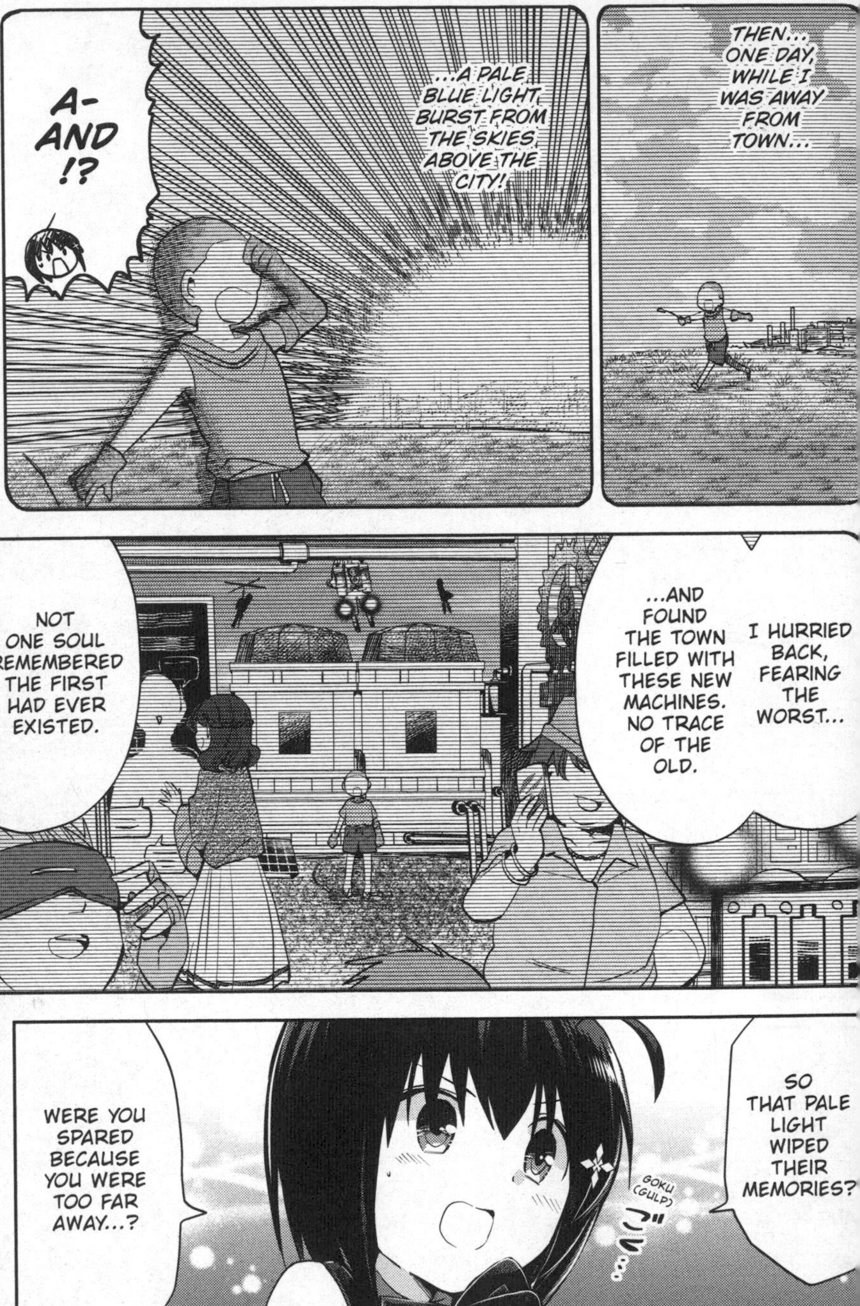
THEN... ONE DAY, WHILE I WAS AWAY FROM TOWN...
...A PALE BLUE LIGHT BURST FROM THE SKIES ABOVE THE CITY!
A-AND !?
I HURRIED BACK, FEARING THE WORST...
...AND FOUND THE TOWN FILLED WITH THESE NEW MACHINES. NO TRACE OF THE OLD.
NOT ONE SOUL REMEMBERED THE FIRST HAD EVER EXISTED.
SO THAT PALE LIGHT WIPED THEIR MEMORIES?
GOKU (GULP)
WERE YOU SPARED BECAUSE YOU WERE TOO FAR AWAY...?

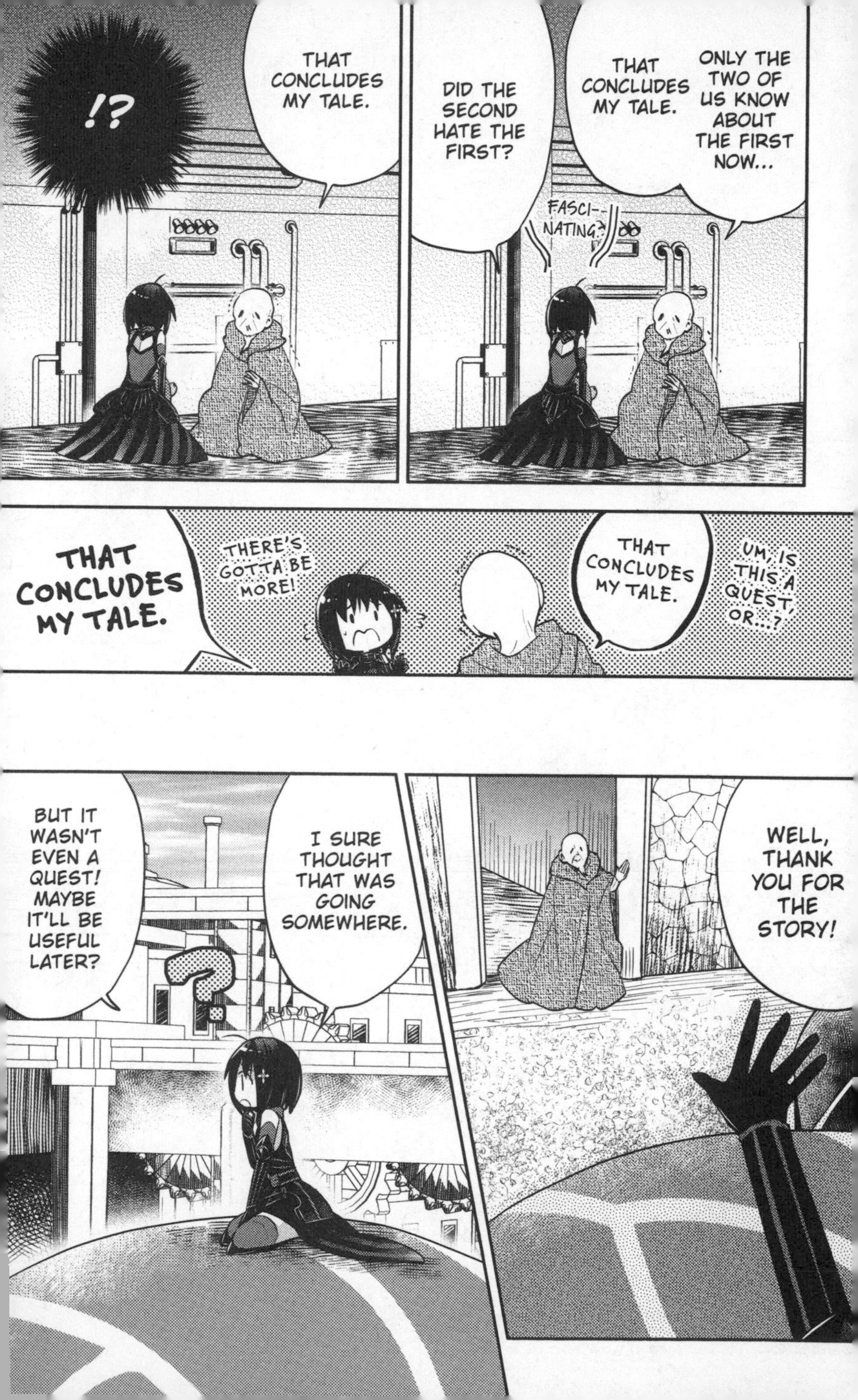
ONLY THE TWO OF US KNOW ABOUT THE FIRST NOW...
THAT CONCLUDES MY TALE.
DID THE SECOND HATE THE FIRST?
FASCI-NATING?
THAT CONCLUDES MY TALE.
!?
UM, IS THIS A QUEST, OR...?
THAT CONCLUDES MY TALE.
THERE'S GOTTA BE MORE!
THAT CONCLUDES MY TALE.
WELL, THANK YOU FOR THE STORY!
I SURE THOUGHT THAT WAS GOING SOMEWHERE.
BUT IT WASN'T EVEN A QUEST! MAYBE IT'LL BE USEFUL LATER?

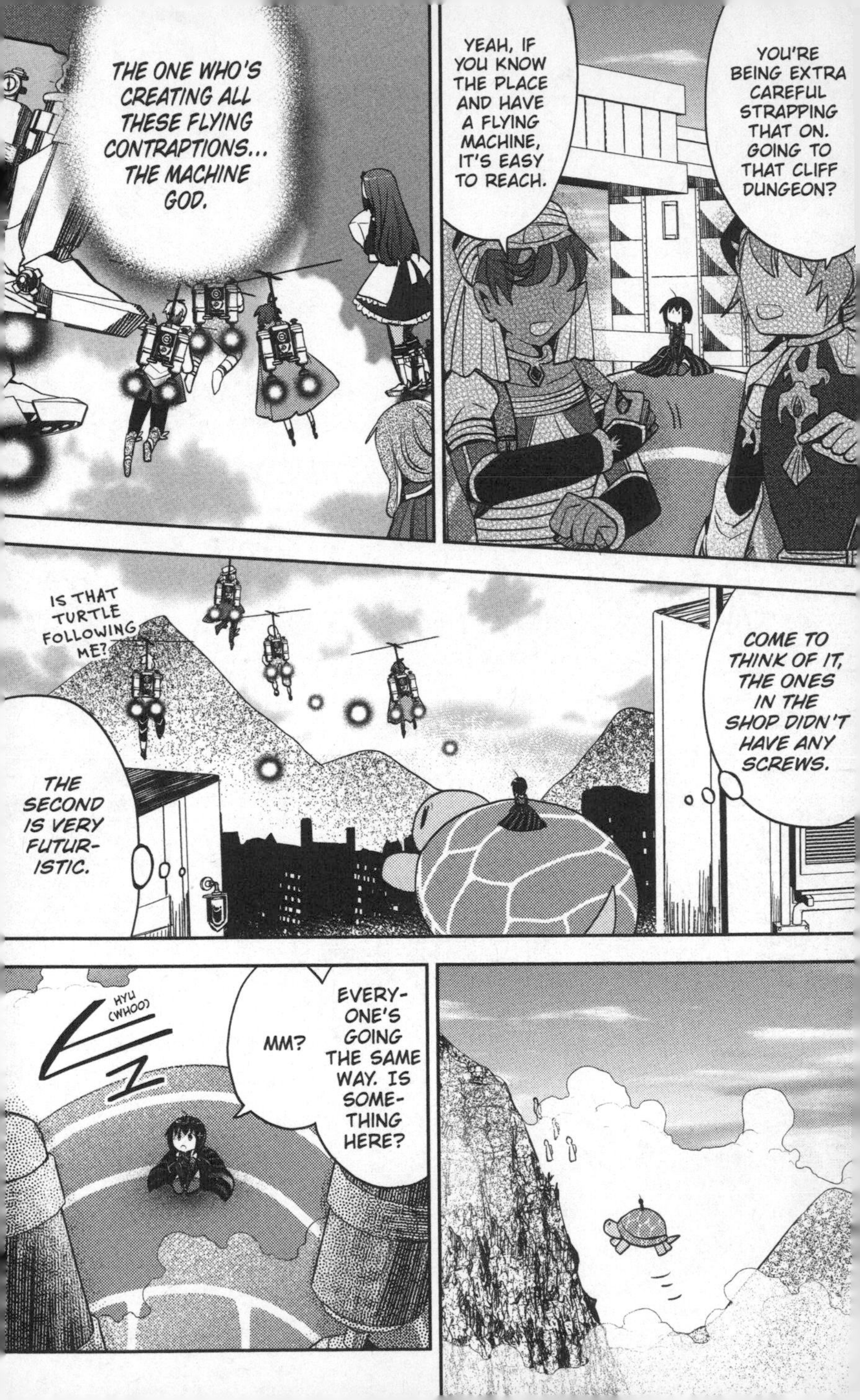
YOU'RE BEING EXTRA CAREFUL STRAPPING THAT ON. GOING TO THAT CLIFF DUNGEON?
YEAH, IF YOU KNOW THE PLACE AND HAVE A FLYING MACHINE, IT'S EASY TO REACH.
THE ONE WHO'S CREATING ALL THESE FLYING CONTRAPTIONS... THE MACHINE GOD.
COME TO THINK OF IT, THE ONES IN THE SHOP DIDN'T HAVE ANY SCREWS.
IS THAT TURTLE FOLLOWING ME?
THE SECOND IS VERY FUTURISTIC.
EVERY-ONE'S GOING THE SAME WAY. IS SOME-THING HERE?
MM?
HYU (WHOO)

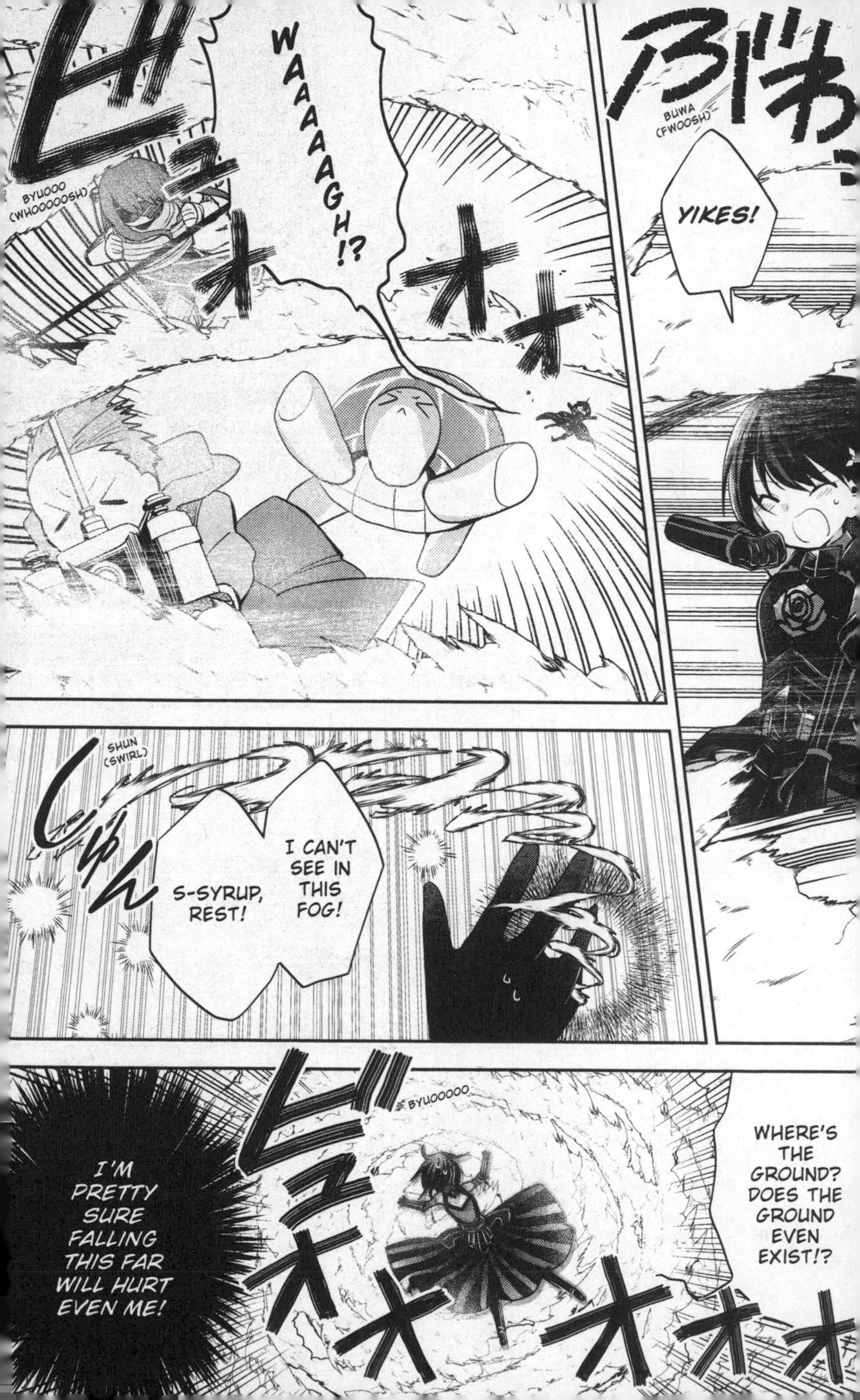
BUWA
(FWOOSH)
YIKES!
WAAAAAAGH!?
BYUOOO
(WHOOOOOSH)
SHUN
(SWIRL)
I CAN'T SEE IN THIS FOG!
S-SYRUP, REST!
WHERE'S THE GROUND? DOES THE GROUND EVEN EXIST!?
BYUOOOO
I'M PRETTY SURE FALLING THIS FAR WILL HURT EVEN ME!

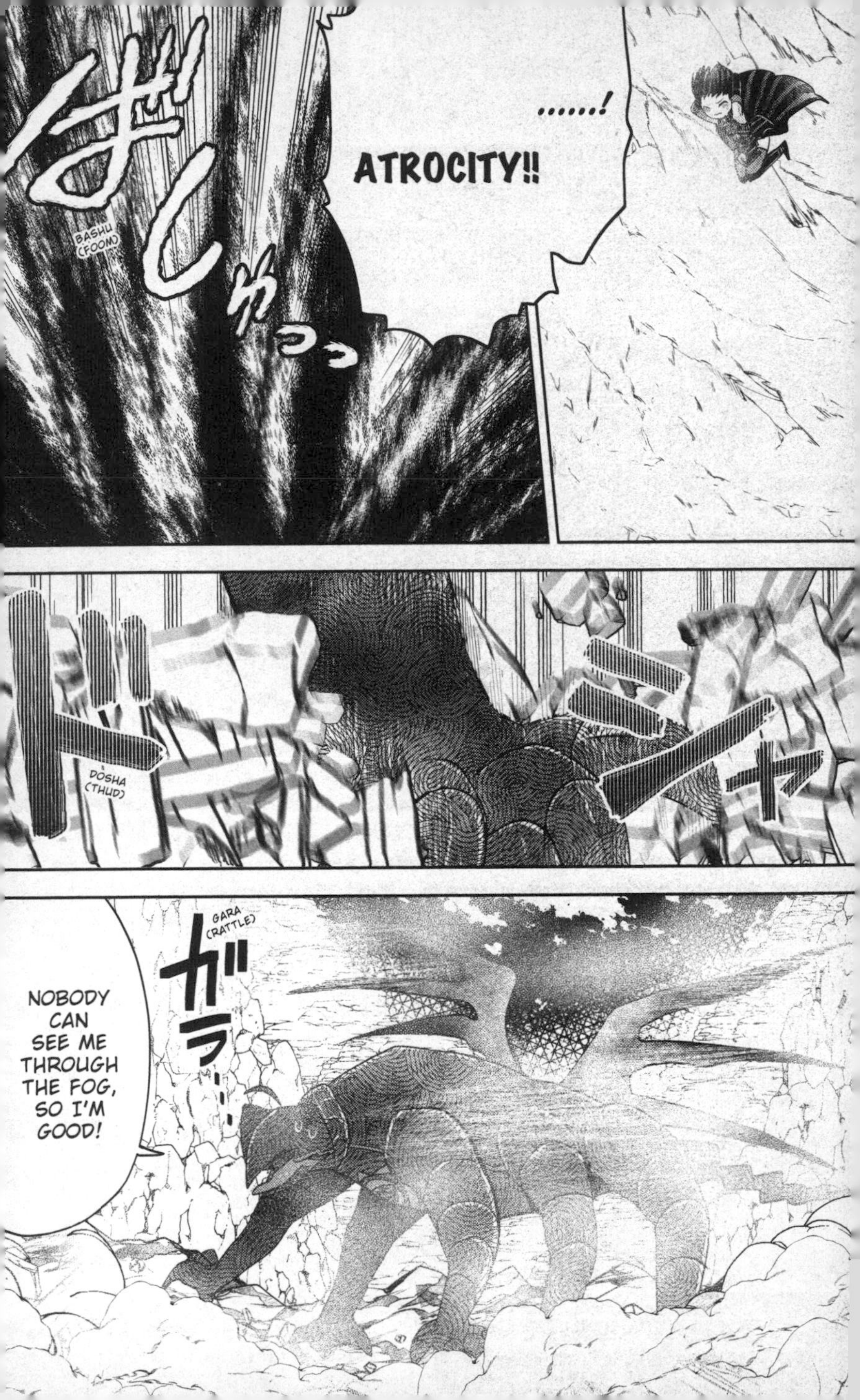
......!
ATROCITY!!
BASHU (FOOM)
DOSHA (THUD)
GARA (RATTLE)
NOBODY CAN SEE ME THROUGH THE FOG, SO I'M GOOD!

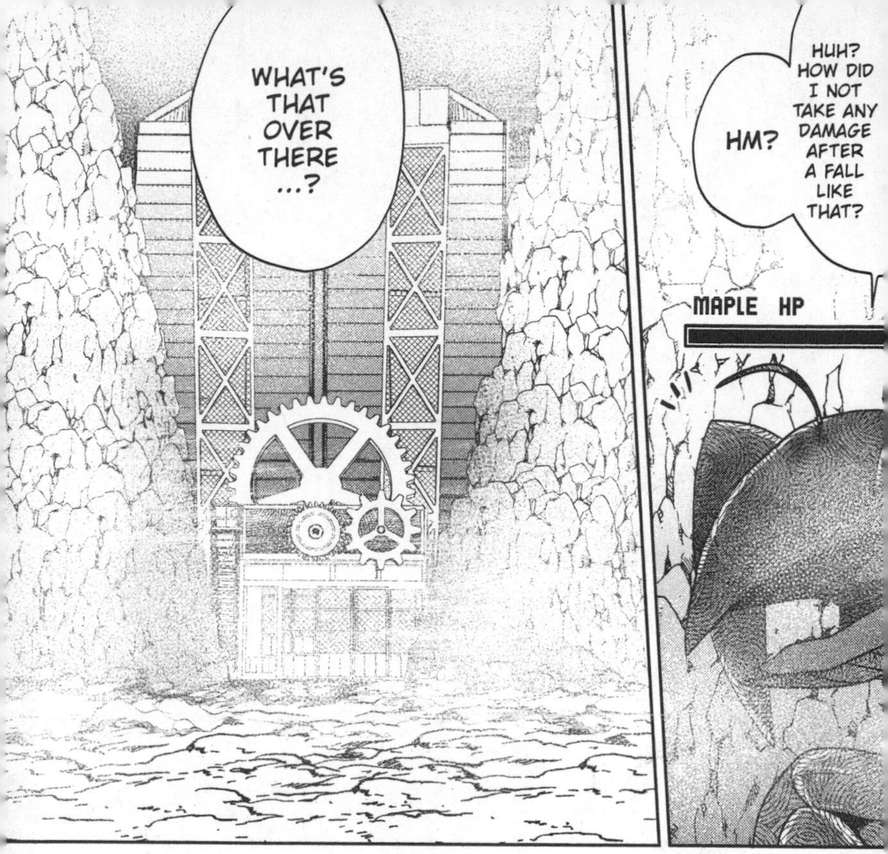
HUH? HOW DID I NOT TAKE ANY DAMAGE AFTER A FALL LIKE THAT?
HM?
MAPLE HP
WHAT'S THAT OVER THERE ...?
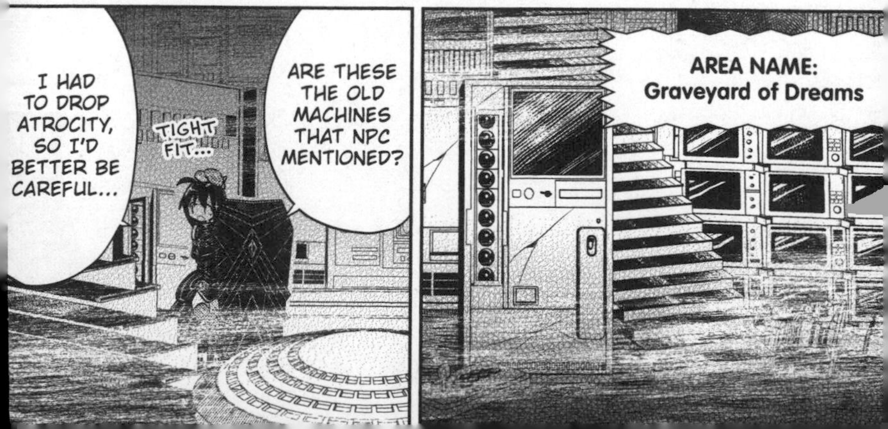
AREA NAME:
Graveyard of Dreams
ARE THESE THE OLD MACHINES THAT NPC MENTIONED?
TIGHT FIT...
I HAD TO DROP ATROCITY, SO I'D BETTER BE CAREFUL...

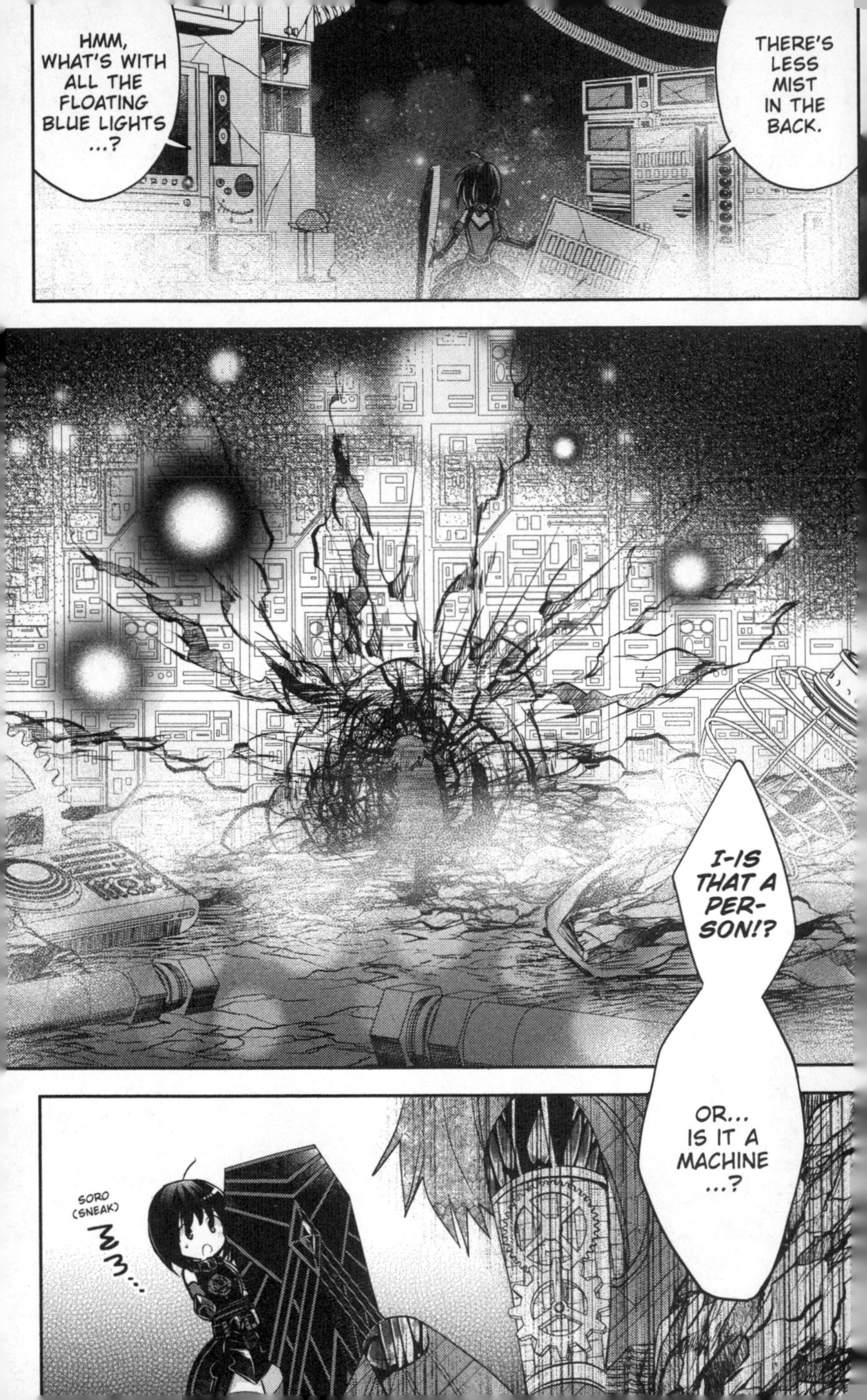
THERE'S LESS MIST IN THE BACK.
HMM, WHAT'S WITH ALL THE FLOATING BLUE LIGHTS ...?
I-IS THAT A PER-SON!?
OR... IS IT A MACHINE ...?
SORO (SNEAK)

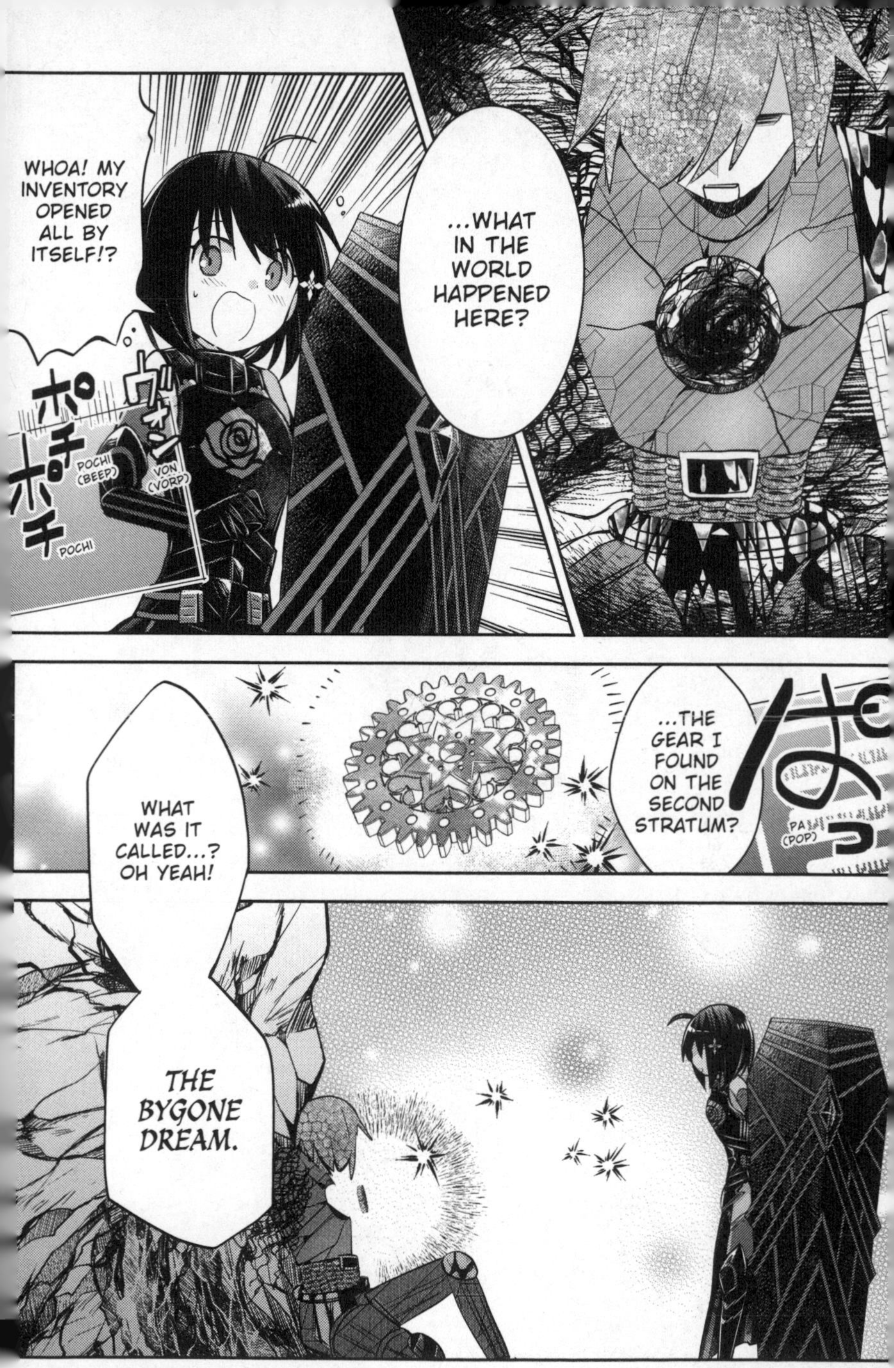
...WHAT IN THE WORLD HAPPENED HERE?
WHOA! MY INVENTORY OPENED ALL BY ITSELF!?
ヴォン
VON (VORP)
ポチポチ
POCHI (BEEP)
ポチ
POCHI
ぱっ
PA (POP)
...THE GEAR I FOUND ON THE SECOND STRATUM?
WHAT WAS IT CALLED...? OH YEAH!
THE BYGONE DREAM.

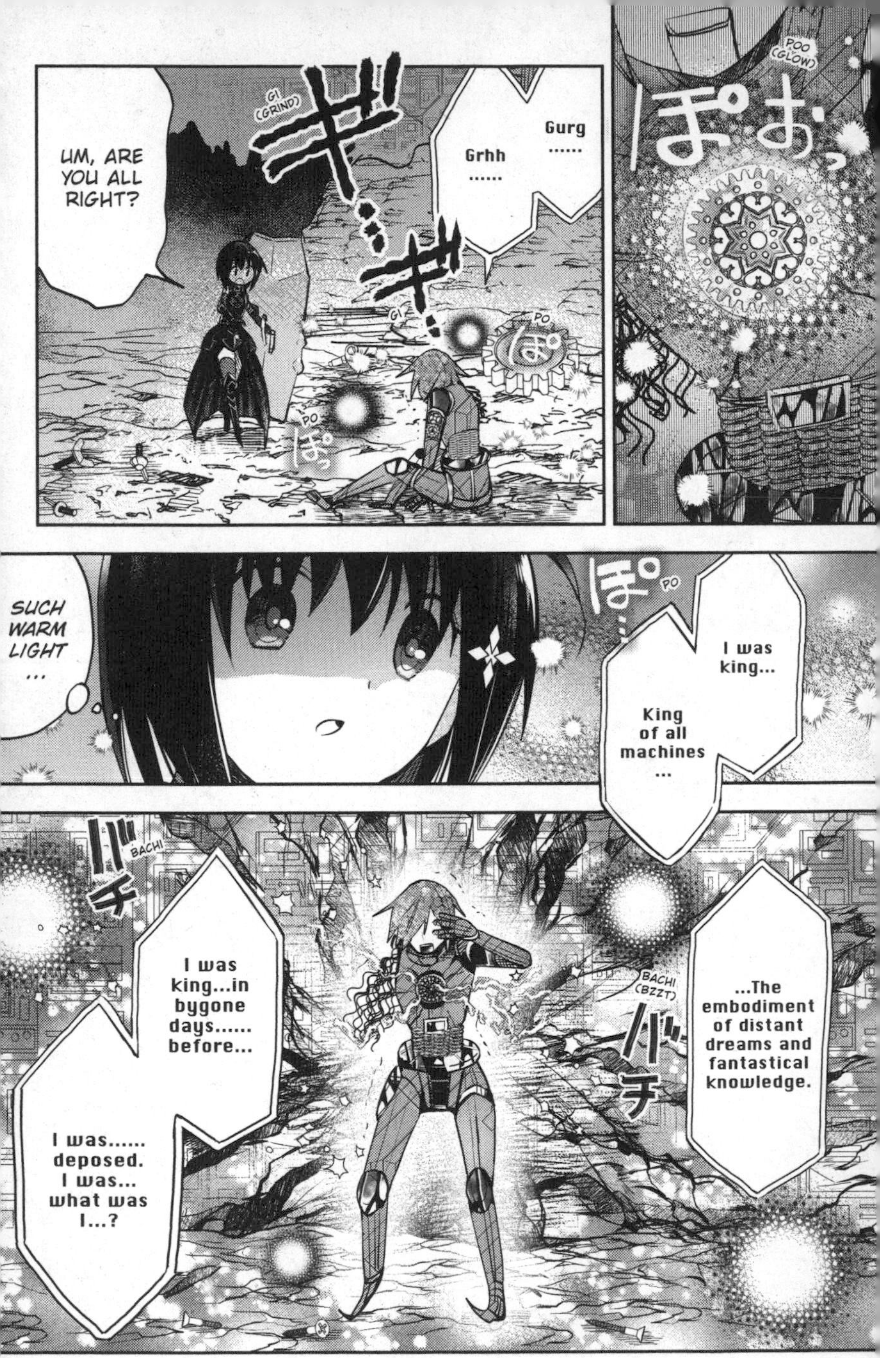
POO (GLOW)
Gurg ......
Grhh ......
GI (GRIND)
UM, ARE YOU ALL RIGHT?
GI
PO
PO
PO
I was king...
King of all machines ...
SUCH WARM LIGHT ...
...The embodiment of distant dreams and fantastical knowledge.
BACHI (BZZT)
I was king...in bygone days...... before...
BACHI
I was...... deposed. I was... what was I...?

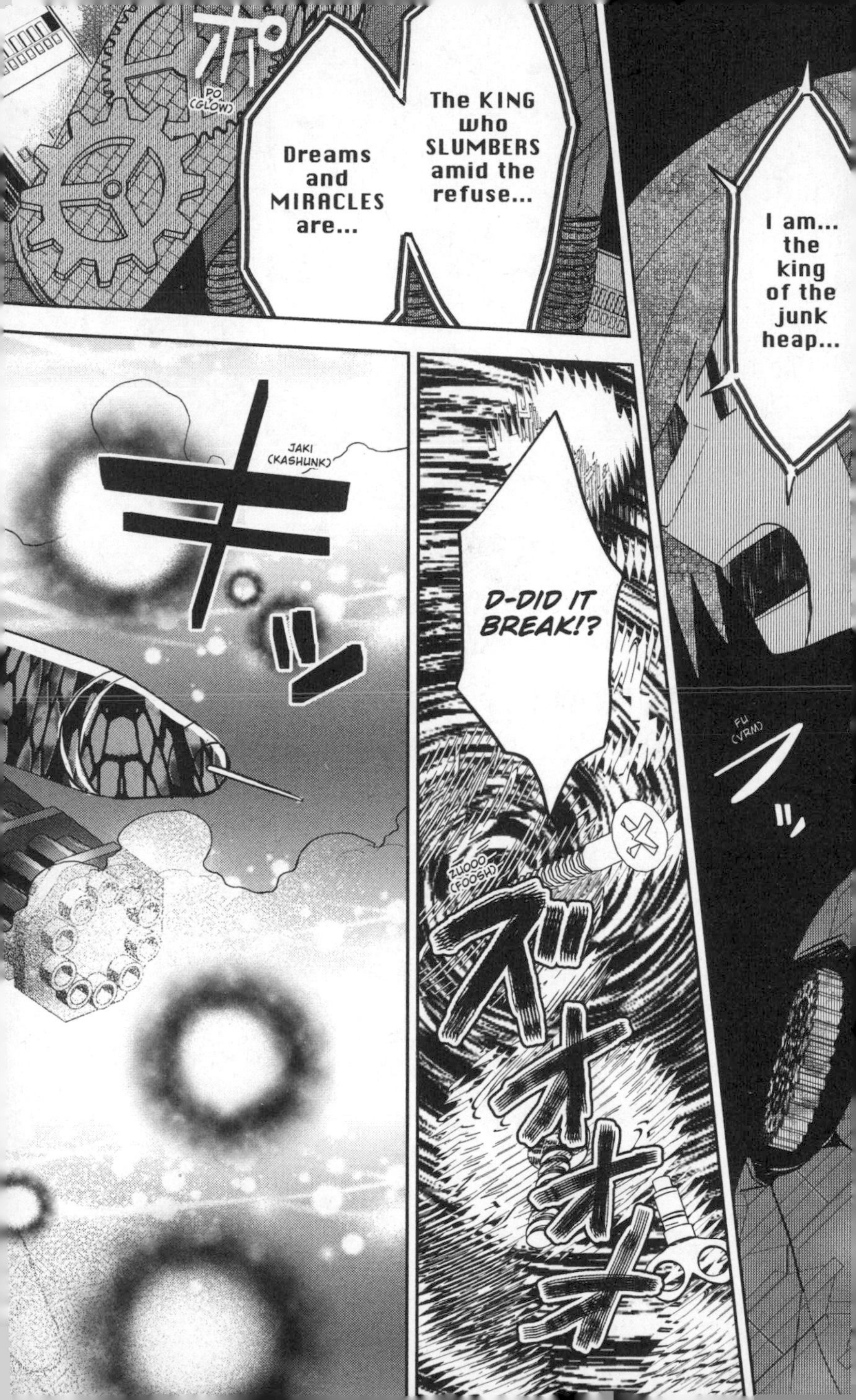
PO (GLOW)
The KING who SLUMBERS amid the refuse...
Dreams and MIRACLES are...
I am... the king of the junk heap...
FU (VRM)
D-DID IT BREAK!?
ZUOOO (FOOSH)
JAKI (KASHUNK)

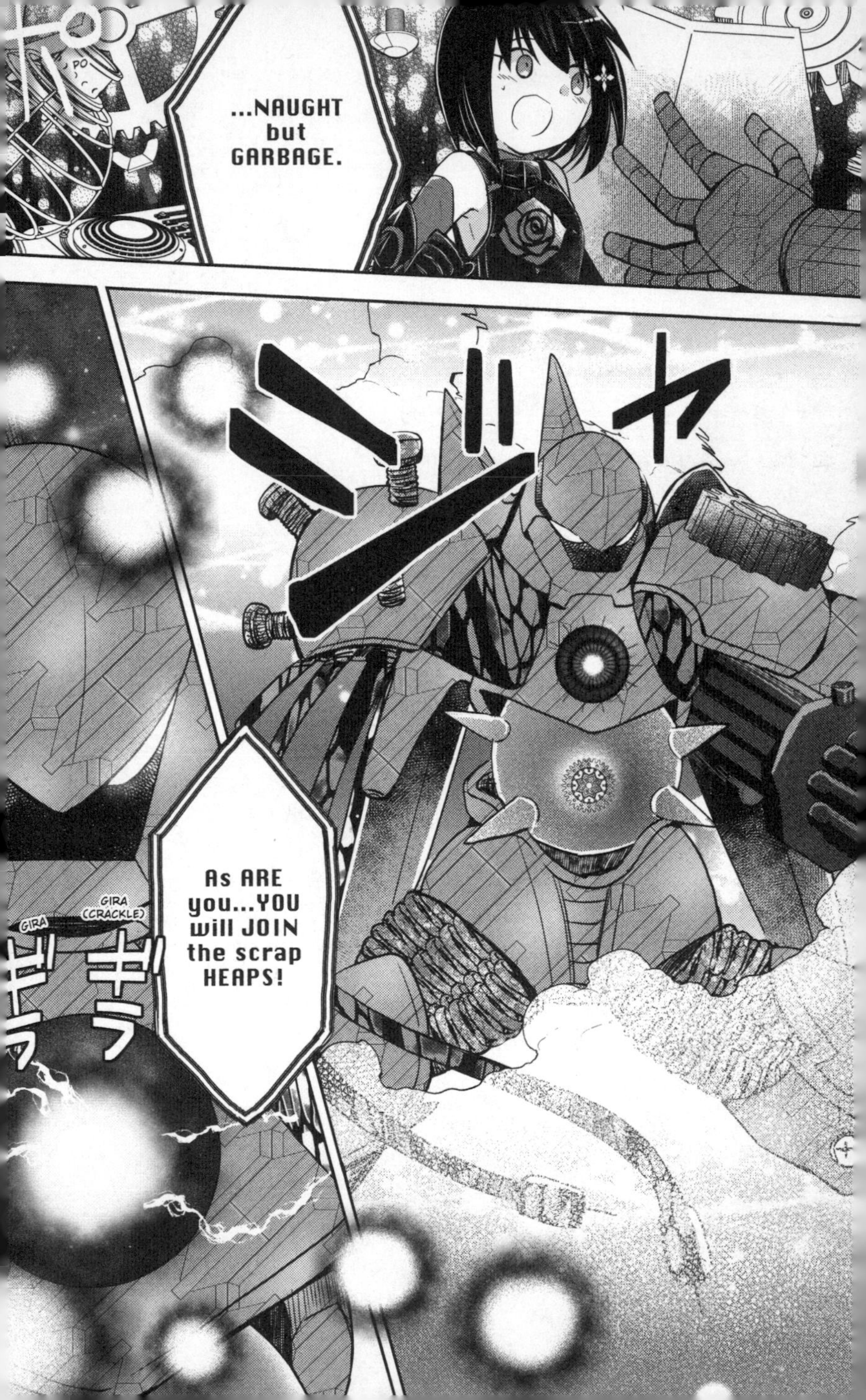
...NAUGHT but GARBAGE.
PO
As ARE you...YOU will JOIN the scrap HEAPS!
GIRA (CRACKLE)
ギラ
GIRA
ギラ

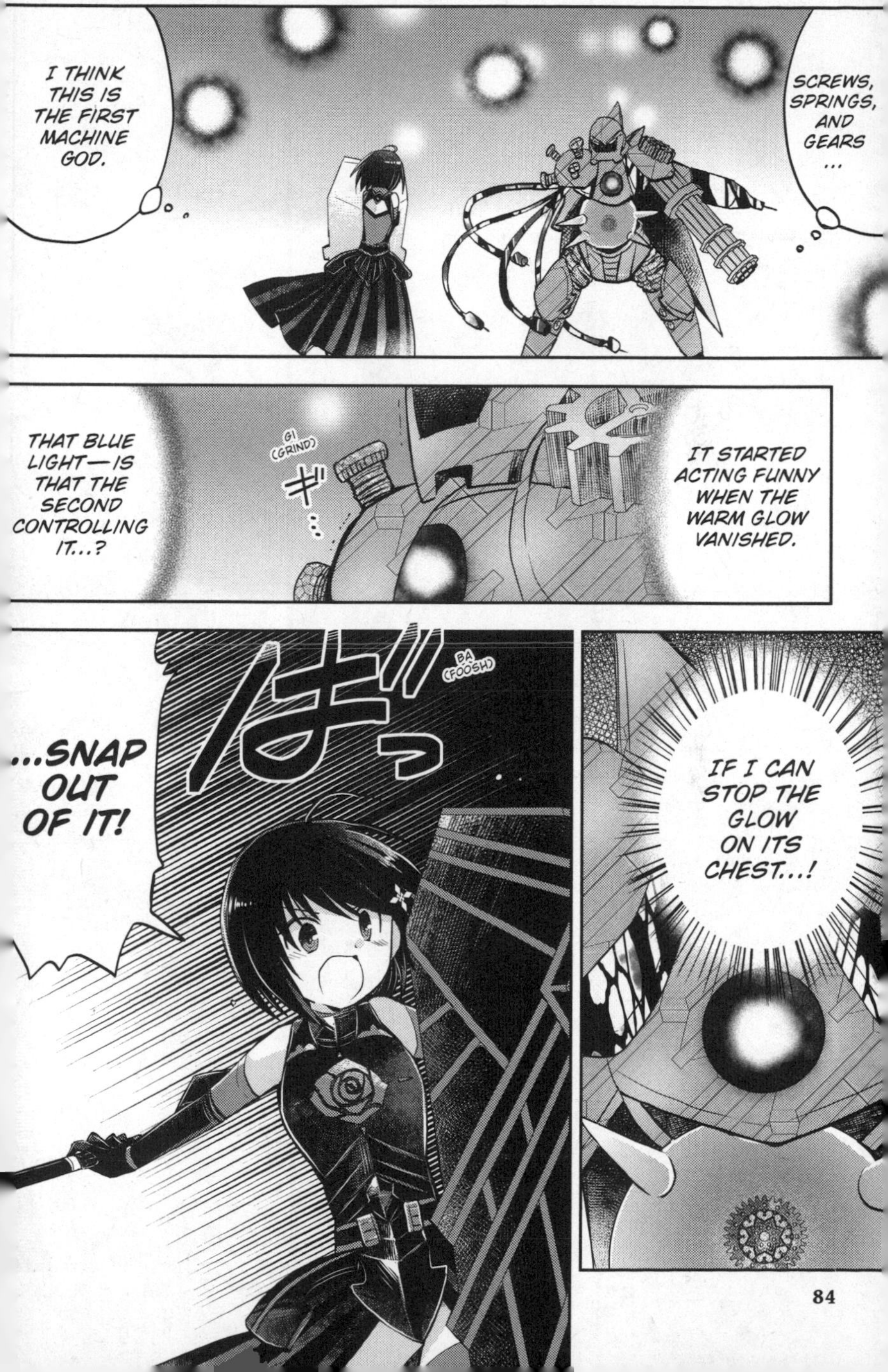
SCREWS, SPRINGS, AND GEARS ...
I THINK THIS IS THE FIRST MACHINE GOD.
IT STARTED ACTING FUNNY WHEN THE WARM GLOW VANISHED.
GI (GRIND)
ギ…
THAT BLUE LIGHT—IS THAT THE SECOND CONTROLLING IT...?
IF I CAN STOP THE GLOW ON ITS CHEST...!
BA (FOOSH)
ばっ
...SNAP OUT OF IT!

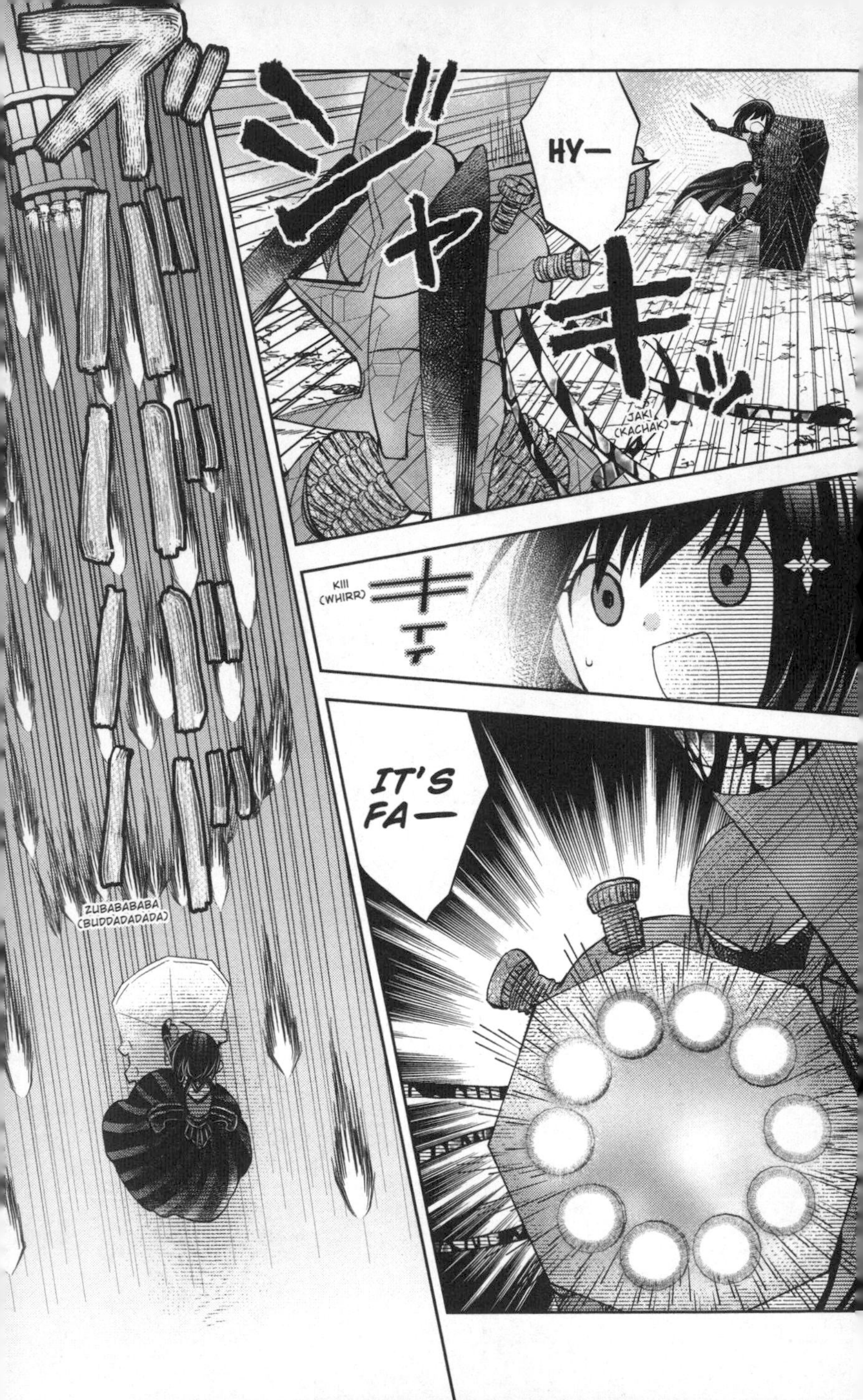
HY—
JAKI (KACHAK)
KIII (WHIRR)
IT'S FA—
ZUBABABABA (BUDDADADADA)

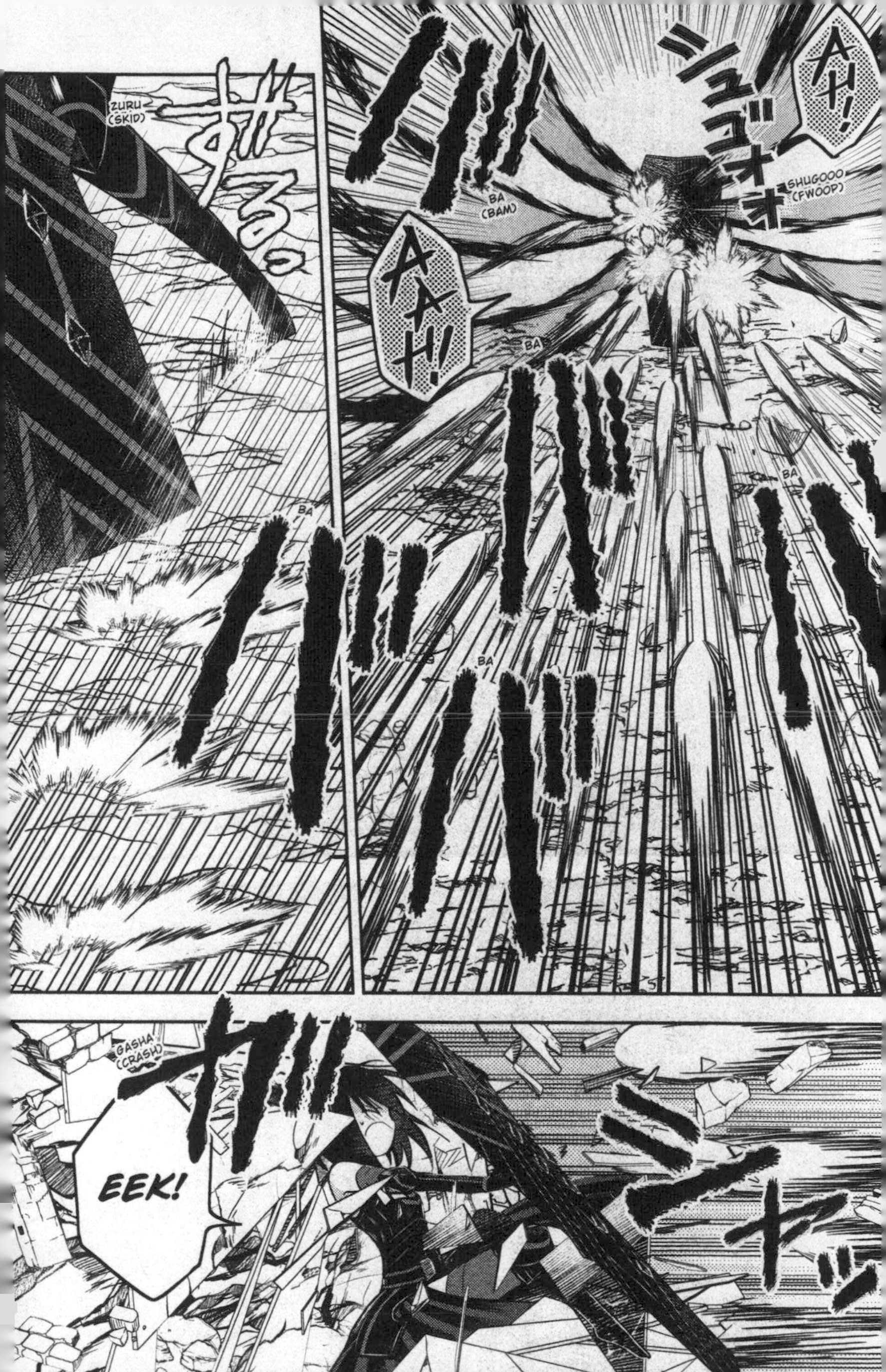
AH!
SHUGOOO (FWOOP)
BA (BAM)
AAH!
BA
BA
BA
BA
ZURU (SKID)
BA
GASHA (CRASH)
EEK!

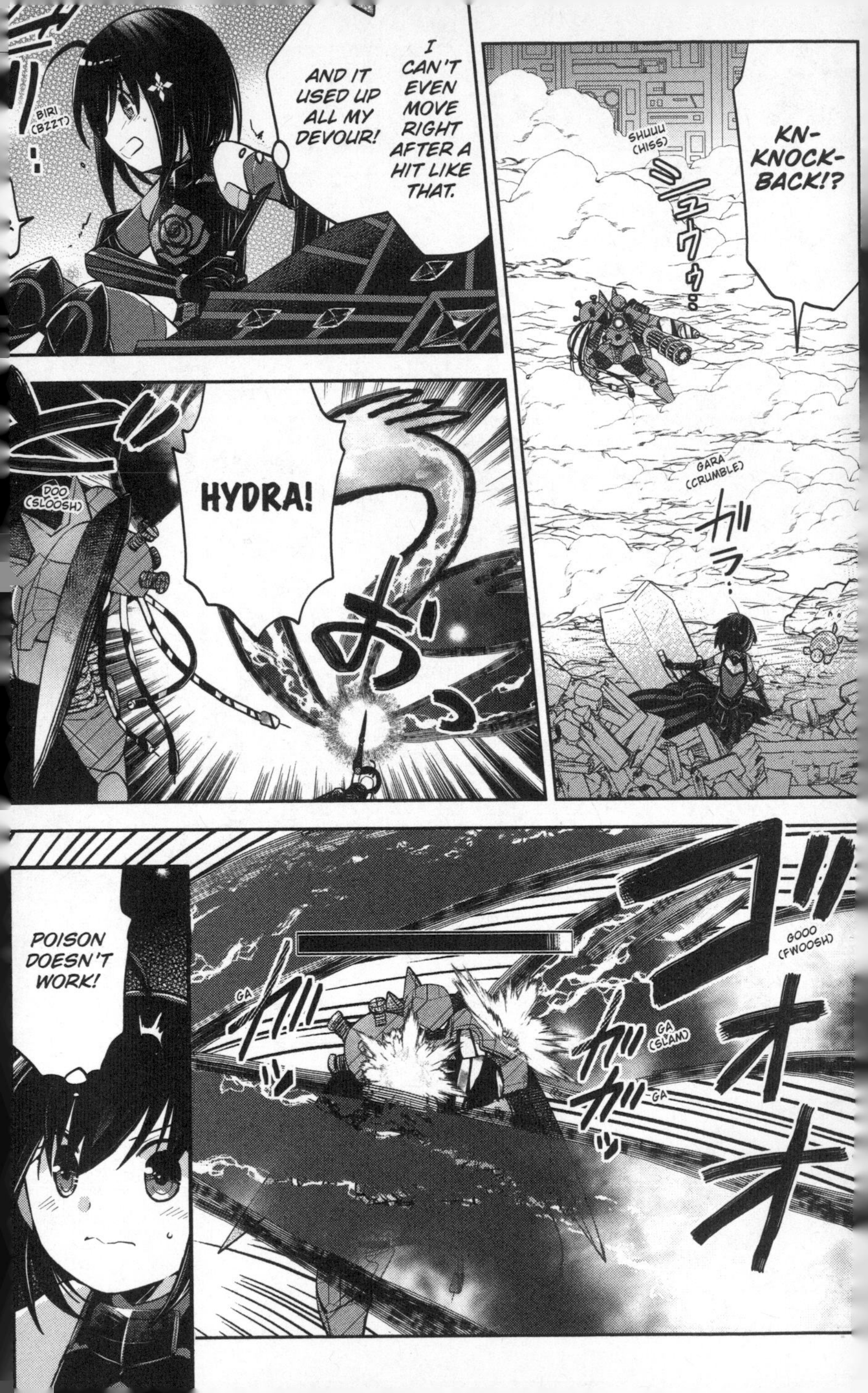
KN-KNOCK-BACK!?
SHUUU (HISS)
GARA (CRUMBLE)
I CAN'T EVEN MOVE RIGHT AFTER A HIT LIKE THAT.
AND IT USED UP ALL MY DEVOUR!
BIRI (BZZT)
HYDRA!
DOO (SLOOSH)
GOOO (FWOOSH)
GA (SLAM)
GA
GA
POISON DOESN'T WORK!

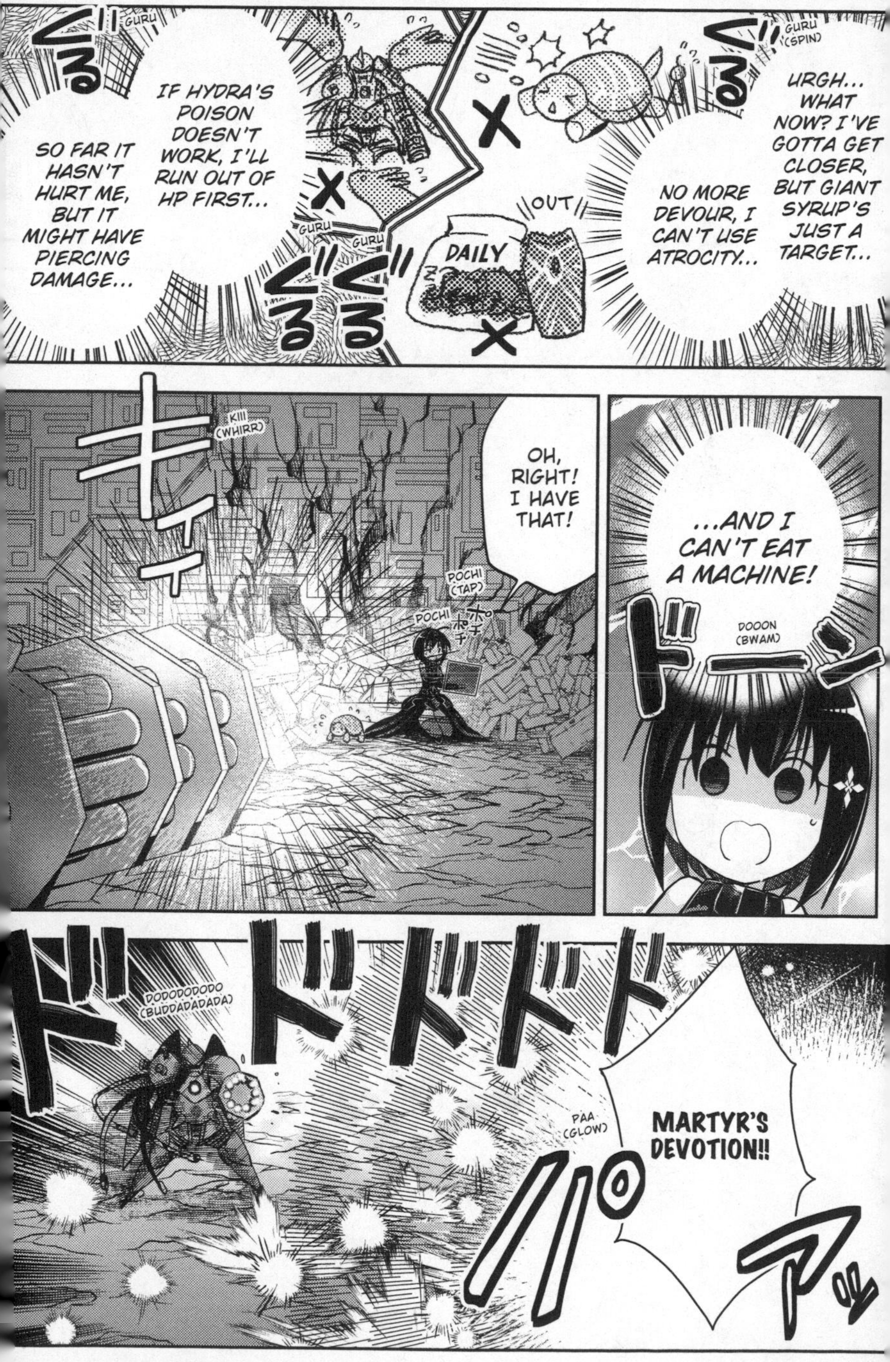
GURU (SPIN)
URGH... WHAT NOW? I'VE GOTTA GET CLOSER, BUT GIANT SYRUP'S JUST A TARGET...
NO MORE DEVOUR, I CAN'T USE ATROCITY...
OUT
DAILY
GURU
IF HYDRA'S POISON DOESN'T WORK, I'LL RUN OUT OF HP FIRST...
SO FAR IT HASN'T HURT ME, BUT IT MIGHT HAVE PIERCING DAMAGE...
GURU
GURU
...AND I CAN'T EAT A MACHINE!
DOOON (BWAM)
OH, RIGHT! I HAVE THAT!
KIII (WHIRR)
POCHI (TAP)
POCHI
MARTYR'S DEVOTION!!
PAA (GLOW)
DODODODODO (BUDDADADADA)

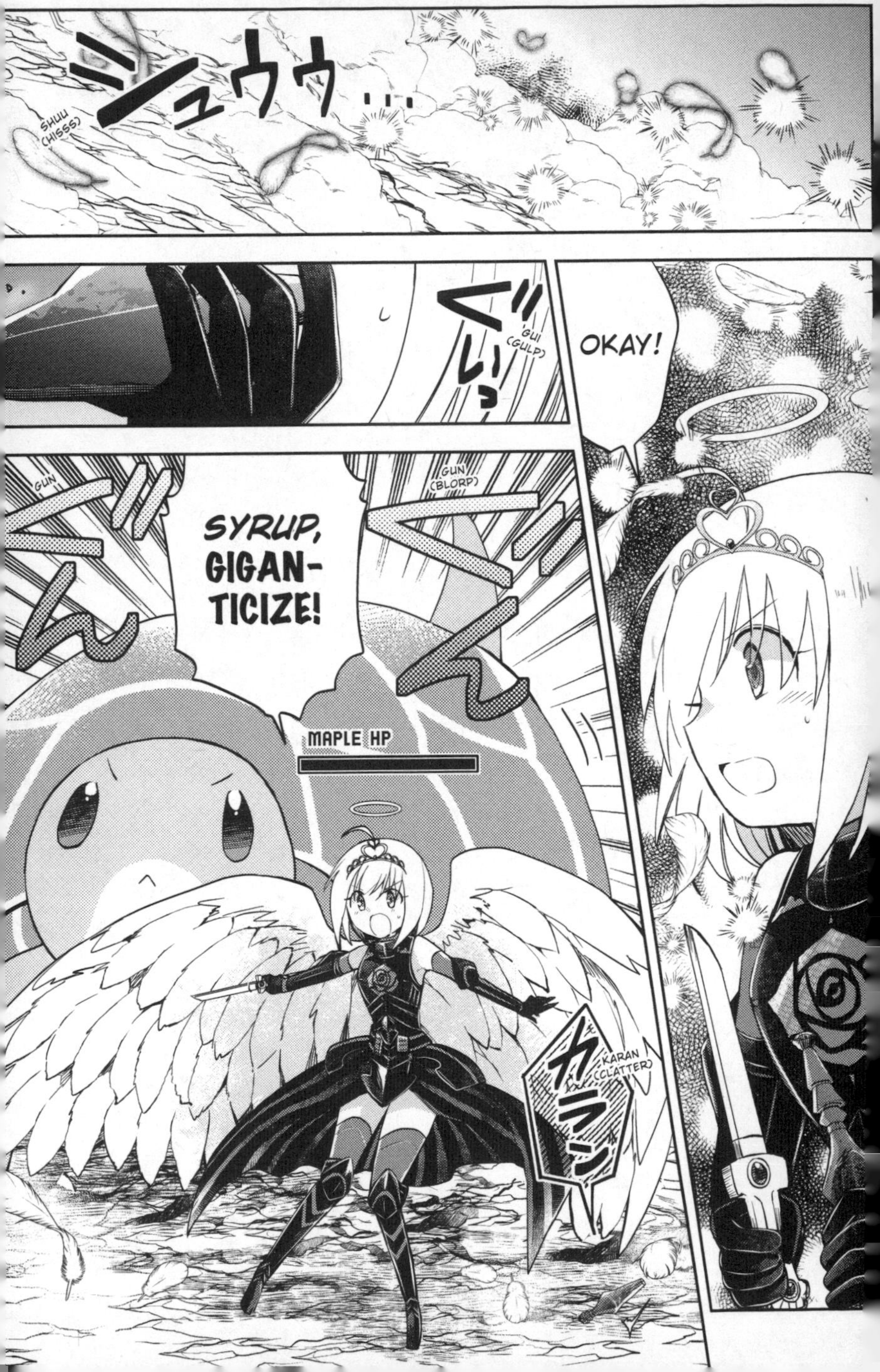
シュウウ…
SHUU (HISSSS)
OKAY!
ぐいっ
GUI (GULP)
GUN (BLORP)
GUN
SYRUP, GIGANTICIZE!
MAPLE HP
カラン
KARAN (CLATTER)

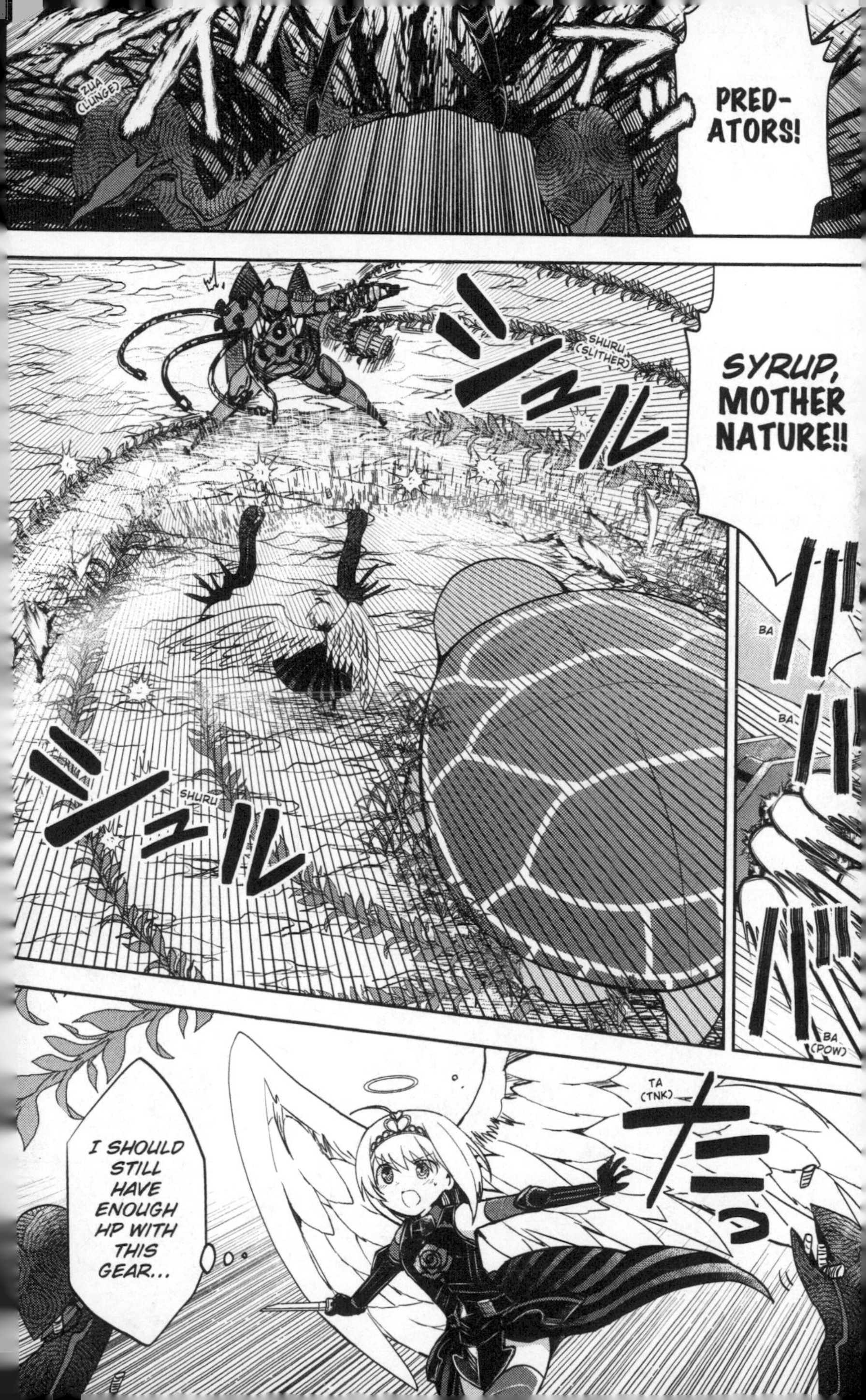
PRED-
ATORS!
ZUA (LUNGE)
SYRUP, MOTHER NATURE!!
SHURU (SLITHER)
SHURU
BA
BA
BA (POW)
TA (TNK)
I SHOULD STILL HAVE ENOUGH HP WITH THIS GEAR...

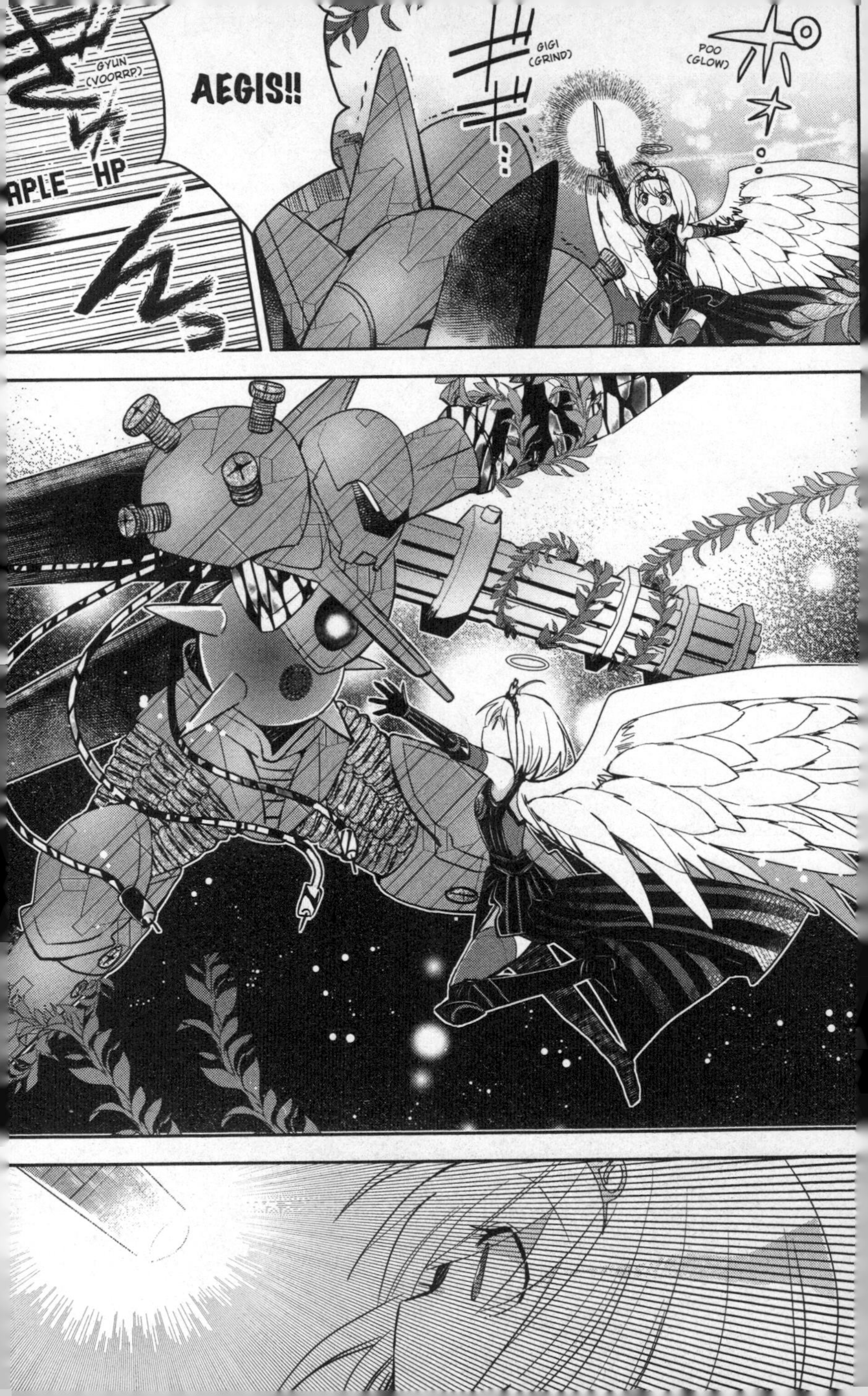
POO (GLOW)
GIGI (GRIND)
AEGIS!!
GYUN (VOORRP)
APLE HP

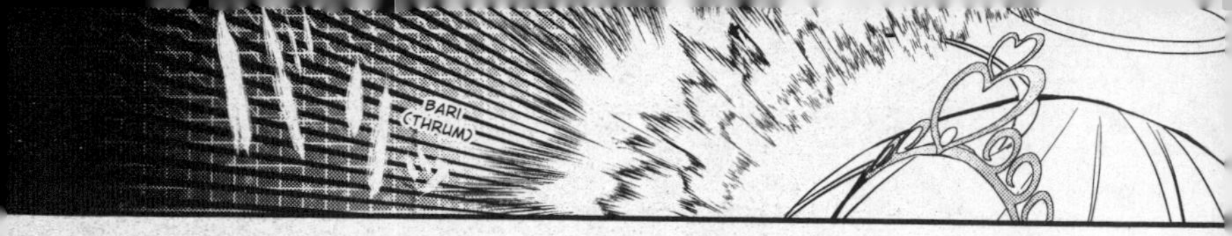
BARI (THRUM)

★**AEGIS:** Martyr's Devotion Subskill. Negates all damage for ten seconds at a high HP cost.

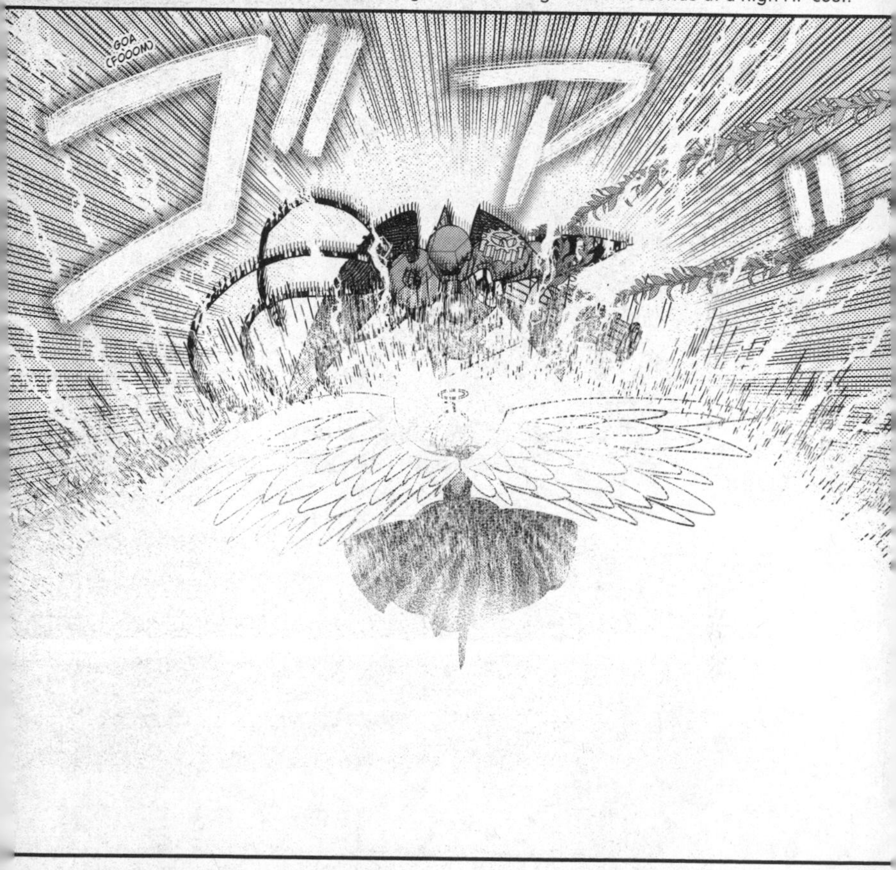
GOA (FOOOM)

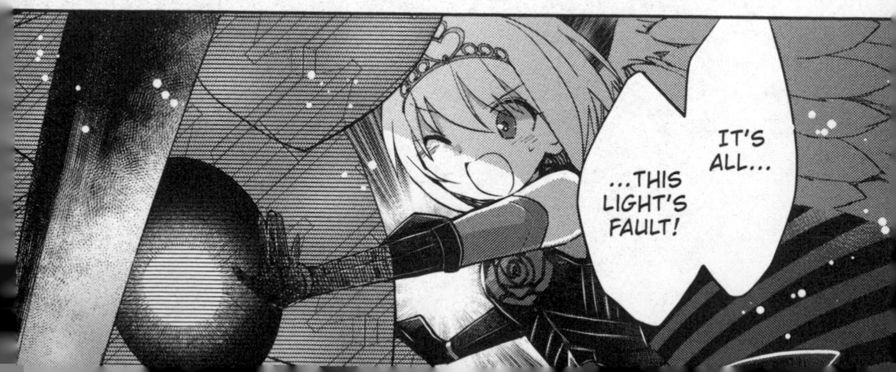
IT'S ALL...
...THIS LIGHT'S FAULT!

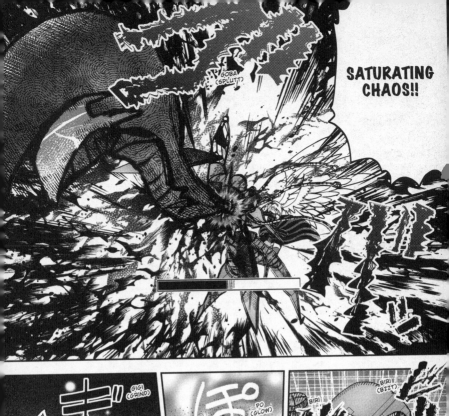

GOBA
(SPLUT!)

SATURATING CHAOS!!

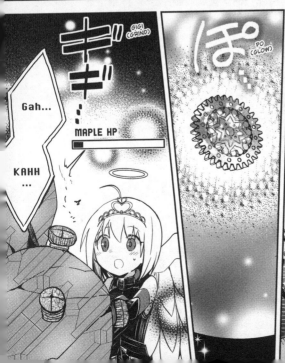

GIGI
(GRIND)

Gah...

KAHH
...

MAPLE HP

PO
(GLOW)

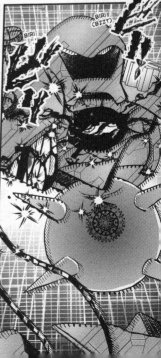

BIRI
(BZZT!)

BIRI

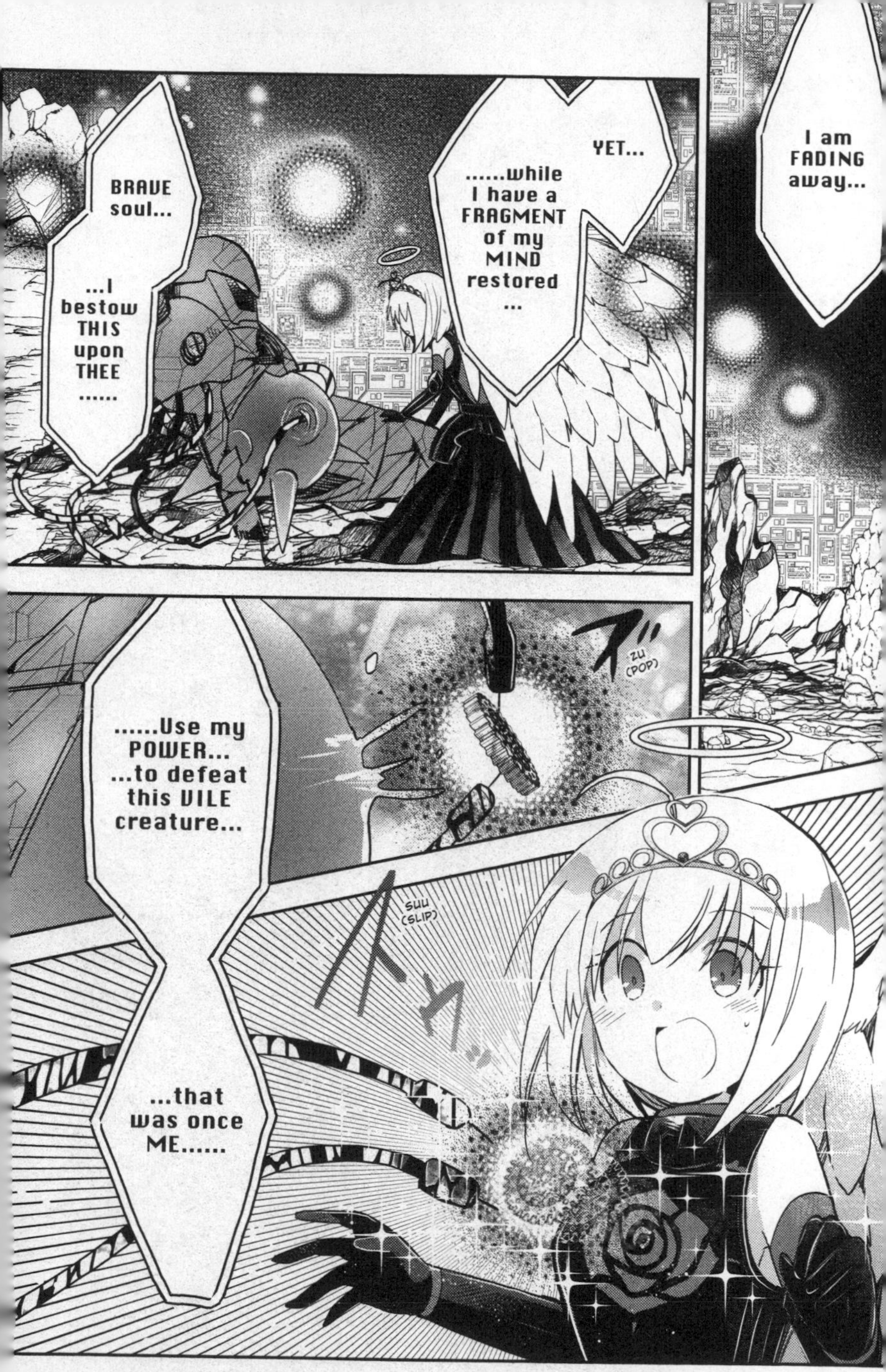
I am FADING away...
YET...
......while I have a FRAGMENT of my MIND restored ...
BRAVE soul...
...I bestow THIS upon THEE ......
ZU (POP)
......Use my POWER... ...to defeat this VILE creature...
SUU (SLIP)
...that was once ME......

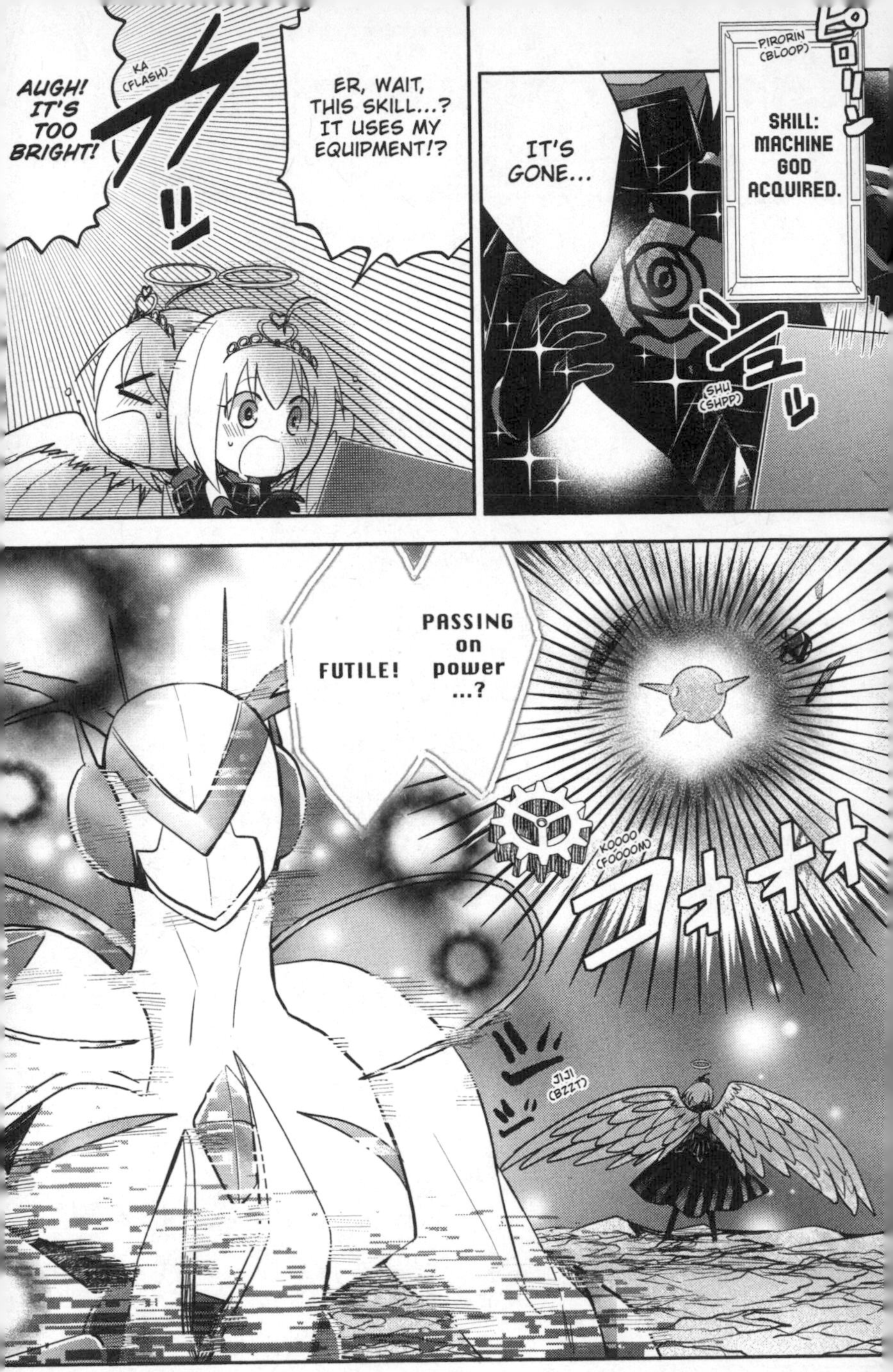
PIRORIN (BLOOP)
SKILL: MACHINE GOD ACQUIRED.
IT'S GONE...
SHU (SHPP)
ER, WAIT, THIS SKILL...? IT USES MY EQUIPMENT!?
KA (FLASH)
AUGH! IT'S TOO BRIGHT!
PASSING on power ...?
FUTILE!
KOOOO (FOOOOM)
JIJI (BZZT)

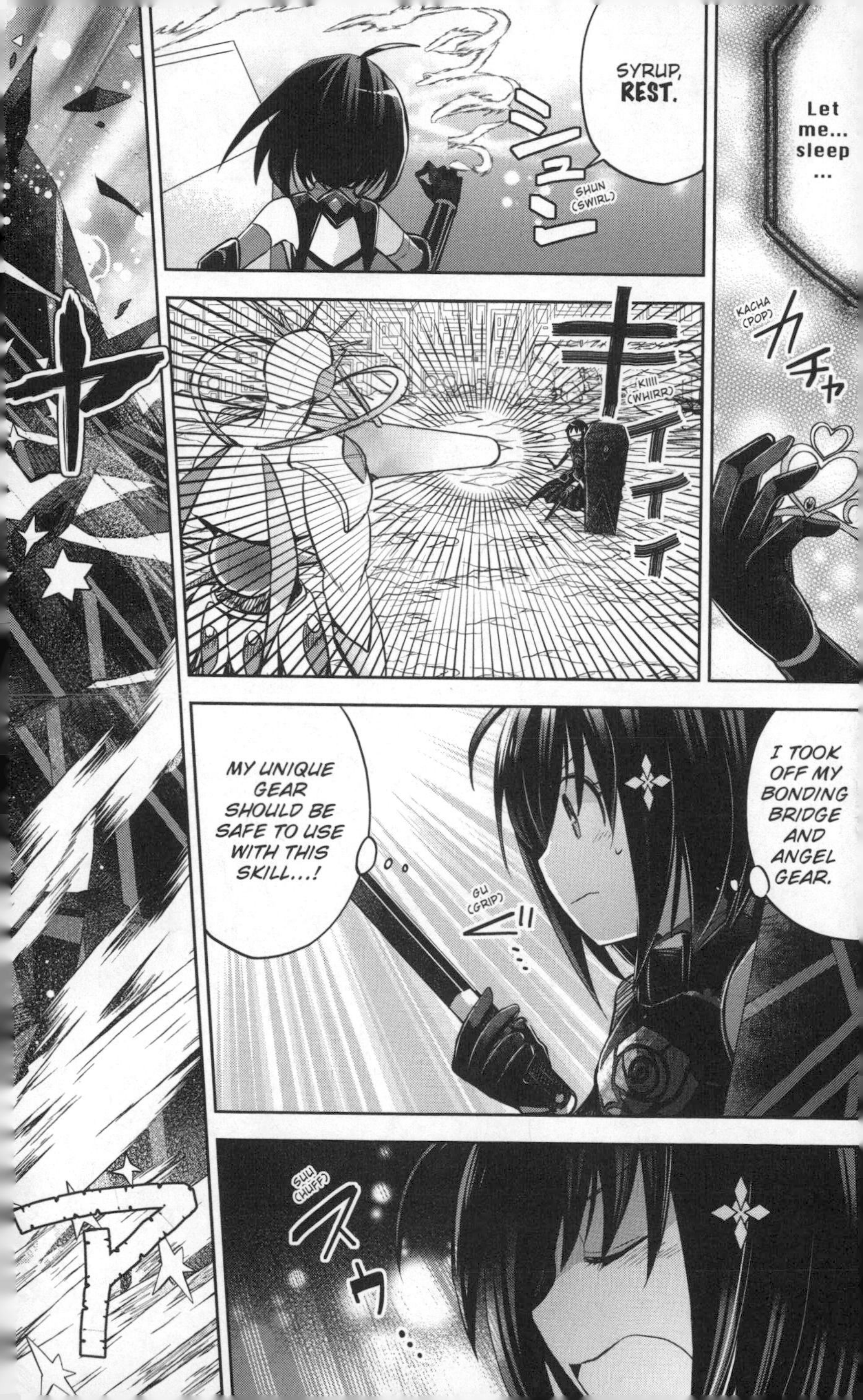
Let me... sleep ...
KACHA (POP)
SYRUP, REST.
SHUN (SWIRL)
KIIII (WHIRR)
I TOOK OFF MY BONDING BRIDGE AND ANGEL GEAR.
MY UNIQUE GEAR SHOULD BE SAFE TO USE WITH THIS SKILL...!
GU (GRIP)
SUU (HUFF)

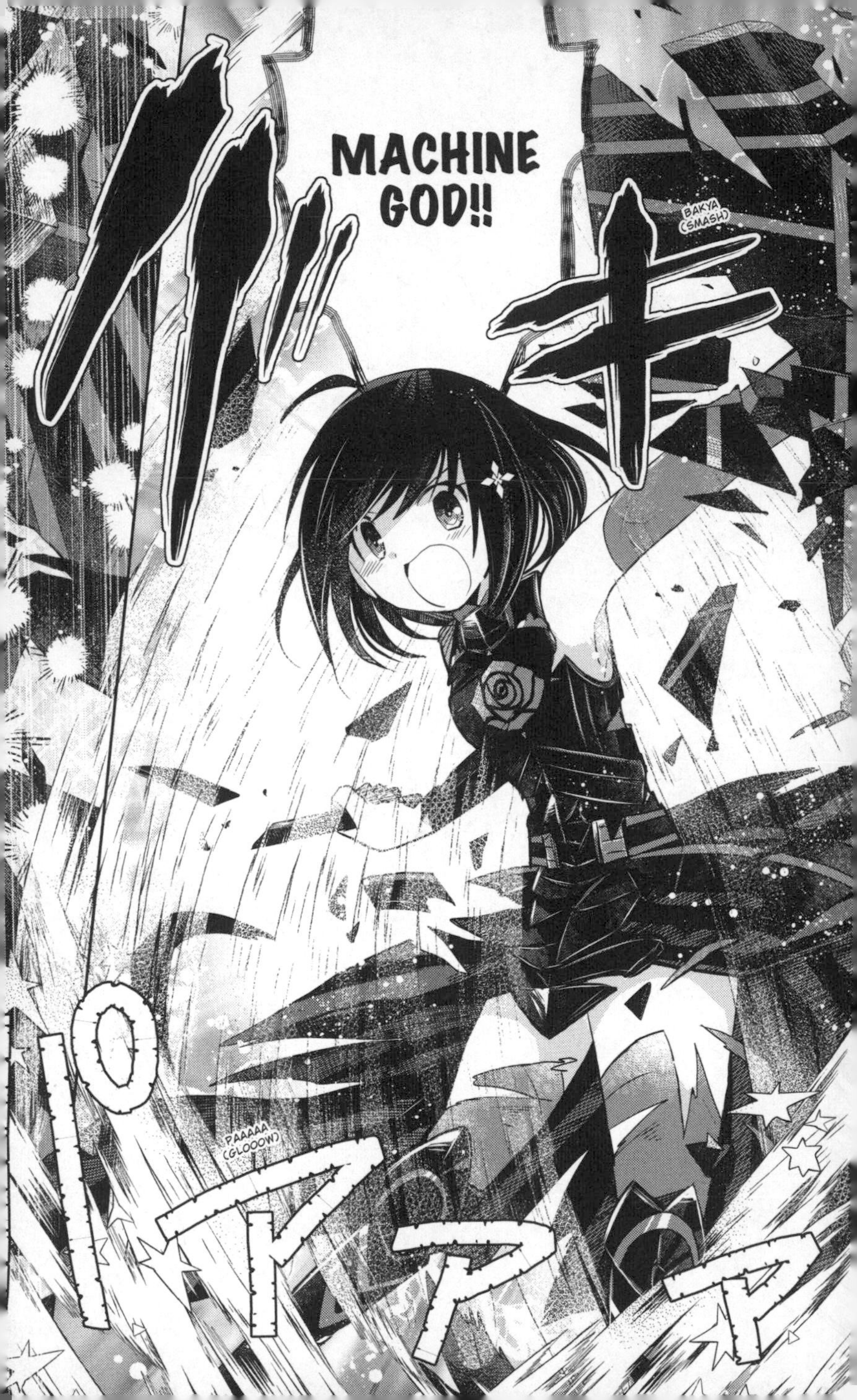
BAKYA (SMASH)
MACHINE GOD!!
PAAAAA (GLOOOW)

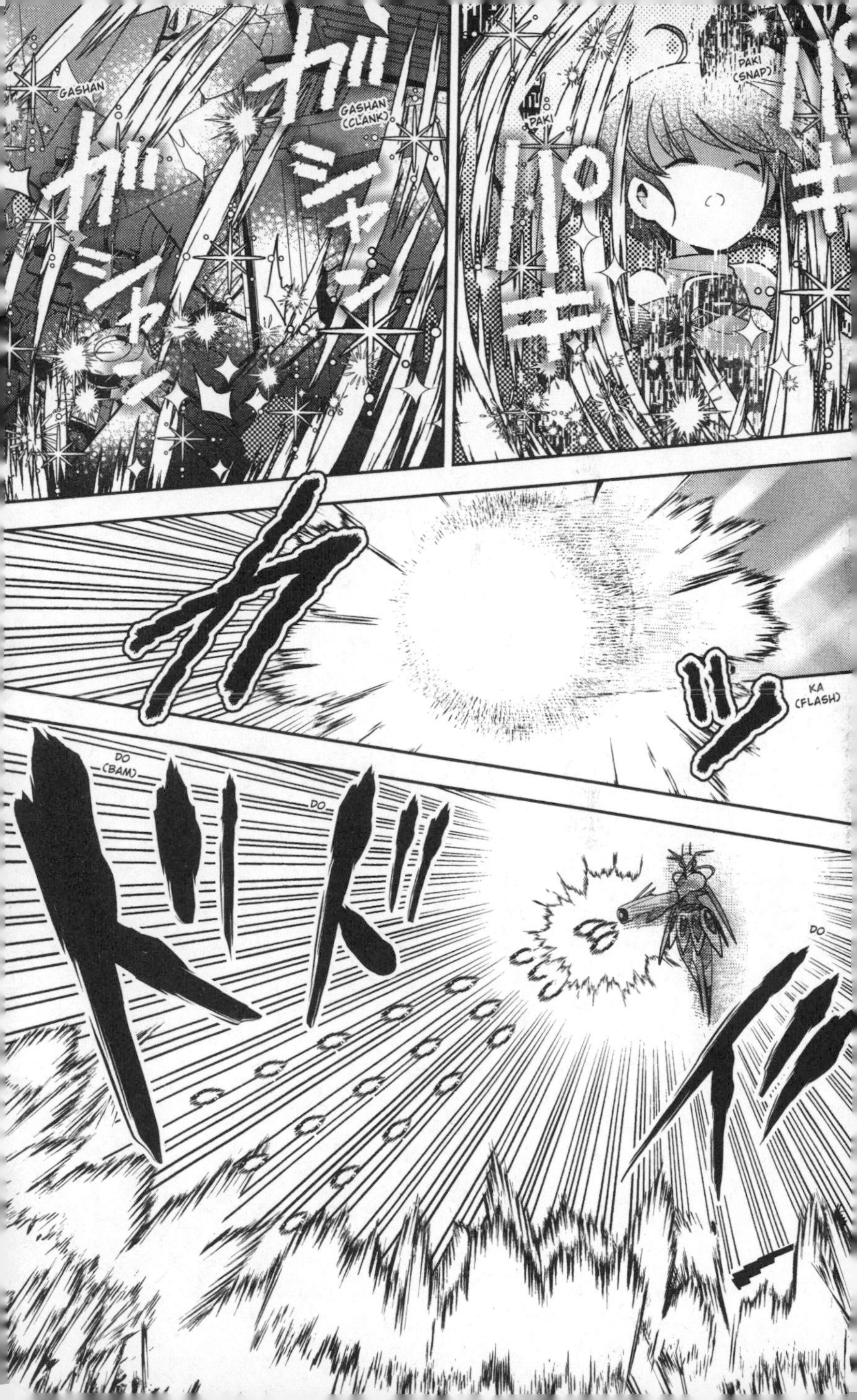
PAKI (SNAP)
PAKI
GASHAN (CLANK)
GASHAN
KA (FLASH)
DO (BAM)
DO
DO

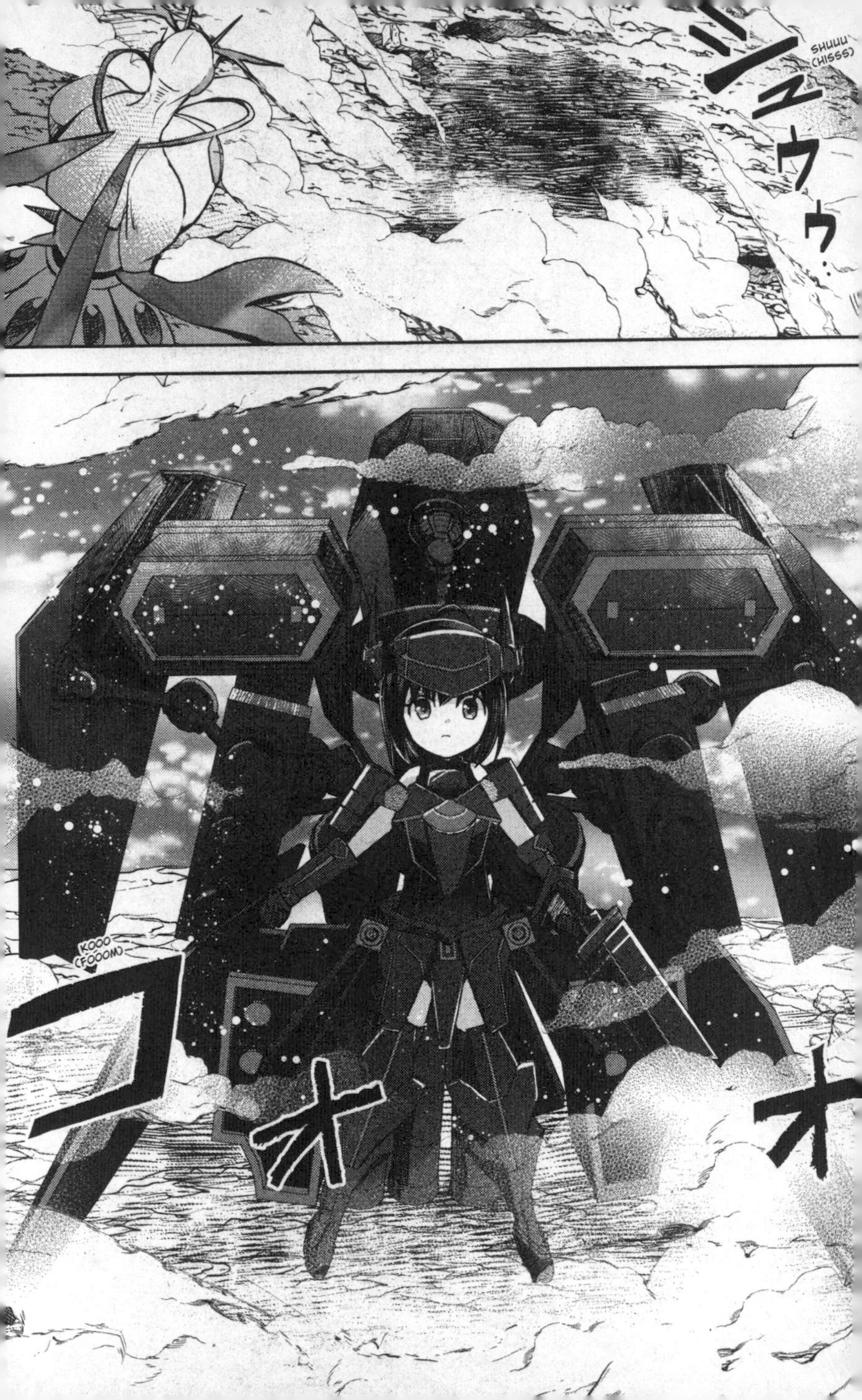

シュウゥ…
SHUUU (HISSS)
コオオ
KOOO (FOOOM)

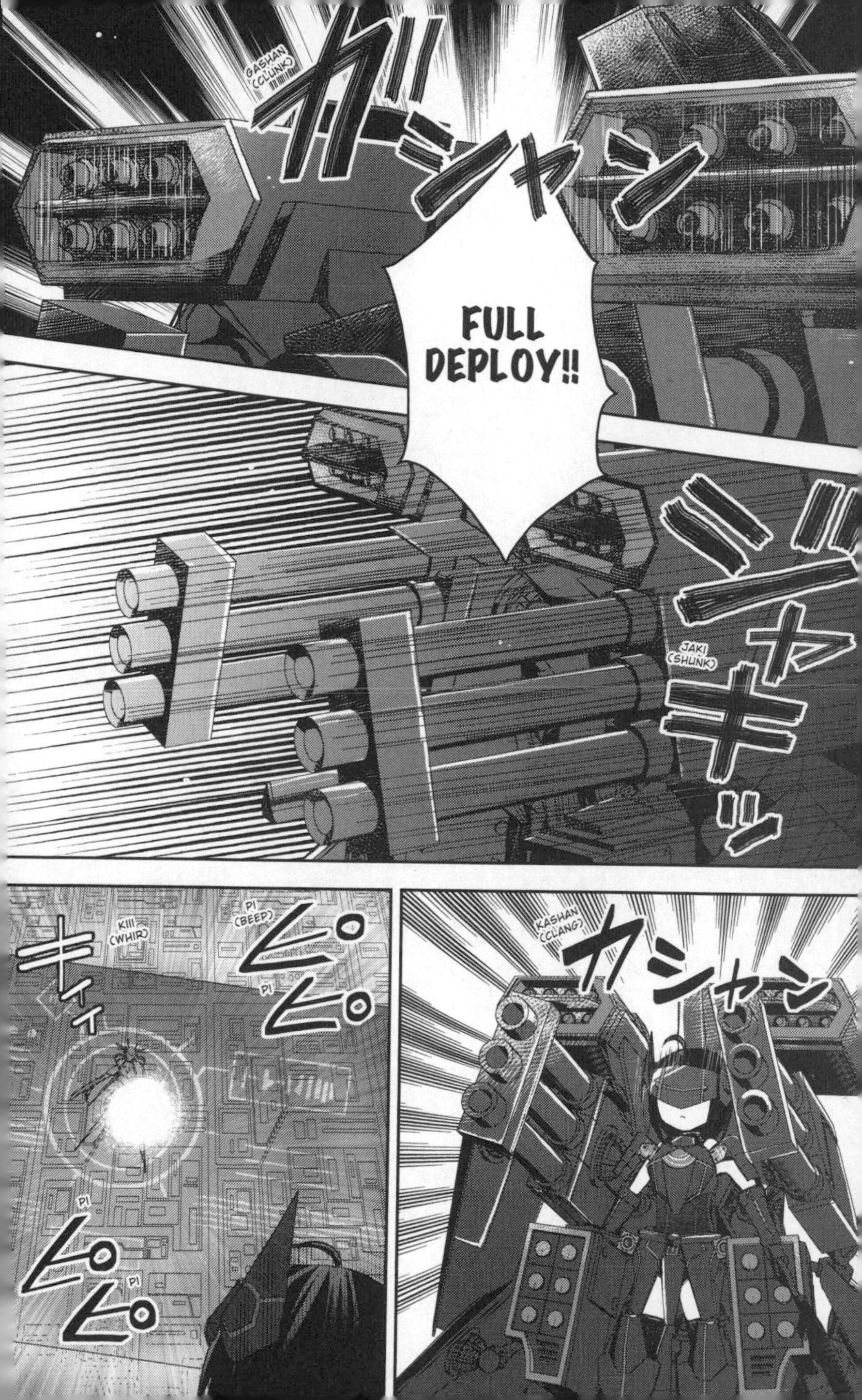
ガシャン
GASHAN (CLUNK)
FULL DEPLOY!!
ジャキッ
JAKI (SHUNK)
カシャン
KASHAN (CLANG)
ピ
PI (BEEP)
ピ
PI
キイイ
KIII (WHIR)
ピ
PI
ピ
PI

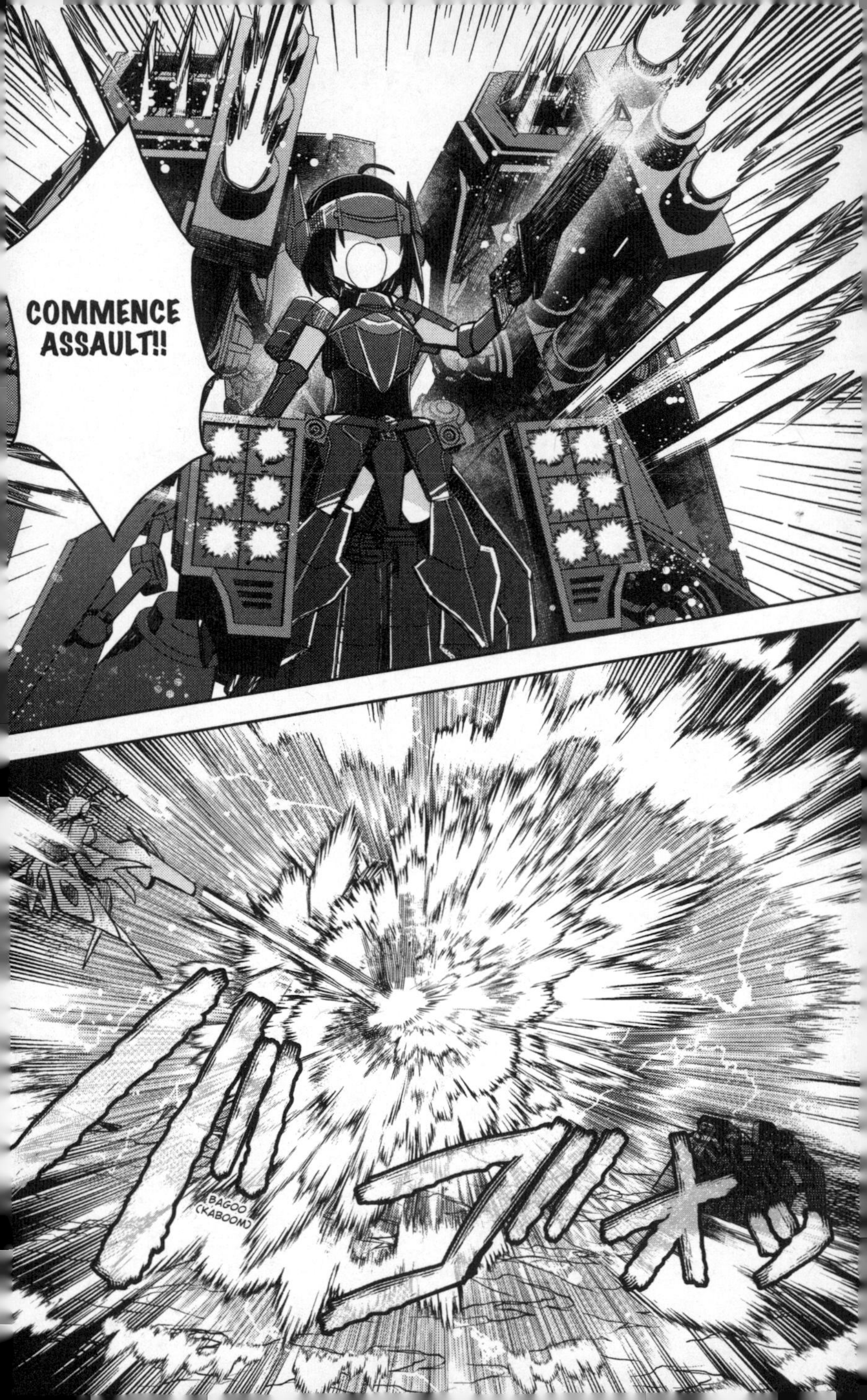
COMMENCE ASSAULT!!
BAGOO (KABOOM)

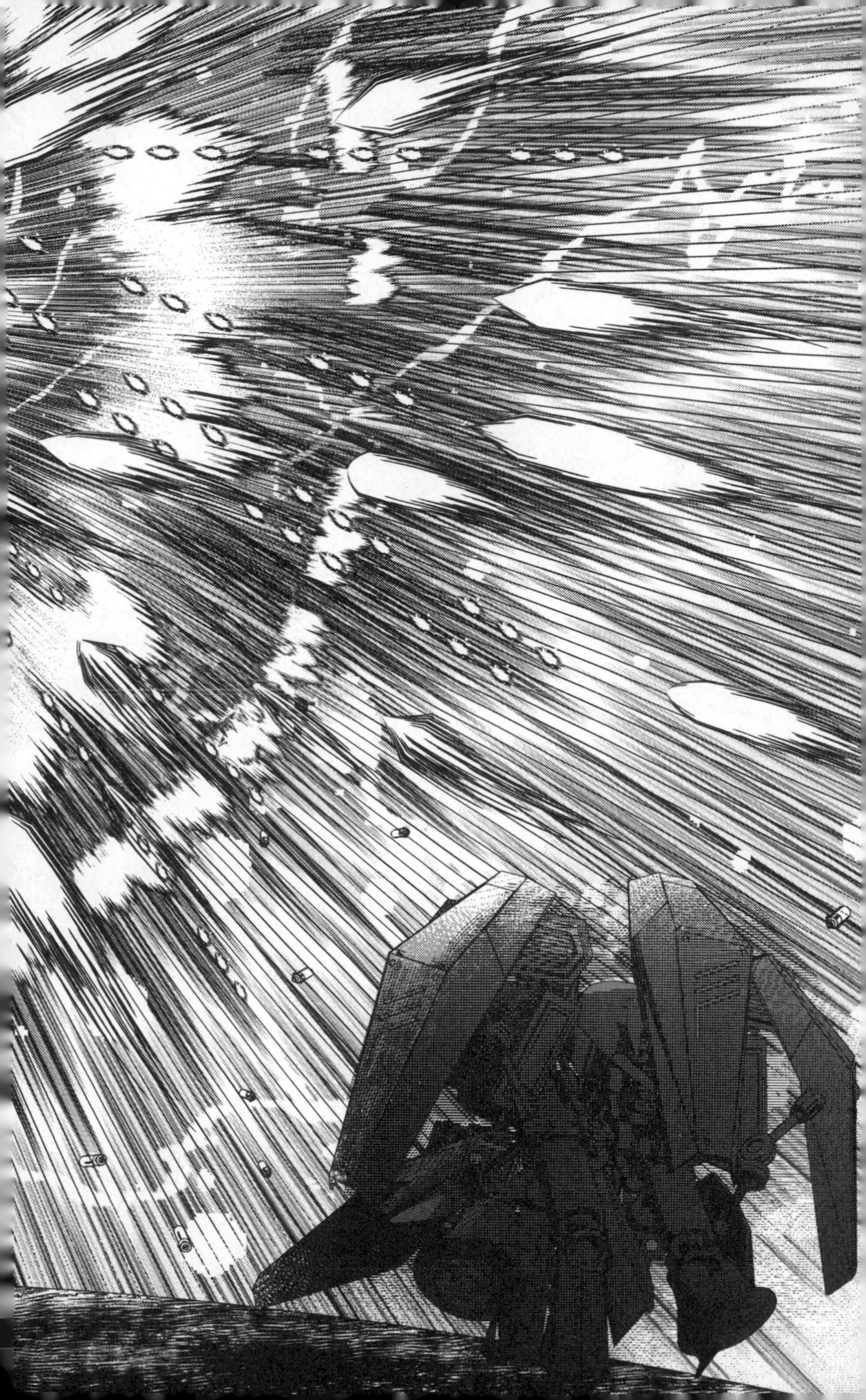

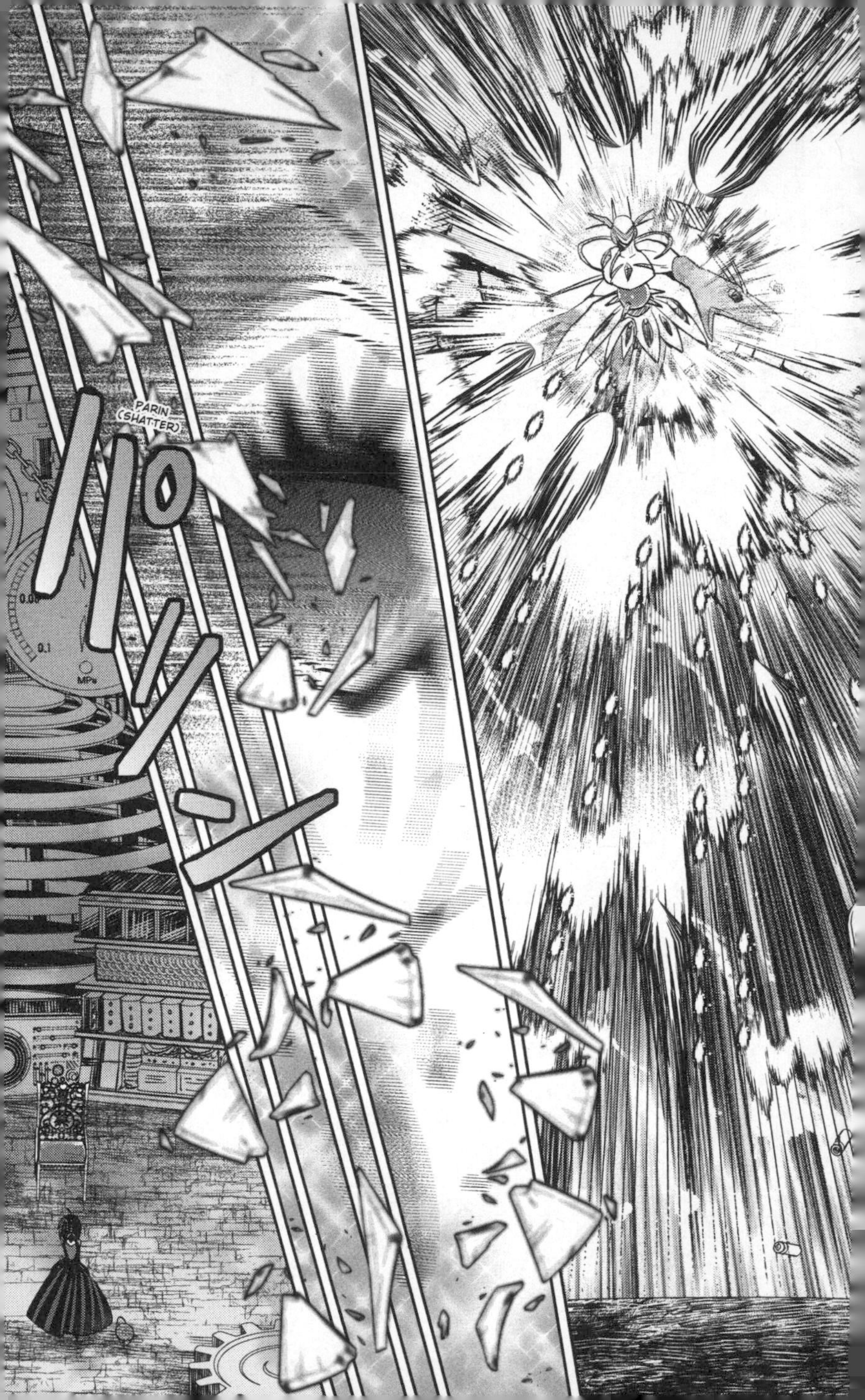
PARIN
(SHATTER)

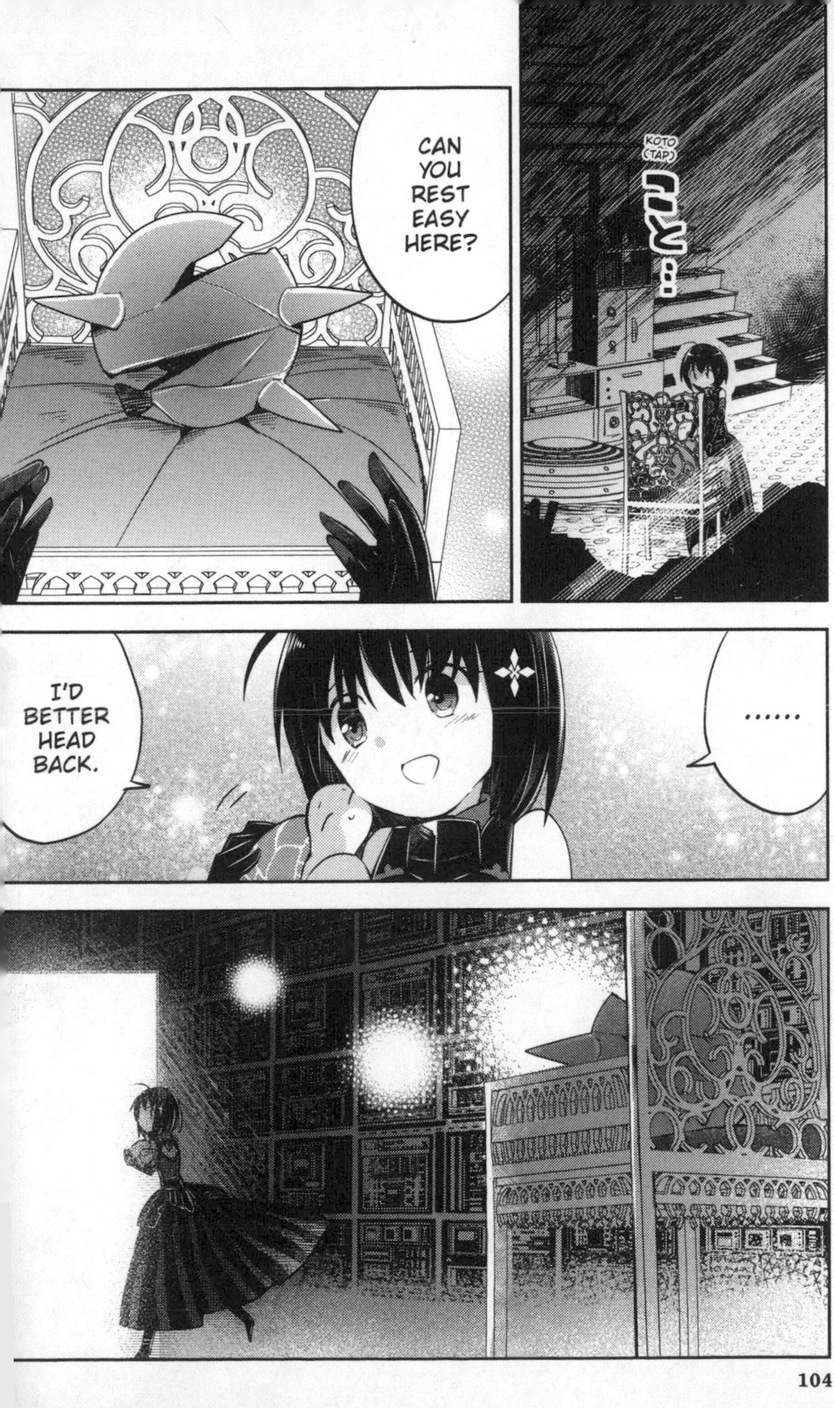
KOTO (TAP)
CAN YOU REST EASY HERE?
......
I'D BETTER HEAD BACK.

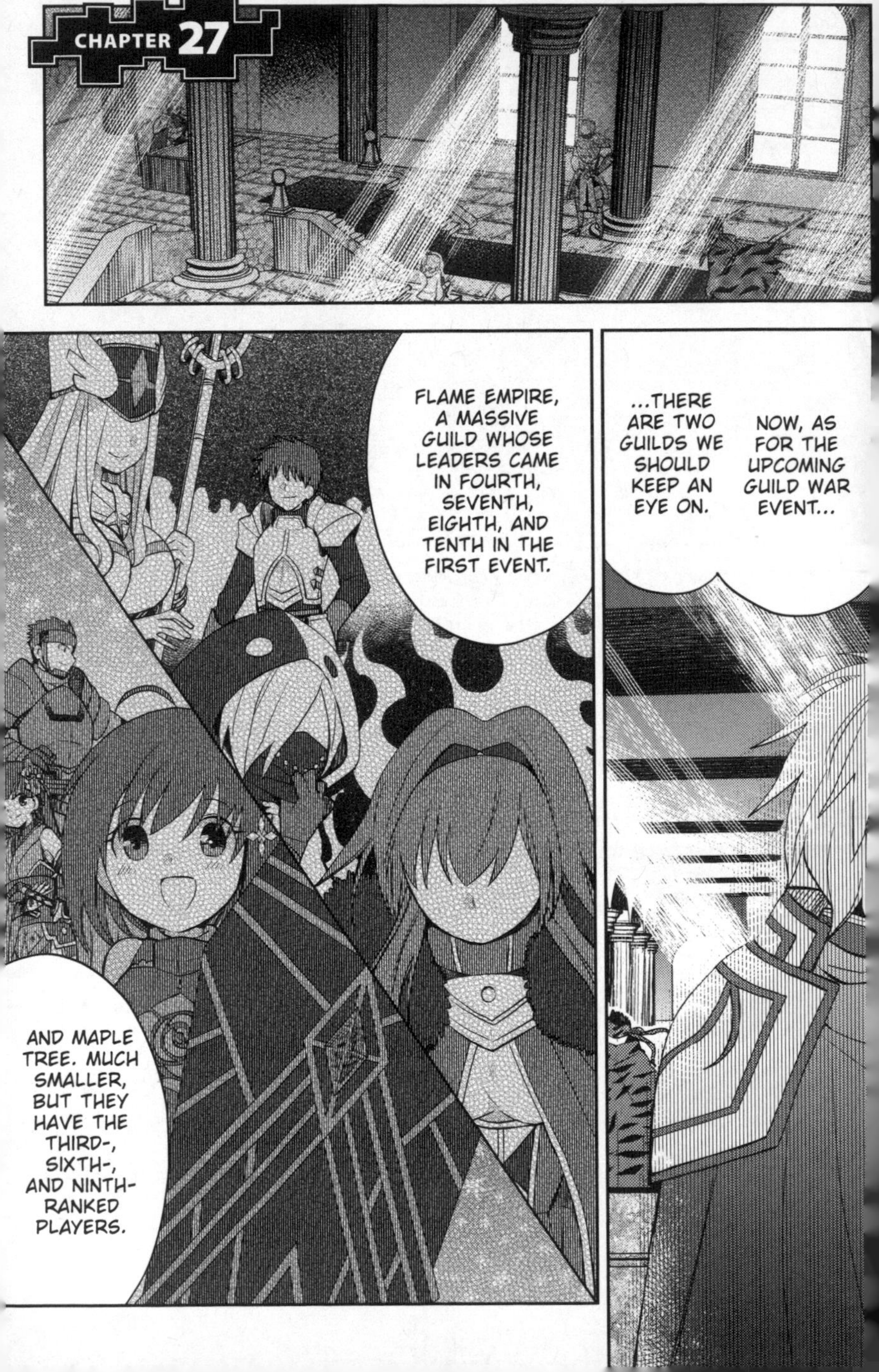
CHAPTER 27
NOW, AS FOR THE UPCOMING GUILD WAR EVENT...
...THERE ARE TWO GUILDS WE SHOULD KEEP AN EYE ON.
FLAME EMPIRE, A MASSIVE GUILD WHOSE LEADERS CAME IN FOURTH, SEVENTH, EIGHTH, AND TENTH IN THE FIRST EVENT.
AND MAPLE TREE. MUCH SMALLER, BUT THEY HAVE THE THIRD-, SIXTH-, AND NINTH-RANKED PLAYERS.

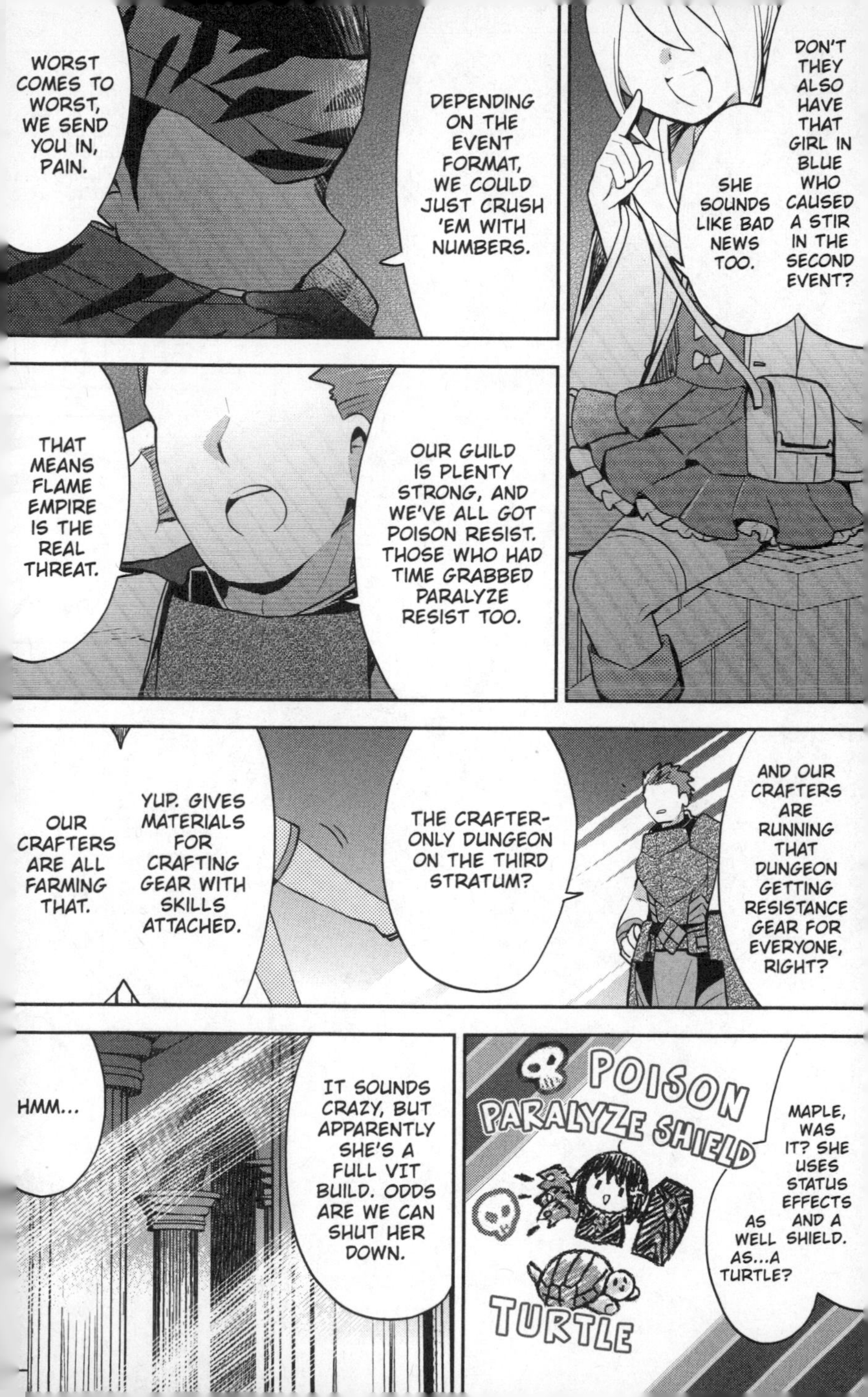
DON'T THEY ALSO HAVE THAT GIRL IN BLUE WHO CAUSED A STIR IN THE SECOND EVENT?
SHE SOUNDS LIKE BAD NEWS TOO.
DEPENDING ON THE EVENT FORMAT, WE COULD JUST CRUSH 'EM WITH NUMBERS.
WORST COMES TO WORST, WE SEND YOU IN, PAIN.
OUR GUILD IS PLENTY STRONG, AND WE'VE ALL GOT POISON RESIST. THOSE WHO HAD TIME GRABBED PARALYZE RESIST TOO.
THAT MEANS FLAME EMPIRE IS THE REAL THREAT.
AND OUR CRAFTERS ARE RUNNING THAT DUNGEON GETTING RESISTANCE GEAR FOR EVERYONE, RIGHT?
THE CRAFTER-ONLY DUNGEON ON THE THIRD STRATUM?
YUP. GIVES MATERIALS FOR CRAFTING GEAR WITH SKILLS ATTACHED.
OUR CRAFTERS ARE ALL FARMING THAT.
MAPLE, WAS IT? SHE USES STATUS EFFECTS AND A SHIELD.
AS WELL AS...A TURTLE?
POISON
PARALYZE SHIELD
TURTLE
IT SOUNDS CRAZY, BUT APPARENTLY SHE'S A FULL VIT BUILD. ODDS ARE WE CAN SHUT HER DOWN.
HMM...

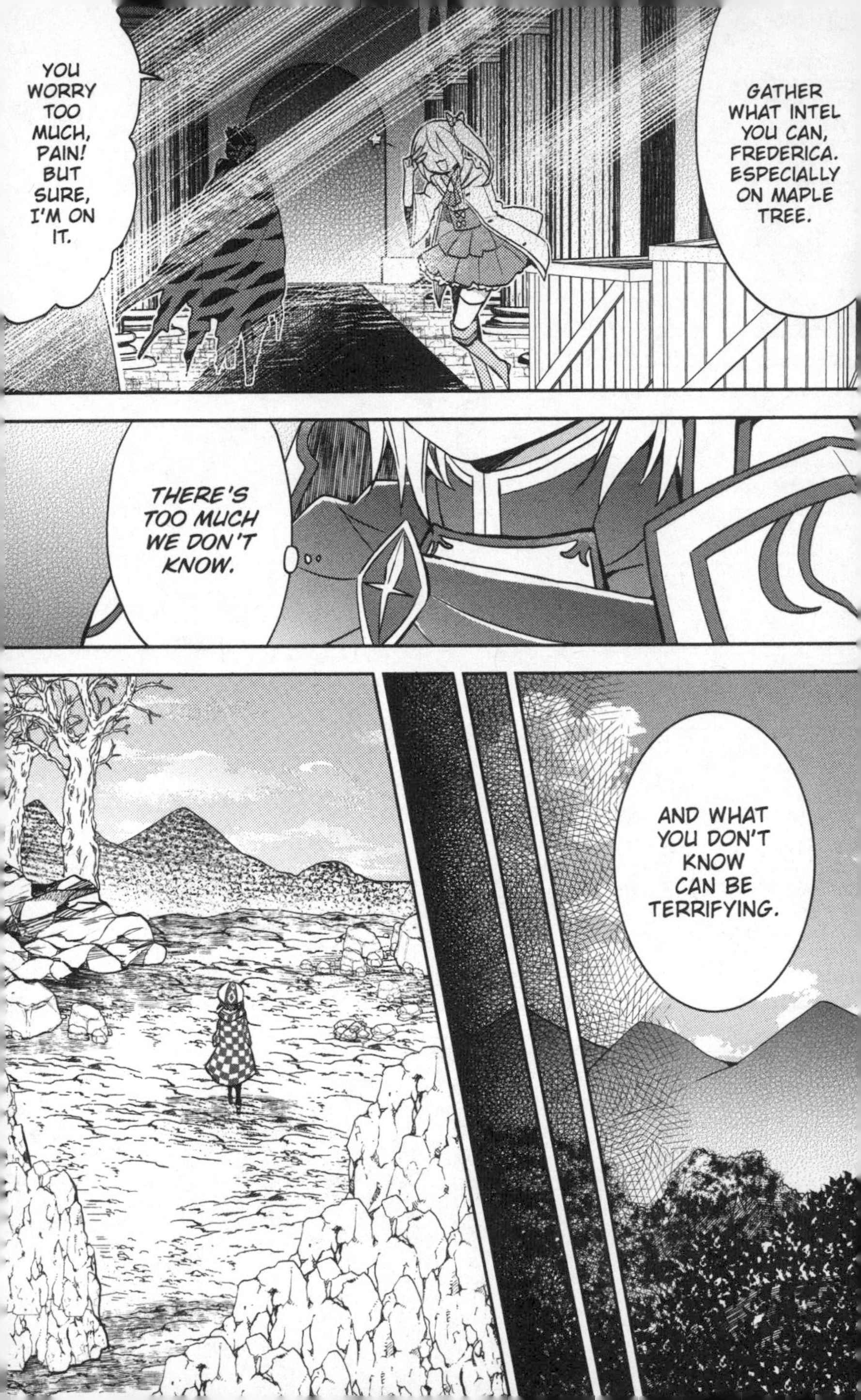
GATHER WHAT INTEL YOU CAN, FREDERICA. ESPECIALLY ON MAPLE TREE.
YOU WORRY TOO MUCH, PAIN! BUT SURE, I'M ON IT.
THERE'S TOO MUCH WE DON'T KNOW.
AND WHAT YOU DON'T KNOW CAN BE TERRIFYING.

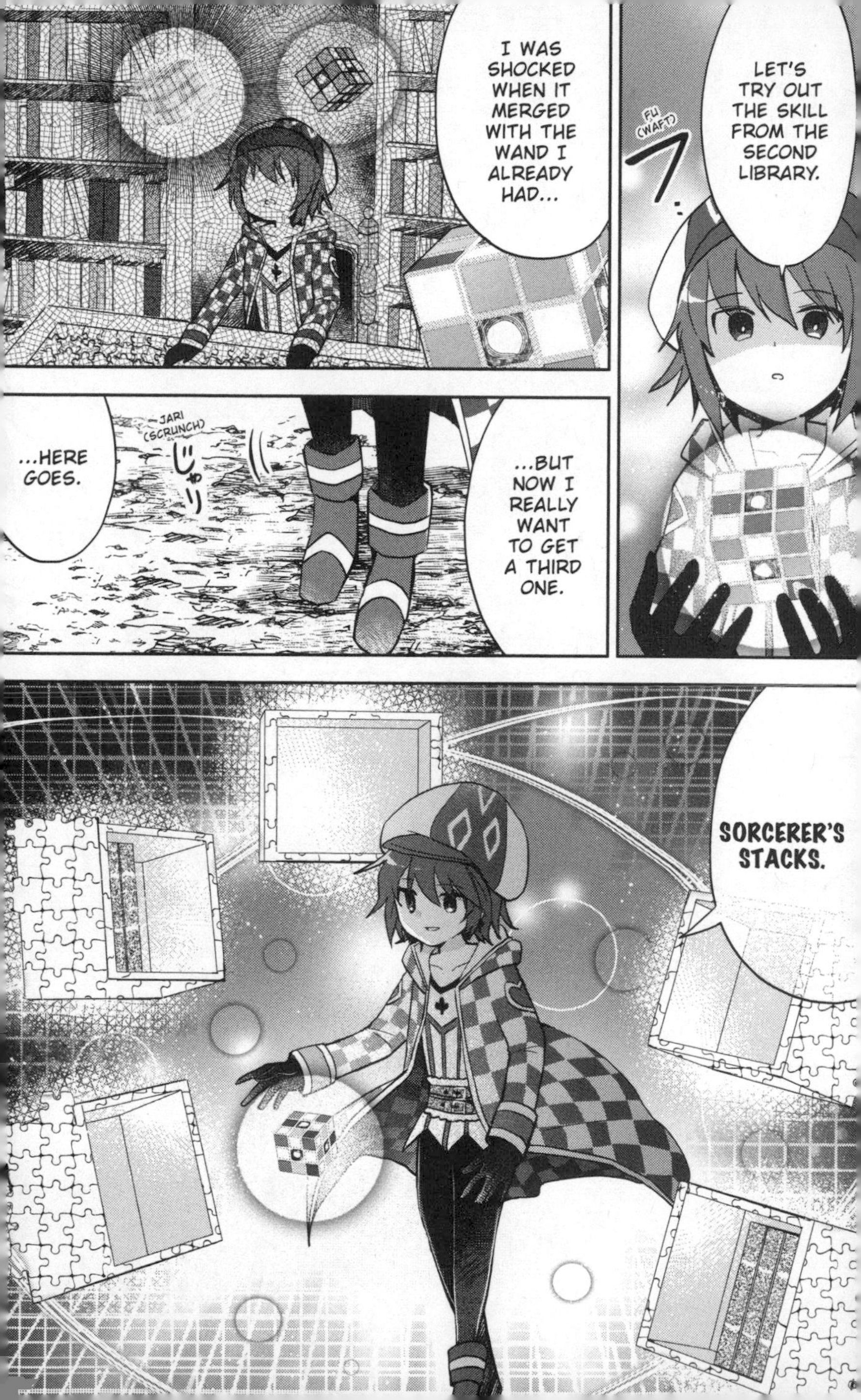
LET'S TRY OUT THE SKILL FROM THE SECOND LIBRARY.
FU (WAFT)
I WAS SHOCKED WHEN IT MERGED WITH THE WAND I ALREADY HAD...
...BUT NOW I REALLY WANT TO GET A THIRD ONE.
JARI (SCRUNCH)
じゃり
...HERE GOES.
SORCERER'S STACKS.

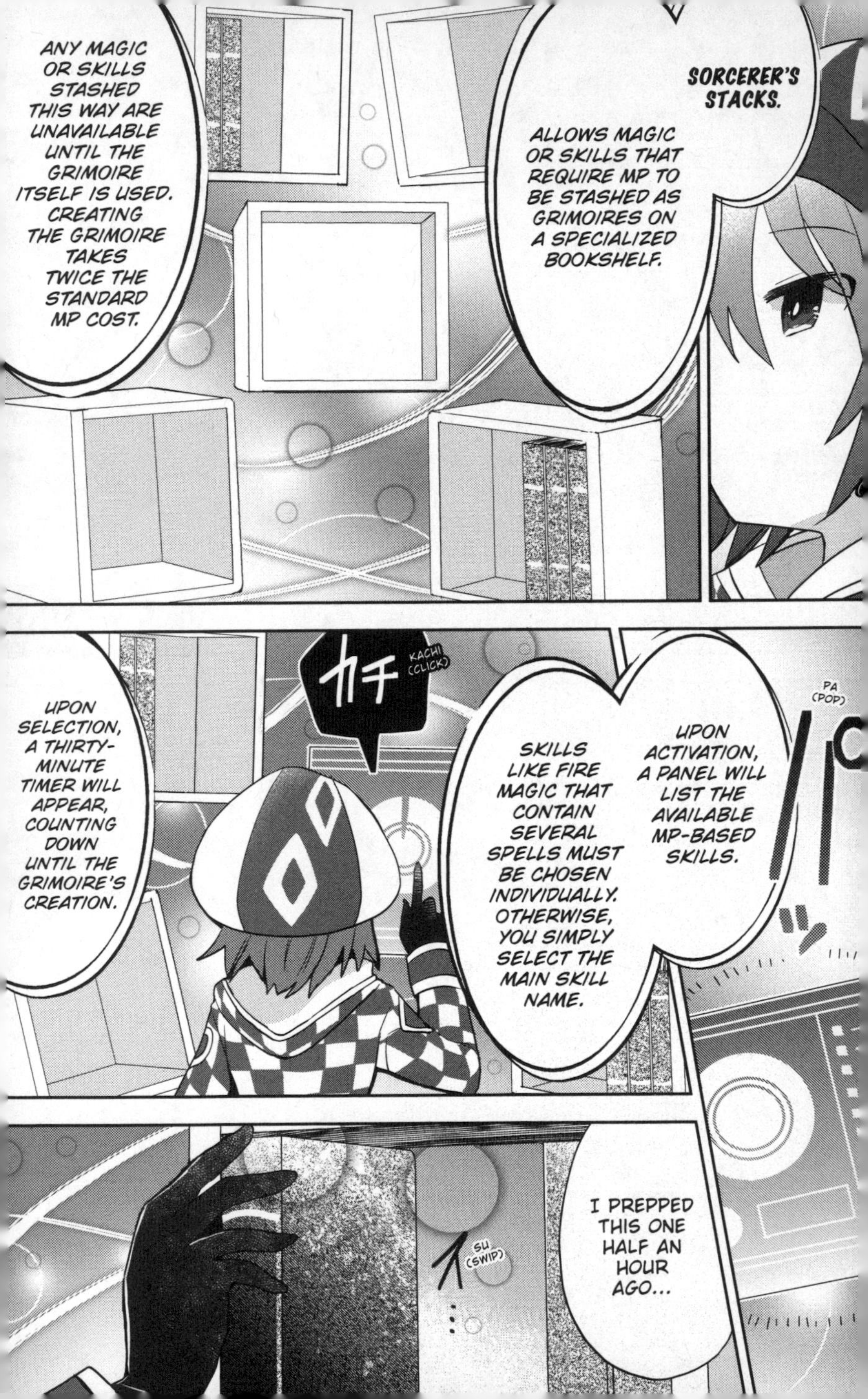
SORCERER'S STACKS.
ALLOWS MAGIC OR SKILLS THAT REQUIRE MP TO BE STASHED AS GRIMOIRES ON A SPECIALIZED BOOKSHELF.
ANY MAGIC OR SKILLS STASHED THIS WAY ARE UNAVAILABLE UNTIL THE GRIMOIRE ITSELF IS USED. CREATING THE GRIMOIRE TAKES TWICE THE STANDARD MP COST.
PA (POP)
UPON ACTIVATION, A PANEL WILL LIST THE AVAILABLE MP-BASED SKILLS.
SKILLS LIKE FIRE MAGIC THAT CONTAIN SEVERAL SPELLS MUST BE CHOSEN INDIVIDUALLY. OTHERWISE, YOU SIMPLY SELECT THE MAIN SKILL NAME.
カチ
KACHI (CLICK)
UPON SELECTION, A THIRTY-MINUTE TIMER WILL APPEAR, COUNTING DOWN UNTIL THE GRIMOIRE'S CREATION.
I PREPPED THIS ONE HALF AN HOUR AGO...
SU (SWIP)

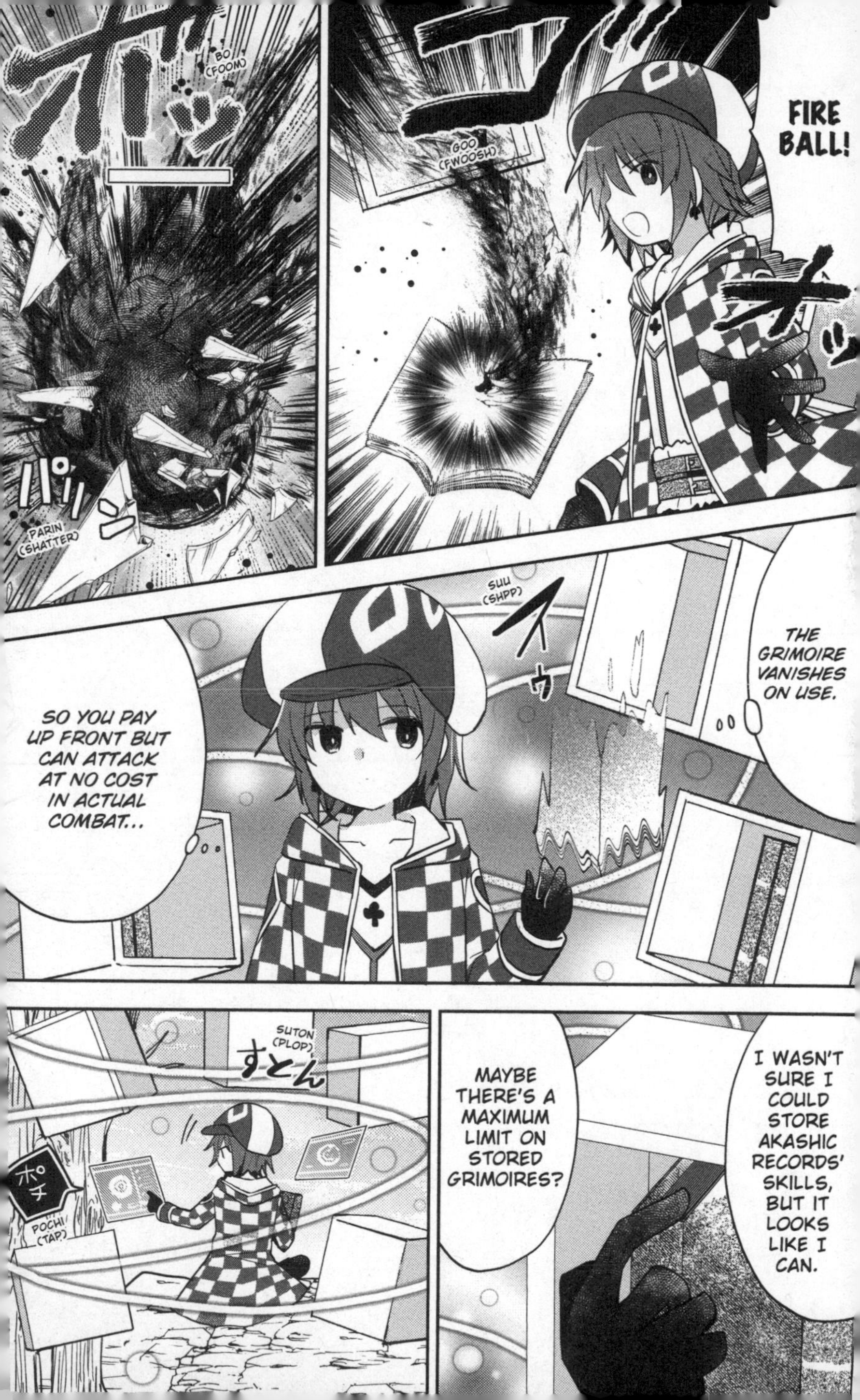
FIRE BALL!
GOO (FWOOSH)
BO (FOOM)
PARIN (SHATTER)
THE GRIMOIRE VANISHES ON USE.
SUU (SHPP)
SO YOU PAY UP FRONT BUT CAN ATTACK AT NO COST IN ACTUAL COMBAT...
I WASN'T SURE I COULD STORE AKASHIC RECORDS' SKILLS, BUT IT LOOKS LIKE I CAN.
MAYBE THERE'S A MAXIMUM LIMIT ON STORED GRIMOIRES?
SUTON (PLOP)
すとん
POCHI (TAP)
ポチ

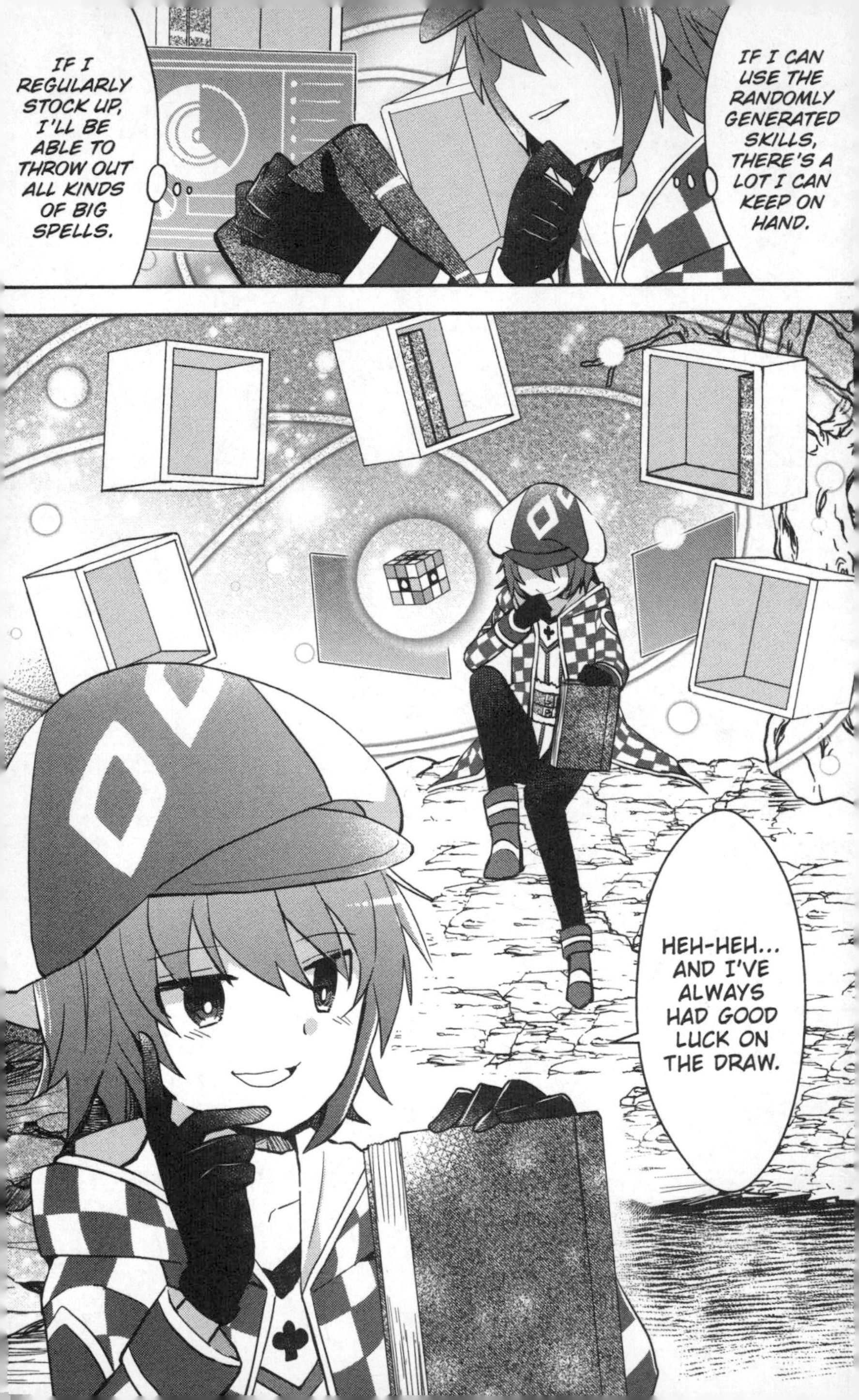
IF I CAN USE THE RANDOMLY GENERATED SKILLS, THERE'S A LOT I CAN KEEP ON HAND.
IF I REGULARLY STOCK UP, I'LL BE ABLE TO THROW OUT ALL KINDS OF BIG SPELLS.
HEH-HEH... AND I'VE ALWAYS HAD GOOD LUCK ON THE DRAW.

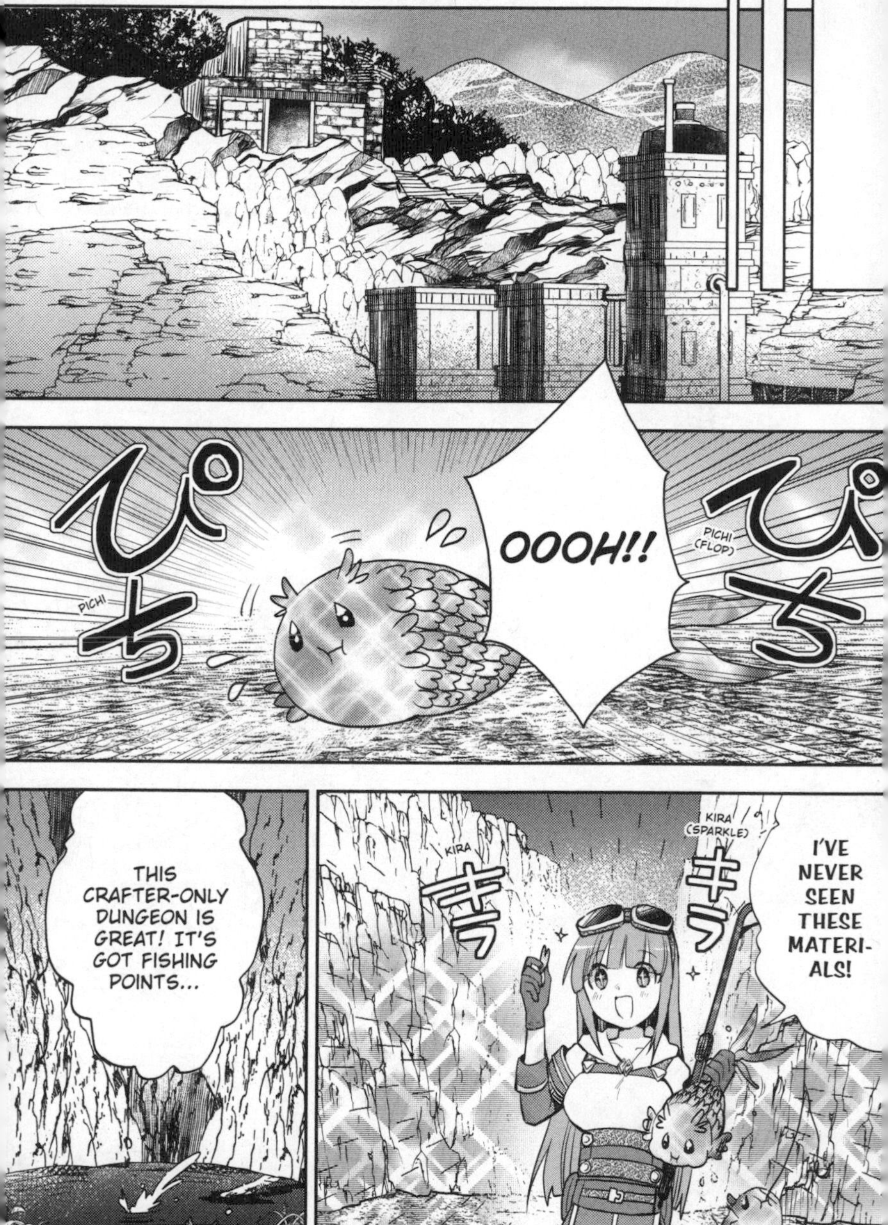
ぴち
PICHI (FLOP)
OOOH!!
ぴち
PICHI
I'VE NEVER SEEN THESE MATERI-ALS!
キラ
KIRA (SPARKLE)
きら
KIRA
THIS CRAFTER-ONLY DUNGEON IS GREAT! IT'S GOT FISHING POINTS...

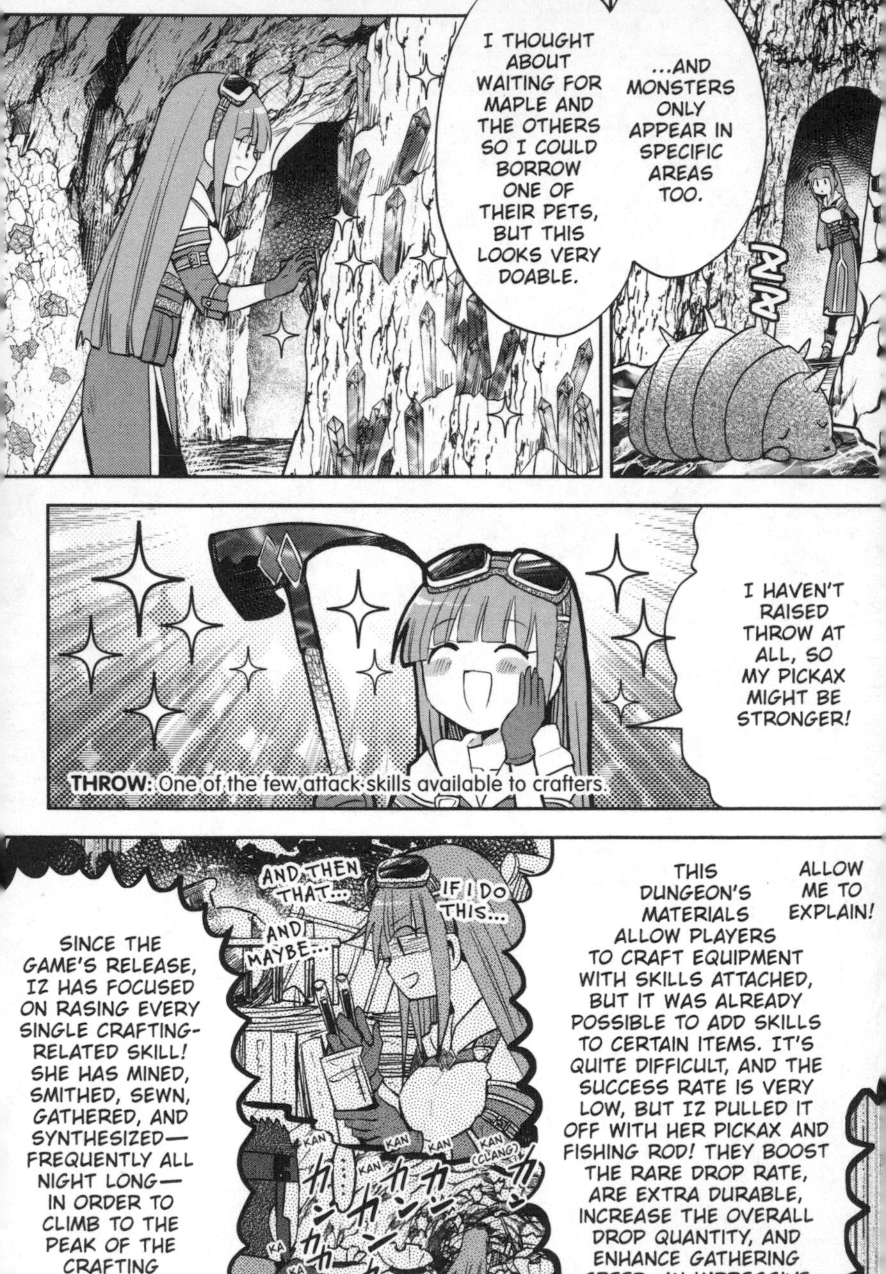
...AND MONSTERS ONLY APPEAR IN SPECIFIC AREAS TOO.
I THOUGHT ABOUT WAITING FOR MAPLE AND THE OTHERS SO I COULD BORROW ONE OF THEIR PETS, BUT THIS LOOKS VERY DOABLE.
I HAVEN'T RAISED THROW AT ALL, SO MY PICKAX MIGHT BE STRONGER!
THROW: One of the few attack skills available to crafters.
ALLOW ME TO EXPLAIN!
THIS DUNGEON'S MATERIALS ALLOW PLAYERS TO CRAFT EQUIPMENT WITH SKILLS ATTACHED, BUT IT WAS ALREADY POSSIBLE TO ADD SKILLS TO CERTAIN ITEMS. IT'S QUITE DIFFICULT, AND THE SUCCESS RATE IS VERY LOW, BUT IZ PULLED IT OFF WITH HER PICKAX AND FISHING ROD! THEY BOOST THE RARE DROP RATE, ARE EXTRA DURABLE, INCREASE THE OVERALL DROP QUANTITY, AND ENHANCE GATHERING SPEED. AN IMPRESSIVE LINEUP!
IF I DO THIS...
AND THEN THAT...
AND MAYBE...
KAN KAN KAN KAN (CLANG)
KA KA KA
SINCE THE GAME'S RELEASE, IZ HAS FOCUSED ON RASING EVERY SINGLE CRAFTING-RELATED SKILL! SHE HAS MINED, SMITHED, SEWN, GATHERED, AND SYNTHESIZED—FREQUENTLY ALL NIGHT LONG—IN ORDER TO CLIMB TO THE PEAK OF THE CRAFTING WORLD!

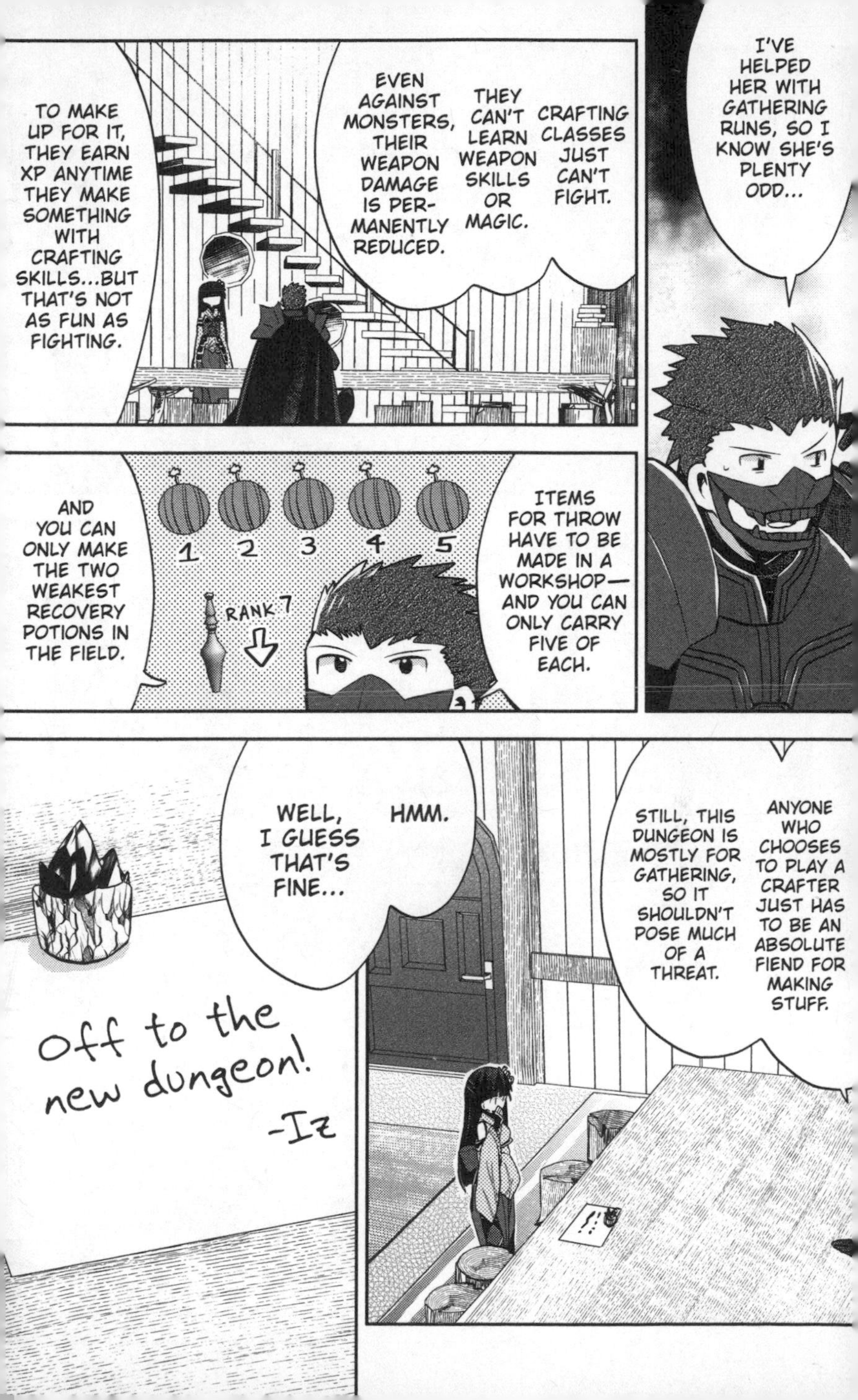
I'VE HELPED HER WITH GATHERING RUNS, SO I KNOW SHE'S PLENTY ODD...
CRAFTING CLASSES JUST CAN'T FIGHT.
THEY CAN'T LEARN WEAPON SKILLS OR MAGIC.
EVEN AGAINST MONSTERS, THEIR WEAPON DAMAGE IS PER-MANENTLY REDUCED.
TO MAKE UP FOR IT, THEY EARN XP ANYTIME THEY MAKE SOMETHING WITH CRAFTING SKILLS...BUT THAT'S NOT AS FUN AS FIGHTING.
ITEMS FOR THROW HAVE TO BE MADE IN A WORKSHOP—AND YOU CAN ONLY CARRY FIVE OF EACH.
1 2 3 4 5
RANK 7
AND YOU CAN ONLY MAKE THE TWO WEAKEST RECOVERY POTIONS IN THE FIELD.
ANYONE WHO CHOOSES TO PLAY A CRAFTER JUST HAS TO BE AN ABSOLUTE FIEND FOR MAKING STUFF.
STILL, THIS DUNGEON IS MOSTLY FOR GATHERING, SO IT SHOULDN'T POSE MUCH OF A THREAT.
HMM.
WELL, I GUESS THAT'S FINE...
Off to the new dungeon! -Iz

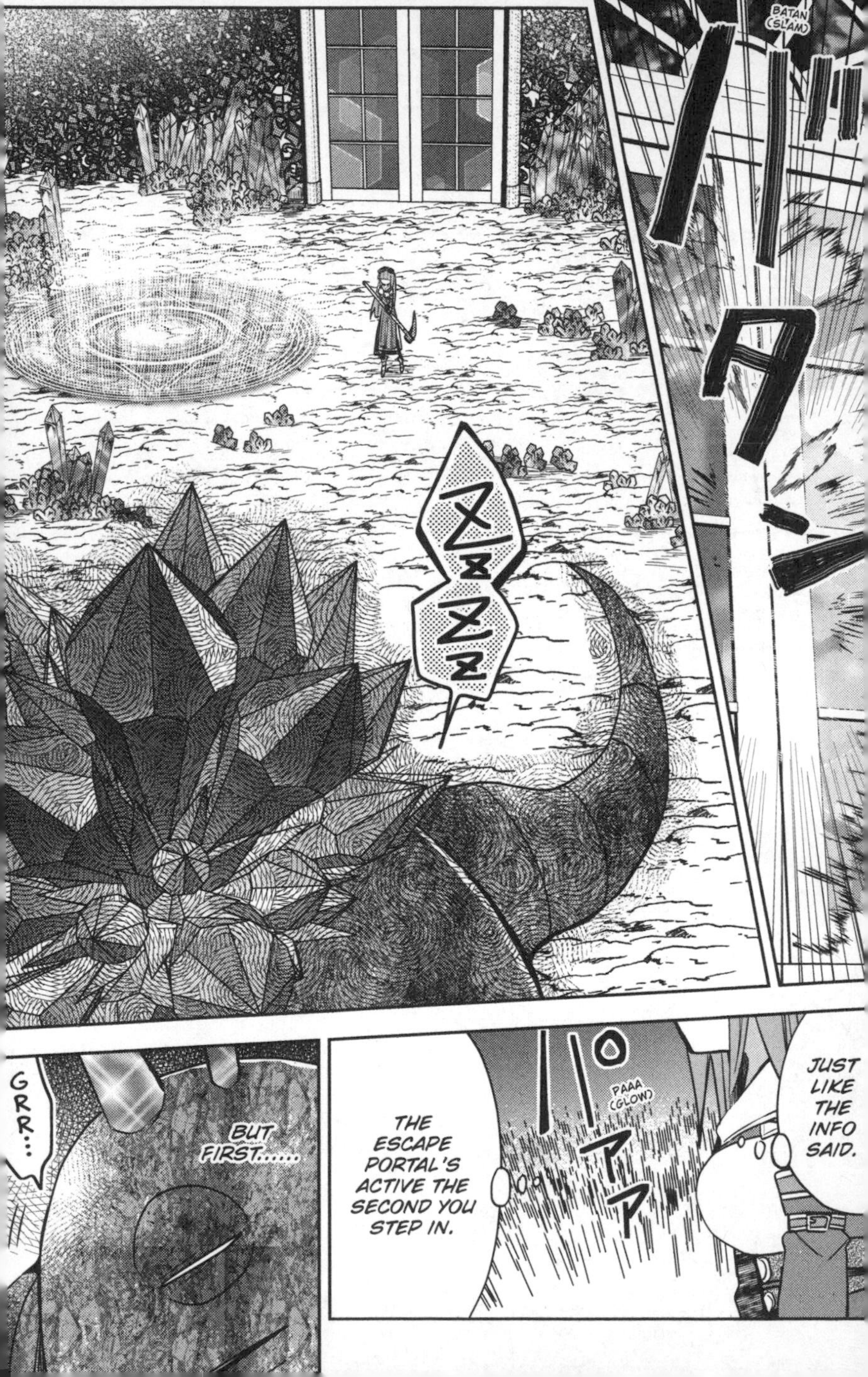
BATAN (SLAM)
Zzz
JUST LIKE THE INFO SAID.
PAAA (GLOW)
THE ESCAPE PORTAL'S ACTIVE THE SECOND YOU STEP IN.
GRR...
BUT FIRST......

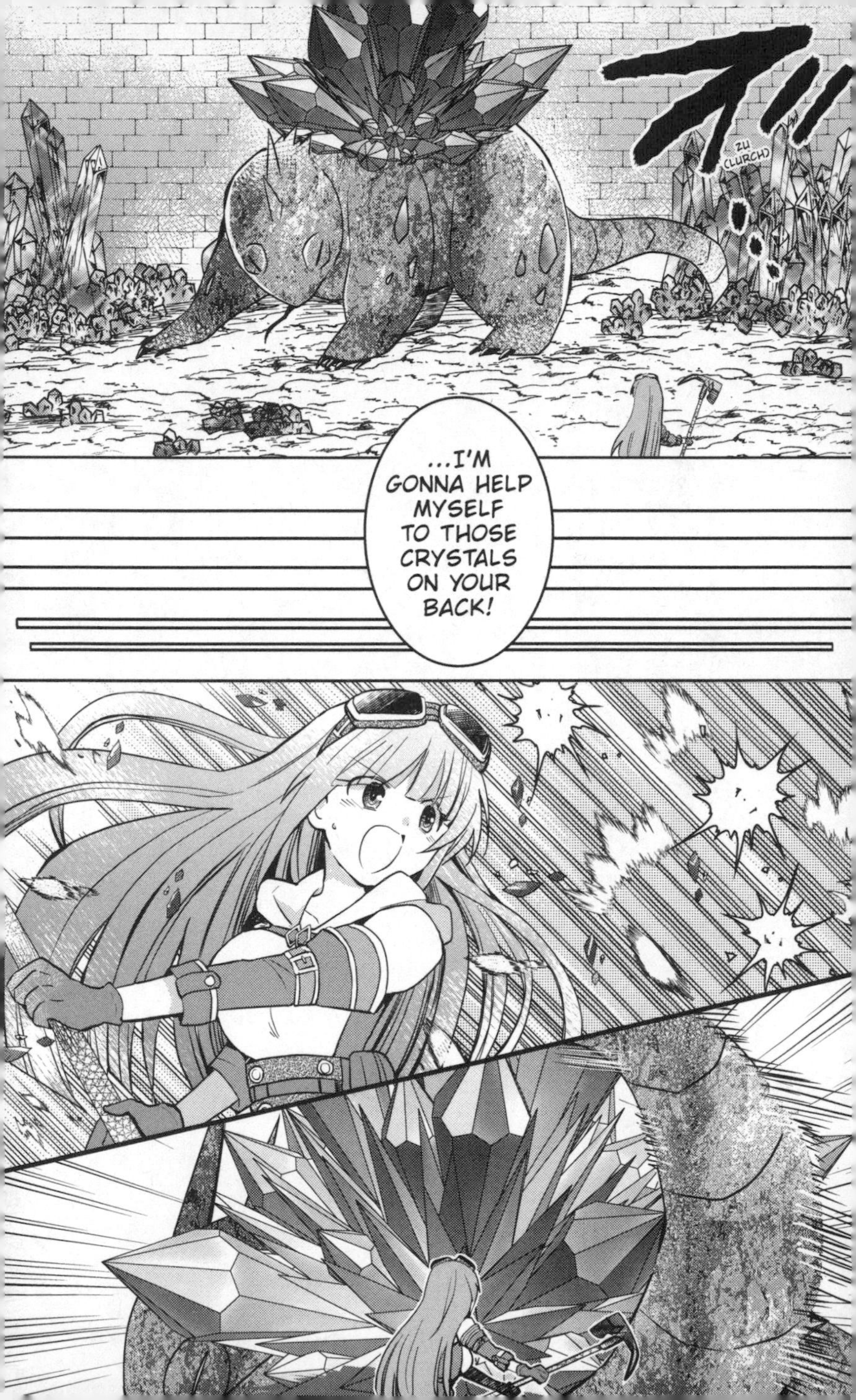
ZU (LURCH)
...I'M GONNA HELP MYSELF TO THOSE CRYSTALS ON YOUR BACK!

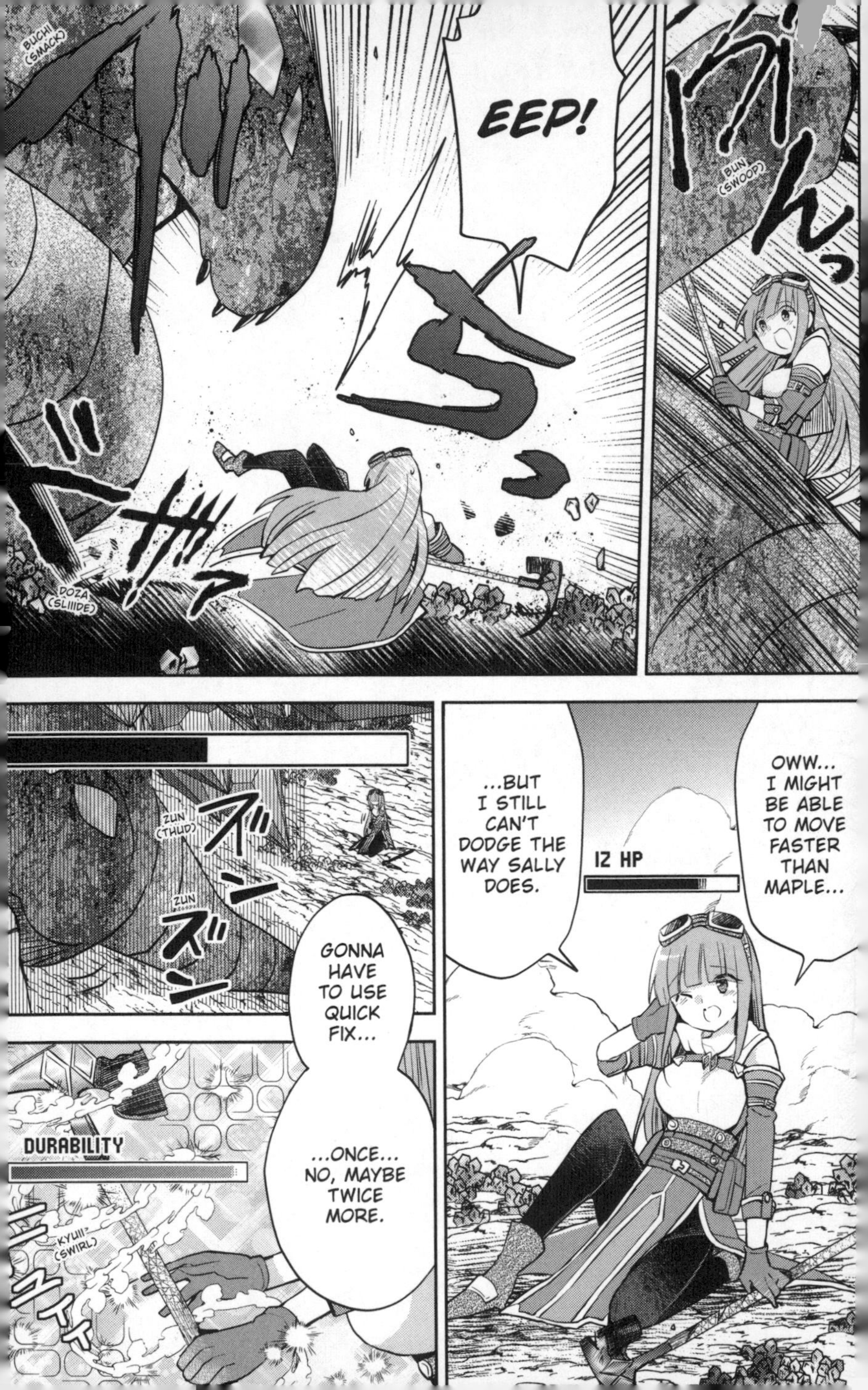
BUN (SWOOP)
EEP!
BUCHI (SMACK)
DOZA (SLIIIDE)
OWW... I MIGHT BE ABLE TO MOVE FASTER THAN MAPLE...
...BUT I STILL CAN'T DODGE THE WAY SALLY DOES.
12 HP
ZUN (THUD)
ZUN
GONNA HAVE TO USE QUICK FIX...
...ONCE... NO, MAYBE TWICE MORE.
DURABILITY
KYUII (SWIRL)

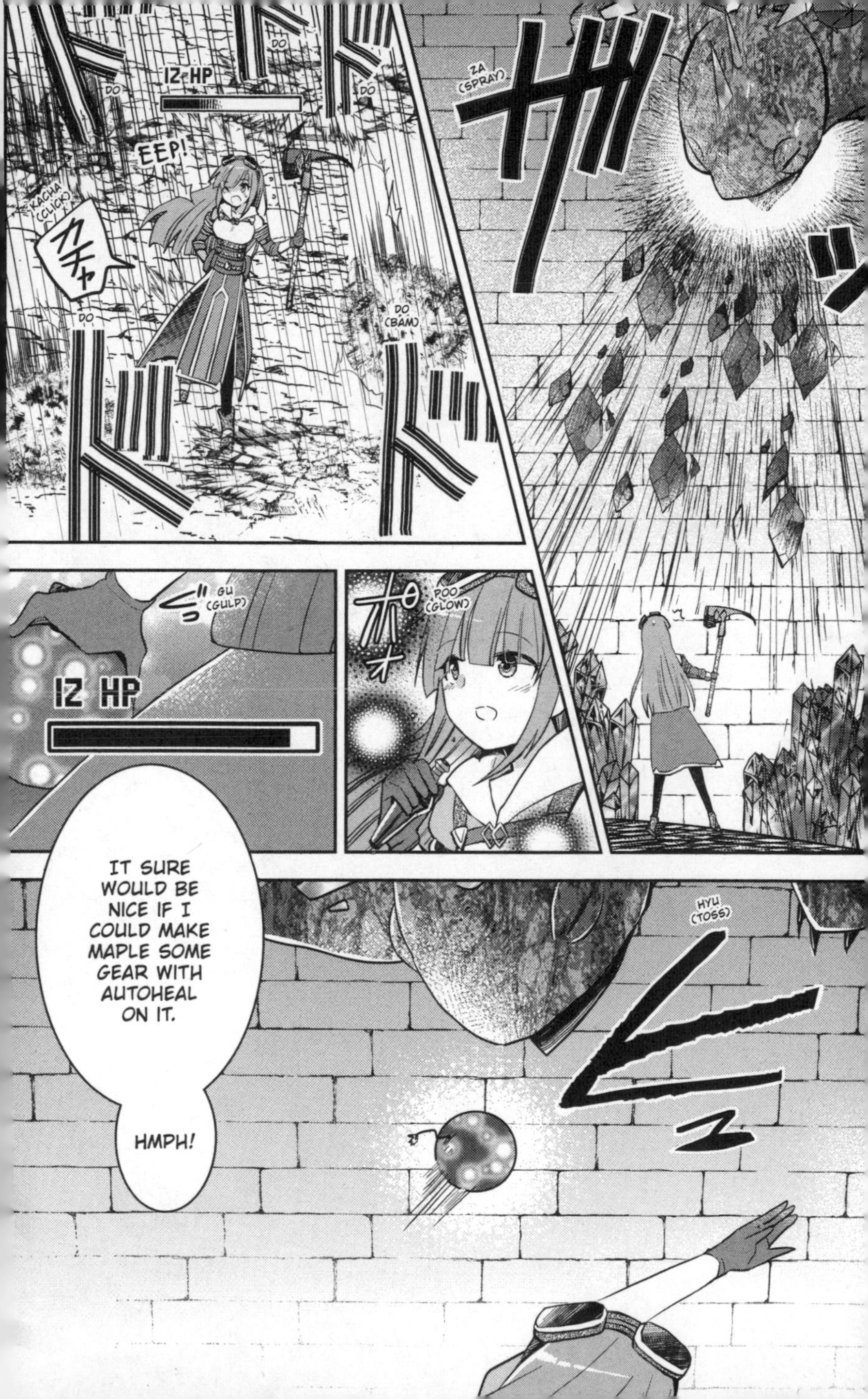
ZA (SPRAY)
DO
DO
12 HP
DO
EEP!
KACHA (CLICK)
カチャ
DO (BAM)
DO
POO (GLOW)
GU (GULP)
12 HP
HYU (TOSS)
IT SURE WOULD BE NICE IF I COULD MAKE MAPLE SOME GEAR WITH AUTOHEAL ON IT.
HMPH!

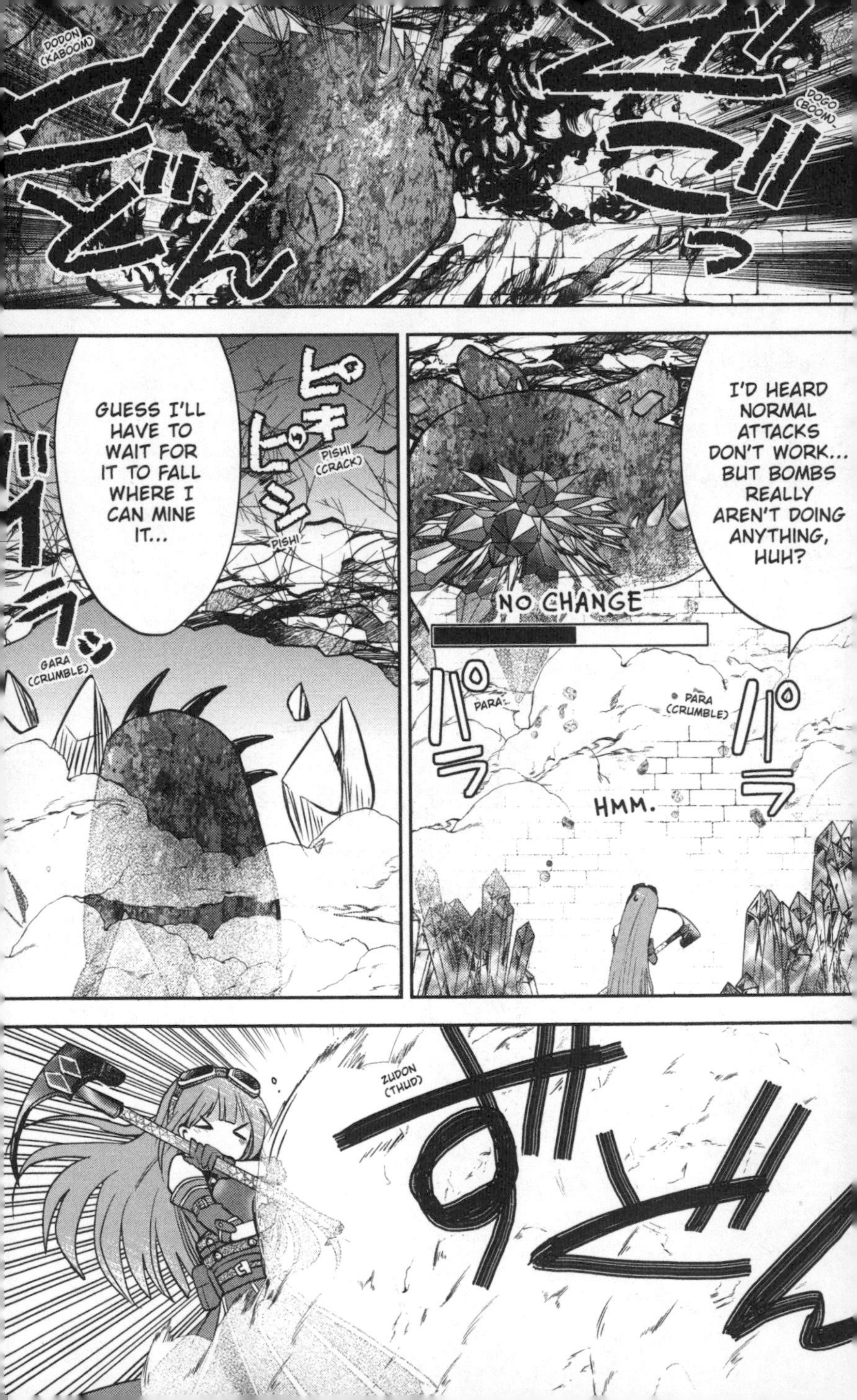
DOGO (BOOM)
DODON (KABOOM)
I'D HEARD NORMAL ATTACKS DON'T WORK... BUT BOMBS REALLY AREN'T DOING ANYTHING, HUH?
NO CHANGE
PARA (CRUMBLE)
PARA
HMM.
PISHI (CRACK)
PISHI
GUESS I'LL HAVE TO WAIT FOR IT TO FALL WHERE I CAN MINE IT...
GARA (CRUMBLE)
ZUDON (THUD)

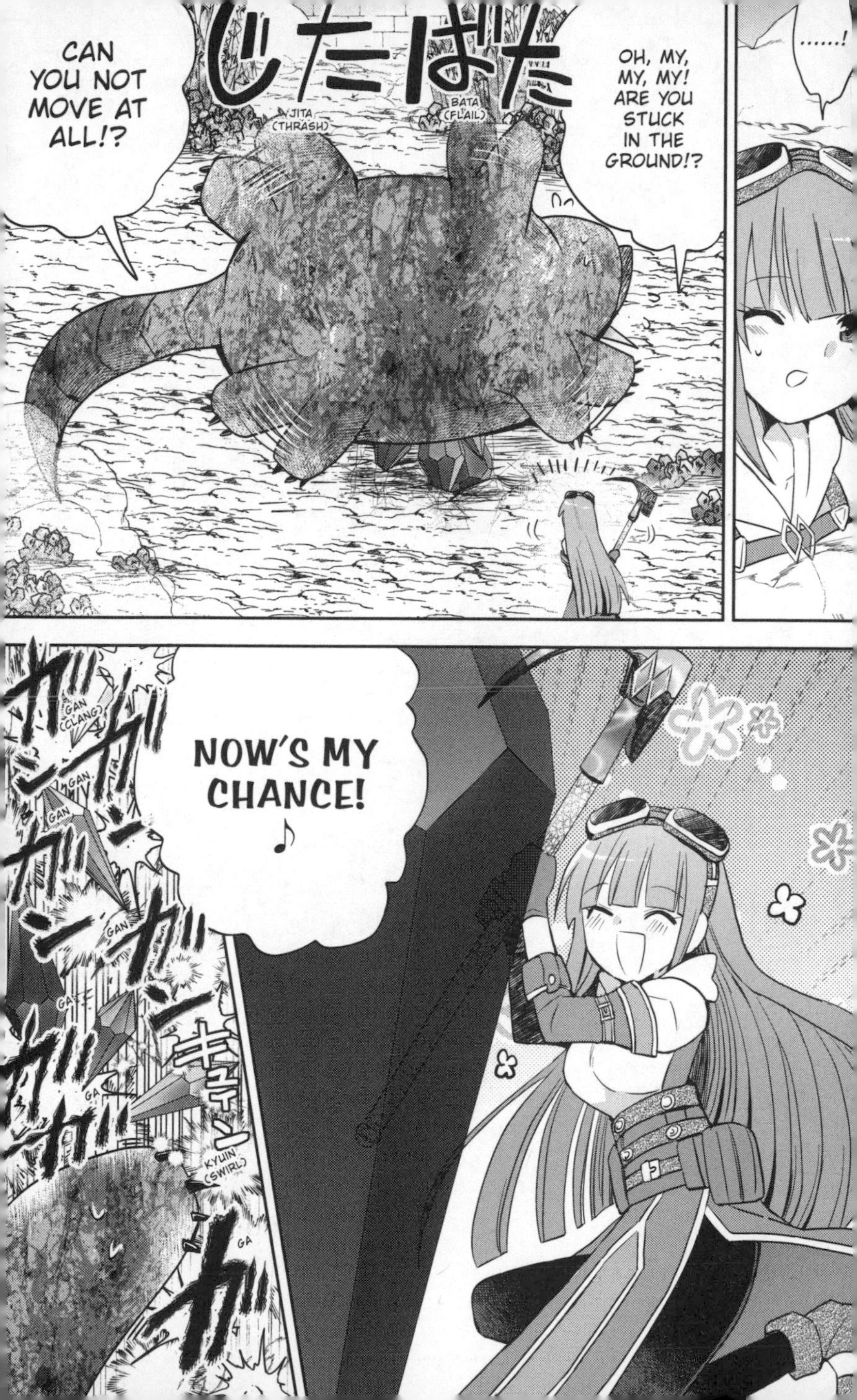
......!
OH, MY, MY, MY! ARE YOU STUCK IN THE GROUND!?
JITA (THRASH)
BATA (FLAIL)
CAN YOU NOT MOVE AT ALL!?
NOW'S MY CHANCE! ♪
KYUIN (SWIRL)
GAN (CLANG)
GAN
GAN
GAN
GA
GA
GA

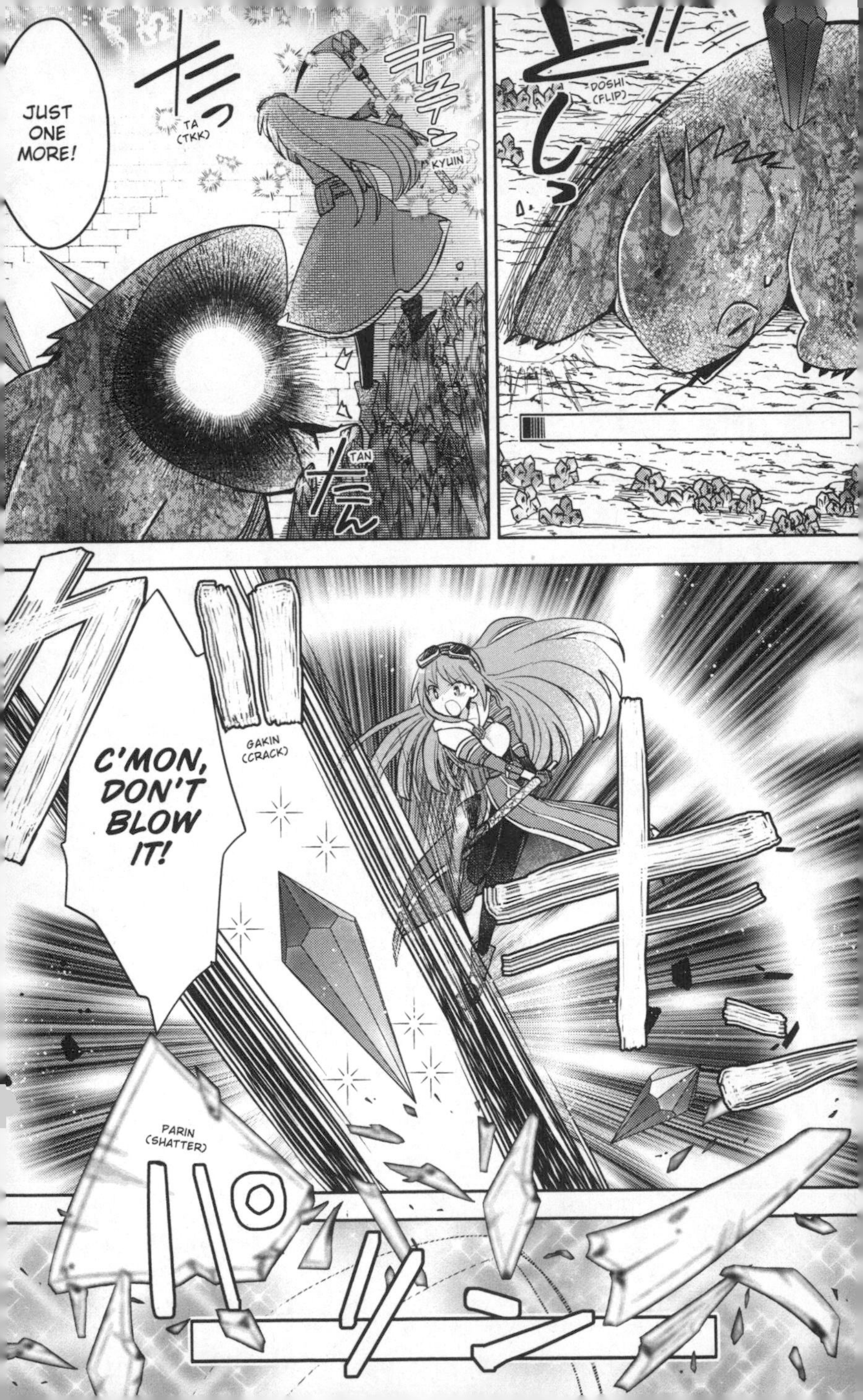

DOSHI (FLIP)
KYUIN
TA (TKK)
JUST ONE MORE!
TAN
GAKIN (CRACK)
C'MON, DON'T BLOW IT!
PARIN (SHATTER)

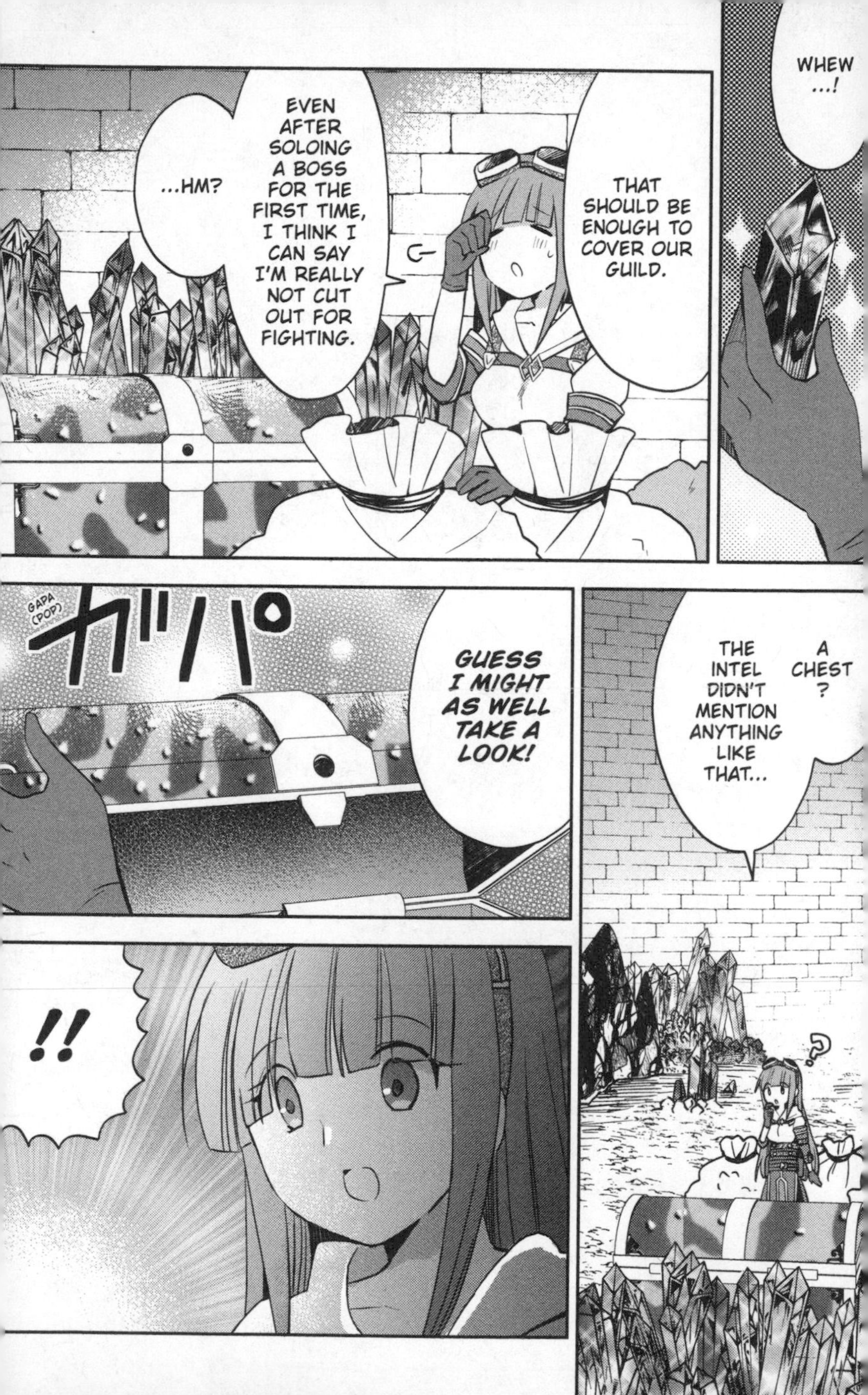
WHEW ...!
THAT SHOULD BE ENOUGH TO COVER OUR GUILD.
EVEN AFTER SOLOING A BOSS FOR THE FIRST TIME, I THINK I CAN SAY I'M REALLY NOT CUT OUT FOR FIGHTING.
...HM?
A CHEST?
THE INTEL DIDN'T MENTION ANYTHING LIKE THAT...
GUESS I MIGHT AS WELL TAKE A LOOK!
GAPA (POP)
!!

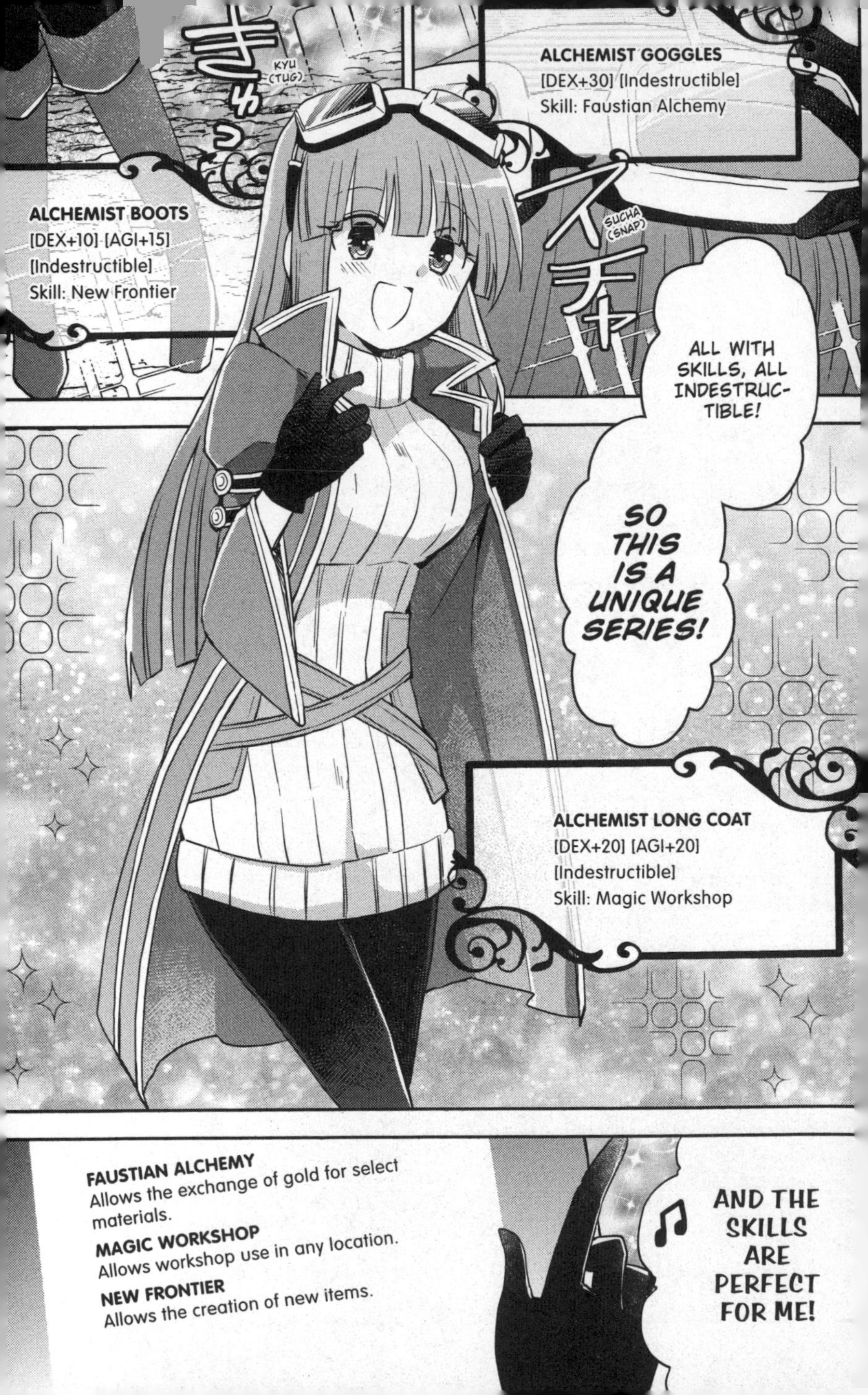
ALCHEMIST GOGGLES
[DEX+30] [Indestructible]
Skill: Faustian Alchemy
スチャ
SUCHA (SNAP)
きゅっ
KYU (TUG)
ALCHEMIST BOOTS
[DEX+10] [AGI+15]
[Indestructible]
Skill: New Frontier
ALL WITH SKILLS, ALL INDESTRUCTIBLE!
SO THIS IS A UNIQUE SERIES!
ALCHEMIST LONG COAT
[DEX+20] [AGI+20]
[Indestructible]
Skill: Magic Workshop
AND THE SKILLS ARE PERFECT FOR ME!
FAUSTIAN ALCHEMY
Allows the exchange of gold for select materials.
MAGIC WORKSHOP
Allows workshop use in any location.
NEW FRONTIER
Allows the creation of new items.

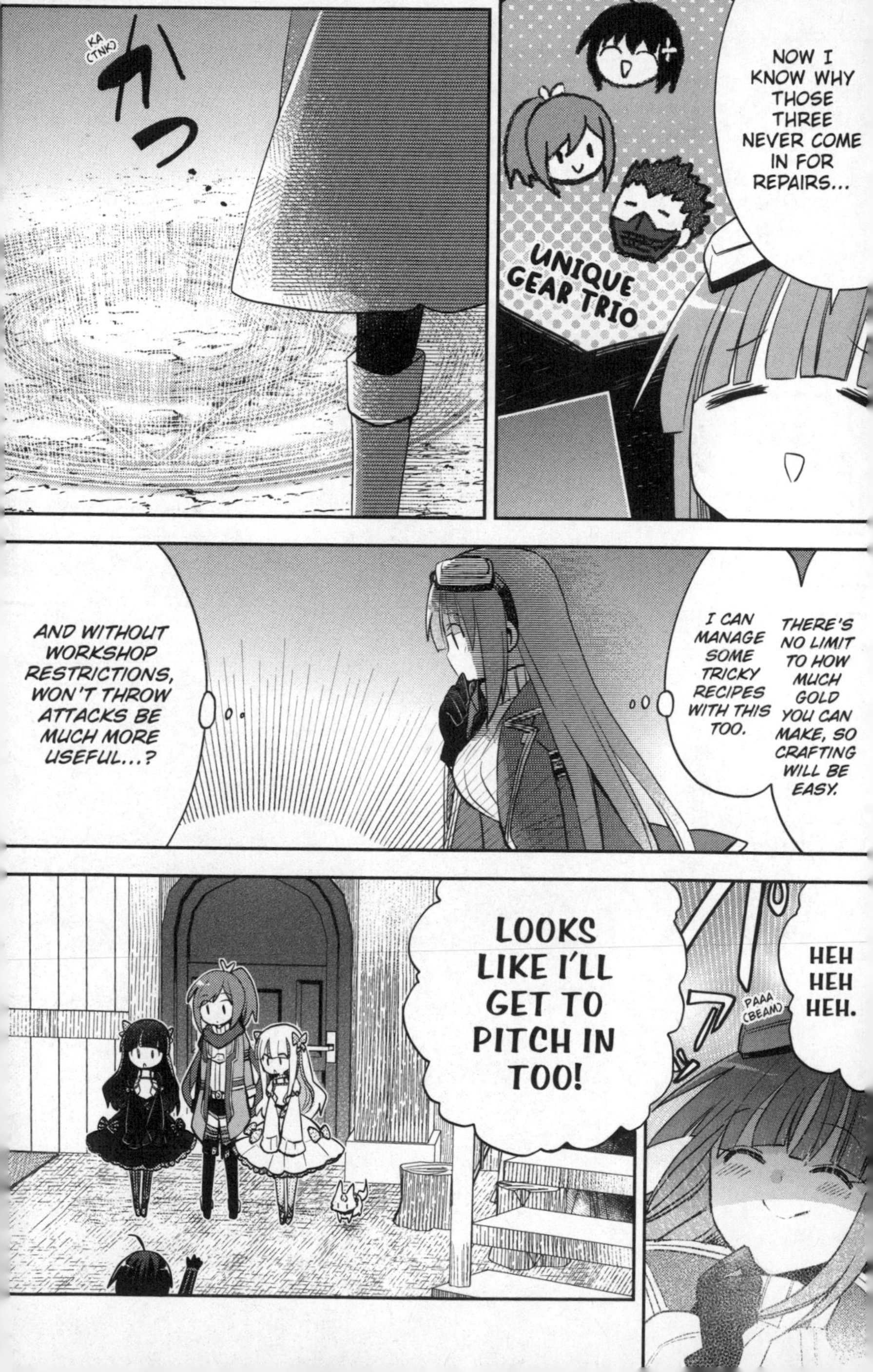
NOW I KNOW WHY THOSE THREE NEVER COME IN FOR REPAIRS...
UNIQUE GEAR TRIO
KA (TNK)
THERE'S NO LIMIT TO HOW MUCH GOLD YOU CAN MAKE, SO CRAFTING WILL BE EASY.
I CAN MANAGE SOME TRICKY RECIPES WITH THIS TOO.
AND WITHOUT WORKSHOP RESTRICTIONS, WON'T THROW ATTACKS BE MUCH MORE USEFUL...?
HEH HEH HEH.
PAAA (BEAM)
LOOKS LIKE I'LL GET TO PITCH IN TOO!

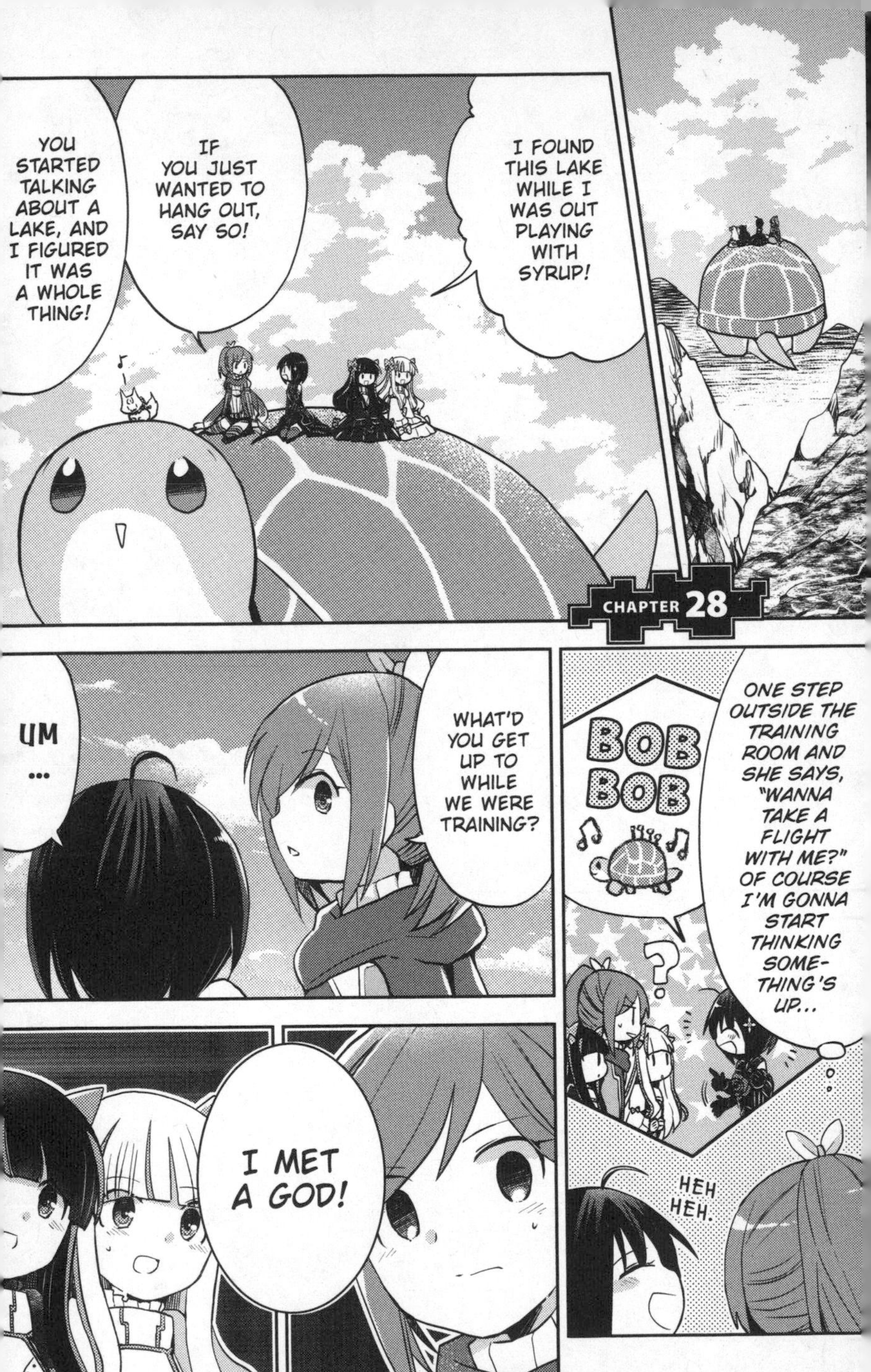
CHAPTER 28
I FOUND THIS LAKE WHILE I WAS OUT PLAYING WITH SYRUP!
IF YOU JUST WANTED TO HANG OUT, SAY SO!
YOU STARTED TALKING ABOUT A LAKE, AND I FIGURED IT WAS A WHOLE THING!
ONE STEP OUTSIDE THE TRAINING ROOM AND SHE SAYS, "WANNA TAKE A FLIGHT WITH ME?" OF COURSE I'M GONNA START THINKING SOME-THING'S UP...
BOB BOB
?
HEH HEH.
WHAT'D YOU GET UP TO WHILE WE WERE TRAINING?
UM ...
I MET A GOD!

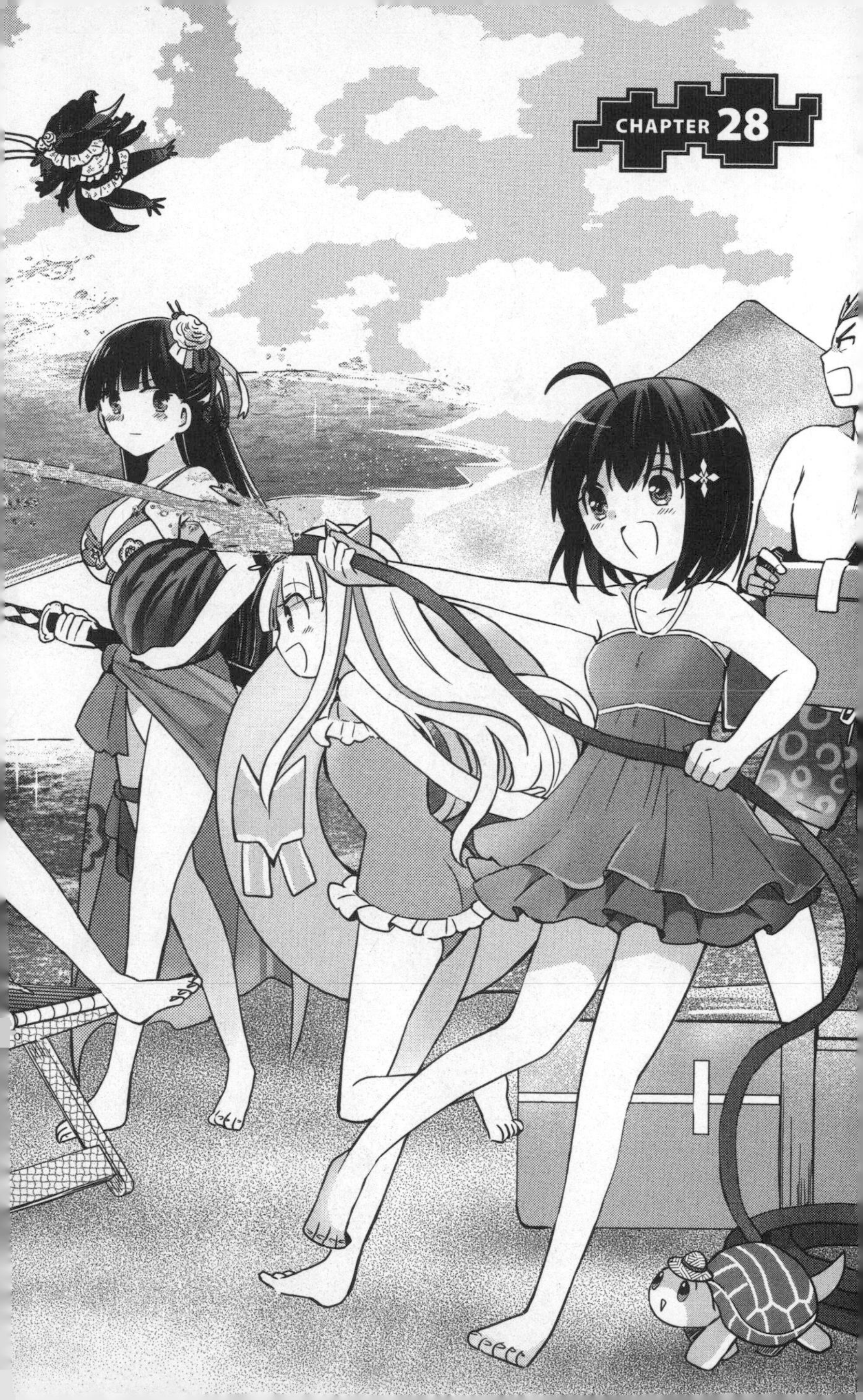
CHAPTER 28

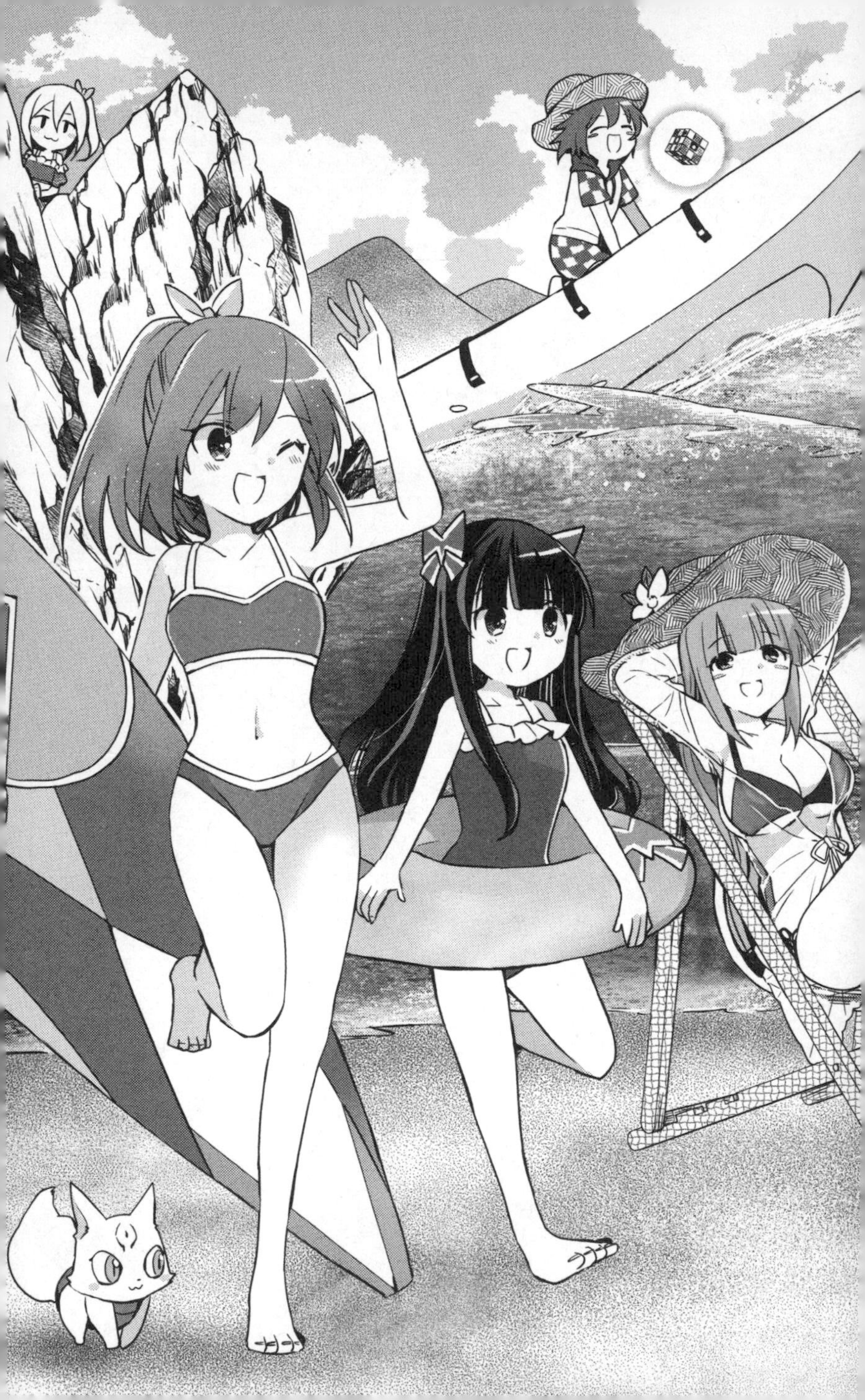

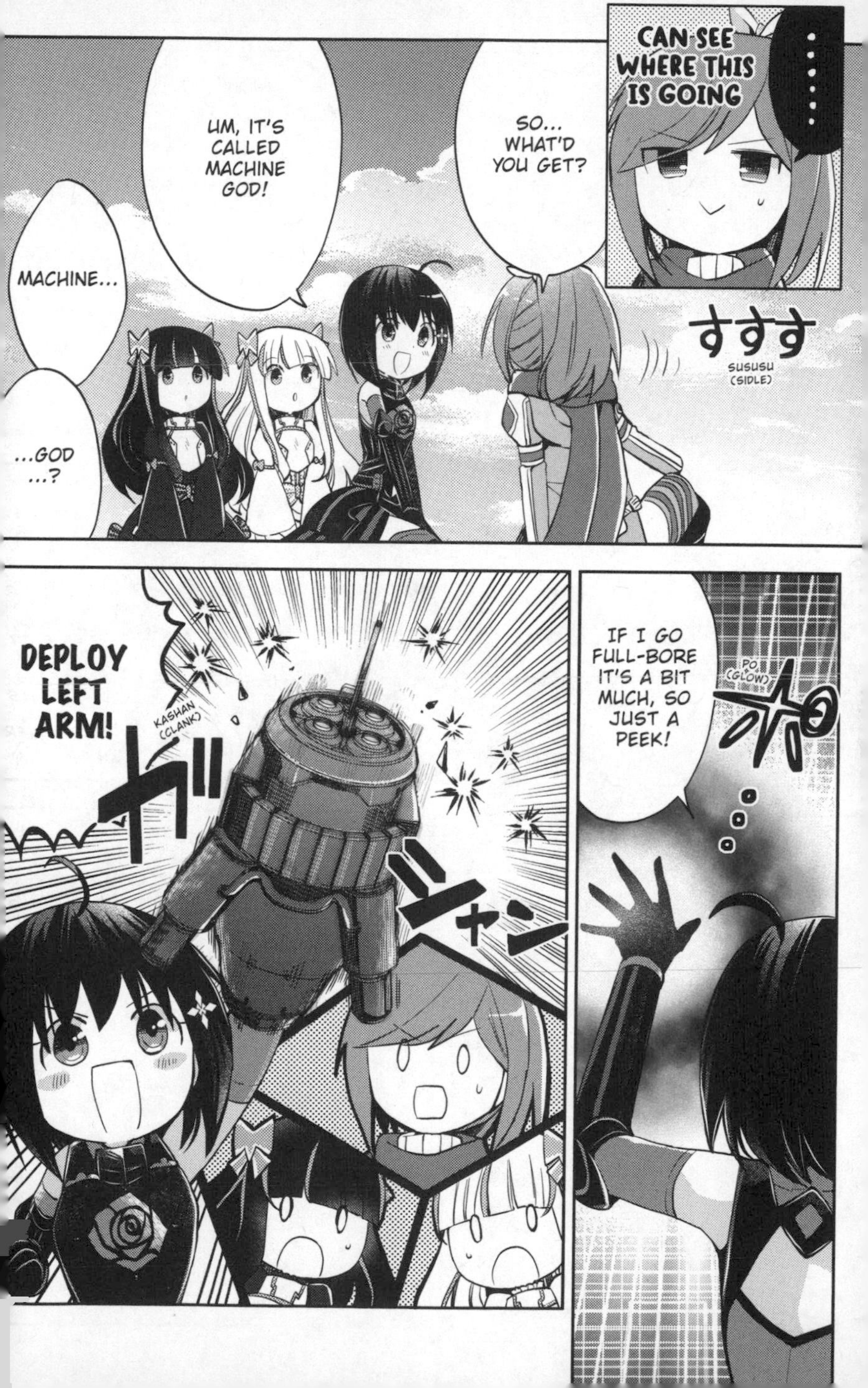
CAN SEE WHERE THIS IS GOING
......
SO... WHAT'D YOU GET?
UM, IT'S CALLED MACHINE GOD!
すすす
SUSUSU (SIDLE)
MACHINE...
...GOD ...?
IF I GO FULL-BORE IT'S A BIT MUCH, SO JUST A PEEK!
PO (GLOW)
DEPLOY LEFT ARM!
KASHAN (CLANK)

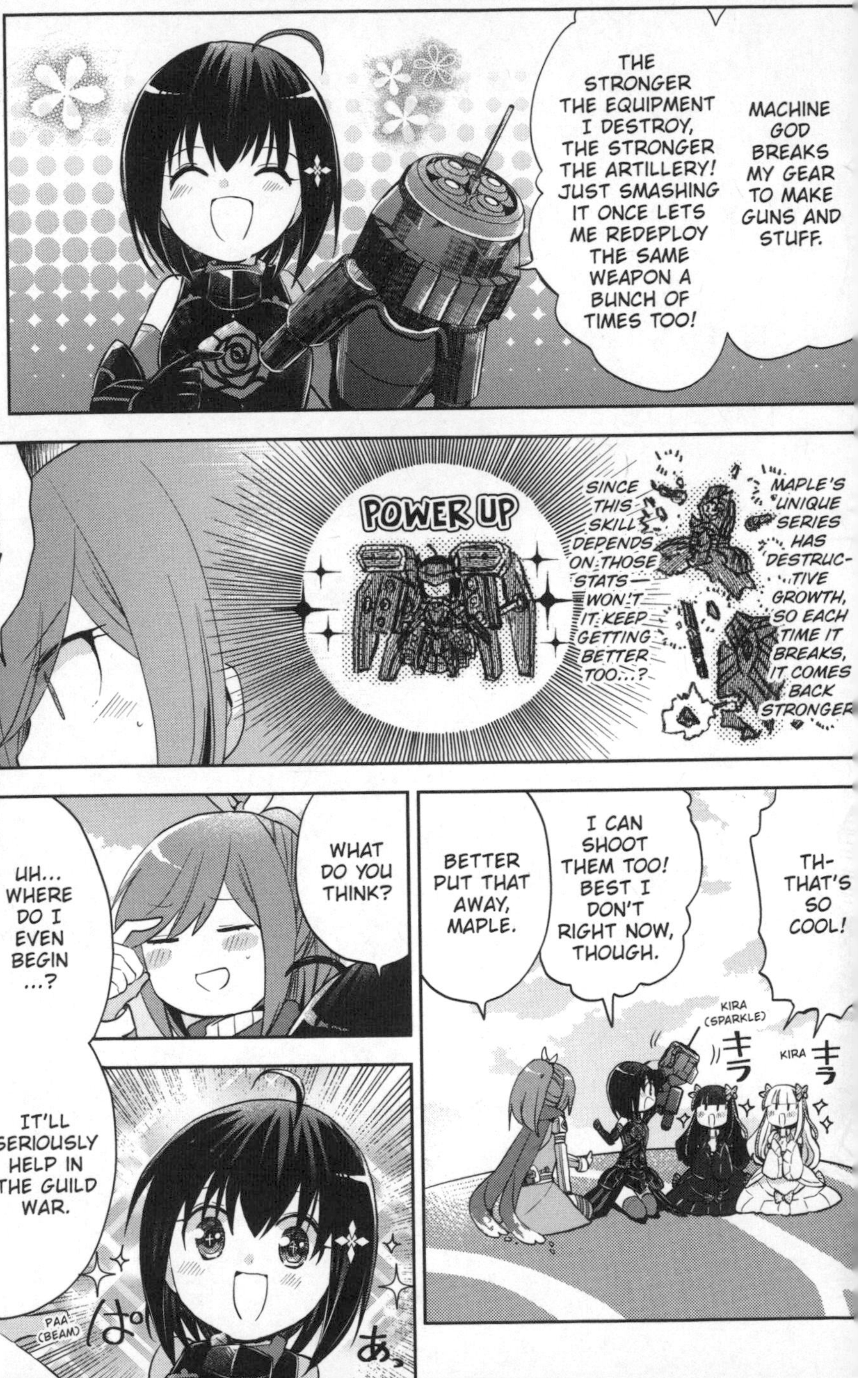
MACHINE GOD BREAKS MY GEAR TO MAKE GUNS AND STUFF.
THE STRONGER THE EQUIPMENT I DESTROY, THE STRONGER THE ARTILLERY! JUST SMASHING IT ONCE LETS ME REDEPLOY THE SAME WEAPON A BUNCH OF TIMES TOO!
MAPLE'S UNIQUE SERIES HAS DESTRUCTIVE GROWTH, SO EACH TIME IT BREAKS, IT COMES BACK STRONGER
SINCE THIS SKILL DEPENDS ON THOSE STATS—WON'T IT KEEP GETTING BETTER TOO...?
POWER UP
......!
TH-THAT'S SO COOL!
I CAN SHOOT THEM TOO! BEST I DON'T RIGHT NOW, THOUGH.
BETTER PUT THAT AWAY, MAPLE.
KIRA (SPARKLE) キラ
KIRA キラ
WHAT DO YOU THINK?
UH... WHERE DO I EVEN BEGIN...?
IT'LL SERIOUSLY HELP IN THE GUILD WAR.
PAA (BEAM) ぱっ
あっ

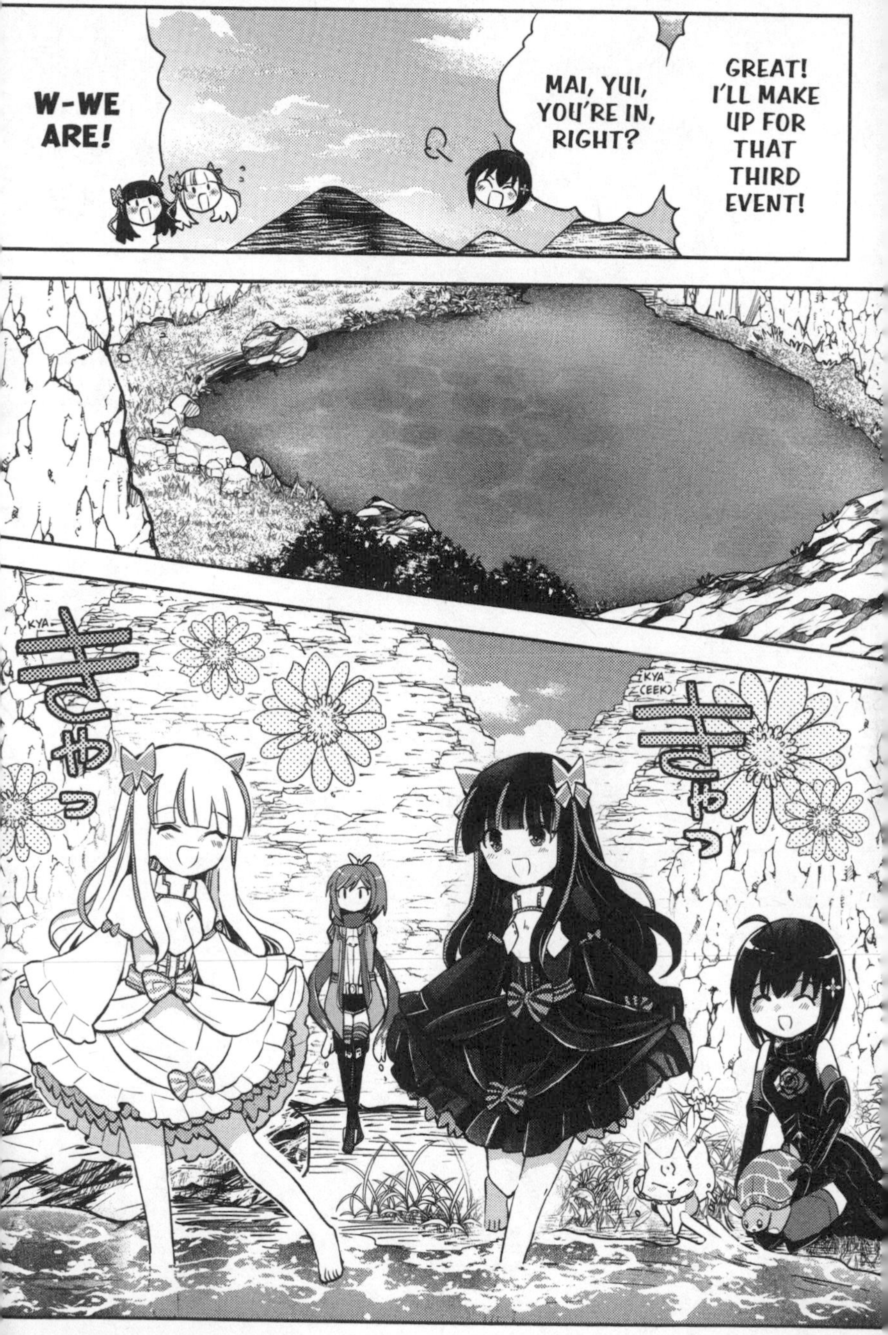
GREAT! I'LL MAKE UP FOR THAT THIRD EVENT!
MAI, YUI, YOU'RE IN, RIGHT?
W-WE ARE!
きゃっ
KYA (EEK)
きゃっ
KYA

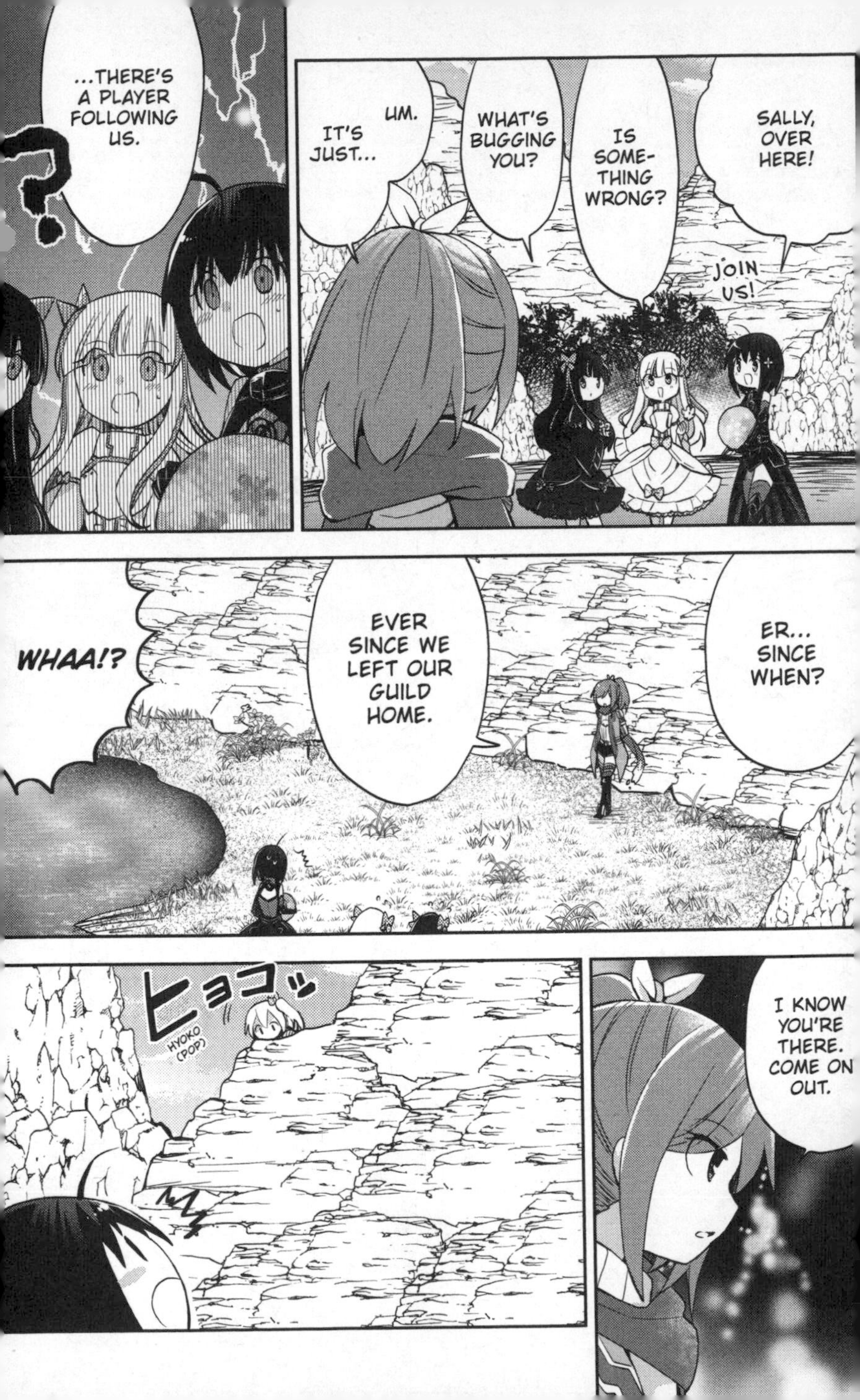
SALLY, OVER HERE!
JOIN US!
IS SOME-THING WRONG?
WHAT'S BUGGING YOU?
UM. IT'S JUST...
...THERE'S A PLAYER FOLLOWING US.
ER... SINCE WHEN?
EVER SINCE WE LEFT OUR GUILD HOME.
WHAA!?
I KNOW YOU'RE THERE. COME ON OUT.
ヒョコッ
HYOKO (POP)

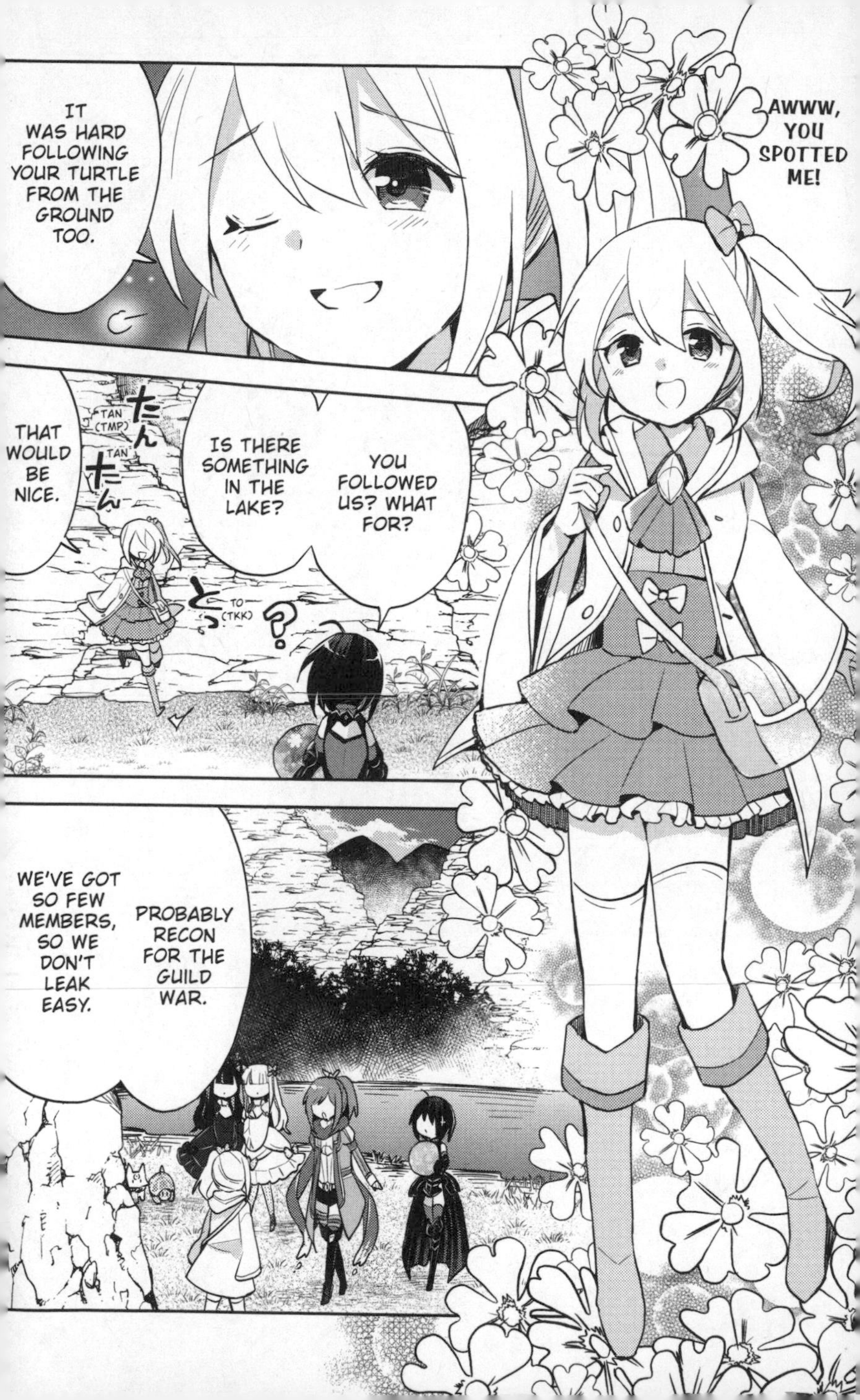
AWWW, YOU SPOTTED ME!
IT WAS HARD FOLLOWING YOUR TURTLE FROM THE GROUND TOO.
YOU FOLLOWED US? WHAT FOR?
IS THERE SOMETHING IN THE LAKE?
とっ TO (TKK)
たん TAN (TMP)
たん TAN
THAT WOULD BE NICE.
PROBABLY RECON FOR THE GUILD WAR.
WE'VE GOT SO FEW MEMBERS, SO WE DON'T LEAK EASY.

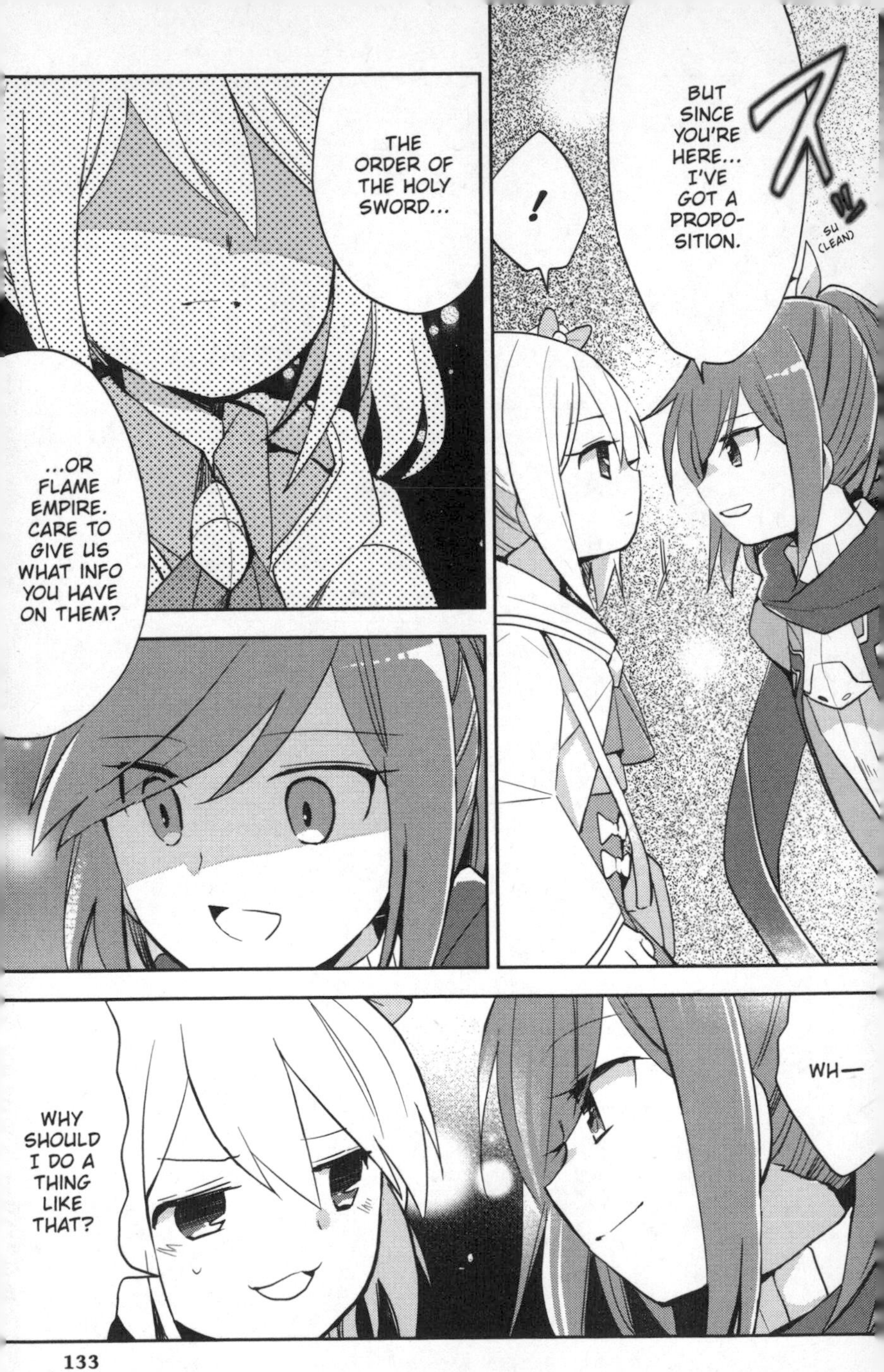
SU (LEAN)
BUT SINCE YOU'RE HERE... I'VE GOT A PROPO-SITION.
!
THE ORDER OF THE HOLY SWORD...
...OR FLAME EMPIRE. CARE TO GIVE US WHAT INFO YOU HAVE ON THEM?
WH—
WHY SHOULD I DO A THING LIKE THAT?

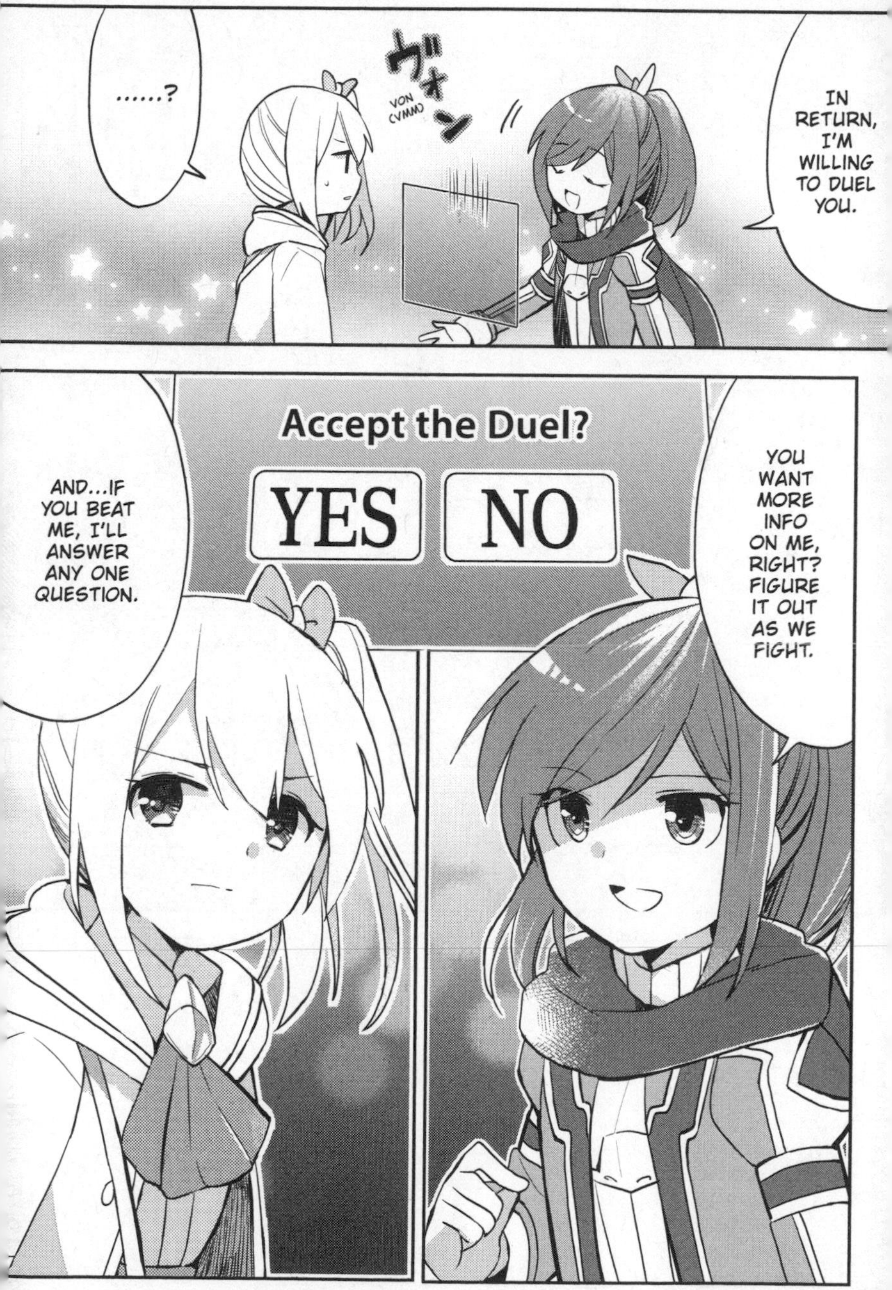
IN RETURN, I'M WILLING TO DUEL YOU.
ヴォン
VON (VMM)
......?
YOU WANT MORE INFO ON ME, RIGHT? FIGURE IT OUT AS WE FIGHT.
Accept the Duel?
YES
NO
AND...IF YOU BEAT ME, I'LL ANSWER ANY ONE QUESTION.

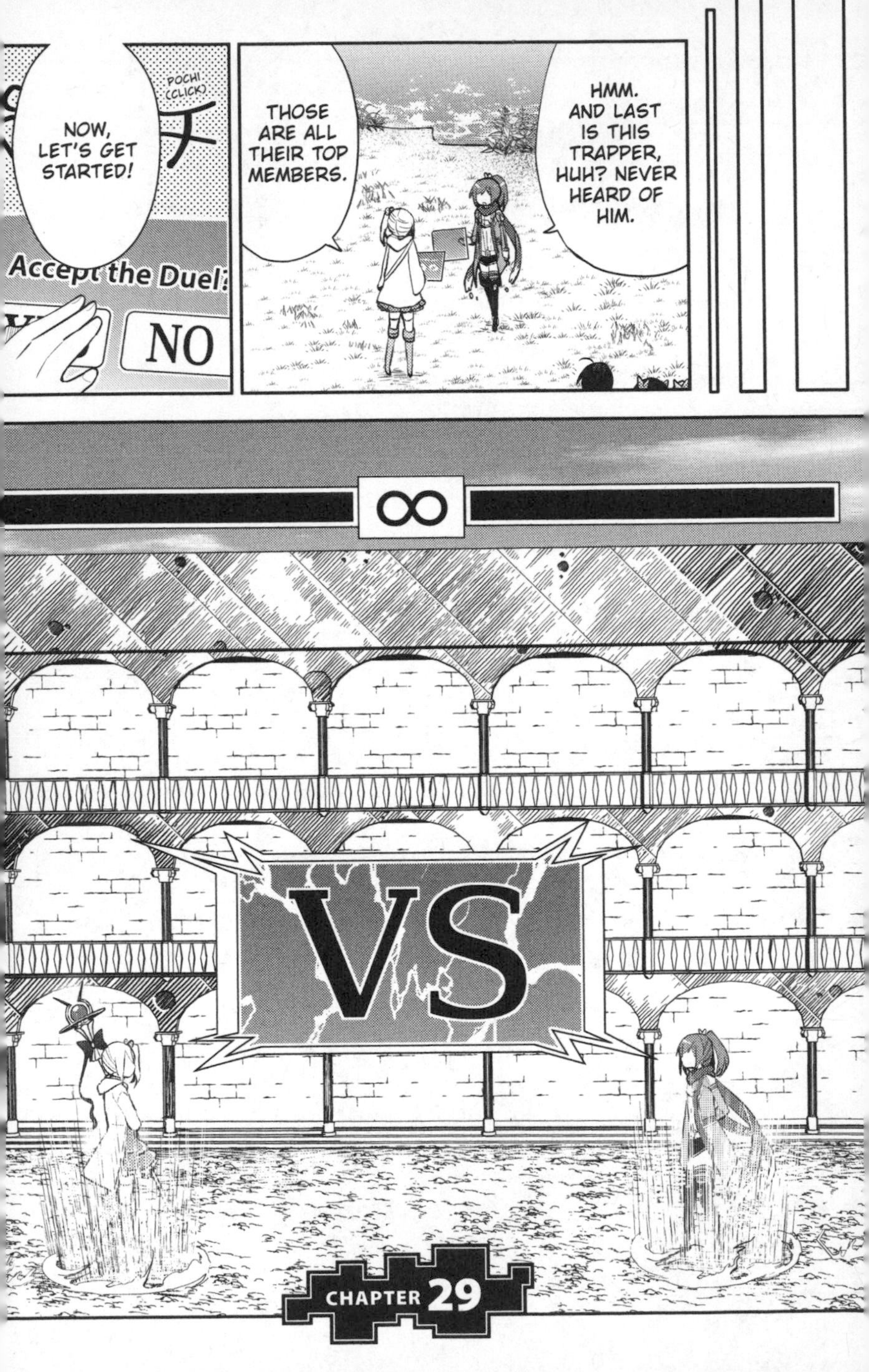
HMM. AND LAST IS THIS TRAPPER, HUH? NEVER HEARD OF HIM.
THOSE ARE ALL THEIR TOP MEMBERS.
POCHI (CLICK)
NOW, LET'S GET STARTED!
Accept the Duel?
NO
∞
VS
CHAPTER 29

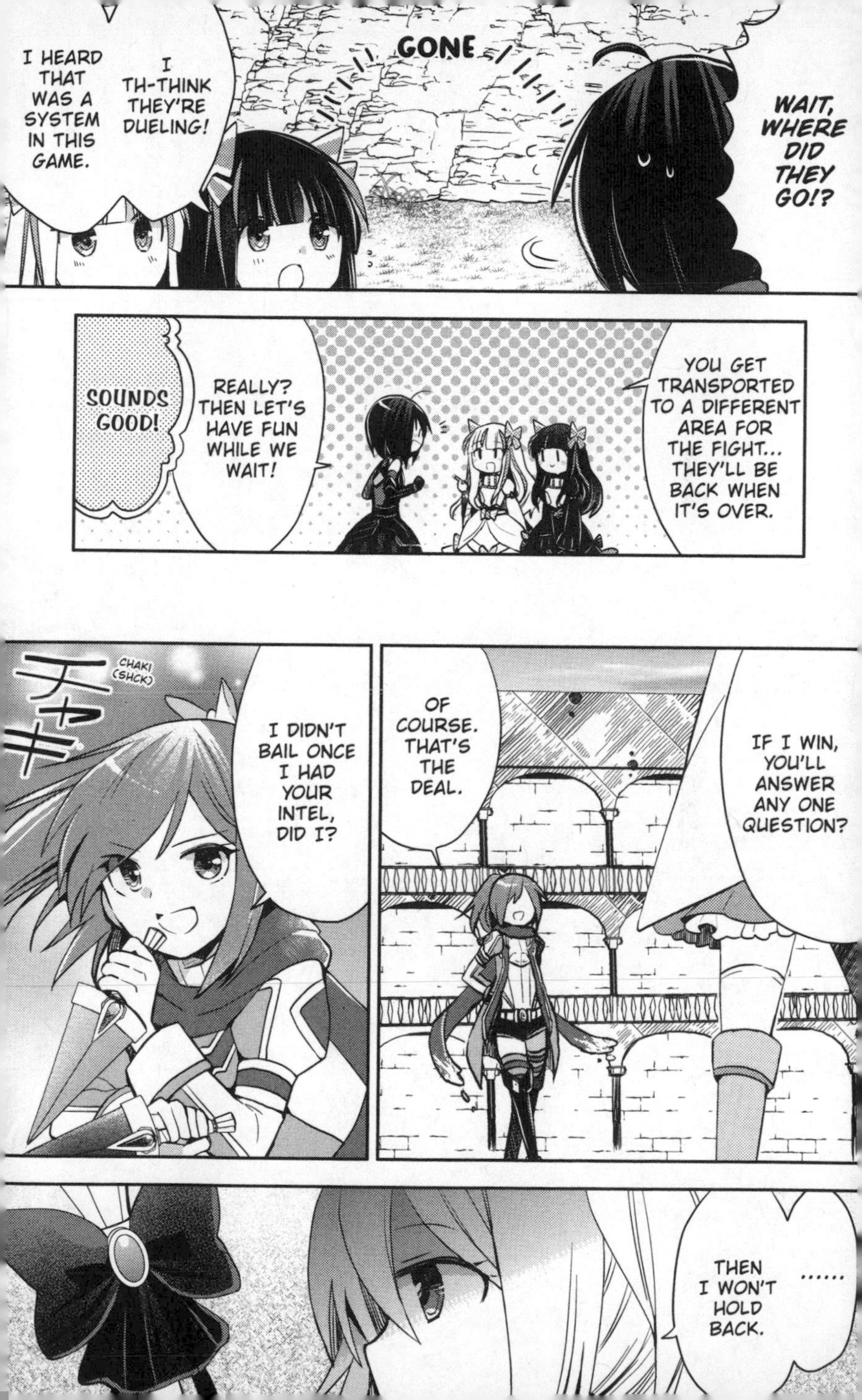
WAIT, WHERE DID THEY GO!?
GONE
I TH-THINK THEY'RE DUELING!
I HEARD THAT WAS A SYSTEM IN THIS GAME.
YOU GET TRANSPORTED TO A DIFFERENT AREA FOR THE FIGHT... THEY'LL BE BACK WHEN IT'S OVER.
REALLY? THEN LET'S HAVE FUN WHILE WE WAIT!
SOUNDS GOOD!
IF I WIN, YOU'LL ANSWER ANY ONE QUESTION?
OF COURSE. THAT'S THE DEAL.
I DIDN'T BAIL ONCE I HAD YOUR INTEL, DID I?
CHAKI (SHCK)
......
THEN I WON'T HOLD BACK.

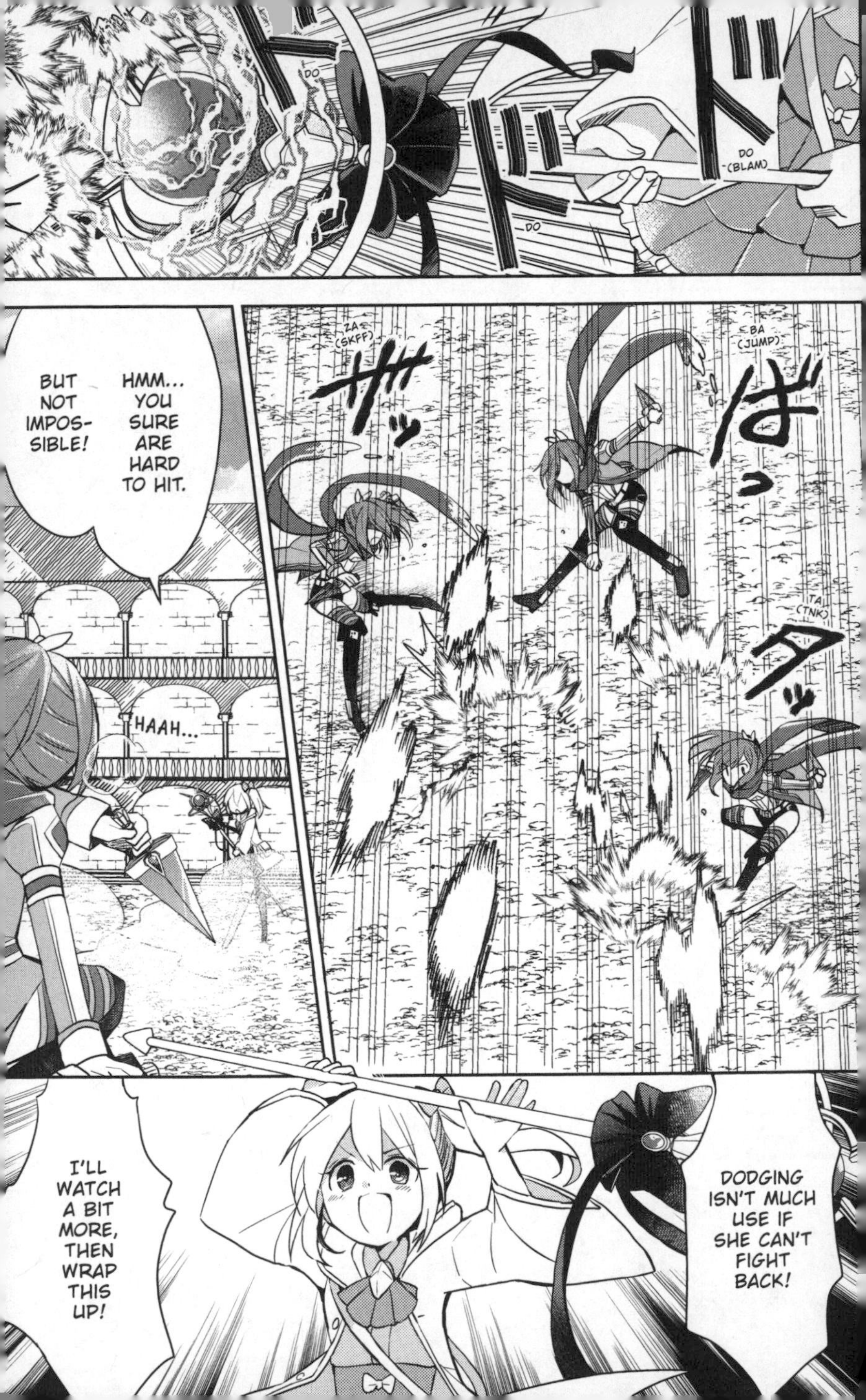
DO (BLAM)
DO
DO
BA (JUMP)
TA (TNK)
ZA (SKFF)
HMM... YOU SURE ARE HARD TO HIT.
BUT NOT IMPOSSIBLE!
HAAH...
DODGING ISN'T MUCH USE IF SHE CAN'T FIGHT BACK!
I'LL WATCH A BIT MORE, THEN WRAP THIS UP!

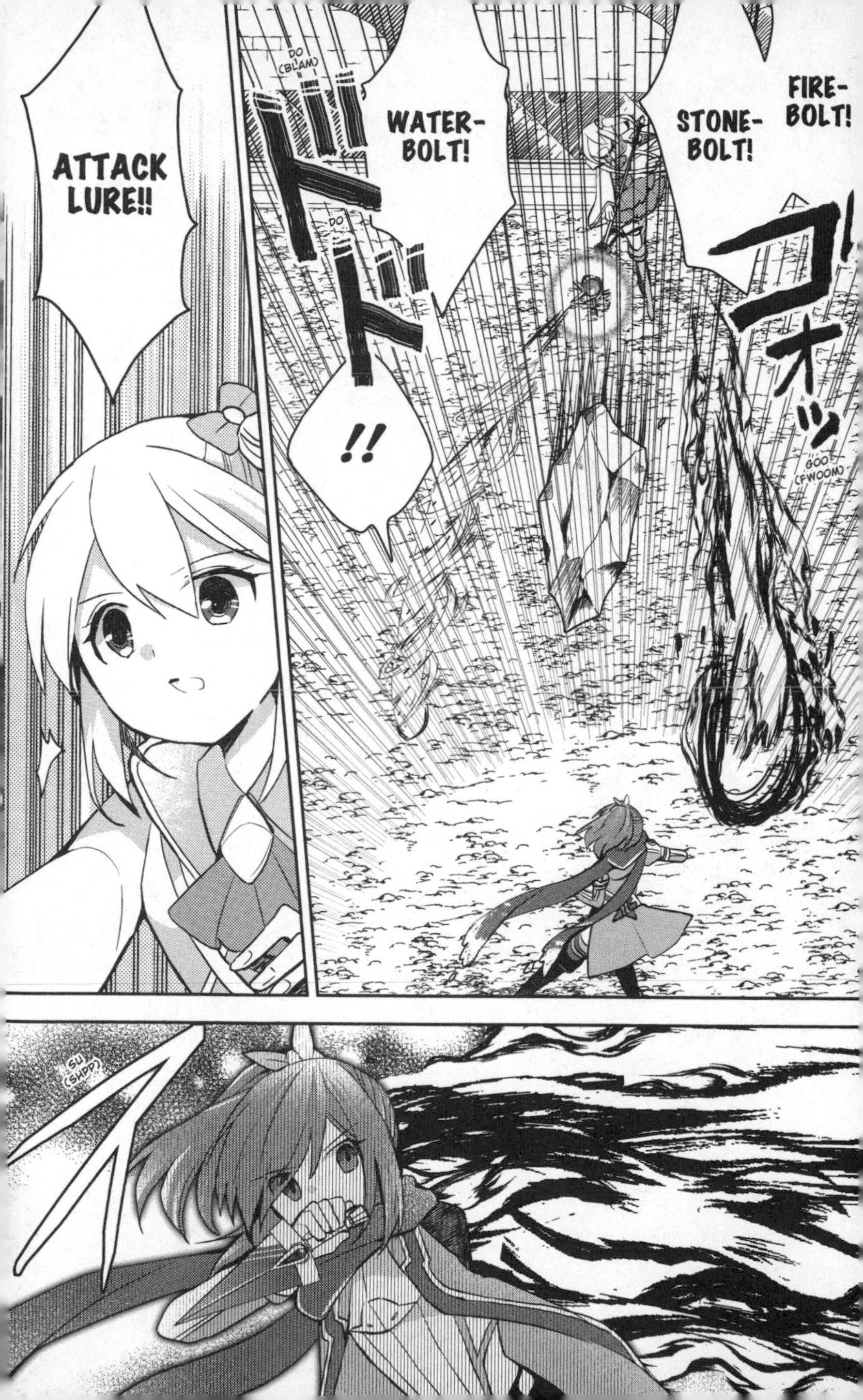
FIRE-BOLT!
STONE-BOLT!
GOO (FWOOM)
WATER-BOLT!
DO (BLAM)
DO
!!
ATTACK LURE!!
SU (SHPP)

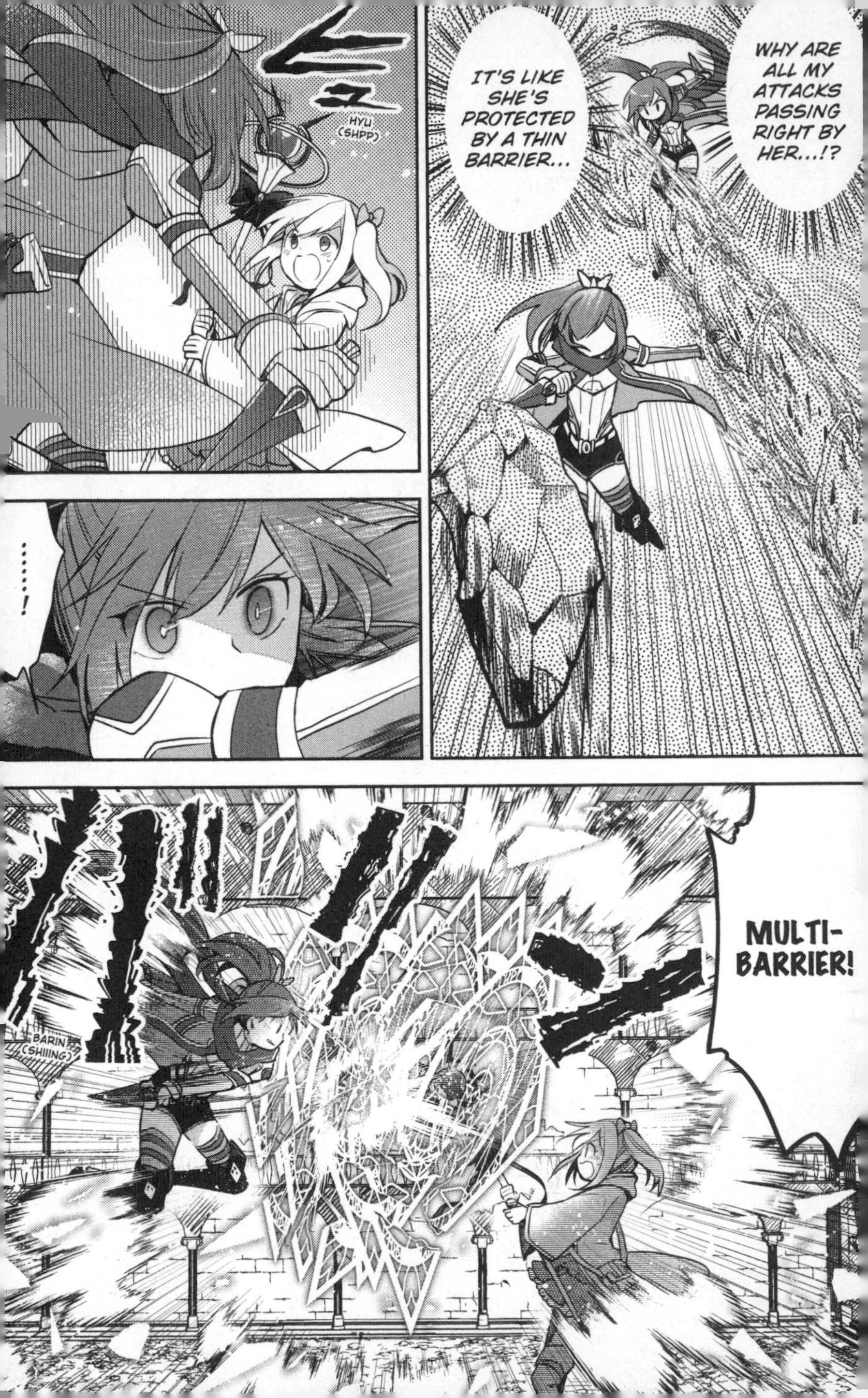

WHY ARE ALL MY ATTACKS PASSING RIGHT BY HER...!?
IT'S LIKE SHE'S PROTECTED BY A THIN BARRIER...
HYU (SHPP)
......!
MULTI-BARRIER!
BARIN (SHIING)

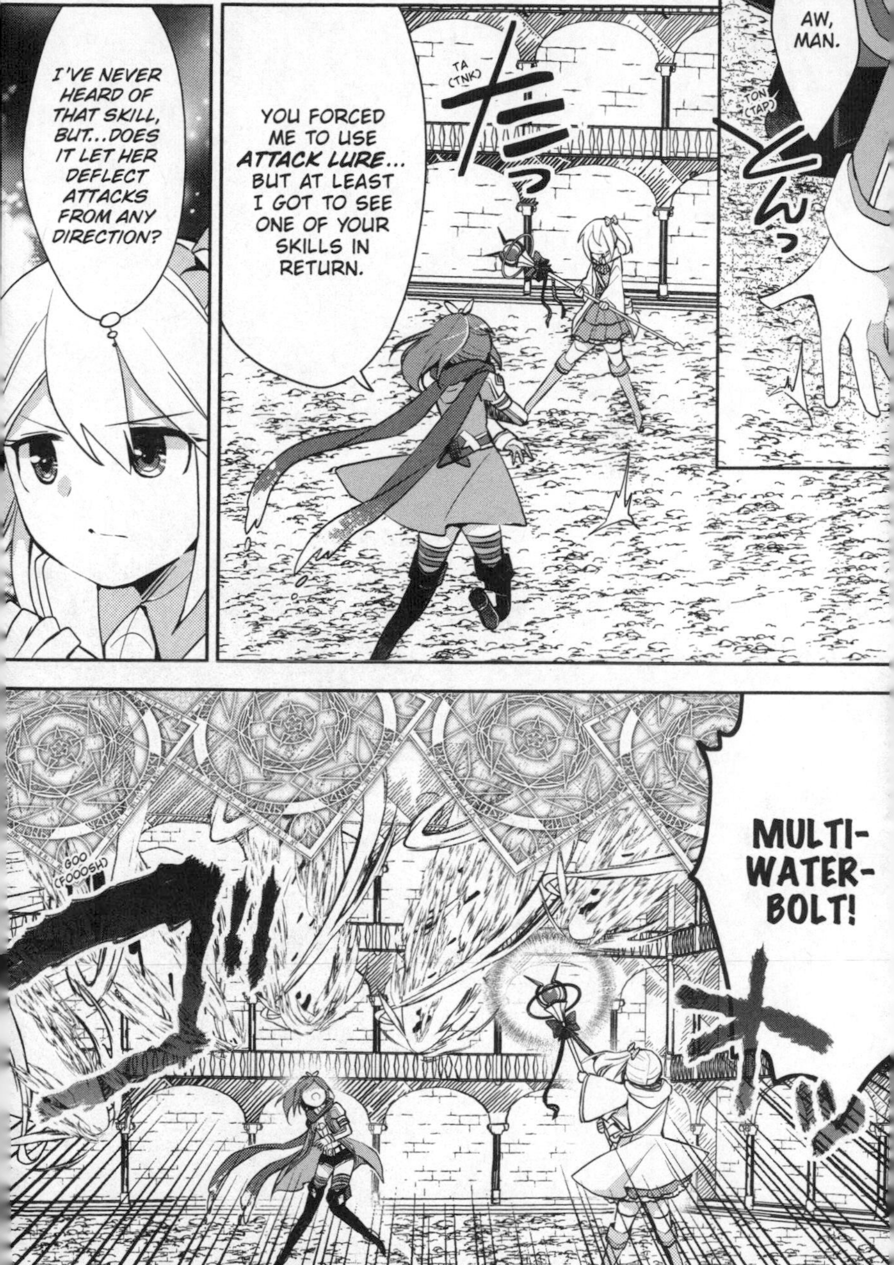
AW, MAN.
TON (TAP)
TA (TNK)
YOU FORCED ME TO USE *ATTACK LURE*... BUT AT LEAST I GOT TO SEE ONE OF YOUR SKILLS IN RETURN.
I'VE NEVER HEARD OF THAT SKILL, BUT...DOES IT LET HER DEFLECT ATTACKS FROM ANY DIRECTION?
MULTI-WATER-BOLT!
GOO (FOOOSH)

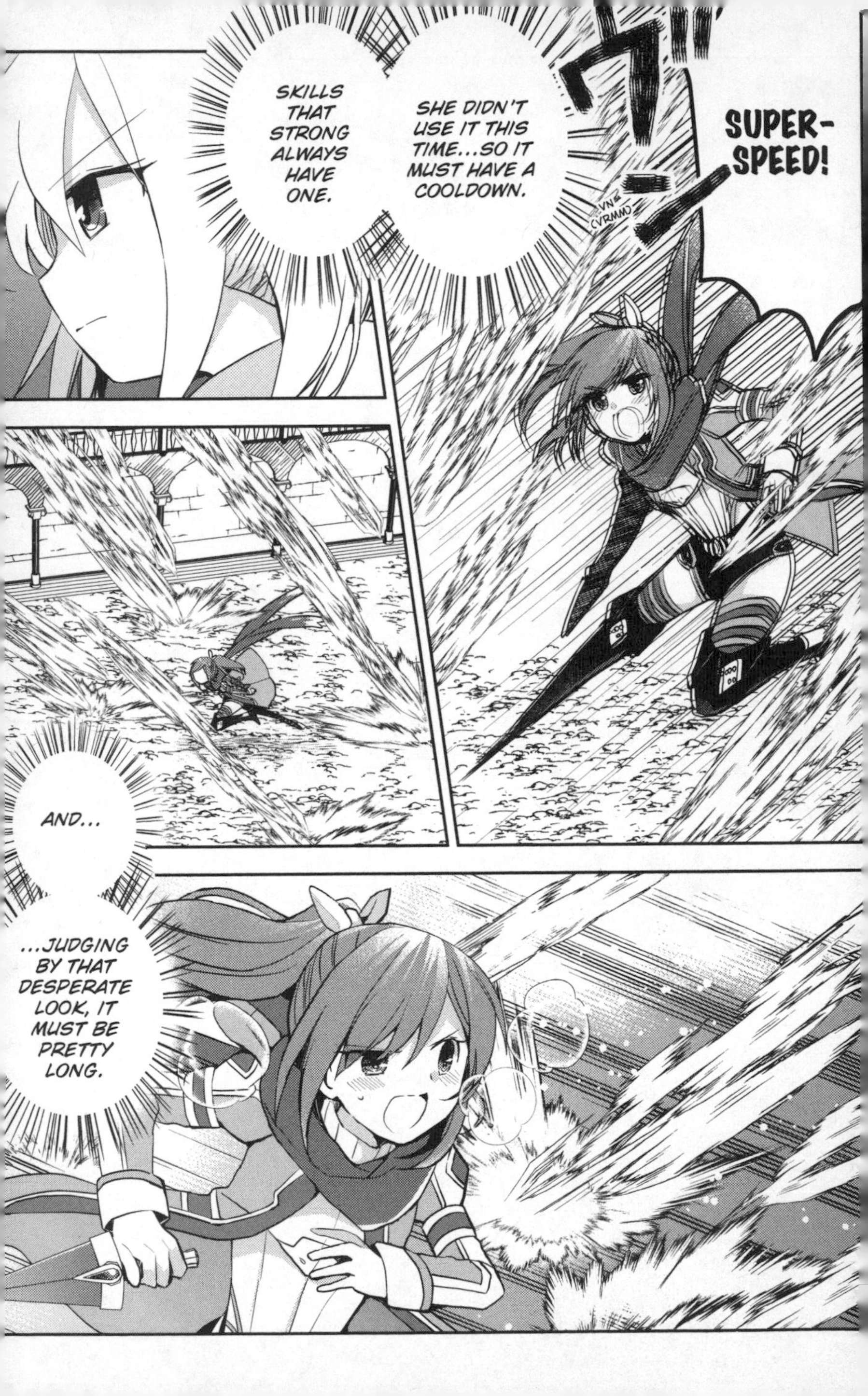
SUPER-SPEED!
VN (VRMM)
SHE DIDN'T USE IT THIS TIME...SO IT MUST HAVE A COOLDOWN.
SKILLS THAT STRONG ALWAYS HAVE ONE.
AND...
...JUDGING BY THAT DESPERATE LOOK, IT MUST BE PRETTY LONG.

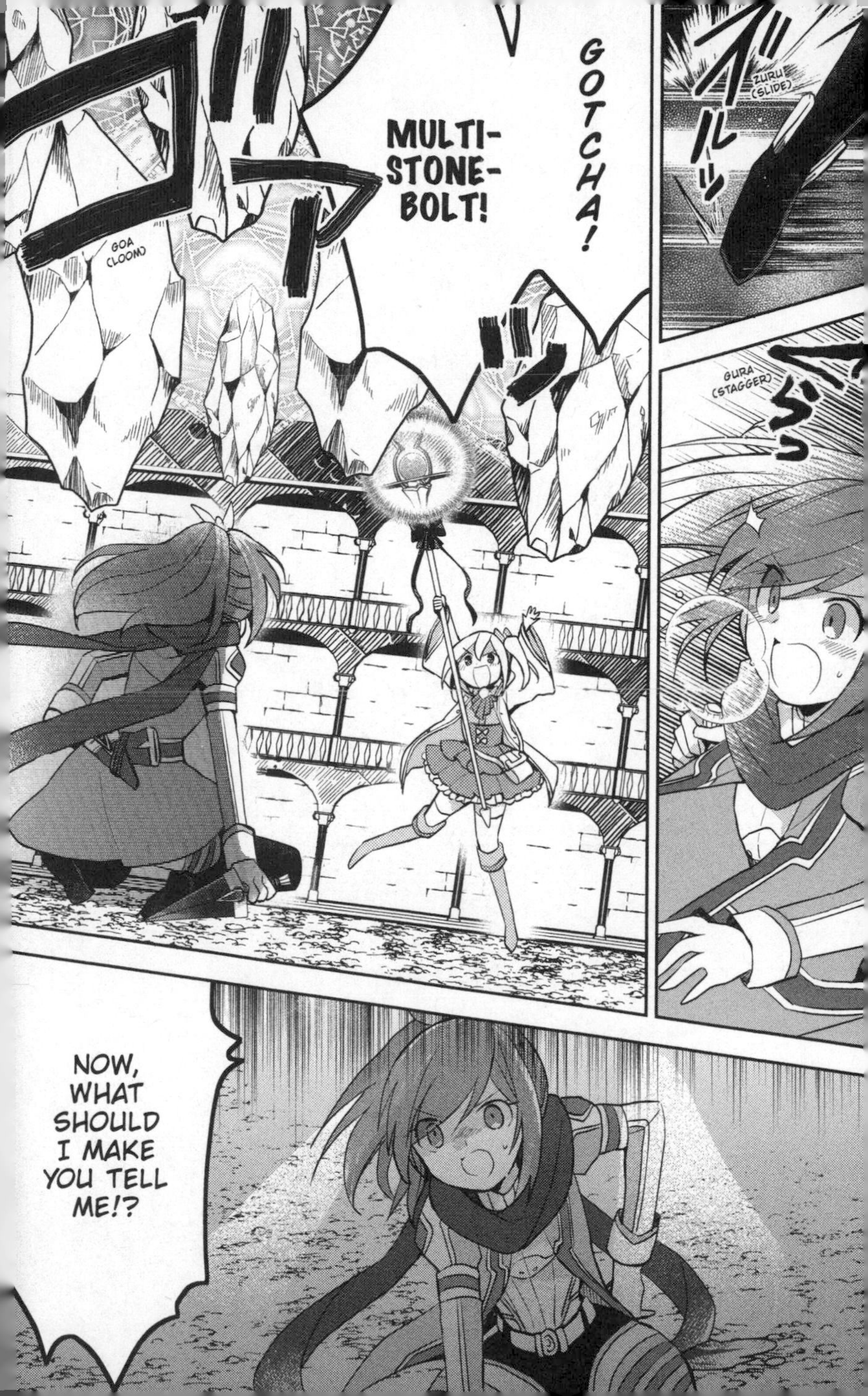
ZURU (SLIDE)
GURA (STAGGER)
GOTCHA!
MULTI-STONE-BOLT!
GOA (LOOM)
NOW, WHAT SHOULD I MAKE YOU TELL ME!?

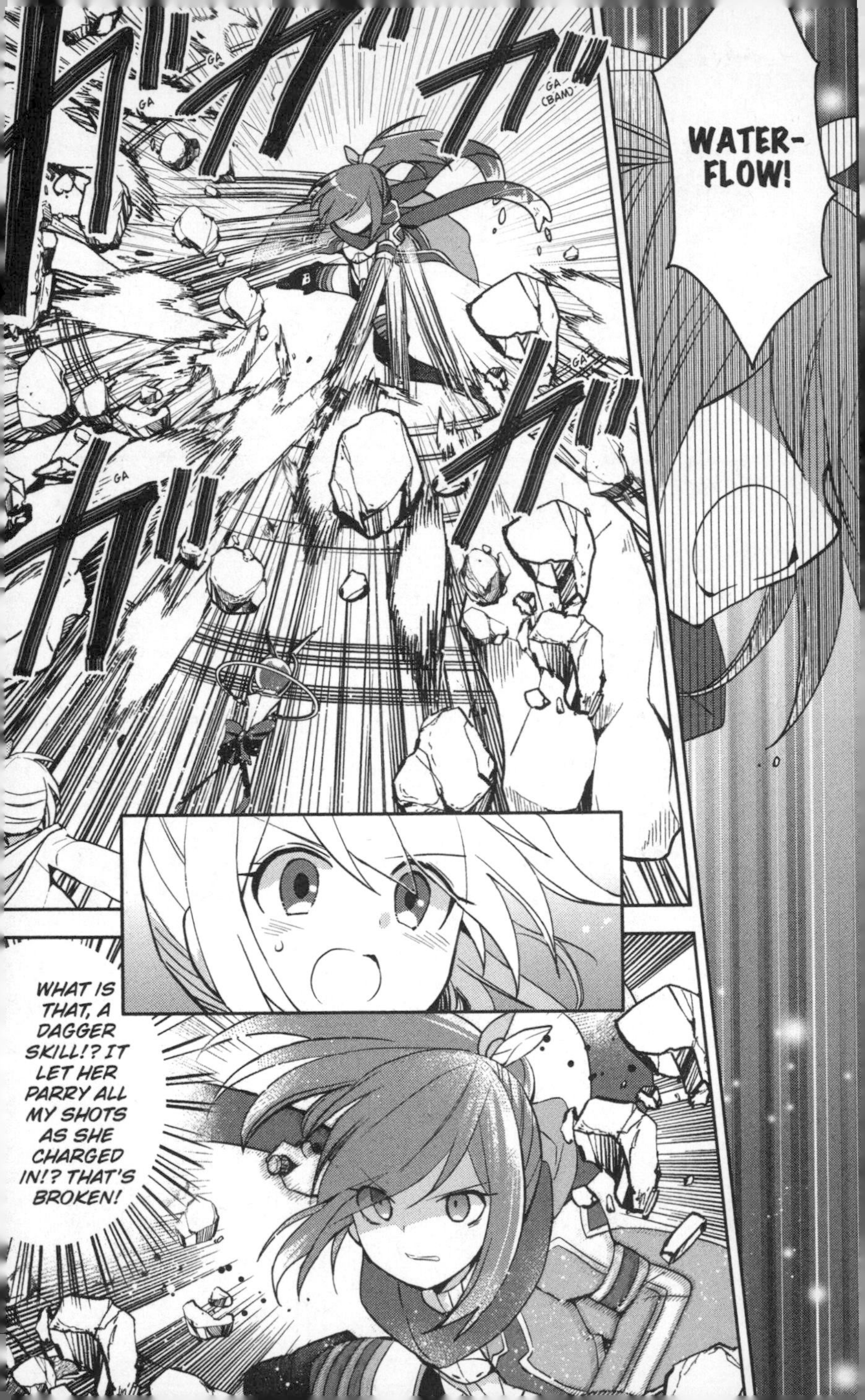
GA
GA
GA (BAM)
WATER-FLOW!
GA
GA
WHAT IS THAT, A DAGGER SKILL!? IT LET HER PARRY ALL MY SHOTS AS SHE CHARGED IN!? THAT'S BROKEN!

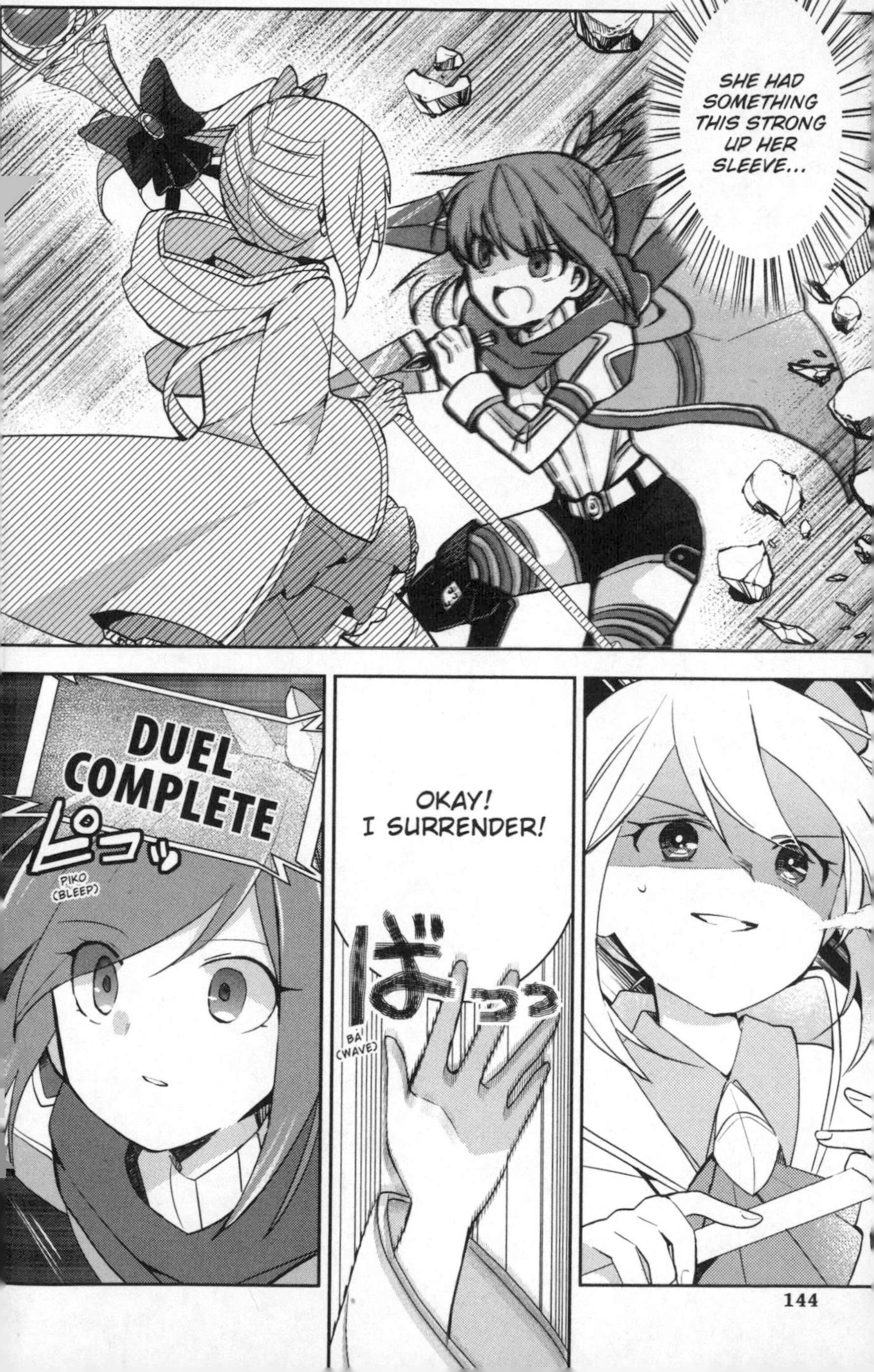
SHE HAD SOMETHING THIS STRONG UP HER SLEEVE...
OKAY! I SURRENDER!
ばっっ
BA (WAVE)
DUEL COMPLETE
ピコッ
PIKO (BLEEP)

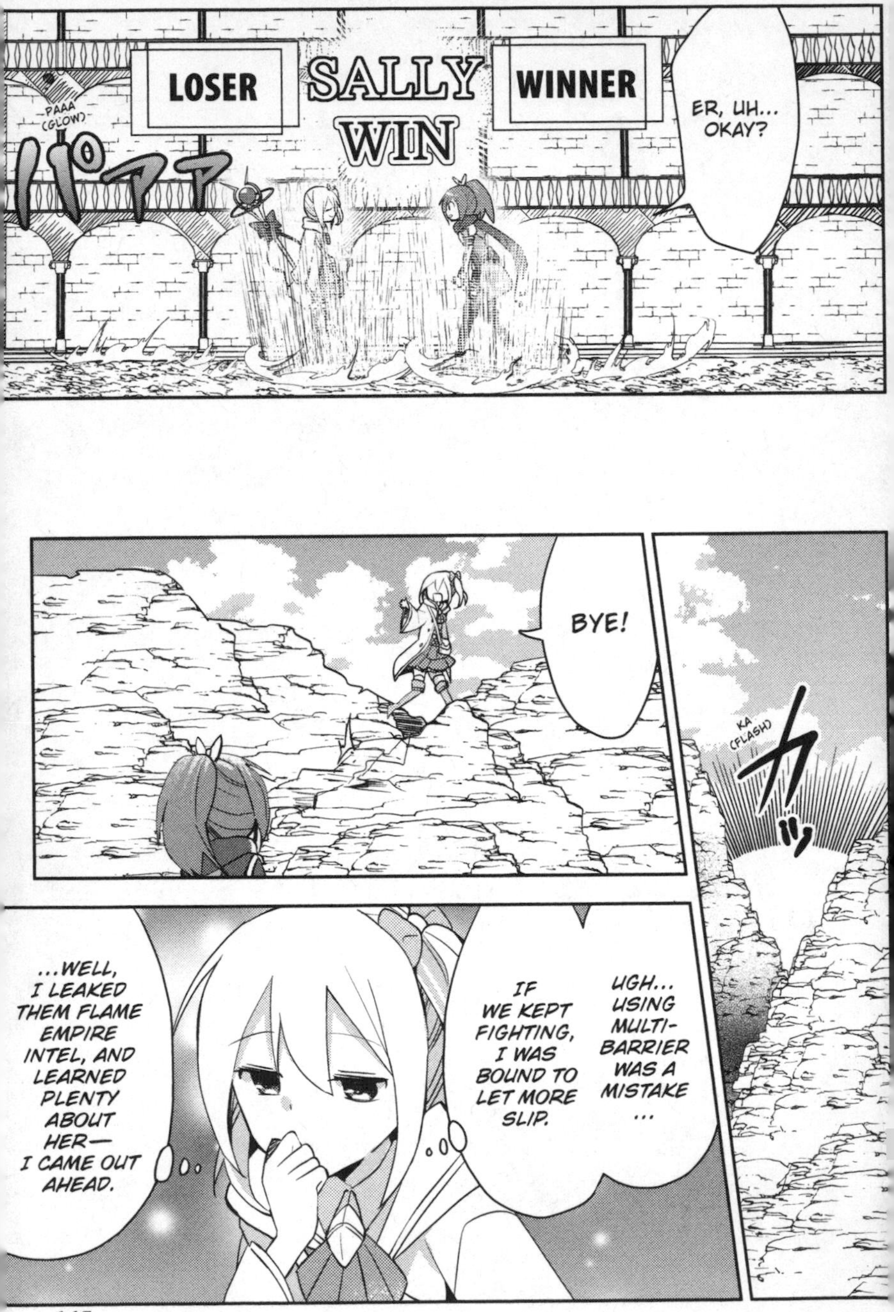
ER, UH... OKAY?
WINNER
SALLY WIN
LOSER
PAAA (GLOW)
KA (FLASH)
BYE!
UGH... USING MULTI-BARRIER WAS A MISTAKE...
IF WE KEPT FIGHTING, I WAS BOUND TO LET MORE SLIP.
...WELL, I LEAKED THEM FLAME EMPIRE INTEL, AND LEARNED PLENTY ABOUT HER— I CAME OUT AHEAD.

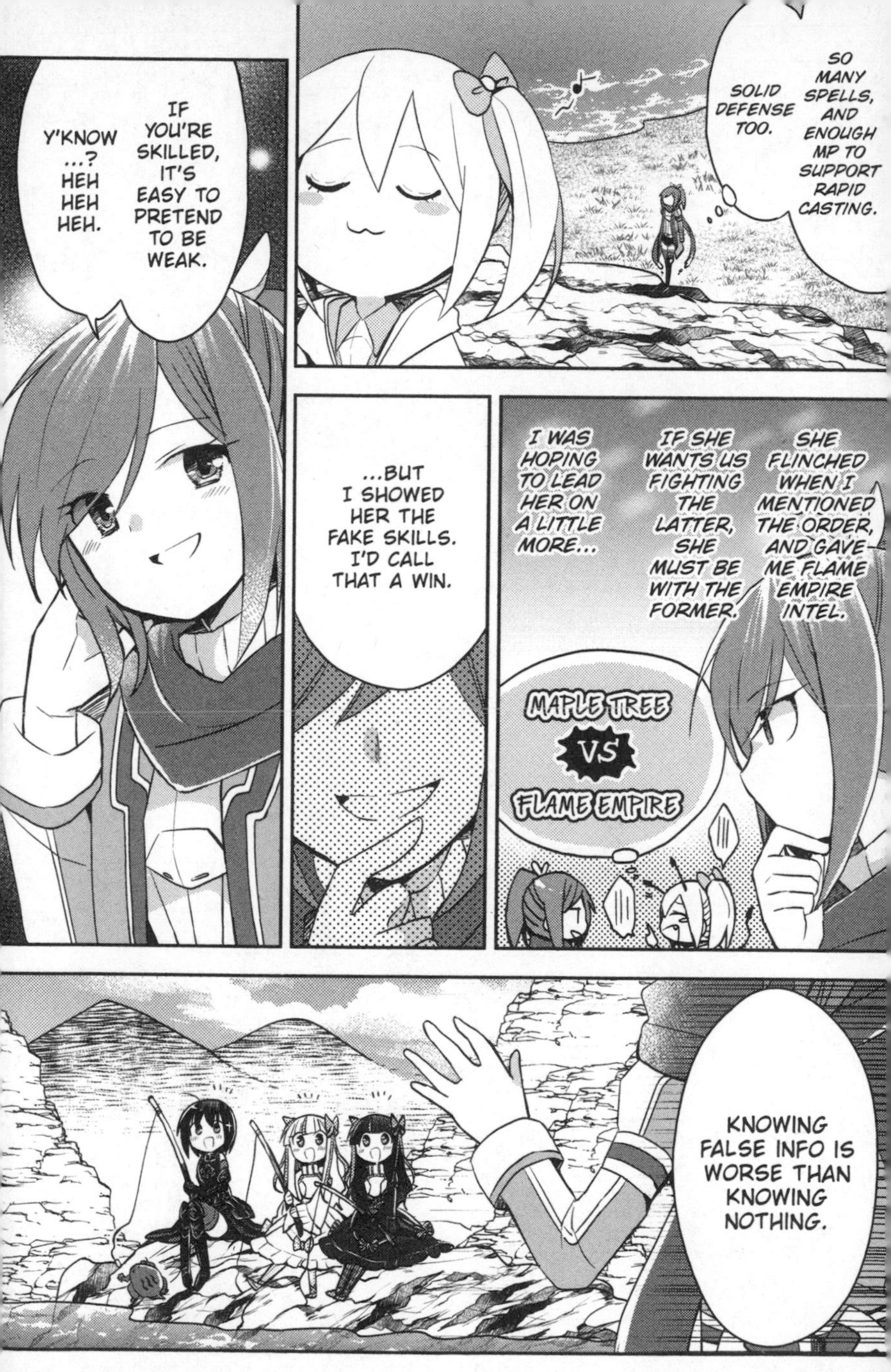
SO MANY SPELLS, AND ENOUGH MP TO SUPPORT RAPID CASTING.
SOLID DEFENSE TOO.
SHE FLINCHED WHEN I MENTIONED THE ORDER, AND GAVE ME FLAME EMPIRE INTEL.
IF SHE WANTS US FIGHTING THE LATTER, SHE MUST BE WITH THE FORMER.
I WAS HOPING TO LEAD HER ON A LITTLE MORE...
MAPLE TREE
VS
FLAME EMPIRE
...BUT I SHOWED HER THE FAKE SKILLS. I'D CALL THAT A WIN.
IF YOU'RE SKILLED, IT'S EASY TO PRETEND TO BE WEAK.
Y'KNOW...? HEH HEH HEH.
KNOWING FALSE INFO IS WORSE THAN KNOWING NOTHING.

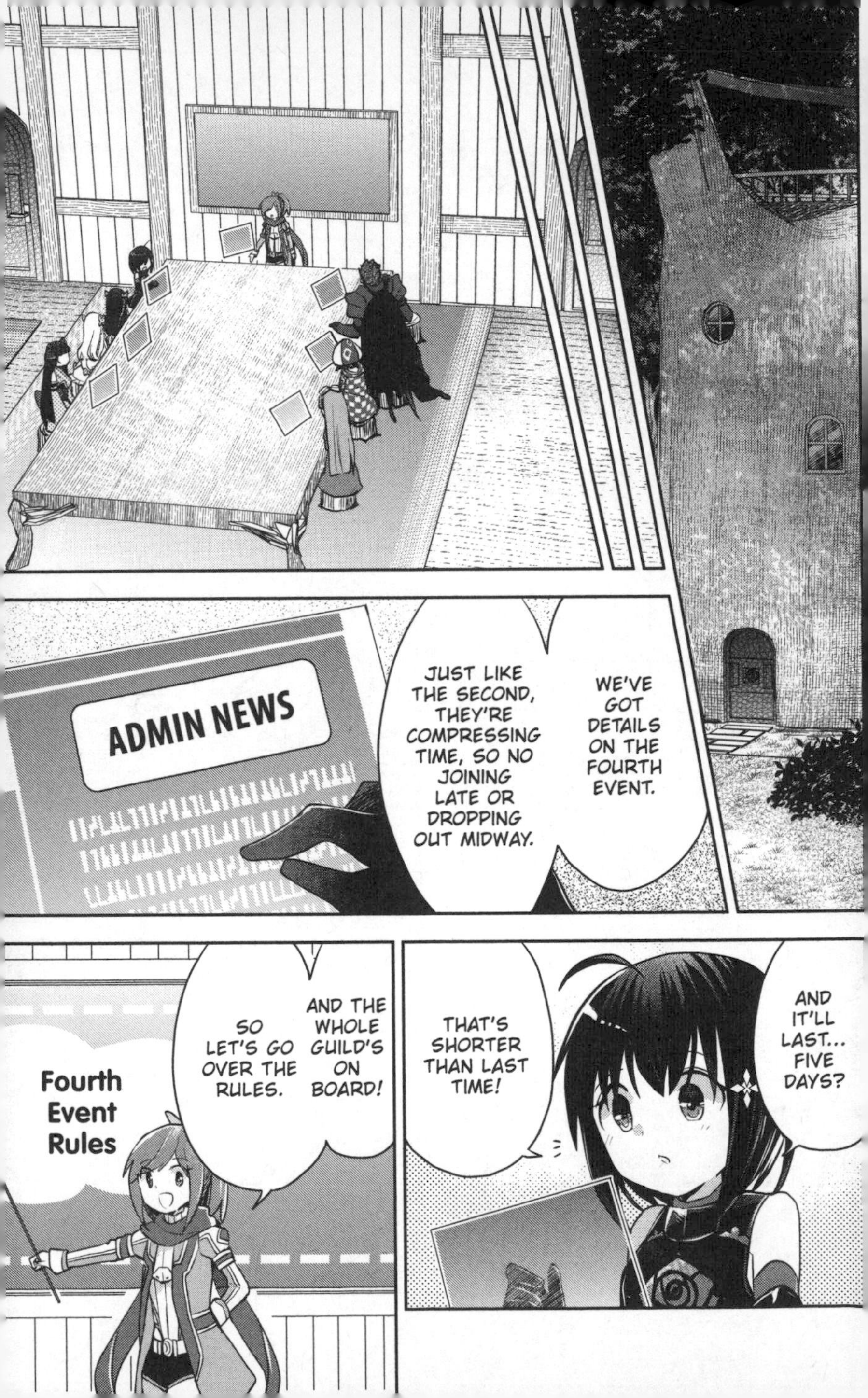
WE'VE GOT DETAILS ON THE FOURTH EVENT.
JUST LIKE THE SECOND, THEY'RE COMPRESSING TIME, SO NO JOINING LATE OR DROPPING OUT MIDWAY.
ADMIN NEWS
AND IT'LL LAST... FIVE DAYS?
THAT'S SHORTER THAN LAST TIME!
AND THE WHOLE GUILD'S ON BOARD!
SO LET'S GO OVER THE RULES.
Fourth Event Rules

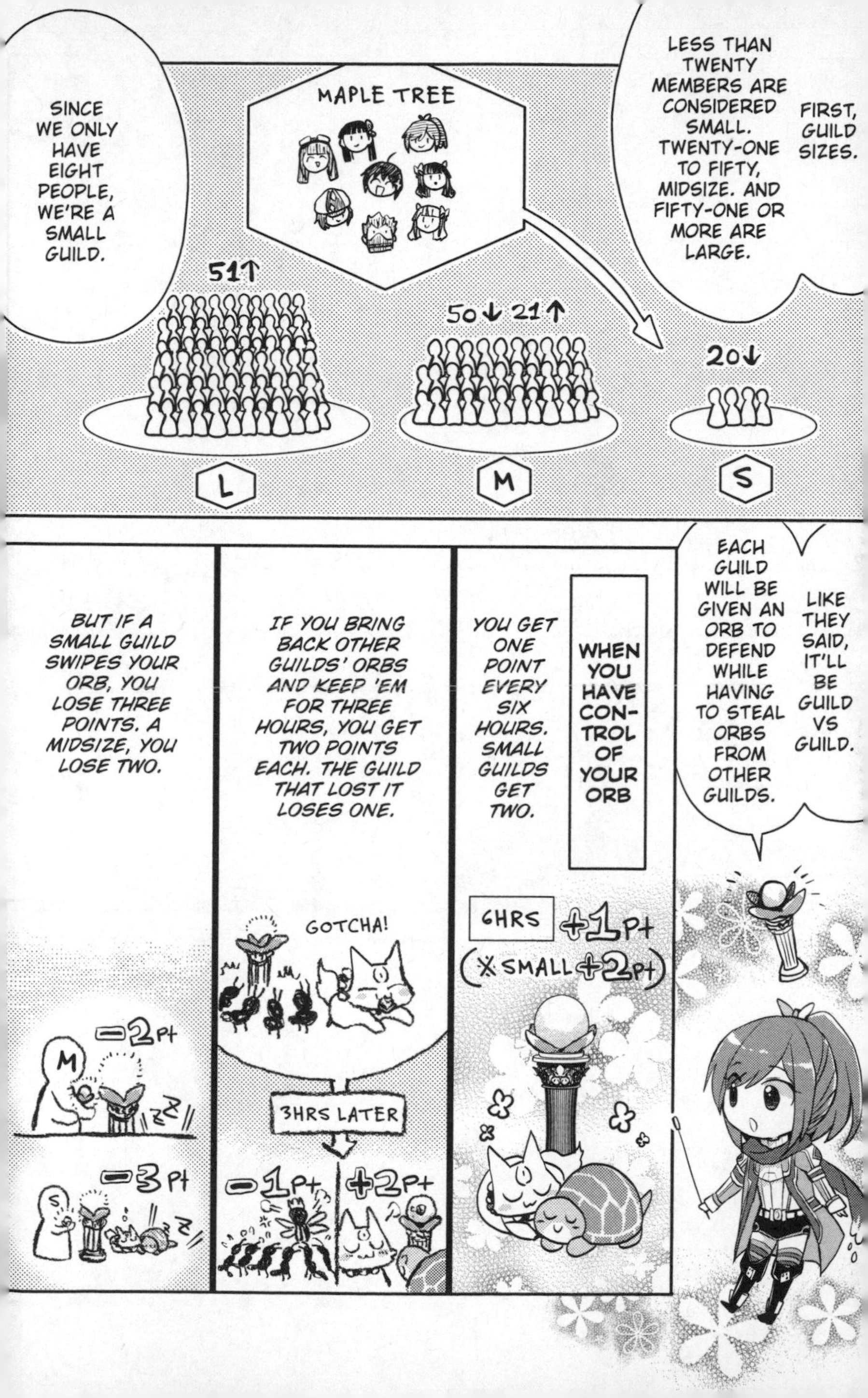
FIRST, GUILD SIZES.
LESS THAN TWENTY MEMBERS ARE CONSIDERED SMALL. TWENTY-ONE TO FIFTY, MIDSIZE. AND FIFTY-ONE OR MORE ARE LARGE.
MAPLE TREE
20↓
50↓ 21↑
51↑
S
M
L
SINCE WE ONLY HAVE EIGHT PEOPLE, WE'RE A SMALL GUILD.
LIKE THEY SAID, IT'LL BE GUILD VS GUILD.
EACH GUILD WILL BE GIVEN AN ORB TO DEFEND WHILE HAVING TO STEAL ORBS FROM OTHER GUILDS.
WHEN YOU HAVE CON-TROL OF YOUR ORB
YOU GET ONE POINT EVERY SIX HOURS. SMALL GUILDS GET TWO.
6HRS +1pt
(※SMALL +2pt)
IF YOU BRING BACK OTHER GUILDS' ORBS AND KEEP 'EM FOR THREE HOURS, YOU GET TWO POINTS EACH. THE GUILD THAT LOST IT LOSES ONE.
GOTCHA!
3HRS LATER
+2pt
-1pt
BUT IF A SMALL GUILD SWIPES YOUR ORB, YOU LOSE THREE POINTS. A MIDSIZE, YOU LOSE TWO.
-2pt
M
-3pt
S

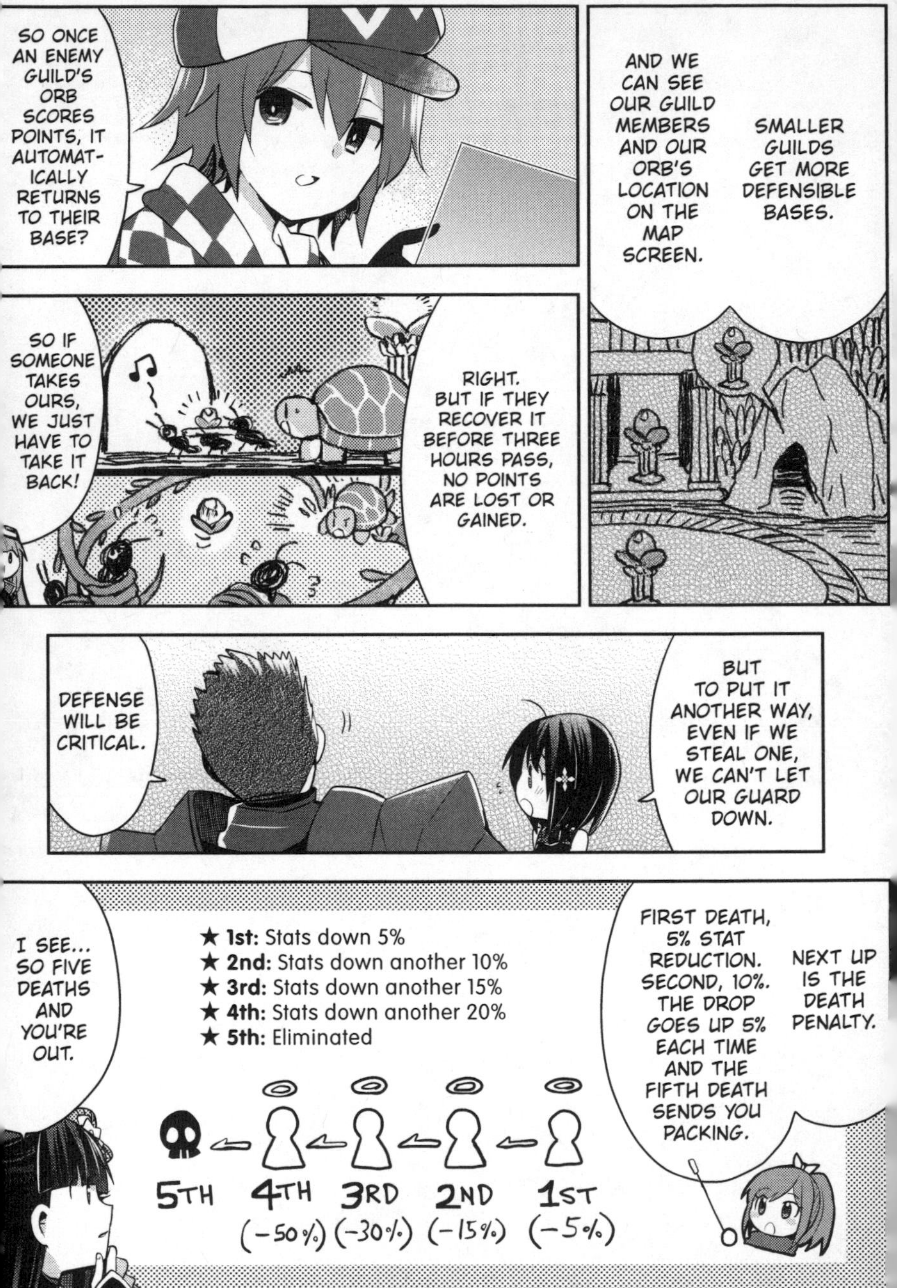
SMALLER GUILDS GET MORE DEFENSIBLE BASES.
AND WE CAN SEE OUR GUILD MEMBERS AND OUR ORB'S LOCATION ON THE MAP SCREEN.
SO ONCE AN ENEMY GUILD'S ORB SCORES POINTS, IT AUTOMAT-ICALLY RETURNS TO THEIR BASE?
RIGHT. BUT IF THEY RECOVER IT BEFORE THREE HOURS PASS, NO POINTS ARE LOST OR GAINED.
SO IF SOMEONE TAKES OURS, WE JUST HAVE TO TAKE IT BACK!
BUT TO PUT IT ANOTHER WAY, EVEN IF WE STEAL ONE, WE CAN'T LET OUR GUARD DOWN.
DEFENSE WILL BE CRITICAL.
NEXT UP IS THE DEATH PENALTY.
FIRST DEATH, 5% STAT REDUCTION. SECOND, 10%. THE DROP GOES UP 5% EACH TIME AND THE FIFTH DEATH SENDS YOU PACKING.
★ 1st: Stats down 5%
★ 2nd: Stats down another 10%
★ 3rd: Stats down another 15%
★ 4th: Stats down another 20%
★ 5th: Eliminated
1ST (−5%)
2ND (−15%)
3RD (−30%)
4TH (−50%)
5TH
I SEE... SO FIVE DEATHS AND YOU'RE OUT.

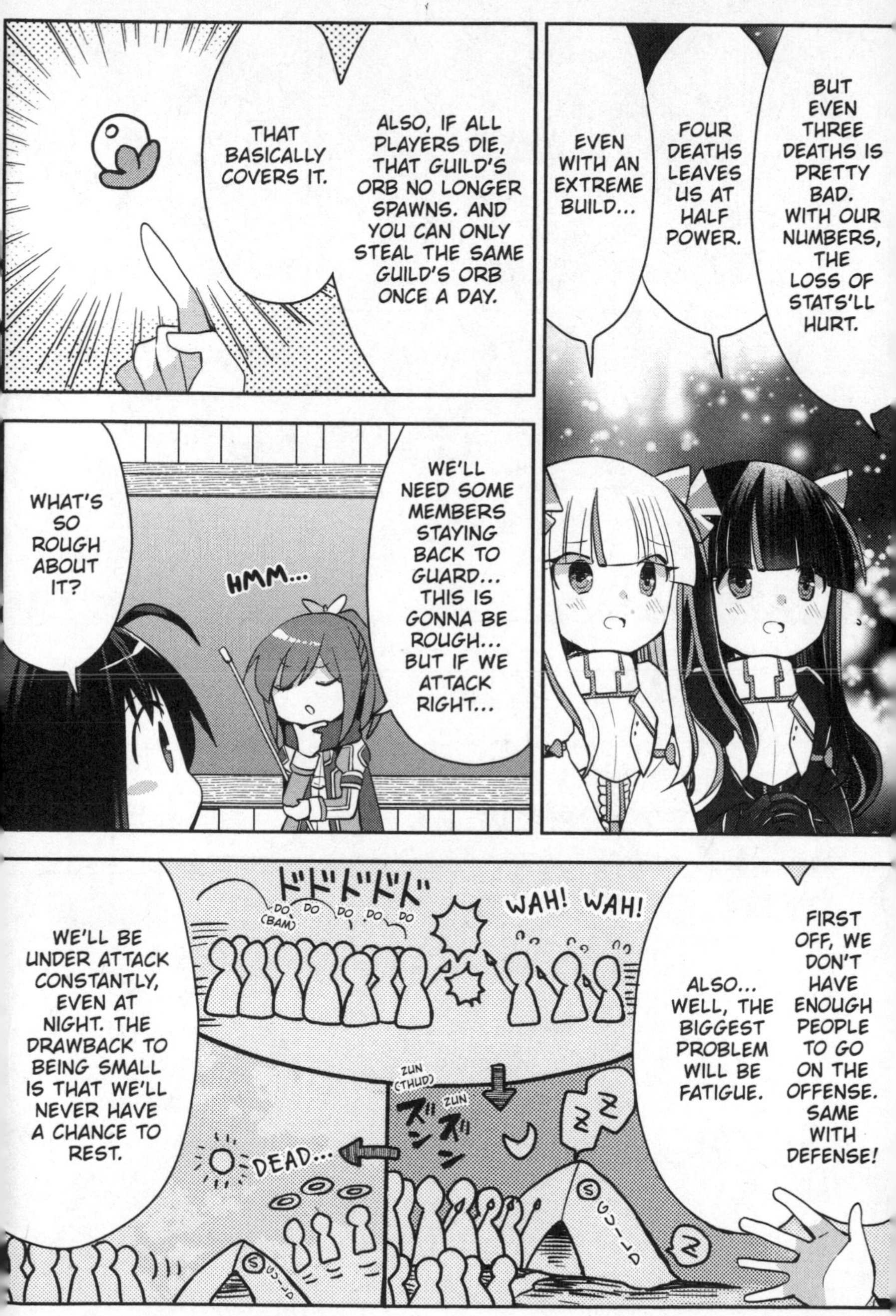
BUT EVEN THREE DEATHS IS PRETTY BAD. WITH OUR NUMBERS, THE LOSS OF STATS'LL HURT.
FOUR DEATHS LEAVES US AT HALF POWER.
EVEN WITH AN EXTREME BUILD...
ALSO, IF ALL PLAYERS DIE, THAT GUILD'S ORB NO LONGER SPAWNS. AND YOU CAN ONLY STEAL THE SAME GUILD'S ORB ONCE A DAY.
THAT BASICALLY COVERS IT.
WE'LL NEED SOME MEMBERS STAYING BACK TO GUARD... THIS IS GONNA BE ROUGH... BUT IF WE ATTACK RIGHT...
HMM...
WHAT'S SO ROUGH ABOUT IT?
FIRST OFF, WE DON'T HAVE ENOUGH PEOPLE TO GO ON THE OFFENSE. SAME WITH DEFENSE!
ALSO... WELL, THE BIGGEST PROBLEM WILL BE FATIGUE.
WAH! WAH!
ドドドドド
DO DO DO DO DO (BAM)
ZUN (THUD) ZUN
ズンズン
GUILD
DEAD...
WE'LL BE UNDER ATTACK CONSTANTLY, EVEN AT NIGHT. THE DRAWBACK TO BEING SMALL IS THAT WE'LL NEVER HAVE A CHANCE TO REST.

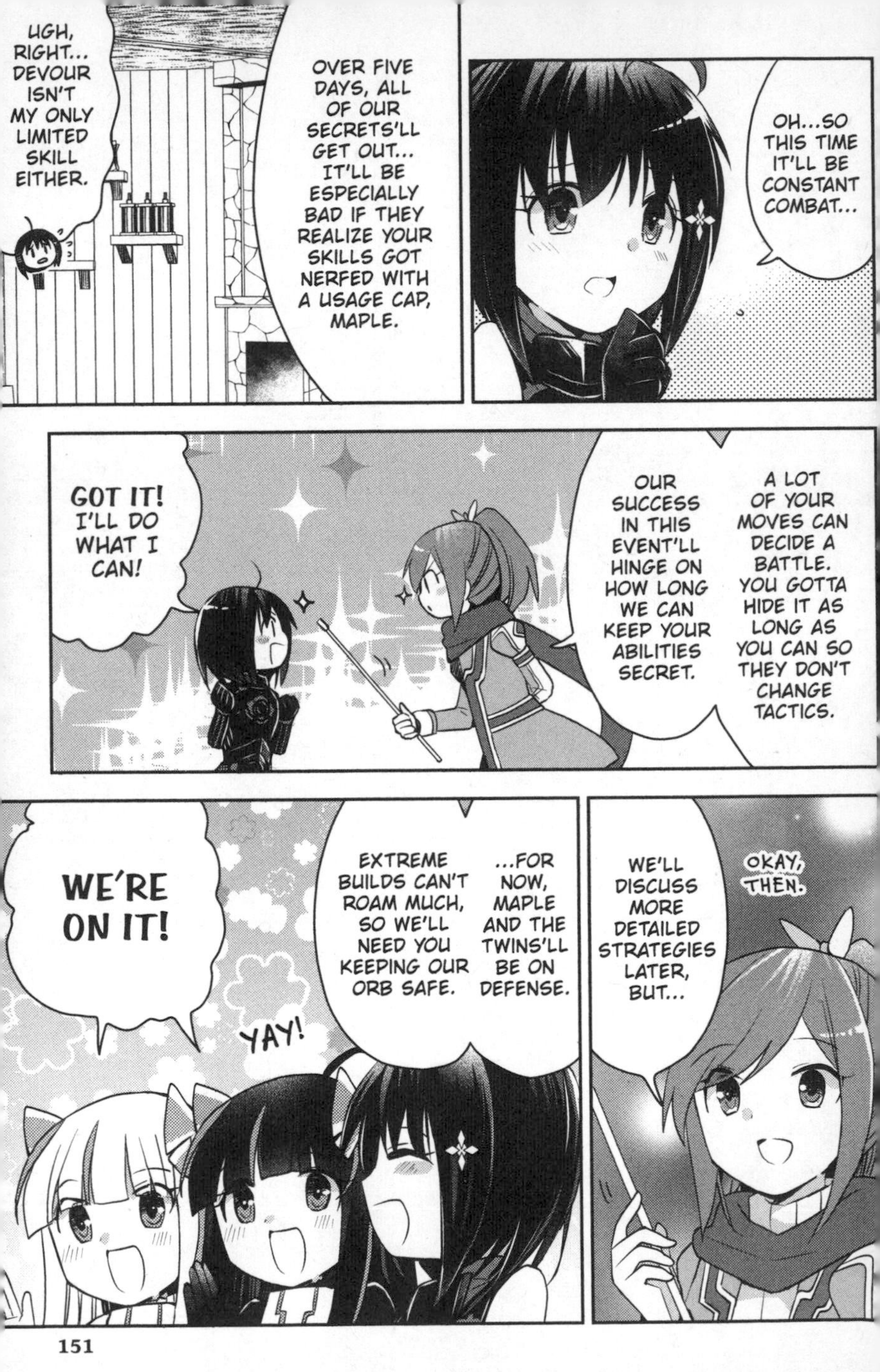
OH...SO THIS TIME IT'LL BE CONSTANT COMBAT...
OVER FIVE DAYS, ALL OF OUR SECRETS'LL GET OUT... IT'LL BE ESPECIALLY BAD IF THEY REALIZE YOUR SKILLS GOT NERFED WITH A USAGE CAP, MAPLE.
UGH, RIGHT... DEVOUR ISN'T MY ONLY LIMITED SKILL EITHER.
A LOT OF YOUR MOVES CAN DECIDE A BATTLE. YOU GOTTA HIDE IT AS LONG AS YOU CAN SO THEY DON'T CHANGE TACTICS.
OUR SUCCESS IN THIS EVENT'LL HINGE ON HOW LONG WE CAN KEEP YOUR ABILITIES SECRET.
GOT IT! I'LL DO WHAT I CAN!
OKAY, THEN.
WE'LL DISCUSS MORE DETAILED STRATEGIES LATER, BUT...
...FOR NOW, MAPLE AND THE TWINS'LL BE ON DEFENSE.
EXTREME BUILDS CAN'T ROAM MUCH, SO WE'LL NEED YOU KEEPING OUR ORB SAFE.
YAY!
WE'RE ON IT!

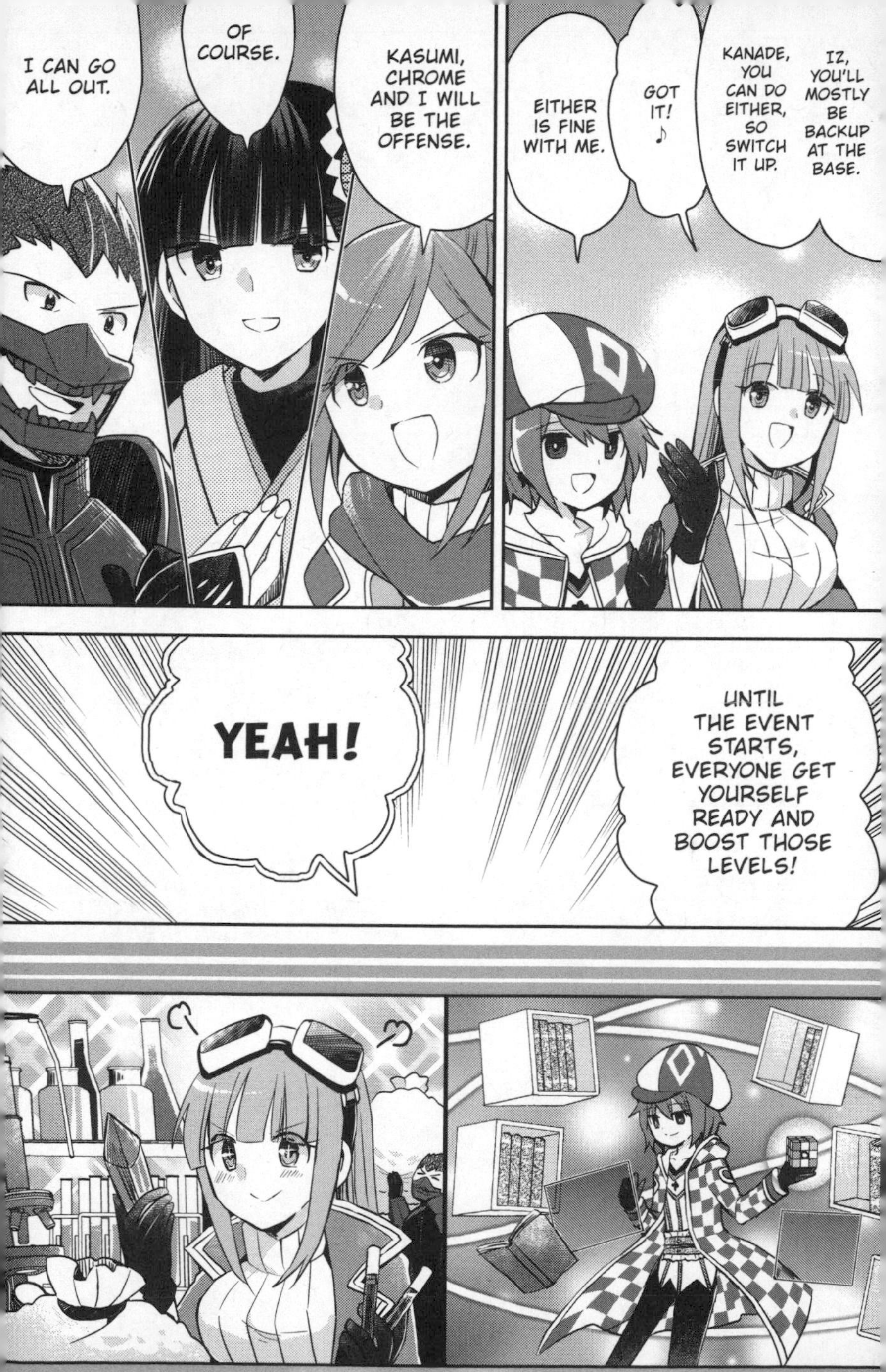
IZ, YOU'LL MOSTLY BE BACKUP AT THE BASE.
KANADE, YOU CAN DO EITHER, SO SWITCH IT UP.
GOT IT! ♪
EITHER IS FINE WITH ME.
KASUMI, CHROME AND I WILL BE THE OFFENSE.
OF COURSE.
I CAN GO ALL OUT.
UNTIL THE EVENT STARTS, EVERYONE GET YOURSELF READY AND BOOST THOSE LEVELS!
YEAH!

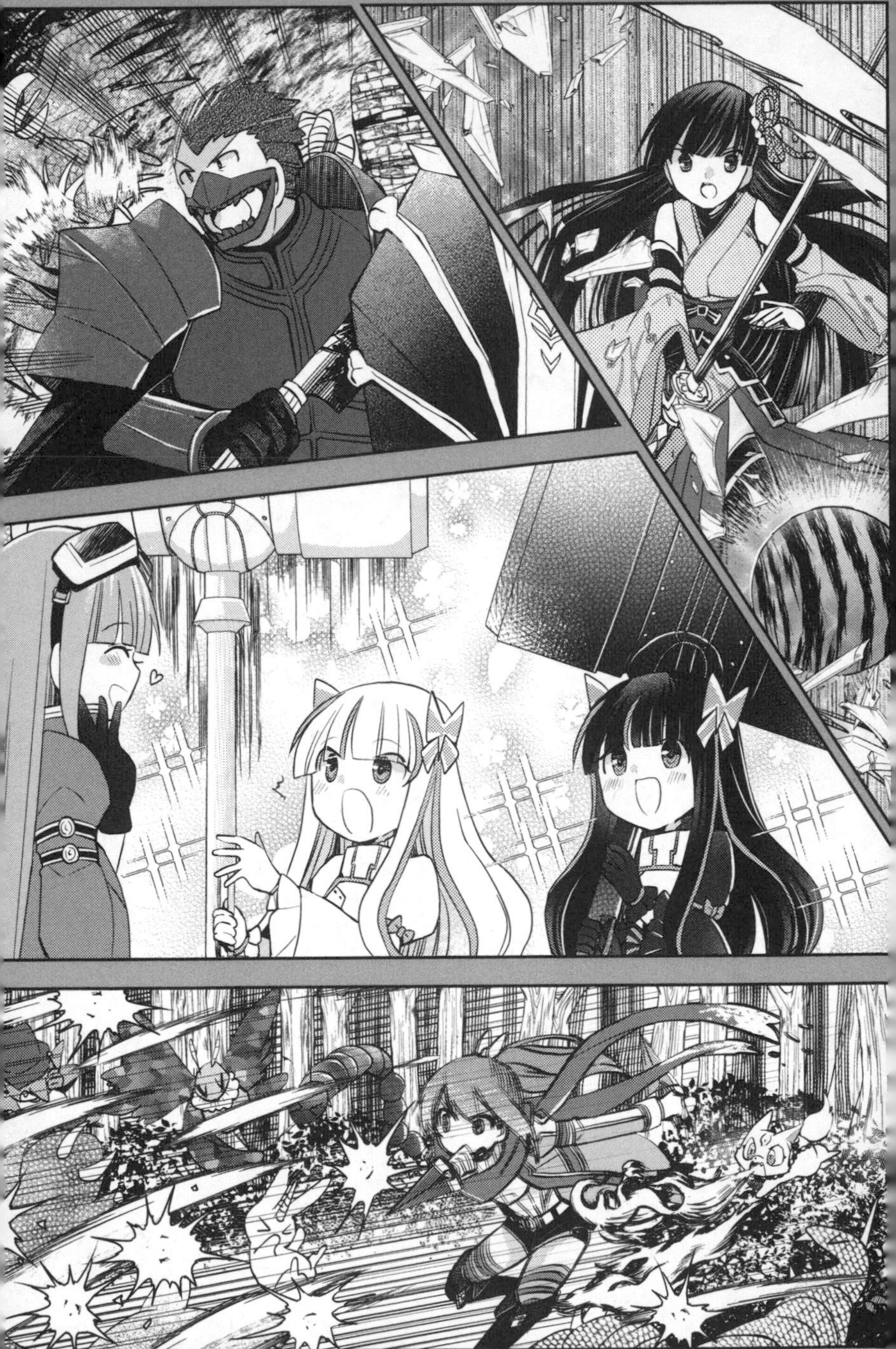

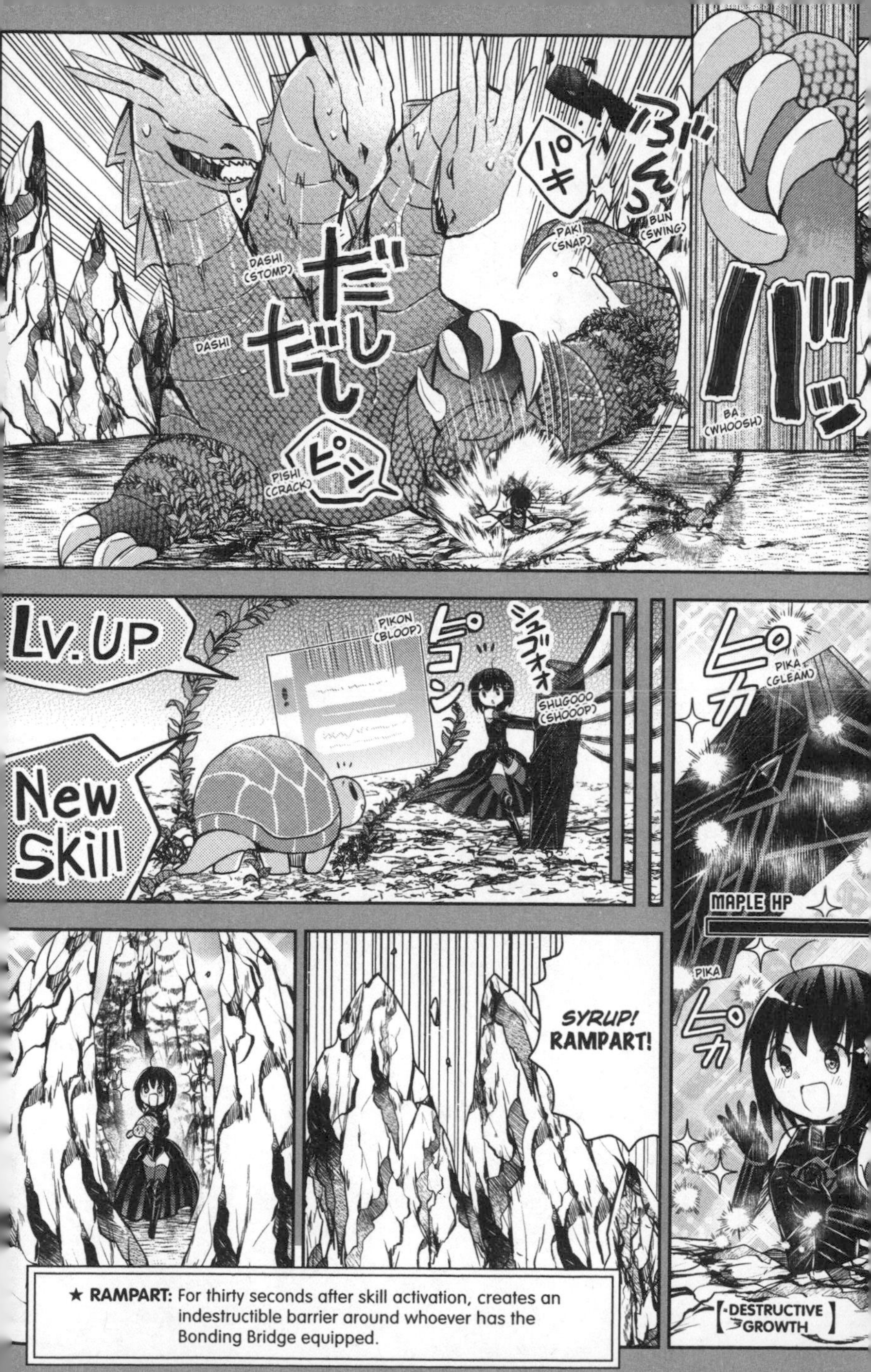
バッ
BA (WHOOSH)
ぶんっ
BUN (SWING)
パキ
PAKI (SNAP)
だしだし
DASHI (STOMP)
DASHI
ピシ
PISHI (CRACK)
ピカ
PIKA (GLEAM)
MAPLE HP
ピカ
PIKA
[DESTRUCTIVE GROWTH]
シュゴオオ
SHUGOOO (SHOOOP)
ピコン
PIKON (BLOOP)
Lv. UP
New Skill
SYRUP! RAMPART!

★ **RAMPART:** For thirty seconds after skill activation, creates an indestructible barrier around whoever has the Bonding Bridge equipped.

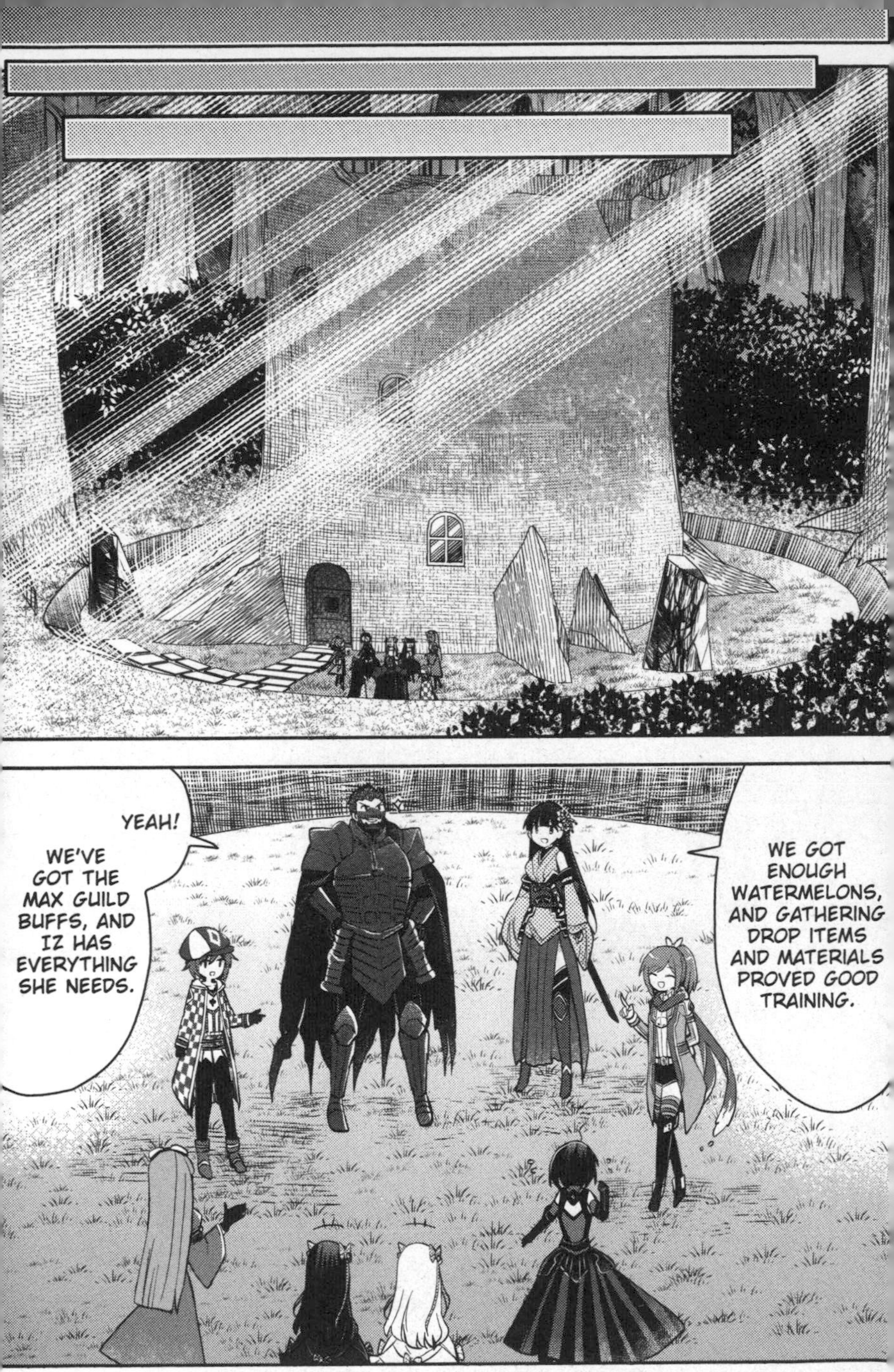
WE GOT ENOUGH WATERMELONS, AND GATHERING DROP ITEMS AND MATERIALS PROVED GOOD TRAINING.
YEAH! WE'VE GOT THE MAX GUILD BUFFS, AND IZ HAS EVERYTHING SHE NEEDS.

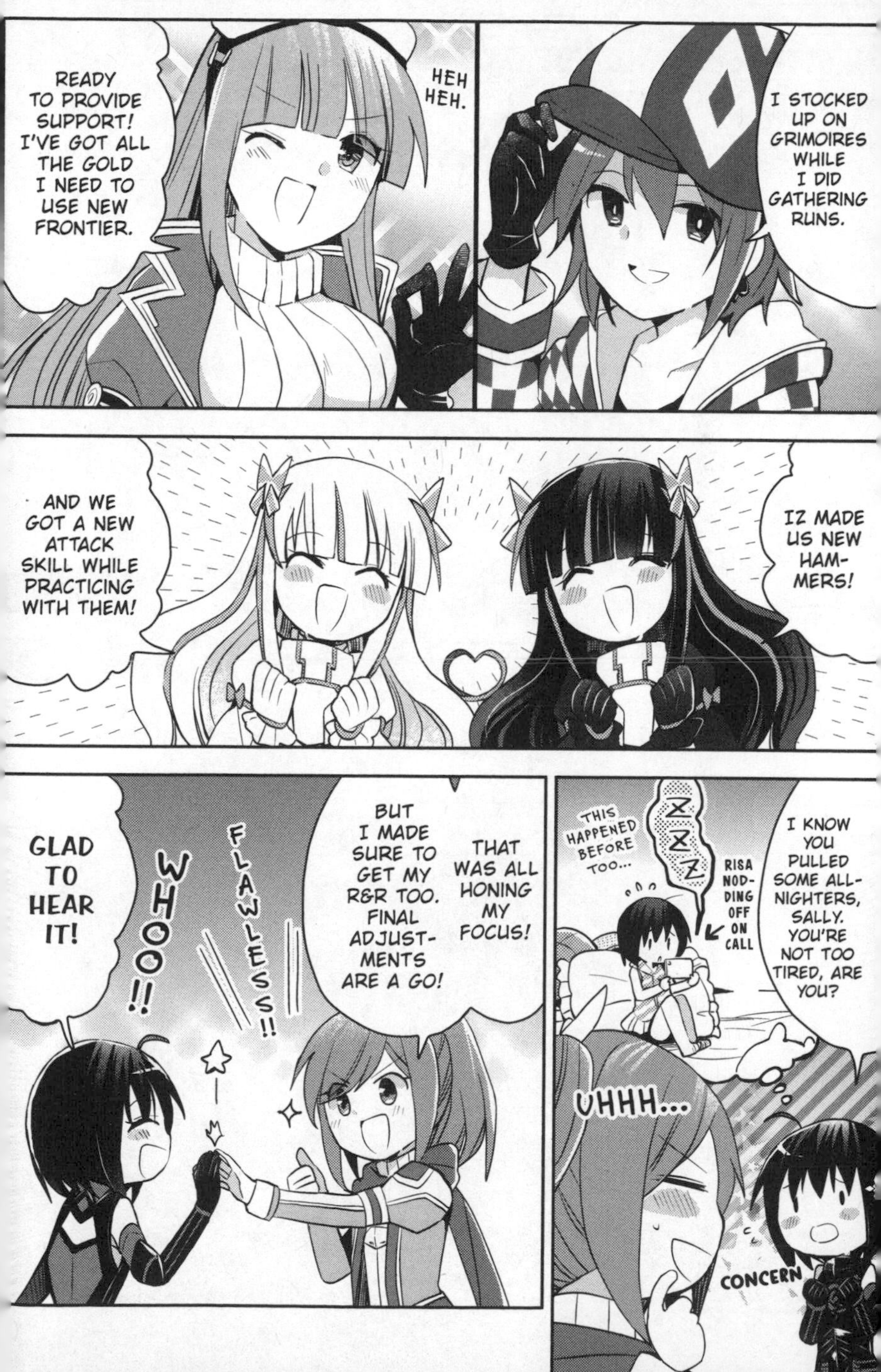
I STOCKED UP ON GRIMOIRES WHILE I DID GATHERING RUNS.
HEH HEH.
READY TO PROVIDE SUPPORT! I'VE GOT ALL THE GOLD I NEED TO USE NEW FRONTIER.
IZ MADE US NEW HAM-MERS!
AND WE GOT A NEW ATTACK SKILL WHILE PRACTICING WITH THEM!
I KNOW YOU PULLED SOME ALL-NIGHTERS, SALLY. YOU'RE NOT TOO TIRED, ARE YOU?
ZZZ
RISA NOD-DING OFF ON CALL
THIS HAPPENED BEFORE TOO...
UHHH...
CONCERN
THAT WAS ALL HONING MY FOCUS!
BUT I MADE SURE TO GET MY R&R TOO. FINAL ADJUST-MENTS ARE A GO!
FLAWLESS!!
WHOOO!!
GLAD TO HEAR IT!

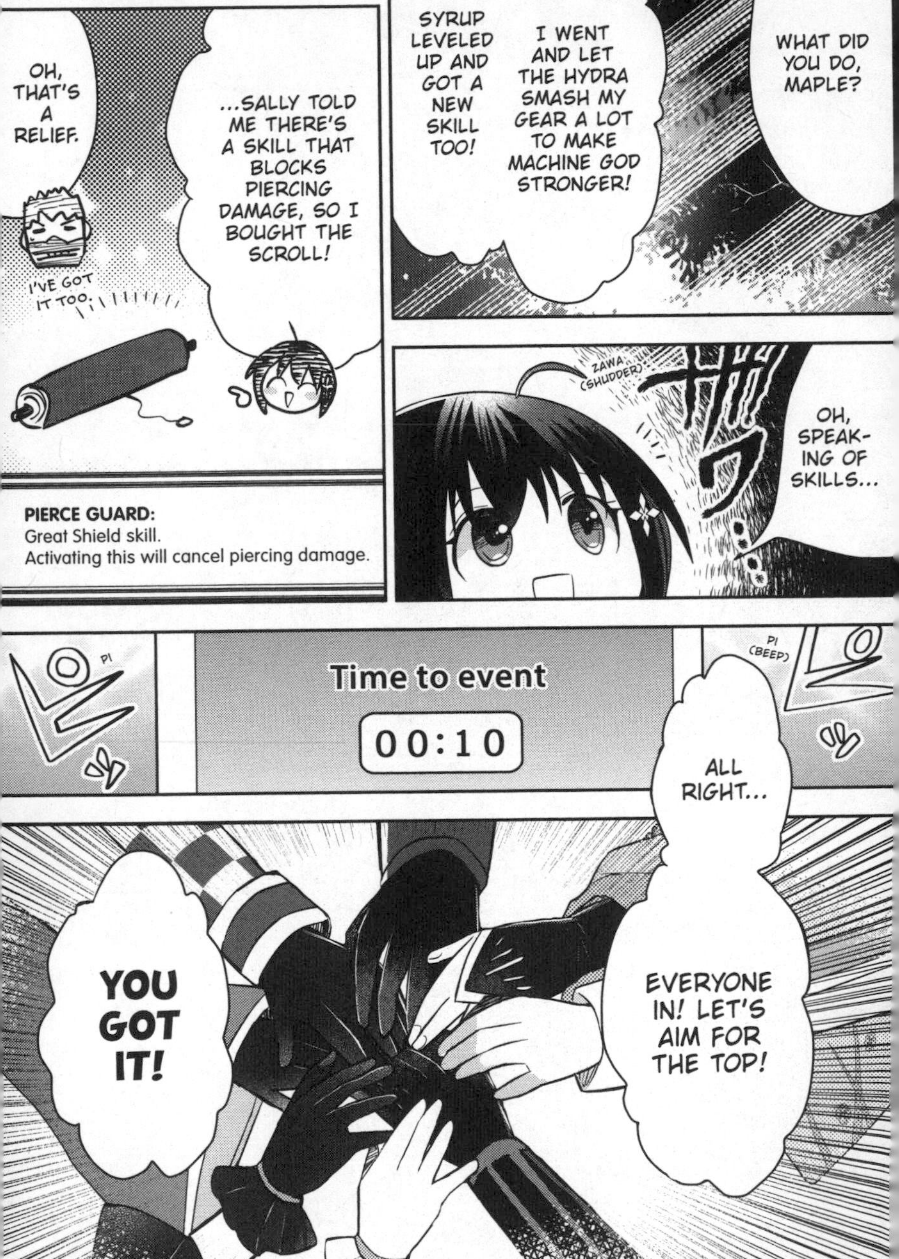
WHAT DID YOU DO, MAPLE?
I WENT AND LET THE HYDRA SMASH MY GEAR A LOT TO MAKE MACHINE GOD STRONGER!
SYRUP LEVELED UP AND GOT A NEW SKILL TOO!
...SALLY TOLD ME THERE'S A SKILL THAT BLOCKS PIERCING DAMAGE, SO I BOUGHT THE SCROLL!
OH, THAT'S A RELIEF.
I'VE GOT IT TOO.
ZAWA (SHUDDER)
OH, SPEAK-ING OF SKILLS...
PIERCE GUARD:
Great Shield skill.
Activating this will cancel piercing damage.
PI (BEEP)
Time to event
00:10
PI
ALL RIGHT...
EVERYONE IN! LET'S AIM FOR THE TOP!
YOU GOT IT!

New World Online

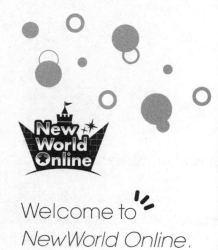

Welcome to *NewWorld Online.*

I Don't Want to Get Hurt, so I'll Max Out My Defense.

presented by: JIROU OIMOTO & YUUMIKAN

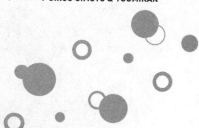

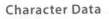

Character Data

[NewWorld Online STATUS]

||| GUILD: **MAPLE TREE** |||

I Don't Want to Get Hurt,

so I'll Max Out My Defense.

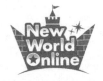

NewWorld Online STATUS

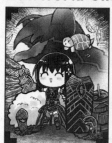

|| NAME **MAPLE**

LV 35

HP 200/200   MP 22/22

STATUS

STR 000   VIT 1235   AGI 000   DEX 000   INT 000

EQUIPMENT

|| New Moon: Hydra || Black Rose Armor: Saturating Chaos

|| Night's Facsimile: Devour || Bonding Bridge

|| Toughness Ring || Life Ring

SKILLS

Shield Attack   Sidestep   Deflect   Meditation   Taunt   Inspire   HP Boost (S)   MP Boost (S)

Great Shield Mastery V   Cover Move II   Cover   Pierce Guard   Counter   Absolute Defense

Moral Turpitude   Giant Killing   Hydra Eater   Bomb Eater   Sheep Eater   Indomitable Guardian

Psychokinesis   Fortress   Martyr's Devotion   Machine God

NewWorld Online STATUS

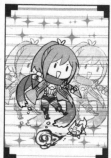

|| NAME **SALLY**

LV 30

HP 32/32   MP 80/80

STATUS

STR 070   VIT 000   AGI 158   DEX 045   INT 050

EQUIPMENT

|| Deep Sea Dagger || Seabed Dagger

|| Surface Scarf: Mirage || Oceanic Coat: Oceanic

|| Oceanic Clothes || Black Boots || Bonding Bridge

SKILLS

Gale Slash   Defense Break   Inspire   Down Attack   Power Attack   Switch Attack

Combo Blade IV   Martial Arts V   Fire Magic II   Water Magic III   Wind Magic III   Earth Magic II

Dark Magic II   Light Magic II   Strength Boost (S)   Combo Boost (S)

MP Boost (S)   MP Cost Down (S)   MP Recovery Speed Boost (S)   Poison Resist (S)   Gathering Speed Boost (S)

Dagger Mastery V   Magic Mastery III

Affliction VI   Presence Block II   Presence Detect II   Sneaky Steps I   Leap III

Cooking I   Fishing   Swimming X   Diving X   Shearing

Superspeed   Ancient Ocean   Chaser Blade   Jack of All Trades   Sword Dance

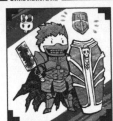

NAME CHROME HP 840/840 MP 52/52 LV 56

STATUS
STR 125 VIT 175 AGI 020 DEX 020 INT 010

EQUIPMENT
| Headhunter: Life Eater | Wrath Wraith Wall: Soul Syphon |
| Bloodstained Skull: Soul Eater | Robust Ring |

Bloodstained Bone Armor: Dead or Alive | Impregnable Ring | Defense Ring

SKILLS
Thrust, Flame Slash, Ice Blade, Shield Attack, Sidestep, Deflect, Great Defense, Taunt, Impregnable Stance, HP Boost (L), HP Recovery Speed Boost (L), MP Boost (S), Great Shield Mastery X, Defense Mastery X, Cover Move X, Cover, Pierce Guard, Counter, Guard Aura, Poison Resist (L), Paralyze Resist (M), Stun Resist (M), Sleep Resist (M), Freeze Resist (M), Burn Resist (S), Mining IV, Gathering V, Spirit Light, Indomitable Guardian, Battle Healing

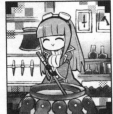

NAME IZ HP 100/100 MP 100/100 LV 40

STATUS
STR 045 VIT 020 AGI 065 DEX 210 INT 030

EQUIPMENT
| Blacksmith Hammer X | Alchemist Goggles: Faustian Alchemy |
| Alchemist Long Coat: Magic Workshop | Blacksmith Leggings X |

Alchemist Boots: New Frontier | Potion Pouch | Item Pouch | Black Gloves

SKILLS
Strike, Crafting Mastery X, Enhance Success Rate Boost (L), Gathering Speed Boost (L), Mining Speed Boost (L), Affliction II, Sneaky Steps III, Smithing X, Sewing X, Horticulture X, Synthesizing X, Augmentation X, Cooking X, Mining X, Gathering X, Swimming IV, Diving V, Shearing, Godsmith's Grace VIII

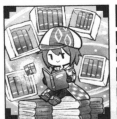

NAME KANADE HP 335/335 MP 290/290 LV 22

STATUS
STR 015 VIT 010 AGI 020 DEX 030 INT 110

EQUIPMENT
| Divine Wisdom: Akashic Records | Diamond Newsboy Cap VIII |
| Smart Coat VI | Smart Leggings VIII | Smart Boots VI |

Spade Earrings | Mage Gloves | Holy Ring

SKILLS
Magic Mastery V, MP Boost (M), MP Cost Down (S), MP Recovery Speed Boost (M), Fire Magic III, Water Magic II, Wind Magic III, Earth Magic II, Dark Magic I, Light Magic II, Sorcerer's Stacks

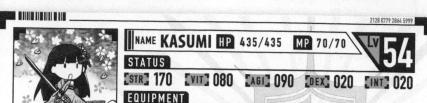

NAME **KASUMI**	HP 435/435	MP 70/70	LV 54

STATUS

STR 170 VIT 080 AGI 090 DEX 020 INT 020

EQUIPMENT

Unsigned Katana	Cherry Blossom Barrette
Cherry Blossom Vestments	Edo Purple Hakama

Samurai Greaves	Samurai Gauntlets	Gold Obi Fastener	Cherry Blossom Crest

SKILLS Gleam Helmsplitter Guard Break Sweep Slice Eye for Attack Inspire Attack Stance
Katana Arts X HP Boost (L) MP Boost (S) Poison Resist (L) Paralyze Resist (L)
Longsword Mastery X Katana Mastery X Mining IV Gathering VI Diving V Swimming VI Leap VII
Keen Sight Indomitable Sword Spirit Dauntless Sinew Superspeed Ever Vigilant

---

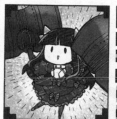

NAME **MAI**	HP 35/35	MP 20/20	LV 24

STATUS

STR 325 VIT 000 AGI 000 DEX 000 INT 000

EQUIPMENT

Black Annihilammer VIII	Black Doll Dress VIII
Black Doll Tights VIII	Black Doll Shoes VIII

Little Ribbon	Silk Gloves

SKILLS Double Stamp Double Impact Attack Boost (S) Hammer Mastery II Throw
Conqueror Annihilator Giant Killing

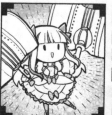

NAME **YUI**	HP 35/35	MP 20/20	LV 24

STATUS

STR 325 VIT 000 AGI 000 DEX 000 INT 000

EQUIPMENT

White Annihilammer VIII	White Doll Dress VIII
White Doll Tights VIII	White Doll Shoes VIII

Little Ribbon	Silk Gloves

SKILLS Double Stamp Double Impact Attack Boost (S) Hammer Mastery II Throw
Conqueror Annihilator Giant Killing

Bofuri

I Don't Want to Get Hurt, so I'll Max Out My Defense.

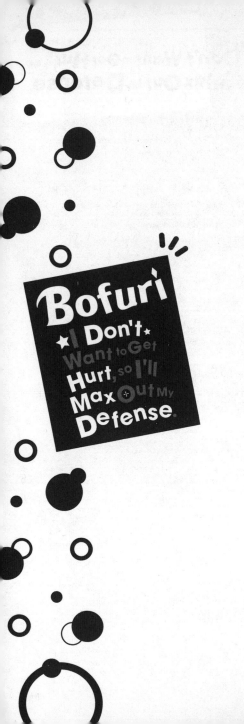

Bofuri ★ I Don't Want to Get Hurt, so I'll Max Out My Defense

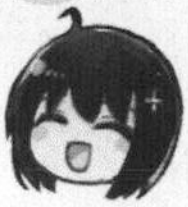

[5]

[Art] **JIROU OIMOTO**
[Original Story] **YUUMIKAN**
[Character Design] **KOIN**

Translation: **Andrew Cunningham** ★ Lettering: **Rochelle Gancio**

ITAINO WA IYA NANODE BOGYORYOKU NI KYOKUFURI SHITAITO OMOIMASU Vol. 5
©Jirou Oimoto 2021 ©Yuumikan 2021 ©Koin 2021
First published in Japan in 2021 by KADOKAWA CORPORATION, Tokyo. English translation rights arranged with KADOKAWA CORPORATION, Tokyo through TUTTLE-MORI AGENCY, INC., Tokyo.

English translation © 2022 by Yen Press, LLC

Yen Press
150 West 30th Street, 19th Floor
New York, NY 10001

Visit us!
yenpress.com • facebook.com/yenpress • twitter.com/yenpress
yenpress.tumblr.com • instagram.com/yenpress

First Yen Press Edition: November 2022
Edited by Yen Press Editorial: Thomas McAlister, Riley Pearsall
Designed by Yen Press Design: Liz Parlett

Yen Press is an imprint of Yen Press, LLC.
The Yen Press name and logo are trademarks of Yen Press, LLC.

Library of Congress Control Number: 2020953028

ISBNs: 978-1-9753-4948-6 (paperback)
978-1-9753-4949-3 (ebook)

10 9 8 7 6 5 4 3 2 1

LSC-C

Printed in the United States of America